FOUNDED 1902

Phoenix, Scottsdale & Sedona

Background **231**
    The Landscape 232
    Plants and Animals 237
    History 241
    Government and Economy 246
    People and Culture 248

Essentials **252**
    Transportation 253
    Travel Tips 254
    Health and Safety 256
    Information and Services 258

Resources **260**
    Glossary 260
    Suggested Reading 262
    Internet Resources 265

Index **267**

List of Maps **272**

Contents

**Discover Phoenix,
  Scottsdale & Sedona** **6**

Planning Your Trip 10

The Best of the Valley of the Sun 13

• 10 Best Hikes 15

Family Road Trip 16

• Beat the Heat 18

• Art in the Desert 20

Desert Luxury 21

• The Valley After Dark 24

Phoenix **25**

Sights 32

Entertainment and Events 52

Shopping 63

Sports and Recreation 70

Food 83

Accommodations 99

Information and Services 105

Transportation 106

Apache Trail and
  Superstition Mountains 107

Scottsdale **115**

Sights 120

Entertainment and Events 126

Shopping 134

Sports and Recreation 140

Food 148

Accommodations 159

Information and Services 165

Transportation 165

Vicinity of Scottsdale 167

Sedona **172**

Sights 177

Entertainment and Events 181

Shopping 185

Sports and Recreation 191

Food 200

Accommodations 208

Information and Services 214

Transportation 214

Vicinity of Sedona 215

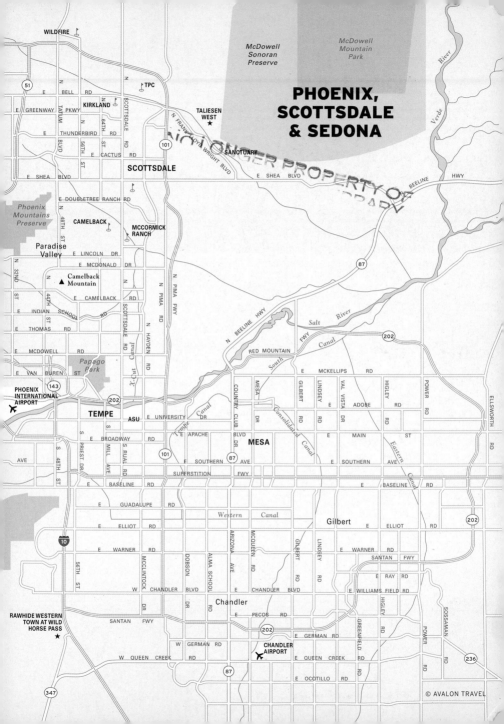

SEP 2 6 2020

PHOENIX, SCOTTSDALE & SEDONA

LILIA MENCONI

O n your flight into Phoenix, you'll notice something that sets it apart from other major cities in the U.S.: space. There's a lot of space to spread out. As the demand for homes, shopping centers, and cultural hotspots continues to rise with every new resident, the sprawling city continues its crawl across the flat desert floor. And with all this space comes a travel experience that can be diverse and unforgettable.

Phoenix, Scottsdale, and the surrounding cities that comprise the "Valley of the Sun" have set aside huge swaths of preserved land in the nearby mountain ranges. These areas have a network of hiking, biking, and equestrian trails offering residents and visitors a glimpse into what this wild desert was once like.

Just as Western expansion began with settlers seeking an escape, today's Valley offers a respite from the hustle and bustle of modern life while still providing some of the posh amenities only found in cosmopolitan cities. Phoenix boasts incredible resorts, and Scottsdale takes the cake as one of

Clockwise from top left: Dia de los Muertos figurine; Sedona city sign; blooming cactus; meditating in the red rocks of Sedona; Paolo Soleri's famous windbells at Cosanti; kayaking in the desert.

the very best spa destinations in the world. Golfers flock to these cities to tee off at more than 200 courses.

Even residents live like they're on vacation, with a hike before work or a late-night swim after a full day. You can join them: Taste the best Sonoran-style cuisine this side of the Mexican border. Wear yourself out partying and shopping in Scottsdale. Join spiritual seekers from far and wide who seek tranquility at one of Sedona's famous retreats. Venture to the leafy respite of Oak Creek Canyon and witness the red-rock monoliths. Discover the rich culture of the Native American people who first settled the Valley and still govern independent tribal land.

First-time visitors may be surprised to find a desert playground that caters to demanding foodies, diehard shoppers, and outdoor adventurers. Get to know this incredible, beautiful place, and you'll discover just how hospitable the desert can be.

Clockwise from top left: shopping in Scottsdale; Canyon Lake in Phoenix; Oak Creek Canyon in Sedona; agave.

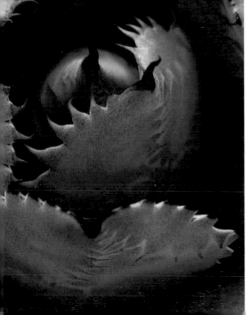

Planning Your Trip

Where to Go

Phoenix

The Sonoran Desert's brilliant light and warmth permeate every aspect of Arizona's state capital, now the sixth-largest city in the country. Thanks to more than 325 days of sunshine a year, it's possible to **dine alfresco, play golf,** or **hike** year-round (although you must hike strategically in the summer). The jagged mountains that surround the Valley of the Sun are prime spots to explore the area's diverse desert landscape. For a little urban fun, **downtown** Phoenix and the college town of **Tempe** offer terrific **museums, cultural attractions,** and popular **restaurants.**

Scottsdale

Phoenix's best-known suburb may call itself the "West's Most Western Town," but visitors are immediately struck by its pleasure-loving attitude. Scottsdale prospers thanks in part to its **chic resorts, restaurants,** and **nightspots,** along with its **desert golf courses** and **eclectic boutiques** selling cowboy boots, trendy brands, and luxury goods. The city's **galleries** support its well-known art market, and its five-star **spas** are among the finest in the world. Even architect Frank Lloyd Wright was seduced by the area, building his winter home, **Taliesin West,** here in the 1930s.

Sedona

As you approach Sedona on the highway, you'll immediately understand why it's called **Red Rock Country.** With monumental formations and intricate spires, its massive crimson buttes lure travelers and outdoor lovers. The city itself is marked by hidden resorts and charming galleries, while rugged **Jeep tours** explore its otherworldly landscape, which is accentuated by deep-green ponderosa pines and leafy cottonwoods. Historic and cultural sights dot the neighboring **Verde Valley,** such as the ancient cliffside dwelling **Montezuma Castle** and the Old West mining town of **Jerome.**

When to Go

Locals like to joke that Phoenix and Scottsdale have three seasons: beautiful, hot, and "I'm never spending another summer here ever again." And although there's some truth to that sentiment, Phoenicians easily adapt in order to take full advantage of the sunny, desert climate year-round.

There's no better time to visit Sedona or the Valley of the Sun than **spring.** Temperatures peak around 70-80°F during the day and cool down to "sweater weather" at night. Residents spend most of their time outdoors, taking advantage of the numerous golf courses, hiking spots, open-air shopping centers, and annual events such as **Major League Baseball spring training** and the **Waste Management Phoenix Open.** Also, the desert explodes with colorful wildflowers and blooming cacti.

You may actually love Phoenix in the **summer** when it sizzles—the nosedive in rates at luxury resorts and spas may help you embrace the heat. The searing temperatures and constant sun leave visitors and residents with little choice but to stake out the closest swimming pool. Cooler mornings and late nights provide relief, and sudden monsoon storms that build in the desert deliver a refreshing reprieve many evenings.

Fall kicks off the social season. Eager to escape their air-conditioned confines, residents return to their outdoor haunts in October and November when temperatures fall back to 70-80°F, filling up patios and gathering for festivals and concerts. Outdoor lovers fill the hiking and biking trails in the surrounding mountains.

By **winter,** the mercury rests between 50-60°F, and the sunny, blue skies make Phoenix a mecca for snow-weary travelers. It can get downright chilly in Sedona, and the occasional light dusting of snow on the red rocks is a spectacular sight.

Winter in Sedona is an incredible sight.

downtown Phoenix

What to Pack

A resort mentality and a Wild West attitude pervade much of Arizona, and overall, visitors will find Phoenix and Sedona to be pretty **casual.** Jeans are acceptable in most places, and in the summer shorts and flip-flops become de rigueur. That said, Scottsdale's nicer restaurants, bars, and clubs require that you **dress to impress,** which basically amounts to collared, pressed shirts (it almost never means a suit or tie). Visitors planning to take advantage of Arizona's myriad **outdoor activities** should come prepared: sneakers and hiking boots, swimsuits, and golf shoes and clubs.

The desert's arid climate can create a bit of confusion, as temperatures can swing as much as 20-30°F from an early-morning low to a late-afternoon high. Fall through early spring, be sure to bring along a **sweater or jacket** if you plan on staying out when the sun goes down. And it can be cold in the winter, with overnight temperatures sometimes falling below freezing.

Oh, and don't forget **sunscreen** with a high SPF, or at least stock up when you get to Phoenix. The Sonoran Desert's powerful sun shouldn't be underestimated, particularly in the summer.

The Best of the Valley of the Sun

Phoenix and Scottsdale make an excellent weekend trip, offering visitors the chance to combine a little culture with their R&R. Don't try to cram in a bunch of "must-see" sights. Instead, savor the Valley like a local—be whimsical and take your pick of activities according to your mood. This is the best way to experience the Valley's unique sensibility.

Day 1

Catch an early flight to **Phoenix Sky Harbor International Airport** and check into your hotel upon arrival. Make your way down to **Tempe** to have lunch at **Four Peaks Brewery** before heading across **Tempe Town Lake** to get to know the Valley from its geographic heart, **Papago Park.** The easy climb up its rounded, red-hued butte to the **Hole-in-the-Rock** formation rewards visitors with a spectacular view of the city. Within the protected reserve, you'll also find the **Desert Botanical Garden,** an impressive collection of the diverse cacti and plants that make their home in the Sonoran Desert. Next, visit **Pueblo Grande Museum and Archaeological Park,** the remains of the ancient Hohokam civilization from which the modern city of Phoenix rose. For dinner, grab a burger in Phoenix's Camelback Corridor at **Delux.** Afterward, grab a beer and play a little bocce ball at **The Vig.**

Day 2

Rise with the sun and pick up some fresh orange juice and a Commuter Sandwich at the popular **La Grande Orange.** Then, head out for a round of **golf** at one of the city's championship desert courses or spend the morning hiking the red-sandstone **Camelback Mountain** or the rocky **Piestewa Peak** for the most spectacular views in town. Spend the rest of your afternoon relaxing, either poolside at your hotel or shopping at the

Hikers take a breather at the amphitheater in Papago Park.

the Desert Botanical Garden

CityScape in downtown Phoenix

open-air **Biltmore Fashion Park.** If you happen to be staying downtown, poke around the shops at **CityScape** after your dip in the pool. Have dinner at **Pizzeria Bianco, The Tuck Shop,** or **Barrio Café,** independent restaurants that regularly earn praise from foodies. Later, join the local art scenesters and hear live music at **The Lost Leaf** or grab a drink and play some old-school board games at **Valley Bar.**

Day 3

Begin your day in North Scottsdale with breakfast at **The Breakfast Joynt** before your tour of **Taliesin West,** Frank Lloyd Wright's winter home and architecture school, which still trains young apprentices. Learn how Wright's revolutionary work blended modern design and the Sonoran Desert landscape. Have lunch in **Old Town Scottsdale** at **Arcadia Farms,** and visit the district's Southwestern boutiques and the **Old Adobe Mission,** Scottsdale's first Catholic church. Head across Scottsdale Road

to the art districts of **Marshall Way** and **Main Street,** where the city's chic galleries showcase contemporary and Western art. Have dinner at one of downtown's numerous restaurants, such as **Cowboy Ciao** or **The Mission,** and barhop among Scottsdale's hip clubs and lounges, including **AZ88, Geisha A Go-Go,** and **The Mint Ultra Lounge.**

Day 4

Have breakfast at **Lo-Lo's Chicken and Waffles** on your last day. Check out the Desert Modernist **Burton Barr Central Library** in downtown Phoenix, then get a dose of culture at the **Phoenix Art Museum** or the **Heard Museum,** one of the nation's finest collections of Native American art and artifacts. Grab a gourmet **Pane Bianco** sandwich for lunch before you have to catch your flight home and consider snagging a couple scoops of ice cream from **Sweet Republic** in Terminal 4 of the airport.

10 Best Hikes

PHOENIX

- Phoenix hikers tend to favor **Piestewa Peak** (page 73) for a huffing, puffing, cardio workout. In a 2.4-mile round-trip, it tops out at 2,600 feet and takes about an hour and a half to complete the craggy, steep trail. It's also connected to the entire trail system of the Phoenix Mountains Preserve, giving stellar views of surrounding desert landscape.

- For the grand tour of the entire Phoenix Mountains Preserve, follow the 11-mile, one-way **Charles M. Christiansen Memorial Trail 100** (page 72), which scales the entire park end-to-end. It is masterfully planned and you'll gain an intimate understanding of the native Sonoran Desert while up, over, and around the dramatic rocky spires of this beloved mountain range. Plan an all-day trek that could last from six to eight hours.

- The **Hole-in-the-Rock Trail** (page 44) in Papago Park is often the very first trail completed by hikers aged three and under. At just 0.3 miles for the round-trip, it amounts to walking up a few flights of stairs and ends at a giant hole in a rock. This weather-eroded hole in the sandstone is so big that you can climb in, find a seat on the rocky sloped sides, and watch the sunset. Plan for 10 minutes of actual hiking followed by at least 30 minutes to enjoy the view.

- **Mormon Trail to Hidden Valley** (page 74) in South Mountain is a 3.6-mile hike with a quick climb at the start followed by a leisurely stroll through a swath of flat, sandy terrain hidden in the mountain. The hike also includes a rock tunnel and a suck-in-your-gut tight squeeze between two boulders called Fat Man's Pass. There's some moderate to advanced trail reading required for this combination of trails so be sure to have a map and pay attention to the trail signs.

SCOTTSDALE

- For a hiker, a visit to Scottsdale would not be complete without a trip up **Echo Canyon Summit Trail on Camelback Mountain** (page 73). At 2.6 miles for the round-trip, it reaches the summit at 2,700 feet and offers a 360-degree view of the valley below. Although it's the most popular trail by far, keep in mind that it is tough, so be prepared!

- For a beautiful, easy, and highly educational walk in the desert, try the **Bajada Nature Trail** (page 144), at McDowell Gateway Trailhead. At just 0.5 miles total for this loop, you could knock it out in 20 minutes but plan for an hour to take in the scenery and read the information signs.

- Hands down, one of the most memorable hikes in all of the McDowell Sonoran Preserve is **Tom's Thumb Trail** (page 145), which is a 4.5-mile round-trip of hard-fought switchbacks cutting right into heart of the mountain range. The final destination of this trail is a blow-your-mind ginormous boulder that juts straight up, up, and up some more. Give yourself about three hours to complete this beast.

SEDONA

- For an easy introduction to Sedona mountain hiking, try the four-mile **Bell Rock Pathway and Courthouse Butte Loop** (page 195) just north of the village of Oak Creek. The popular trail allows hikers to get up close and personal with some of the area's best-known rock formations.

- Speaking of rock formations, strap on your climbing shoes and scale the slick sides of **Cathedral Rock Trail** (page 195), which provides hand-and foot-holds to assist in your ascent. It may only be a 1.6-mile walk but don't be fooled, this short hike goes straight up for one heck of a workout and some incredible views.

- Ready for the best hike of your life? **West Fork of Oak Creek Trail** (page 218) in Oak Creek Canyon is an eight-mile epic round-trip that crosses the West Fork tributary waterway 13 times. It ends at a serene beach where hikers can take a dip or continue for additional miles wading through the watery canyon.

the Bajada Nature Trail

Family Road Trip

Phoenix, Scottsdale, and Sedona offer too much to do for the whole family—which is a great problem to have. Start in the Valley of the Sun and explore downtown Phoenix's museums and parks. Then head north to Sedona for a series of outdoor adventures before making your way back to Scottsdale's resorts and Old West fun.

Day 1

Fly into **Phoenix Sky Harbor International Airport** and check into your resort. You've got plenty of time to explore the city, so spend the afternoon taking advantage of the resort's amenities, which range from water parks and tennis courts to game rooms for kids.

Day 2

There's no better place to begin your trip to Phoenix than at its ancient foundations, the **Pueblo Grande Museum and Archaeological Park.** Explore inside reconstructed pit homes and learn how archaeologists

dig for artifacts by getting your own hands dirty. Head to neighboring **Tempe Town Lake,** where you can rent boats or take a relaxing stroll around the lake's edge. Have lunch at one of downtown's many restaurants, such as **The Chuckbox.** Cross back over the lake to **Papago Park** to tour **Phoenix Zoo,** where you can touch stingrays or duck into the walk-through Monkey Village. In the evening, sample the tacos, chimichangas, and fajitas at **Macayo's Depot Cantina.**

Day 3

Begin your third day in the Valley at **Matt's Big Breakfast,** a downtown Phoenix breakfast joint known for its fresh orange juice, hash browns, thick-cut bacon, and scrambled eggs with salami. Afterward, visit the **Arizona State Capitol,** restored to its original look in 1912, the year of Arizona's statehood. Consider a picnic lunch at **Civic Space Park,** where kids play in the grass or splash around in the water features, or **Encanto Park,** home of **Enchanted Island Amusement**

Montezuma Castle National Monument

Cathedral Rock

Park. Spend your afternoon at the **Arizona Science Center** nearby, which is a delightfully interactive museum in **Heritage and Science Park.** Younger kids may prefer the **Children's Museum of Phoenix,** across 7th Street. Older teens will enjoy a tour of Phoenix's progressive art and design at the **Phoenix Art Museum** and the **Burton Barr Central Library,** which offers brilliant views of the Phoenix skyline. Tonight, try dinner at one of downtown's pizzerias, like **Cibo Urban Pizzeria** or the renowned **Pizzeria Bianco.**

Day 4

It's time to immerse in the Sonoran Desert, with a morning hike in **South Mountain Park,** the world's largest municipal park. Hunt for ancient Native American petroglyphs or explore the pristine trails on horseback. Reward your adventurous spirit with a hearty, gourmet meal at the open-air **The Farm at South Mountain.** Explore more of South Phoenix at the mountainside **Mystery Castle,** a private house built from objects found in the desert, or you may want to take the children to **Rawhide Western Town.** The 1880s'-themed Old West town features dusty streets, stagecoach rides, and old-fashioned carnival games. After lunch, pan for "gold," visit a territorial jail, and

scope out the three-story Dinosaur Mountain at the **Arizona Museum of Natural History** in Mesa. Later, have dinner at **Caffe Boa,** followed by a stroll along **Mill Avenue.**

Day 5

Today, discover Arizona's rich Native American history. Start out at the **Heard Museum,** an impressive introduction to the state's original inhabitants and culture. Next, head north on I-17 to **Montezuma Castle National Monument.** The stunning five-story pueblo is perched on a cliffside near Camp Verde and was once inhabited by the ancient Sinagua people. Just up the interstate, you can witness more of their ingenuity at **Montezuma Well,** one of Arizona's unique geological wonders, which is fed by 1.5 million gallons of water by underground springs every day.

From there, take I-17 to Highway 179 and explore the red rocks of **Sedona.** As you drive into town, admire the monolithic **Bell Rock, Courthouse Butte,** and **Cathedral Rock.** Pull over in the Village of Oak Creek to have lunch at the **Red Rock Cafe.** Fortified, stop in at **Chapel of the Holy Cross,** an elegant, Modernist church that appears to rise out of the red rocks and offers panoramic views of Sedona. Check into your

Beat the Heat

PHOENIX

- The **water parks** (page 80) of Phoenix are simply massive, with features like wave pools, tubing areas, lazy rivers, white water rafting, and more slides than you'll know what to do with. Gather up the kids and take your pick from the most popular three: **Big Surf, Mesa Golfland-Sunsplash,** and **Wet 'n' Wild.**

- For a quick, free cool down that doesn't really even require a swimsuit, head to any number of **splash playgrounds** around town. Located at many large retail centers and city parks, the most convenient for downtown guests is at **Cityscape** (page 63). And at **Phoenix Zoo** (page 45), the kids can bombard one of three water play areas with the price of entry.

- Alternatively, head out to the northeast side of the Valley for a day of **tubing in the Salt River** (page 80). The breathtaking scenery where shoreline meets desert has moments of serenity as you float with the river's flow. The overall experience, however, is raucous, booze-guzzling, and slightly degrading as you frequently lift your hindquarters to avoid scraping the riverbed in shallow areas.

- Hike the **Hieroglyphic Trail in the Superstition Mountains** (page 114), where the trail ends in a canyon peppered with tanks—deep holes in the rock floor filled with rainwater. If there's been a good downpour in the last 24 hours, the water is fresh enough for a dip.

- For more ways to beat the heat in Phoenix, see page 75.

SCOTTSDALE

- For the party crowd, **resort pool parties** become a way of life in the summer. With DJs spinning and pop-up bars near the pool, the best bronzed bodies in all the Valley swarm to such events. Most of the Scottsdale resorts have a set schedule for these all-day drink-a-thons from June through August.

- It's no secret that Scottsdale has incredible spas but the whirlpools, showers, and plunge pools are a godsend, especially in the dry summer heat. Go to the **Joya Spa** (page 146) at the Omni Scottsdale Resort & Spa for the cold

Oak Creek Canyon

deluge shower, which will chill you to the bone in a most delicious way.

SEDONA

- Take the plunge at Arizona's best swimming hole in **Slide Rock State Park** (page 215), situated seven miles north of Sedona. Glide down the 80-foot-long natural rockslide, which was carved into the granite and red sandstone canyon floor by Oak Creek.

- Head to **Oak Creek Canyon** (page 215) for refreshing hiking, fishing, wading, and swimming.

- Phoenix isn't the only place that has cornered the market for splash pads. In the summer months, visit **Sunset Park** (page 180), where the kids can get hosed down at the dragon-themed splash pad and then dry off at the two playgrounds.

hotel, and after dinner at **Elote Cafe,** consider a **stargazing** adventure with an astronomer who will guide you around Arizona's nighttime sky.

Day 6

Have breakfast at **Coffee Pot Restaurant** and explore one of Sedona's protected parks, like **Red Rock State Park** or **Crescent Moon Recreation Area,** which features postcard views of **Oak Creek** and **Cathedral Rock.** Also, you can't come to Sedona without venturing into the backcountry on one of the ubiquitous **Jeep tours.** These guided journeys are a fun way to explore out-of-the-way formations and learn about Sedona's unique geology and wildlife. After lunch at **Oak Creek Brewery & Grill** at **Tlaquepaque,** head north on Highway 89A to the leafy refuge of **Oak Creek Canyon.** Hike the picturesque forest trails or plunge down the 80-foot-long natural chute at **Slide Rock State Park.**

Day 7

Take a side trip to the Old West mining town of **Jerome.** The hillside community was once called

Slide Rock State Park

the "Wickedest Town in the West," and today it's a National Historic Landmark, welcoming visitors with a host of small cafés, shops, galleries, and saloons. Have lunch at **Mile High Grill & Spirits** and visit the **Mine Museum** before driving back to the Valley of the Sun. Consider a stop at **Dead Horse Ranch State Park,** a lush stretch of the **Verde River** that offers hiking, mountain biking, fishing, and equestrian areas. Make the 90-minute drive back to **Scottsdale** and check into one of the city's sprawling resorts.

Day 8

Reacquaint yourself with the Valley of the Sun at **Camelback Mountain.** The difficult summit trails are among the best in the area, although you may want to take the kids to **McCormick-Stillman Railroad Park,** where they can ride the popular train or beautifully restored carousel. After lunch at **Chloe's Corner,** head to Frank Lloyd Wright's desert masterpiece, **Taliesin West,** for a tour of the architect's winter home. Then, keep heading north on Scottsdale Road to **Frontier Town** in **Cave Creek.** Embrace the Wild West spirit and have dinner at **El Encanto,** the area's best-known Mexican restaurant, which has a peaceful ambience bordering a lagoon.

Day 9

Today, camp out at your resort to enjoy the pools, tennis courts, and golf courses. However, if you're looking for a little adventure, rent some tubes and float down the **Salt River.** Tonight, have dinner at **Old Town Tortilla Factory,** then take in the night's sky with a **Stargazing Adventure** hosted by Stellar Adventures.

Day 10

On your last day in Scottsdale, dine at **The Breakfast Club** and explore the Western-themed streets of **Old Town** to pick up last-minute souvenirs and gifts. Hop on and off the free **Scottsdale Trolley,** which stops in the three arts districts and at **Scottsdale Fashion Square.** Grab lunch and an old-timey banana split at **The Sugar Bowl** before you have to catch your flight home.

Art in the Desert

PHOENIX

- **Civic Space Park** (page 36): *Her Secret Is Patience,* a massive fabric-net sculpture that hangs over the park from steel rings, resembles a saguaro cactus blossom—or a giant jellyfish, depending on your perspective. Visit at night to see the sculpture literally glow as it is illuminated from the ground up.

- **Heard Museum** (page 39): You'll find an unbeatable collection of Native American artifacts, fine art, and contemporary works at this museum.

- **Phoenix Art Museum** (page 39): The city's largest art museum has it all: western, eastern, ancient, modern, contemporary, painting, sculpture, fashion, and so on. Don't dare miss the incredible light installation by Yayoi Kusama.

- **Mystery Castle** (page 51): The late Mary Lou Gulley used to welcome visitors into her home, an eccentric "castle" her father built in the 1930s and 1940s from found objects like rocks, adobe, glass, auto parts, and even petroglyphs. Now open for tours, it's a wild place to see.

- **Roosevelt Row** (page 63): Tour this eclectic area downtown, which stretches from 7th Street

Roosevelt Row

to 7th Avenue along Roosevelt Street and features funky retail shops, art galleries, and some of the best mural artwork you'll ever see. Visit in the evening on the first and third Fridays of the month for the art walk, when all the galleries and businesses are open.

SCOTTSDALE

- **Scottsdale Museum of Contemporary Art** (page 123): With just a handful of galleries in the small museum, rotating exhibitions are often bold, highly conceptual, and well executed. The museum regularly hosts artist talks, art performances, and storytelling nights that bring in the crowds.

- **Cosanti** (page 124): Visit this small artists' village and bell foundry by Paolo Soleri, Frank Lloyd Wright's former student, which includes a subterranean "Earth House," outdoor studios, and student dorms. Visitors can often spy students pouring liquid bronze into molds to create the Soleri windbells.

- **Art Galleries** (page 138): Marshall Way, Main Street, Old Town, and Civic Center Park have a heavy concentration of art galleries, many of which feature Southwestern culture—making this the perfect place to find a souvenir piece.

- **Cave Creek** (page 167): This artistic community manages to retain much of its 1880s' character at Frontier Town, where you can spend the better part of an afternoon soaking in the artsy culture and poking around for funky tchotchkes.

SEDONA

- **Art Galleries** (page 188): Pull over along Route 179 as you approach the "Y" intersection and pop in and out of the many art galleries that line the road—don't skip the Tlaquepaque Arts and Crafts Village.

- **The Red Rocks** (page 179): Make your own art by spending a day among the red rocks as a landscape photographer. You're pretty much guaranteed to take amazing photos.

- **Jerome** (page 221): Hippies, artists, and bikers have transformed this old mining town into an eclectic mix of galleries, hotels, restaurants, and saloons.

Desert Luxury

Brilliant light, rugged mountains, sculptural plant life—few landscapes create such an evocative setting, but the Sonoran Desert also has a luxurious, cosmopolitan side, which lures pleasure-seekers and stressed-out vacationers to its resorts, golf courses, award-winning restaurants, and five-star spas. Sip prickly pear margaritas amid the boulders and adobe villas of Scottsdale before retreating north to Sedona's red rocks.

Day 1

Arrive at **Phoenix Sky Harbor International Airport** and head to **Papago Park** to get your bearings in this sprawling city. The park's rounded, red-rock formation is an easy ascent, and its views of the desert metropolis are well worth the little bit of effort. Visit the park's **Desert Botanical Garden** to learn about spiny cacti, green-bark palo verde trees, and colorful wildflowers. Afterward, head north on Scottsdale Road to see these indigenous plants in

their native environment at the **Four Seasons Resort Scottsdale at Troon North,** a desert sanctuary nestled into the foothills of Pinnacle Peak and inspired by old adobe villas. Relax on the veranda overlooking the Valley of the Sun and enjoy—literally—the fruits of the desert in a delicious prickly pear margarita. Have dinner at one of the resort's restaurants or order room service for a romantic meal on your private balcony.

Day 2

Wake up early to experience the desert at sunrise. Consider a leisurely hike up Pinnacle Peak or a round of golf at **Troon North Golf Club,** one of the Valley's best championship desert courses. Have lunch at **Chloe's Corner,** and reward your efforts and soothe any aching muscles at one of Scottsdale's deluxe spas, like the intimate **Spa at the Four Season Resort Scottsdale** or the renowned **Spa at The Boulders Resort,** which is set against the namesake rock formation and

the luxurious pool at Sanctuary on Camelback Mountain Resort & Spa

Troon North Golf Club in Scottsdale

features treatments rooted in Native American traditions. The spa also offers rock-climbing clinics for the more adventurous. Once you're feeling relaxed, head over to **Kierland Commons,** an outdoor shopping center in North Scottsdale, to browse for gifts or to find a cozy restaurant for dinner.

Day 3

Spend the morning shopping at **Scottsdale Fashion Square** in downtown Scottsdale. Grab brunch at **Arcadia Farms,** a charming cottage that serves fresh sandwiches, soups, and salads. Afterward, drive across Scottsdale Road to **Old Town** for more shopping. You can also get a dose of historical and modern culture at the **Old Adobe Mission** and the **Scottsdale Museum of Contemporary Art,** which is highlighted by *Knight Rise,* a Skyspace installation by artist James Turrell that frames Arizona's changing sky beautifully. If you're hungry for more art, downtown's **galleries** are among the finest in the country, showcasing edgy modern pieces along with traditional Southwestern art. You're

in the heart of Scottsdale's dining and **nightlife** scene, so spend your evening sampling the city's numerous options, such as **Café Monarch** or **Roaring Fork.**

Day 4

Horseback ride this morning through the desert and mountain passes of Tonto National Forest with **Spur Cross Stables.** Customize your horseback adventure or select one of several guided options. Afterward, enjoy lunch at **Zinc Bistro** and perhaps a quick siesta. Re-energized, drive south on Scottsdale Road to **Paradise Valley,** where Paolo Soleri's quirky **Cosanti** bell foundry and artist community reveals the architect's theories on environmentally responsible design. As evening approaches, enjoy a handcrafted cocktail at Sanctuary on Camelback Mountain Resort & Spa's stylish **Jade Bar,** where you can catch Mummy Mountain bathed in a desert sunset. Enjoy a Western-inspired dinner at the historic **LON's at the Hermosa Inn** or go modern at the sleek **Bourbon Steak.**

hot-air balloon above Sedona's red rocks

Day 5

Even that quintessentially American architect, Frank Lloyd Wright, was seduced by the desert. Tour his winter home, **Taliesin West,** a stone, sand, and glass masterpiece that incorporates indigenous materials and blends indoor and outdoor spaces. Afterward, get out of the sun and take in a massive musical history lesson at **Musical Instrument Museum,** which showcases more than 6,500 musical instruments from around the world. Have lunch at the charming **El Encanto,** then drive north to the high desert of **Sedona,** where massive red-rock buttes reveal Arizona's rich geological diversity. Once you get into town, head west on Highway 89A to Boynton Canyon, where the hacienda-inspired **Enchantment Resort** and **Mii amo Spa** are enveloped by the canyon's soaring cliff walls. You may never want to leave, although you should, if only for dinner at **Mariposa Latin Inspired Grill.**

Day 6

This morning, survey the red-rock buttes from the sky while floating in a **hot-air balloon** over Sedona, giving a perspective of the vast scale of the region's rocky formations. Once you descend and enjoy the complimentary champagne breakfast, be sure to visit the **Chapel of the Holy Cross,** where a local artist created a stunning church that seems to emerge from its red-rock foundations. You then have plenty of time to shop the small boutiques and galleries at **Tlaquepaque Arts and Crafts Village.** Make a reservation in advance so that you can dine by the creek at **Cress on Oak Creek.**

Day 7

For breakfast, scoot up Oak Creek Canyon to **Garland's Indian Gardens Café & Market** and enjoy a delicious breakfast on their back patio, which kisses the canyon walls. Stop by **Hoel's Indian Shop** to select a one of a kind, exquisite piece of Native American jewelry from this retail space housed in an enormous vault. Spend the rest of your morning perusing the shops in **Uptown,** enjoy a picnic lunch at **Sedona Memories,** and drive back to Phoenix to catch a late flight home.

The Valley After Dark

SEE AN OUTDOOR MOVIE

- Bring blankets, fold out chairs, and snacks to watch a family-friendly movie for free, hosted at places like **CityScape** (page 63) and **Biltmore Fashion Park** (page 64).

HIKE BY MOONLIGHT

- **Piestewa Peak** (page 73) trailheads close at 7pm but remain open until 11pm for those already hiking and looking to experience the desert after hours.

- In **McDowell Mountain Regional Park** (page 144), rangers take groups on sunset walks, moonlight hikes, and early-morning moonset hikes. The rangers are expert guides and will point out all the good stuff along the way. You're guaranteed to see a lot of wildlife action, which may include scorpions, coyotes, rattlesnakes, and desert tortoises. Families are welcome.

CRUISE THE MOUNTAINS

- In the summer months, **McDowell Mountain Regional Park** (page 141) hosts special moonlit biking events for experienced bikers to cruise along the park's incredible trails.

HUNT FOR SCORPIONS

- **Maricopa County Parks and Recreation** (www.maricopacountyparks.net/events/scorpion-hunt/) hosts events in which rangers help guests find scorpions because, you know, who doesn't want to look for creepy, poisonous critters with pincers and stingers?

LOOK AT ART

- During the Valley's **monthly art walks,** art galleries and businesses open their doors and sidewalks fill with people. Art walks take place every first and third Friday from 6pm-10pm in downtown Phoenix (page 64) and every Thursday from 7pm-9pm in Scottsdale (page 138).

- Check out James Turrell's art installation *Knight Rise* at the **Scottsdale Museum of Contemporary Art** (page 123), which stays open until 9pm Thursday through

Knight Rise at the Scottsdale Museum of Contemporary Art

Saturday. It's a particularly special experience as the sun goes down.

GAZE AT THE STARS

- Study the desert sky with a professional astronomer on a three- to four-hour tour with **Stellar Adventures** (page 140); it's $185 per person, and transportation, snacks, and beverages are provided.

GO CLUBBING IN SCOTTSDALE

- Hit up **Old Town Scottsdale** (page 120) on a weekend night for some of the hottest clubbing in the country.

Phoenix

Sights 32

Entertainment and Events 52

Shopping. 63

Sports and Recreation 70

Food 83

Accommodations. 99

Information and Services 105

Transportation. 106

Apache Trail and
    Superstition Mountains 107

Look for ★ to find recommended sights, activities, dining, and lodging.

Highlights

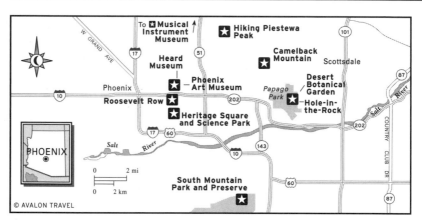

© AVALON TRAVEL

★ **Heritage Square and Science Park:** Heritage Square's eight historic homes now house small museums and popular restaurants and bars, while the futuristic Arizona Science Center is the perfect spot to escape the summer heat (page 36).

★ **Heard Museum:** Perhaps the finest collection of Native American art in the world, this museum is one of Arizona's great treasures. Learn about the rich culture of the state's original inhabitants (page 39).

★ **Phoenix Art Museum:** This sleek, stylish museum features a wide range of international art. And you can't miss Yayoi Kusama's mind-blowing room of light—one of the coolest art installations ever created (page 39).

★ **Camelback Mountain:** You can't miss the iconic "kneeling camel" profile of this mountain. The red-sandstone-and-granite peak rising at the center of the Valley of the Sun is a top draw for hikers and rock climbers (page 42).

★ **Musical Instrument Museum:** 6,500 musical instruments from 200 countries are beautifully displayed via a multi-media self-guided tour (page 43).

★ **Hole-in-the-Rock:** Join Phoenicians who gather in Papago Park to hike this rounded, red-rock formation once used by the ancient Hohokam civilization for astronomy (page 44).

★ **Desert Botanical Garden:** This garden easily claims the world's largest collection of desert plants, with some 50,000 cacti, shrubs, trees, and colorful wildflowers (page 44).

★ **South Mountain Park and Preserve:** Many Valley residents escape the city to hike, bike, horseback ride, and picnic in this large desert park. You can even take a scenic drive up to the summit (page 50).

★ **Roosevelt Row:** The creatives of Phoenix have joyously taken over an entire street and filled it with funky wall murals, fine-art galleries, cozy bars, independent shops, and tasty restaurants. Take a lively tour during the monthly art walks (page 63).

★ **Hiking Piestewa Peak:** The Summit Trail is steep, but you'll be rewarded with views in every direction and a chance to commune with saguaros, lizards, and other denizens of the desert (page 73).

S mug is the sun-kissed face of a Phoenix tourist wearing shorts and flip-flops in December. Yes, the city has temperatures over 110°F in summer, but the place is a paradise the rest of the year. The city and its neighboring suburbs are a

haven for fair weather activities like golfing, hiking, swimming, museum hopping, and gourmet patio dining.

You may have to traverse endless roadways lined with suburban buildings, but the art, food, music, and curious cultural quirks are worth hunting down. Explore downtown to discover areas packed with shopping and cultural happenings like theater or music shows, sports events, and the art walks that happen on the first and third Fridays of the month. Take an obligatory selfie by a saguaro cactus in the 33,000 acres of Sonoran Preserve, which boast 180 miles of hiking trails. And don't forget to treat yourself to authentic Mexican cuisine while guzzling refreshing margaritas.

The Valley of the Sun is a recreational nirvana, where warm days by the pool or on the links melt into a blazing sea of color at sunset. This heady mix of sun and fun has tempted many people to make a permanent move to

the city. But Phoenix-dwellers are not content to waste away in a dreamy haze of margaritas. Their pioneering spirit is alive and well in the sixth-largest city of the United States, and they are determined to create a vibrant, culturally relevant city on a par with its Sun Belt sisters in Miami, Austin, and Los Angeles.

The dramatic landscape and Western spirit of Phoenix have conspired to create a unique destination. Sure, you'll find prickly cacti, lots of sunshine, and all the things you think you already know about Phoenix, but you'll also discover a unique sensibility. Get to know the city and its residents by having brunch at the Farm at South Mountain or by lounging at the pool to savor "the dry heat," a favorite Phoenician punch line.

Don't try to explore Phoenix as a succession of tourist sites as if you were in New York or Washington DC. Instead, think of the city as a collection of experiences: smelling orange

---

Previous: downtown Phoenix; hiking the Peralta Trail. **Above:** the Desert Botanical Garden.

Phoenix

To Sedona

101

W UNION HILLS DR
7TH AVE
7TH ST
CAVE CREEK RD
★ MUSICAL INSTRUMENT MUSEUM
McDowell Sonoran Preserve

51
W BELL RD
E BELL RD
TPC

KIRKLAND
SCOTTSDALE RD
W GREENWAY RD
E GREENWAY PKWY
TALIESIN WEST ★

W THUNDERBIRD RD
84TH ST
56TH ST
E THUNDERBIRD RD
BLVD
N FRANK LLOYD WRIGHT BLVD

17
W CACTUS RD
North Mountain Park
E CACTUS RD
101

W PEORIA RD
ORANGE TREE
SCOTTSDALE
E SHEA BLVD
W OLIVE RD
Arizona Canal
E SHEA BLVD

W NORTHERN AVE
Phoenix Mountains Preserve
E DOUBLETREE RANCH RD
CAMELBACK
MCCORMICK RANCH
TALKING STICK

W GLENDALE AVE
BLACK CANYON FWY
19TH AVE
7TH AVE
7TH ST
16TH ST
PIESTEWA FWY
★ HIKING PIESTEWA PEAK
Paradise Valley
E LINCOLN DR
PAVILION LAKES

W BETHANY HOME RD
E MCDONALD DR

60
51ST AVE
43RD AVE
35TH AVE
27TH AVE
CENTRAL AVE
24TH ST
32ND ST
44TH ST
51
▲ CAMELBACK MOUNTAIN
E CAMELBACK RD
PIMA FWY

E INDIAN SCHOOL RD
SCOTTSDALE RD
HAYDEN RD
N BEELINE HWY

Encanto Park
★ HEARD MUSEUM
E THOMAS RD
DESERT BOTANICAL GARDEN

N GRAND AVE
★ PHOENIX ART MUSEUM
E MCDOWELL RD
Papago Park
87

PAPAGO FWY ★ ROOSEVELT ROW
E VAN BUREN ST
PHOENIX ZOO
★ HOLE-IN-THE-ROCK
COUNTRY CLUB DR

HERITAGE SQUARE AND SCIENCE PARK
PUEBLO GRANDE MUSEUM AND ARCHAEOLOGICAL PARK
Tempe Canal

W BUCKEYE RD
PHOENIX
202

10
PHOENIX INTERNATIONAL AIRPORT
143
TEMPE
E UNIVERSITY DR
ARIZONA MUSEUM OF NATURAL HISTORY ★

51ST AVE
35TH AVE
Salt
River
7TH AVE
7TH ST
24TH ST
48TH ST
ASU
E BROADWAY RD
E APACHE BLVD

W BROADWAY RD
PRIEST DR
MILL AVE
RURAL RD
101
E SOUTHERN AVE

19TH AVE
E SOUTHERN AVE
SUPERSTITION FWY

60
E BASELINE RD

E GUADALUPE RD

SOUTH MOUNTAIN ENVIRONMENTAL EDUCATION CENTER ★
MYSTERY CASTLE ★
Western Canal
E ELLIOT RD

Western Canal
★ SOUTH MOUNTAIN PARK AND PRESERVE
10
E WARNER RD

Phoenix South Mountain Park
56TH ST
MCCLINTOCK DR
DOBSON RD
ALMA SCHOOL RD
ARIZONA AVE

0   5 mi
0   5 km
KAI ▼
CHANDLER BLVD
CYCLO ▼
Chandler
101

RAWHIDE WESTERN TOWN AT WILD HORSE PASS ★
SANTAN FWY
SAN MARCOS RESORT

BELTLINE RD
W QUEEN CREEK RD
W GERMAN RD

blossoms in the spring, hearing gravel beneath your feet as you climb Piestewa Peak, tasting authentic corn tortillas and carne asada at a small *taqueria*, discovering the ancient culture of the region's Native American people at the Heard Museum. These subtle—often hidden—pleasures will linger long after a suntan begins to fade.

ORIENTATION

When people say "Phoenix," they are often referring to the mass of roadways, highways, urban, and suburban developments that encompasses the city limits and the connected neighboring cities as well. So for the purposes of this book, here's how we've split up the city.

Downtown Phoenix may be small by comparison to the downtown areas of other cities but it is still easily recognizable by its tall buildings and heavy pedestrian traffic (by Phoenix standards anyway). "Downtown" is typically referred to as the generous swath of property that includes the arts district, a west-to-east span of 15th Avenue to 15th Street, and a north-to-south spread of McDowell Road to Buckeye Road.

Heading north and slightly east from downtown is what this book designates as Central Phoenix. What once were the "outskirts" of Phoenix are now extensions of the heart of the city, including neighborhoods North Central Phoenix, Biltmore, and Arcadia. These neighborhoods are less populated by art galleries and museums but are heavy with restaurants, shopping, and outdoor recreation.

Keep heading north from these neighborhoods and you'll hit the rest of the city, which is broadly referred to as North Phoenix. Attractions are certainly more spread out among the many miles of this area, which are mostly filled by office buildings, suburban neighborhoods, strip malls, and city parks.

To the south and east of downtown Phoenix sits the city of Tempe, and further east are the cities of Mesa, Chandler, and Gilbert, which comprise the East Valley. Each has its own downtown complete with shopping, museums, restaurants, and bars.

PLANNING YOUR TIME

You'll need at least three days to see Phoenix, balancing a few cultural sights with the bounty of outdoor activities. Consider a hike or round of golf in the morning and afternoon visits to the Phoenix Art Museum, Heritage Square, or the world-renowned Heard Museum, which has a rich repository of Native American art and artifacts. However, you should really take a week to make the most of a trip to the Valley of the Sun. Phoenix, Scottsdale, and the surrounding suburbs each offer pockets of pedestrian-friendly neighborhoods to explore, and you'll want to make sure you have plenty of time to relax and enjoy the sunshine.

The Valley of the Sun is huge and its 4.5 million residents crisscross the city daily, thanks to a large web of freeways. Fortunately for visitors, many of the best sights, parks, restaurants, and shops are clustered in a central strip running from South Mountain through downtown Phoenix and Tempe to North Scottsdale. To explore the city, you'll definitely need a car—and you'll become quite familiar with the main commuter arteries: I-10, SR 51, Highway 101, Highway 202, Central Avenue, and Camelback Road.

Families, couples, and groups of friends won't struggle to find activities that appeal to their tastes. Most of the year, kids will want to spend morning, noon, and—yes—night, in the Valley's pools and water parks, recreational specialties found at many resorts. When the weather is cooler, however, Phoenix Zoo and the Old West-themed Rawhide Western Town are entertaining diversions. Adults, too, won't mind spending time poolside with a tasty beverage and good book in hand, but should take time to immerse themselves in the Sonoran Desert landscape. Hikers, mountain bikers, and horseback riders of all levels will appreciate the cactus-dotted peaks that rise throughout the city—get a taste of this rugged landscape without leaving the city's paved sidewalks at the Desert Botanical Garden and Papago Park.

The weather, in all likelihood, will shape what you do and when you do it. Phoenix is heavenly October through April, when warm days and cool evenings attract most visitors. It can even get a little cold in the winter, with the occasional nighttime temperature dropping below freezing. Summer is a very different story. Count on temperatures over 86°F from June through September, making a swimming pool or air-conditioned escape mandatory. Don't be frightened, though. The desert's arid climate means you'll actually be shivering when you emerge from a pool, and an early morning hike or round of golf means you won't be trapped inside. Summer is also the opportunity to indulge at luxury resorts for bargain prices.

HISTORY

Phoenix is called a "young" city so often that it's easy to forget that there's an entire ancient civilization buried underneath it. Native Americans have called the Sonoran Desert home for thousands of years, with the Hohokam people digging the first irrigation canals fed by the Salt River about 2,000 years ago. They improved and expanded the system over the centuries using nothing but wood and stone tools, simple leveling devices, and their own labor. Some canals were as long as 20 miles and carried thousands of gallons of water through a complex series of main lines, laterals, and small ditches. At its height around AD 1300, the system watered more than 10,000 acres scattered across the present-day metro Phoenix. The Hohokam's corn, beans, squash, and cotton crops supported as many as 50,000 people, making the Salt River valley one of the largest settlements in prehistoric North America. But after 1,500 years of growth, Hohokam society began a slow collapse, probably triggered by a combination of drought, environmental stresses, and

war. By the end of the 1400s, the people had abandoned their pueblos and canals for small farming villages scattered across the region.

Modern Phoenix wasn't born until 1867, when a man named Jack Swilling passed through and recognized that the Salt River Valley looked like a good place for farming. The broad, fertile valley was filled with desert grasses, mesquite, willow, and cottonwood trees, and best of all, the wide, winding river that flowed down out of the mountains to the northeast. So after this one-time army scout, gold miner, cattle rancher, and saloon owner returned home to Wickenburg (a mining town about 50 miles northwest of present-day Phoenix) he got financial backing from a group of local residents and organized a company to dig irrigation canals and establish farms in the remote valley.

It wasn't long before he and the dozens of settlers who followed discovered that digging up the Hohokam canal system was an easier way to bring water to their fields than starting from scratch. So it was that an erudite settler named Lord Darrell Duppa suggested they name their new town Phoenix, after the mythical bird that rises from its own ashes after being consumed by flame.

By 1900, the young town's population had grown to 5,554, thanks to a long growing season and new railroads centered on the historic Union Station downtown, which delivered crops all across the United States. Technology didn't solve all the settlers' problems, though; snowmelt and rain regularly sent the Salt River over its banks, including the worst flood on record in February 1901, which swelled the river to three miles wide in some places, wiping out crops, houses, and the all-important railroad bridge. The brand-new territorial capitol west of downtown was inundated, too, destroying many early records. Luckily, President Theodore Roosevelt rode to the rescue with a bold plan and several million dollars.

In 1911, Roosevelt tasked the newly formed Bureau of Reclamation with building a

The Valley of the Sun

Phoenix, now the sixth-largest city in the country, is a part of an immense metropolitan area known as the Valley of the Sun—and it's not just a tourism slogan, thanks to 300 days of sun per year. "The Valley," as locals call it, is surrounded by a series of mountain ranges, and after decades of development, the suburban sprawl is creeping beyond the valley floor. Census estimates consistently name Phoenix as one of the fastest growing cities year over year and developers have consumed huge swaths of agricultural land and pristine desert. Formerly independent cities and towns now blend from one into another, connected by a giant grid of freeways.

The East Valley was the first to experience a huge surge of arrivals in the 1980s and 1990s, when small cities like Chandler and former agricultural centers including Gilbert, Queen Creek, and Apache Junction became stucco-home boomtowns. Bedroom communities like Fountain Hills and Ahwatukee practically sprang up overnight. Scottsdale in the Northeast Valley also experienced significant growing pains, annexing huge portions of land.

A decade later, master-planned communities—like Anthem in the north, Gold Canyon in the east, and Maricopa in the south—pushed further into the desert. Developers in the West Valley turned huge tracts of land into subdivisions that now house hundreds of thousands of people. The retirement community of Sun City and Glendale were both engulfed by Surprise, Avondale, Goodyear, Peoria, and Buckeye, and civic leaders had to scramble to find the best ways to turn their small towns in big ones. However, the housing bust in 2008 complicated matters, with the West Valley becoming one of the hardest-hit areas in the country.

However, much like the rest of the country, Phoenix has been marching on the road to recovery from the whole real-estate crash. With a resurgence of cultural value towards homes built mid-century, developers and buyers have shifted their focus to remodeling and revitalizing existing neighborhoods that are more centrally located.

hydroelectric dam on the Salt River to control flooding and generate electricity. It was the first project the new agency tackled, and although it tamed the free-flowing river by diverting the whole flow from its banks into an expanded canal system, it led to one of Phoenix's first big boom periods. With an economy fueled by the "Five Cs"—citrus, cotton, cattle, copper, and climate—the city's population mushroomed to nearly 30,000 people by 1920 and added almost 20,000 more by 1930, matching the Hohokam's previous record of 50,000 inhabitants in just 50 years. Even then, the boom had barely begun.

Following World War II, returning soldiers—of whom many had trained at airbases around Phoenix, thanks to its sunny, flying-friendly weather—flocked to the city and its burgeoning aerospace industry. As air-conditioning became widely available and early technology and manufacturing companies also moved west in search of cheap land, the population grew past 100,000 by 1950 and neared an almost-unimaginable 440,000 by 1960.

Today, some 1.5 million live in Phoenix proper, making it the sixth-largest city in the nation behind New York City, Los Angeles, Chicago, Houston, and Philadelphia, whose recent growth was just large enough to nudge Phoenix down from the fifth spot. Phoenix has had tremendous growth and it has come at a price. Many residents see pollution and the destruction of pristine desert sapping their quality of life as suburban sprawl forces them to spend hours commuting or going about everyday tasks. But the same spirit that drove Phoenicians to build a metropolis in less than 150 years is pushing them to dream up new solutions, and it's anyone's guess what seemingly impossible feats the residents of this dynamic city will tackle next.

Sights

Phoenix, now the sixth-largest city in the United States, is a sprawling expanse of neighborhoods and suburbs, and its attractions are scattered throughout the city. You'll need a car to navigate the Valley of the Sun, although the new light-rail system conveniently connects some of the most popular sights, including the Heard Museum, the Phoenix Art Museum, the Arizona Science Center, and Tempe's Mill Avenue neighborhood.

DOWNTOWN AND THE ARTS DISTRICT

Like any Old West town worth its salt, Phoenix has had to endure the boom and bust of life in the desert since its founding in 1870. However, unlike some of its ghost-town brethren, Phoenix has a knack for emerging from hard times. Tombstone may be "the town too tough to die," but downtown Phoenix is the metropolis that always seems to rise again.

Following decades of suburban flight and urban decay, businesses and, more importantly, people, are returning to downtown Phoenix. An estimated $4 billion has been spent redeveloping the 90-block area known as **Copper Square,** and it seems to be paying off, albeit slowly. Much as in the city's early days, when farmers and ranchers would come to town for a show or to pick up supplies, suburbanites are flocking to downtown's stadiums, museums, and concert venues, and supporting new restaurants and bars. The construction of a convention center, Arizona State University's downtown campus, CityScape shopping and residential center, and countless other revitalizations to existing buildings has brought some nighttime pedestrian traffic to the once-empty streets. Plus, the light rail has given downtown another steroid shot in the arm.

If you have any questions or need directions, **Downtown Phoenix Inc.** (dtphx.org, 602/495-1500) has got everything covered.

Visit their website for a live chat or look for one of the Downtown Phoenix "ambassadors," easily identifiable in an orange shirt printed with the words "Ask Me." They roam the streets seven days a week, 365 days per year.

Arizona State Capitol

Arizona's territorial capital bounced between Prescott and Tucson before finally settling on Phoenix in 1889. In an effort to prove to the federal government that Arizona was ready for statehood, the territorial legislature constructed the capitol building between 1898 and 1901. The design, based on a rejected concept for the Mississippi State Capitol, was scaled back in size and appropriated for Arizona's desert climate, with additions such as thick masonry walls for insulation and ventilating windows. They also painted the dome copper as a tribute to the mineral that served as an essential local economic resource.

As the state grew, so did the demands on the building. Part-time Arizona resident Frank Lloyd Wright submitted plans in 1957 for a massive Arizona Capitol Complex, which would have transferred the legislature, governor, and Supreme Court from downtown to Papago Park at a whopping cost of $5 million. It was immediately rejected. One of the proposed 125-foot-tall spires for the project is now visible at Scottsdale and Frank Lloyd Wright Boulevards in North Scottsdale. Instead, the State House and Senate were relocated into bunker-like buildings on either side of the capitol in 1960, and the governor moved to the Executive Tower behind the capitol.

A renovation in 1981 restored the building to its original look from 1912, the year of Arizona's statehood, and the dome was finally given a proper copper plating: $4.8 million-worth, a fitting number for the 48th state. That same year, the **Arizona Capitol Museum** (1700 W. Washington St., 602/926-3620, www.azlibrary.gov/azcm, 9am-4pm

Downtown Phoenix

To Melrose
Shopping District

PHOENIX ✴
ART MUSEUM

BUNKY
BOUTIQUE

MCDOWELL RD

To
✴ HEARD MUSEUM

To
America's
Taco Shop

E WILLETTA ST

ST. MARY'S
BASILICA

E   MONROE   ST

ROSSON
HOUSE

CHILDREN'S
MUSEUM
OF PHOENIX

PHOENIX
MUSEUM ★
OF HISTORY

✚ HERITAGE SQUARE
AND SCIENCE PARK

▼ ROSE & CROWN

BURTON BARR
CENTRAL LIBRARY

2ND ST

PAPAGO   FWY

PAPAGO   FWY   10

BAR
BIANCO ▼

PIZZERIA
BIANCO

E   MORELAND   ST

N 5TH ST

ARIZONA
SCIENCE CENTER

7TH ST

E   WASHINGTON   ST

Deck Park
Japanese
Friendship
Garden

CARLY'S
BISTRO ▼

2ND ST

E   PORTLAND   ST

W   PORTLAND   ST

CENTRAL
AVE

THE
NASH ▼

ROOSEVELT ROW ✚

ROOSEVELT   ST

TAMMIE COE
CAKES

LOLA
COFFEE ▼

REVOLVER
RECORDS ▼

BLISS
REBAR ▼

MADE ART
BOUTIQUE/EYE LOUNGE

MATT'S
BIG BREAKFAST ▼

FILM BAR ▼

THE
LOST LEAF

W   MCKINLEY   ST

THE BREADFRUIT ▼

ANTIQUE SUGAR ▼

5TH ST

7TH ST

7TH
AVE

CHAMBERS ON
FIRST/POMO
PIZZERIA

COBRA
ARCADE
BAR

3RD
ST

CIBO ▼

6TH AVE

5TH AVE

4TH AVE

3RD AVE

PHOENIX
PUBLIC MARKET ★

WESTWARD HO ✴

E   FILLMORE   ST

1ST ST

To
Arizona Capital
& Museum

CIVIC
SPACE
PARK

1ST AVE

ARIZONA

CENTER

To
Super 8
Phoenix

RODEWAY
INN

CRESCENT
BALLROOM

SHERATON
GRAND

E   VAN   BUREN   ST

HOTEL
SAN
CARLOS

THE
WESTIN

HYATT
REGENCY

HERBERGER
THEATER

SEE DETAIL

SEAMUS MCCAFFREY'S
IRISH PUB ▼ ★

HILTON
GARDEN INN

MONROE   ST

HERITAGE SQUARE ✚
AND SCIENCE PARK

★

VALLEY
BAR ▼

RENAISSANCE
HOTEL

ORPHEUM
THEATRE ★

HANNY'S ▼

PHOENIX
SYMPHONY
HALL

COMERICA ■
THEATRE

WELLS FARGO ★
HISTORY MUSEUM

HOTEL
PALOMAR ▼

CARTEL
COFFEE
LAB

E WASHINGTON   ST

MRS. WHITE'S
GOLDEN RULE CAFE ▼

GABBA
GREEN

CITYSCAPE ★

HISTORIC ★
CITY HALL

STAND
UP LIVE ★ ▼

ARROGANT
BUTCHER

JEFFERSON   ST

0   400 yds

3RD

LUHRS
TOWER

BITTER &
TWISTED
COCKTAIL
PARLOUR

TALKING STICK ■
RESORT ARENA

CHASE

FIELD

0   400 m

1ST AVE

CENTRAL

E   BUCHANAN   ST

7TH ST

To Lo-Lo's Chicken and Waffles,
Last Exit Live, and New Garden Cafe

THE
▼ DUCE

E   LINCOLN   ST

© AVALON TRAVEL

Exploring Phoenix's Architecture

Changing architectural styles in Phoenix's neighborhoods and commercial districts are like tree rings tracking the city's growth. Because it grew so big so fast, many neighborhoods in Phoenix were built at the same time by developers. The resulting "master-planned communities" can make it seem like all the city has to offer are cookie-cutter ranch houses or red-tile roofs, but that's not the whole truth. The warm, sunny climate has encouraged architectural innovation since the first people moved to the Sonoran Desert, and today is no exception.

PHOENIX PREHISTORY (AD 1-1450)

More than 2,000 years ago, the Hohokam people started building a system of irrigation canals fed by the Salt River. For the next millennium and a half, they built villages, pit houses, and walled pueblos that housed as many as 50,000 people in what is now metro Phoenix, making it one of the largest ancient population centers in North America. Their society collapsed in the mid-1400s and most of their buildings are gone or buried, but visitors can walk through the ruins of a large, 800-year-old platform mound at **Pueblo Grande Museum**

Luhrs Tower in downtown Phoenix

and Archaeological Park (4619 E. Washington St., 602/495-0901, www.pueblogrande.com, 9am-4:45pm Mon.-Sat., 1pm-4:45pm Sun., closed Sun.-Mon. May-Sept., $6 adults, $3 children 6-17). The earthen-walled structure evokes how these resourceful people adapted to life in the desert.

TURN OF THE 20TH CENTURY (1880-1915)

The 19th-century houses huddled on **Heritage Square and Science Park** (113 N. 6th St., 602/262-5070, www.heritagesquarephx.org) show the roots of the modern city. Home to the merchants and traders who served what was then a valley of farmers and ranchers, they are the only extant residential structures from the city's original townsite. The sturdy, red-brick houses with ample verandahs (also known as "sleeping porches" where residents would sleep on summer nights) are now inhabited by a mix of restaurants, bars, and museums. At the park is the **Rosson House** (10am-4pm Wed.-Sat., noon-4pm Sun., $7.50 adults, $4 children 6-12), a Victorian mansion built in 1895 and is open for public tours.

THE ROARING TWENTIES (1920-1935)

A half-mile stretch of Central Avenue between Jefferson and Fillmore Streets downtown displays the architectural ambitions from this perennial boomtown's first growth spurt in the 1920s. The renaissance-revival **Hotel San Carlos** (220 N. Central Ave., 602/253-4121, www.hotelsancarlos.com) and the Art Deco **Westward Ho** (618 N. Central Ave.) both debuted in 1928 as luxury hotels that have attracted Hollywood stars, gangsters, and politicians over the ensuing decades. The 14-story, Art Deco **Luhrs Tower** (11 W. Jefferson St.) rose a year later in 1929; it now houses the popular Bitter & Twisted Cocktail Parlour (602/340-1924, www.bitterandtwistedaz.com, 4pm-2am Tues.-Sat.). Across the street, Phoenix's 1928 **City Hall** (125 W. Washington St.) makes the idea of occupying one of the jail cells on the upper levels almost appealing. The **Orpheum Theatre** (203 W. Adams St., 602/495-7139, www.phoenixconventioncenter.com/orpheum-theatre) was built in 1929 as a vaudeville theater and injects Spanish Revival with Spanish Baroque embellishment. Free theater tours run frequently, but visit the Friends of the Orpheum Theatre (www.friendsoftheorpheumtheatre.org) to confirm dates and times.

MIDCENTURY IDENTITY (1948-1970)

Phoenix came of age following World War II as its population exploded, and the city's wealth of midcentury architecture shows it. Frank Lloyd Wright lived in Arizona for decades, designing a number of buildings around town, including his winter home and workshop, **Taliesin West** (12345 N. Taliesin Dr., 480/627-5340, www.franklloydwright.org, 8:30am-6pm Thurs.-Mon.). It's open for tours daily, as is **Cosanti** (6433 E. Doubletree Ranch Rd., 800/752-3187, www.cosanti.com, 9am-5pm Mon.-Sat., 11am-5pm Sun., free), designed by visionary architect Paolo Soleri. Good examples of midcentury commercial buildings include the 1964 **Phoenix Financial Center** (3443 N. Central Ave.), which has a facade designed to look like a computer punch card, and **Hanny's** (40 N. 1st St., 602/252-2285, www.hannys.net), which was downtown's first modernist department store in 1948 and now houses a restaurant/bar of the same name. But the best places to see how new owners have updated that icon of the Atomic Age, the ranch house, are two neighborhoods near the Phoenix Mountains Preserve. A drive around **Paradise Gardens**—generally bounded by 36th and 33rd Streets to the east and west and Gold Dust and Mountain View Roads to the north and south—shows off the work of locally revered architect Al Beadle. **Marlen Gardens**—which sits between Bethany Home and Montebello Roads along 10th and 11th Streets—was designed and built by the equally beloved Arizona architect Ralph Haver. The group Modern Phoenix (www.modernphoenix.net) arranges tours of residences several times a year.

DESERT MODERN (1990-PRESENT)

Dozens of Phoenix offices and houses have earned the attention of the design world over the past few years, thanks to their blending of indoor and outdoor spaces, innovative use of materials, and embracing of light and space. But a lot of it is, unfortunately, private. The best publicly accessible examples of this Desert Modernism are a trio of public libraries (www.phoenixpubliclibrary.org):

the Will Bruder-designed **Burton Barr Central Library** (1221 N. Central Ave.), the Richard+Bauer-designed **Desert Broom Library** (29710 N. Cave Creek Rd.), and the Gould Evans and Wendell Burnette-designed **Palo Verde Branch Library** (4402 N. 51st Ave.). Other ways to catch a glimpse of spectacular houses include driving around neighborhoods near the mountains, or scanning real estate websites such as www.azarchitecture.com for open houses.

Contributed by David Proffitt, architectural journalist

Burton Barr Central Library

Mon.-Fri., 10am-2pm Sat. Sept.-May, free) was opened, allowing visitors to see the old House and Senate chambers, offices of the governor, and exhibitions on Arizona's history. There is also a small display chronicling the USS *Arizona.*

Civic Space Park

Part of an effort by city leaders to transform downtown into a vibrant urban space, **Civic Space Park** (424 N. Central Ave., 602/262-7490, www.phoenix.gov/parks, 5am-11pm daily, free) brings some green design to the neighborhood, with rolling lawns, dancing water fountains, and leafy trees that are expected to shade as much as 70 percent of the park once they mature.

What you'll surely notice first is a massive fabric-net sculpture that hangs over the park from steel rings. This public artwork, *Her Secret is Patience,* initially garnered some controversy, both because of its abstract shape and its $2.4 million price tag. Artist Janet Echelman—who named the piece after a line in a Ralph Waldo Emerson poem: "Adopt the pace of nature; her secret is patience,"—says Arizona's monsoon clouds and saguaro cactus blossoms inspired her, although some have likened the funnel-shaped sculpture to a giant jellyfish or purple tornado. As with many public art pieces, time has proven its worth and the dynamic structure is now a point of pride for downtown Phoenix. The piece is best viewed in the evening while lying in the grass and staring up at the netting. Massive lights create a dramatic electric glow to the net's color and its flexible support cables allow the entire piece to dance in the breeze.

In fact, it's the three-acre park's transformation when the sun sets that makes it so enticing. A dozen LED-lit poles put on a light show at the southern end of the park while whimsical water features for kids glow purple. There is even space for movies and small concerts, which attract students from Arizona State University's adjacent downtown campus. The requisite energy demands are offset by solar panels on the park's shade structures during the day.

Visit on the second or fourth Wednesday of the month for Wednesday Wind Up, which takes place between 11am to 1:30pm for live entertainment and a chance to try out the cooking from local food trucks.

Wells Fargo History Museum

For a quick snapshot of the Wild West, duck into the **Wells Fargo History Museum** (145 W. Adams St., 602/378-1852, www.wellsfargohistory.com/museums/phoenix, 9am-5pm Mon.-Fri., free), where you'll be greeted by an icon of Arizona's history—an authentic 19th-century stagecoach that still bears the scars of a hard life roaming the West's bumpy trails. The small collection of memorabilia includes antique guns, Western artwork by N. C. Wyeth, and a display showing how gold bars were made. Kids can climb aboard a replica stagecoach or try their hands at working the telegraph.

St. Mary's Basilica

When Phoenix's citizens built their first Catholic church in 1881, only the most devout could have imagined a papal visit some 100 years later. That original structure was constructed from hand-formed adobe and was replaced in 1902 by **St. Mary's Basilica** (231 N. 3rd St., 602/354-2100, www.saintmarysbasilica.org, 9am-4pm Mon.-Fri., 10am-6pm Sat., 8am-1pm Sun., free), a Mission Revival-style church that still holds Mass every day. Pope John Paul II named St. Mary's a minor basilica in 1985, and two years later he visited the church on a trip to Phoenix. The inspiring collection of stained-glass windows is the largest in the state and its spacious, bright interior is worth a quick stop.

★ Heritage Square and Science Park

Heritage Square and Science Park (113 N. 6th St., 602/262-5070, www.heritagesquarephx.org) is something of an anomaly in tear-it-down-and-build-something-new

The Arts District

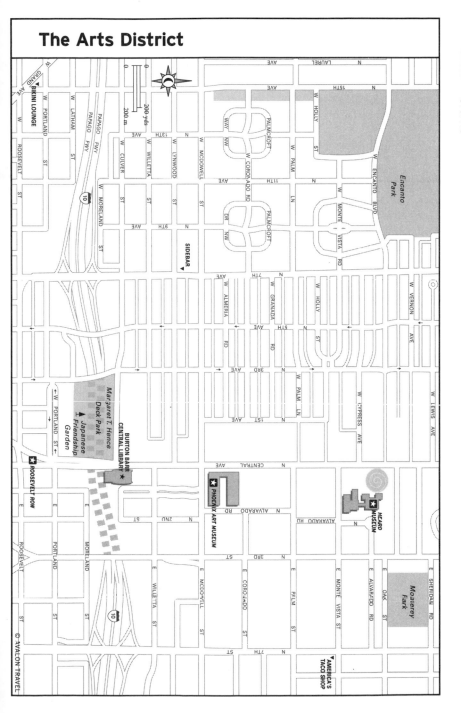

Phoenix. The historic park protects the only remaining residential buildings from Phoenix's original 1870 townsite. Today, the eight historic structures house small museums, offices, shops, and restaurants. **Rosson House** (113 N. 6th St., 602/262-5070, www.heritagesquarephx.org, 10am-4pm Wed.-Sat, noon-4pm Sun., $7.50 adults, $4 children 6-12) is the most ornate, and even when it was built by Roland and Flora Rosson in 1895 for $7,525, the Victorian house's octagonal turret and shaded veranda were considered extravagant. Flora, who came from a wealthy family, had bought the entire city block, allowing plenty of space for the 4,200-square-foot home's 10 rooms, which have been restored with period furnishings and pressed-tin ceilings. Docent-guided tours are available.

Arizona Science Center

One of the best museums in the Valley and a hit with kids, the **Arizona Science Center** (600 E. Washington St., 602/716-2000, www.azscience.org, 10am-5pm daily, $18 adults, $13 children 3-17) packs more than 300 interactive exhibits into 98,000 square feet of gallery space, making science a hands-on, physical experience. Here children can ride a high-wire bike, race up a pulley system,

make clouds, or lie on a bed of 1,000 nails. Noted architect Antoine Predock designed the sprawling concrete-and-metal building, creating soaring spaces for the huge displays. The museum's high-tech, five-story IMAX theater and Dorrance Planetarium feature a series of shows throughout the day, and nationally traveling exhibitions regularly make a pit stop here. The on-site **Lab Café** (10am-4pm daily, $6-11) is a great place to grab an after-museum lunch, with salads, burgers, and snacks.

Children's Museum of Phoenix

It seems fitting that Jackson Pollock's old elementary school should find new life as the splashy **Children's Museum of Phoenix** (215 N. 7th St., 602/253-0501, www.childrensmuseumofphoenix.org, 9am-4pm Tues.-Sun., $11), a hands-on, 70,000-square-foot gallery dedicated to youngsters aged 10 and under. Would-be Picassos and Pollocks will find more than finger-paints here, though. In 2008, the historic Monroe School Building, once the largest elementary school west of the Mississippi, was transformed into a playground designed to "engage the minds, muscles, and imaginations of children." Kids can navigate through the Noodle Forest, climb up a makeshift tree house, pedal through a

the Arizona Science Center

tricycle car wash, or simply enjoy a little reading in the comfy Book Loft. It's one of the top ten children's museums in the country and you'll instantly understand why when you see the unbridled energy released as children engage in this environment, which encourages play-based learning and liberated exploration. It's also a great option for the family on a hot summer's day.

★ Heard Museum

Talk to a native Phoenician and they surely have memories of grinding corn with a stone at the **Heard Museum** (2301 N. Central Ave., 602/252-8840, www.heard.org, 9:30am-5pm Mon.-Sat., 11am-5pm Sun., 6pm-10pm first Friday of the month, $18 adults, $7.50 children 6-17). For thousands of years, people made their home in the Southwest, creating an incredibly rich culture. The Heard Museum documents their millennia-old traditions, offering an impressive introduction to Native American art and Arizona's original inhabitants. Experience what it is like to live in a Navajo hogan, or learn how the intricate weavings and beadwork found in many clothes, baskets, and rugs reflect a tribe's precious history. There are also intricate sand paintings and boldly imaginative works by contemporary artists, as well as exhibitions documenting the indignities of those forced to live on reservations and in boarding schools in the 19th and 20th centuries.

The museum started as the personal collection of Dwight and Maie Heard, who built the first incarnation of the Spanish Colonial building on their private grounds in 1929 to house the art and artifacts that had begun to overtake their home. Dwight died of a heart attack as the display cabinets were being installed, but Maie forged ahead, overseeing the museum until her death in 1951. The Heard has been significantly expanded over the years, and its grounds, beautifully landscaped with native plants and trees, also provide space for music and dance performances, special events, and festivals, including the annual Indian Fair and Market held in March. The gift shop sells art and jewelry by Native American artisans, and its seasonally inspired restaurant, **Courtyard Café** (602/251-0204, 11am-3pm daily, 6pm-8:30pm first Friday of the month, $9-13), serves fresh and delicious meals.

★ Phoenix Art Museum

One of the most amazing art spaces on planet Earth (although it will transport you off the

the Heard Museum

planet) exists at the **Phoenix Art Museum** (1625 N. Central Ave., 602/257-1880, www. phxart.org, 10am-9pm Wed., 10am-5pm Thurs.-Sat., noon-5pm Sun., $15 adults, $6 children ages 6-17). Yayoi Kusama's *You Who Are Getting Obliterated in the Dancing Swarm of Fireflies* is a dark, mirrored room with a forest of hanging LED lights that seem to stretch into infinity. The installation disrupts your expected sensory experience through the limitless reflections of sparkling light, thus disorienting your sense of time and space. Walking around this room will crack your senses open to a whole new level.

But Phoenix couldn't always brag about this piece. Like many regional art museums, the museum limped by for years with a small but respectable collection of art, featuring secondary works by well-known masters and a few excellent pieces by lesser-known artists. That all changed in 1996, when an ambitious makeover was launched that has transformed the institution, nearly tripling its size and bringing new focus to its acquisitions and exhibitions. A later $50 million expansion added a grassy sculpture garden and a dramatic, glass-enclosed lobby and entry plaza.

Throughout the museum, there's a broad cross-section of art, with pieces by American, European, and Latin American artists including Claude Monet, Pablo Picasso, Georgia O'Keeffe, Mark Rothko, and Frida Kahlo, as well as a well-curated Asian art gallery. A new four-level wing has added space for large-scale contemporary pieces, photography, and the museum's renowned design collection, featuring garments by Balenciaga, Chanel, Dior, and Yves Saint Laurent. Be sure to make time to see the exhibition *The Art of Philip Curtis,* which highlights the work of the former WPA artist who moved to Arizona in 1937 to spearhead the Phoenix Art Center, the precursor to today's museum. His whimsical and provocative paintings are reminiscent of Norman Rockwell and they reveal his love of Arizona's mining towns.

The museum regularly hosts film screenings and live concerts, as well as blockbuster

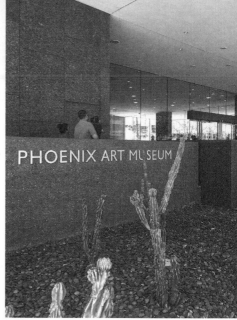
the Phoenix Art Museum

traveling exhibitions, which have featured Impressionism, Rembrandt, Richard Avedon, and Andy Warhol. The museum's restaurant, **Palette** (602/257-2191, 11am-3:30pm Thurs.-Sun., 11am-8pm Wed. and first Friday of the month, $9-16), is a great place to grab lunch.

Encanto Park
Encanto Park (2605 N. 15th Ave., 602/261-8991, www.phoenix.gov/parks, 5:30am-11pm, free) has been a Phoenix favorite for generations. On most weekends, you'll see kids running toward the playground, young couples lying under shady trees, and families hauling coolers and bags of food to the picnic tables. The 222-acre "enchanted" park was designed to be a leafy oasis for escaping the summer heat, and its quaint neighborhood of Spanish Colonial homes and historic bungalows still feels connected to the Phoenix of 50 years ago. There are plenty of amenities—basketball and tennis courts, softball fields, a municipal swimming pool, and a golf course—but it's the small lagoon that gives the park its unique

Phoenix Indian School

In 1891, the **Phoenix Indian School** opened, part of the federal government's plan to assimilate Native Americans. It was one of several boarding schools established around the country to force Native American children to speak English, cut their hair, wear Anglo clothes, and attend church. Students were also required to abandon their tribal traditions and leave their families behind, a particularly difficult sacrifice for the close-knit Native American communities.

By 1900, the co-ed school had grown to 698 students from 23 tribes across the West. Its 160-acre campus had a large schoolhouse, dining hall, several dormitories, and workspace to teach vocation skills. It finally closed in 1990, and a decade later, a third of the land was redeveloped as the **Steele Indian School Park** (300 E. Indian School Rd., 602/534-4810, www.phoenix.gov/parks, 6am-10pm daily, free). Only three of the school's original buildings remain, including the restored Memorial Hall, an auditorium that now hosts events and galas. Fittingly, Native Americans now gather at the park for tribal celebrations and festivals, and it's also the site of Phoenix's annual Fourth of July fireworks event.

It's also a great place to spend an afternoon with sprawling lawns, gazebos, gardens, and picnic tables. A lagoon is stocked with fish for urban anglers who cast their lines and there's a playground for young children.

---

character, so head down to the boathouse and rent a pedal boat. Encanto also is home to the **Enchanted Island Amusement Park** (1202 W. Encanto Blvd., 602/254-1200, www.enchantedisland.com, open 10am-2pm Wed.-Thurs. 10am-8pm Fri.-Sun., hours vary seasonally, free admission, $1.25 per ticket), which offers a charming collection of rides, bumper boats, games, a splash zone, and a carousel. Check the website for detailed information on hours and ride prices.

Burton Barr Central Library

Phoenix embarked on a cultural renaissance in 1988, when voters approved an ambitious, architecturally daring series of public-works projects that included the **Phoenix Art Museum** and **Burton Barr Central Library** (1221 N. Central Ave., 602/262-4636, www.phoenixpubliclibrary.org, 9am-5pm Mon., 9am-9pm Tues.-Thurs., 9am-5pm Fri.-Sat., 1pm-5pm Sun.). The iconic building's rectangular, rusted-steel facade resembles a red-hued mesa. Phoenix architect Will Bruder, a pioneer in the region's Desert Modernism movement, gracefully incorporated natural daylight throughout the design, including a glass-and-steel central stairwell and elevator atrium known as the Crystal Canyon. On

the equinox, the sun shines directly through overhead skylights into the fifth-floor reading room, lighting its graceful, white columns and creating a stunning show.

Japanese Friendship Garden

If you don't want to feel like you're in Phoenix, the tranquil **Japanese Friendship Garden** (1125 N. 3rd Ave., 602/274-8700, www.japanesefriendshipgarden.org, 10am-4pm Tues.-Sun., closed Jun.-Sept., $5 adults, children under 6 free) is a pleasant contrast to the desert cityscape that surrounds it, with some 50 varieties of plants, flowing streams, a koi pond, and a 14-foot waterfall. This joint effort between Phoenix and its sister city, Himeji in Japan, is tucked into the southwestern end of **Margaret T. Hance Deck Park** (on top of the I-10 freeway tunnel, between Central and 3rd Aves.). Enter through the bamboo gate and follow the pathway through the perfectly manicured grounds, which feature yellow and purple irises, lush water lilies, and artfully placed boulders. Some allowances for the desert climate have been made, like the neatly trimmed bonsai trees that are shaped from hardy olive trees. You can join a tea ceremony the third Saturday of the month during regular public hours, although reservations are required and best made well in advance. The ceremony coasts $30 per person and includes a docent greeting and quick tour with tea volunteers presenting the tea ceremony while dressed in beautiful kimonos.

CENTRAL PHOENIX

Central Phoenix straddles the borders of Scottsdale and Paradise Valley. All three areas share the valley's most iconic natural landmark.

★ Camelback Mountain

It doesn't require a great deal of imagination to make out the "kneeling camel" profile. **Camelback Mountain,** the Valley's most iconic landmark, straddles the communities of Phoenix, Scottsdale, and Paradise Valley, luring some 400,000 hikers to its red-sandstone and granite cliffs every year.

The park preserves a 76-acre piece of the Sonoran Desert in the heart of the city, where bighorn sheep once scaled the dramatic rock formations and the ancient Hohokam civilization practiced religious rituals.

The federal government set aside Camelback as an Indian reservation until the late 1800s, and it slipped into private hands in the 1940s. Finally, in 1968, private citizens led by Senator Barry Goldwater arranged a land exchange that protected the mountain from future development. The event was marked by President Lyndon B. Johnson and Lady Bird Johnson, who walked the mountain in high heels.

Today, a good portion of Camelback has been protected for recreation, although multimillion-dollar homes and top-end resorts climb its base. For visitors not heading out to the desert, it's an excellent opportunity to see Sonoran critters like spiny lizards, roadrunners, rabbits, and, yes, the possible rattlesnake, in their native environment.

To get an up-close view of Camelback, explore the **Echo Canyon Recreation Area** (4925 W. McDonald Dr., 602/261-8318, www.phoenix.gov/parks/trails/locations/camelback-mountainphoenix.gov) at the "camel's head," where you'll find the **Praying Monk rock.** The freestanding, 80-foot-high rock tower, which looks like the camel's eyelashes from a distance, is a popular spot for rock climbers.

Taking one of the two trails to the 2,704-foot summit is not recommended for novice hikers and not recommended for anyone in the summer except at dawn or dusk. Confident climbers in good weather will be

Echo Canyon Recreation Area

rewarded with 360-degree views of the Valley and the surrounding mountain ranges. The trailheads are open daily from sunrise to sunset and are always busy; parking can be a bit of a zoo.

NORTH PHOENIX

North Phoenix is yet another area that solidifies the greater Phoenix area as a sea of suburbia. But among the houses and outdoor malls is an attraction that should not be missed: a museum for music lovers across the world.

★ Musical Instrument Museum

Music lovers, get ready to freak out. This is a rare treat for you. North Phoenix is home to the **Musical Instrument Museum** (4725 E. Mayo Blvd., 480-478-6000, www.mim.org, 9am-5pm daily, $20 adult, $15 ages 13-19, $10 children ages 4-12, free ages 3 and under), which is home to more than 6,500 instruments from across the world. Explore most instruments via audio and video technologies to hear the sounds and see how they are played by their native musicians.

Pop culture is also on display here, with instruments from the likes of John Lennon, Elvis Presley, and Carlos Santana (just to name-drop a few).

Although much of this pristine collection falls under the "look-y but no touch-y" category, be sure to head to the Experience Gallery, where guests of all ages are free to bang, strum, pluck, and jam with instruments like the gong, Burmese harp, and guitars galore. For more noise of the professionally arranged type, the museum hosts a robust line-up of live concerts booked almost daily. Check the events calendar for excellent activities that keep little hands busy like building your own stringed instrument or learning a simple tune on the ukulele. Grab a bite at the on-site Café Allegro, serving tasty lunch from 11am-2pm with beverages and snacks also available throughout the day.

All this is the brainchild of former Target CEO, Robert J. Ulrich and friend Marc Felix. With Ulrich's obsessive instrument collection acting as the impetus for the museum, the collection has grown to 16,000 instruments total (though not all are on display). Enlisting the award-winning architect Rich Varda to design the museum, visitors experience this incredible place via architecture that evokes the topography, materials, and ambience of the Southwest.

PAPAGO PARK

Papago Park (625 N. Galvin Pkwy., 602/495-5458, www.phoenix.gov/parks, 6am-7pm daily, free) is a natural refuge in the middle of the city, where residents can hike, fish, or play a round of golf. The large desert sanctuary's paved trails, small lake, baseball stadium, and softball fields as well as its museums and cultural attractions have made it a popular destination.

AZ Heritage Center at Papago Park

Some wild things have happened in Arizona— Old West gunfights, copper rushes, gubernatorial impeachments—and the state's version of the National Archives has been there to document events from the beginning. The first territorial legislature created the Arizona Historical Society in 1864, and, since then, the institution has been chronicling the state's history as it happened. Today, eight museums across Arizona preserve over three million artifacts, with the **AZ Heritage Center at Papago Park** (1300 N. College Ave., 480/929-0292, www.arizonahistoricalsociety.org, 10am-4pm Tues.-Sat., noon-4pm Sun., $12 adults, $7 children ages 7-17) specializing in the Phoenix area and the 20th and 21st centuries. A particularly interesting exhibition documents how the state came of age during World War II with the bombing of the USS *Arizona* at Pearl Harbor. In fact, you can learn how Camp Papago Park, not too far from the museum, experienced the largest mass escape of POWs in the United States.

Papago Park

★ Hole-in-the-Rock

The short, easy trek to the landmark **Hole-in-the-Rock,** a natural formation through which you can survey the city, is often a Phoenix child's very first hike and holds a special place in many local hearts. You can see Papago's rounded, red-hued buttes from the surrounding communities of Phoenix, Tempe, and Scottsdale, but the sandstone formations should be explored up close, especially the unique "holes" formed by weather erosion over millions of years. Phoenix's first residents, the Hohokam, used the Hole-in-the-Rock formation for astronomy and to track the seasonal movements of the sun. You can also make the short walk to Hunt's Tomb, a white pyramid that serves as the final resting place of Arizona's first governor, George W. P. Hunt.

★ Desert Botanical Garden

People seem to think of a desert as a lifeless wasteland, but nothing could be further from the truth. A trip to the **Desert Botanical Garden** (1201 N. Galvin Pkwy., 480/941-1225, www.dbg.org, 8am-8pm daily Oct.-Apr., 7am-8pm daily May-Sept., $22 adults, $10 children ages 3-12) quickly dispels any misconceptions and shows off how truly lush this environment can be. With around 50,000 cacti, agaves, succulents, shrubs, trees, and colorful wildflowers, the garden easily claims the world's largest, if not finest, collection of desert plants, including 289 rare, threatened, or endangered species. About a third of the living collection is native to the region, with the remaining plants originating from Africa, Australia, South America, and Mexico. The park began in 1939 with a mission "to exhibit, to conserve, to study,

Hole-in-the-Rock

and to disseminate knowledge of the arid-land plants of the world." Since then, it has evolved beyond a plant refuge, offering classes and hosting a series of social events throughout the year that range from spring concerts to arts festivals.

Try to come early in the day or late in the evening, when the sunlight is incredible. For a different perspective, flashlight tours are held during the summer, which are an entertaining opportunity for children to see the nocturnal desert's nighthawks, snakes, insects, and night-blooming flowers. Of course, the springtime wildflowers are always a highlight, and the annual Las Noches de las Luminarias in November has become a Phoenix holiday tradition.

Phoenix Zoo

The **Phoenix Zoo** (455 N. Galvin Pkwy., 602/286-3800, www.phoenixzoo.org, 9am-5pm daily Oct.-May; 7am-2pm Mon.-Fri., 7am-4pm Sat.-Sun. June-Sept., $20 adults, $14 children ages 3-13) is one of the nation's largest non-profit organizations and boasts a diverse variety of nature experiences with some 1,400 birds, slithering reptiles, and furry mammals from around the world. You'll find lions and tigers, a vast savannah filled with frolicking zebras and giraffes, and animal habitats with elephants, tigers, and playful orangutans. But it's the highly interactive exhibits that are blurring the boundaries of the animal kingdom like Monkey Village, where visitors can walk through an enclosure while a dozen squirrel monkeys hop from tree to tree. Children can also roam free on the farm, complete with petting zoo and a real tractor to climb. With the purchase of a Total Experience Ticket ($36 adults, $30 children ages 3-13), you can plunge your hand into Stingray Bay and feed a school of small sharks and stingrays, experience the 4-D Theater, and take a camel ride.

Pueblo Grande Museum and Archaeological Park

Like Rome's Forum or Beijing's Forbidden City, this is where the modern metropolis of Phoenix honors the ancient foundations from which it rose. **Pueblo Grande Museum and Archaeological Park** (4619 E. Washington St., 602/495-0901, www.pueblogrande.com, 9am-4:45pm Mon.-Sat., 1pm-4:45pm Sun., closed Sun.-Mon. May-Sept., $6 adults, $3 children ages 6-17) is the site of a Hohokam village that stood here from about AD 450 to 1450, supporting as many as 1,000 people. It now sits in the middle of a desert metropolis, but the Valley looked quite different then, when water flowing through the Salt River fed lush plants along its banks as well as a complex system of canals that irrigated crops. Those well-engineered waterways served as a framework for the rebirth of Phoenix in the 1860s—and today's canals still parallel their original paths.

The Hohokam lived in wood-framed homes, built over shallow pits and covered with adobe. Because these natural materials were so vulnerable to erosion, none of Phoenix's early dwellings still exist, although you're now able to go inside full-size replicas of these adobe pit houses. You can also see an excavated ball court and an example of an adobe compound, homes that families would surround with large walls to create private courtyards—a practice adopted into Mexican architecture and modern suburban housing developments. The recently renovated museum highlights the Hohokam's tools, shell and stone jewelry, and unique red-on-buff pottery. There are also interactive exhibits that examine how archaeologists dig at sites and sort through artifacts to piece together the history of an ancient civilization. A warning: There isn't much shade at the site, so be sure to visit on a cool day or early in the morning.

Tovrea Castle and Carraro Cactus Garden

Many Phoenicians regularly drive by **Tovrea Castle** (5025 E. Van Buren St., 800/838-3006, www.tovreacastletours.com, tour times vary, $15 adult, children under 2 free) on Highway 202 (Loop 202) and have no idea what it is, but the three-tier wedding cake-style house is hard to miss. In 1928, Italian immigrant Alessio Carraro purchased 277 acres of undeveloped land east of downtown Phoenix, armed with grand plans for the desert hilltop. He envisioned a luxury housing development that would be crowned by a massive cactus garden and a posh resort, which he designed as a rococo castle inspired by his native Italy.

Pueblo Grande Museum and Archaeological Park

Carraro had the vision but was short on the know-how and his grand plans never came to full fruition. Still, he spent a year in the mansion before selling it in 1931 to Edward and Della Tovrea, a couple who ranched the land adjacent to his would-be oasis (there's some theorizing that their addition of a slaughterhouse nearby may have spoiled Carraro's plans). Edward died the following year, but Della went on live in the castle until 1969, when she died of pneumonia two months after she survived a break-in by two burglars. Today, with help from volunteers and preservationists, the city of Phoenix has renovated the abandoned home and garden, which has been replanted with thousands of cacti, including over 300 saguaros. The garden opened to the public for the first time in 2012, and the restored castle is available for tours led by guides who offer a riveting history of the castle and its 44 acre-gardens. Check the website for tour dates and times as they vary depending on time of year, and be sure to book well in advance.

Hall of Flame Fire Museum

Little kids will love you forever if you take them to the **Hall of Flame Fire Museum** (6101 E. Van Buren St., 602/275-3473, www. hallofflame.org, 9am-5pm Mon.-Sat., noon-4pm Sun., $7 Adults, $5 students 6-17, $2 children ages 3-5, free children under 3). The grown-ups will be fascinated by the galleries, which showcase restored fire trucks and fire-safety clothing dating right back to the 18th century. With more than 130 vehicles and 10,000 smaller objects to peruse, big-time fire-fighting fans could easily spend a few hours here. The most popular engine, by far, is the 1952 American La France Model 700, which is available for boarding and makes the perfect Instagram shot.

TEMPE AND THE EAST VALLEY

The vibrant college town of Tempe came of age during the early 21st century, staking its claim as a progressive, culturally minded community. Surrounded by the cities of Phoenix, Scottsdale, Mesa, and Chandler, the 40-square-mile Tempe is unable spread into the desert like other Valley suburbs. Instead, it's meeting the demands of a growing population by slowly casting away the shackles of suburbia to become a city where residential, retail, and commercial buildings coexist rather than retreat into their respective neighborhoods. The city's developers, recognizing the success of pedestrian-orientated **Mill Avenue**—a popular spot for dining and shopping—are now moving beyond the street's nostalgic red-brick buildings and creating a modern cityscape along Tempe Town Lake.

That said, the city isn't new to experimental design. In 1971, the **Tempe Municipal Building** (31 E. 5th St., 480/350-4311, www. tempe.gov) was unveiled, an inverted glass-walled pyramid that shades itself from the summer sun. Subsequently, the **Tempe Center for the Arts** (700 W. Rio Salado Pkwy., 480/350-2822, www.tempe.gov/TCA, 10am-6pm Tues. & Thurs., 10am-7pm Wed.,

10am-7:30pm Fri., 11am-6pm Sat., free) made a splash on the banks of Tempe Town Lake, with an elaborate silver roof reminiscent of the local mountain ranges.

Still, Tempe hasn't bulldozed its past. At the northern end of Mill Avenue, you can see the tall silos and remains of the river-powered **Hayden Flour Mill,** which was built by Charles Hayden in 1874. His Hayden Ferry connected Phoenix across Salt River to its south banks, where the road eventually led to Tucson. A small community grew up along this road, which became the origins of Mill Avenue—many of the original brick buildings, quaint bungalows and ranch houses that popped up here have been repurposed as retail and restaurant space.

Tempe Town Lake

If you build it, they will come—or so city leaders hoped in 1989 when they adopted the ambitious Rio Salado Master Plan, which converted two miles of the usually dry Salt River into a reservoir lake for boating, rowing, and fishing. The resulting **Tempe Town Lake** (620 N. Mill Ave., 480/350-5200, www. tempe.gov/lake, free) opened a decade later, created by inflatable rubber dams (which famously burst in 2010) and encircled by five miles of paths for biking and jogging. The adjacent **Tempe Beach Park** has become one of the Valley's prime spots for festivals, concerts, and events.

Arizona State University

Much of Tempe's progressive attitude—and the abundance of cheap restaurants, bars, and shops—can be credited to the main campus of **Arizona State University** (University Dr. and Mill Ave., 480/965-7788, www.asu. edu). ASU was founded as the Tempe Normal School in 1885 while Arizona was still a territory. Since then, it has mushroomed into the largest public research university in the country, with 67,000 students on four campuses in the Valley. The school reached joke status in the early 21st century when it landed on top lists of party schools, but has since tried to

Tempe

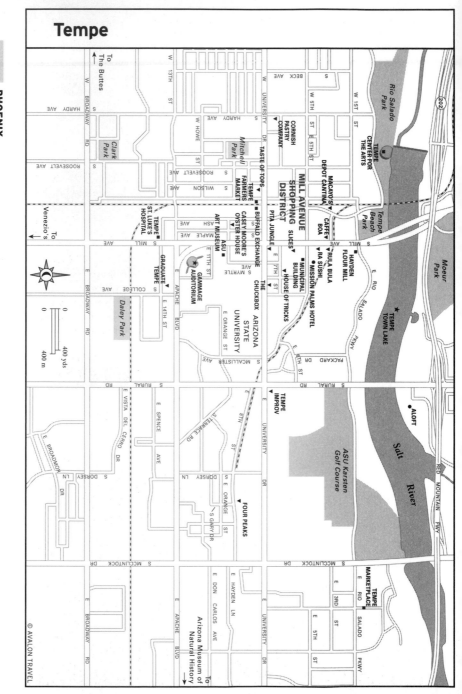

© AVALON TRAVEL

showcase its education in an attempt to shake off the unwanted attention.

Walks of shame aside, the university has much to offer visitors. Those interested in design and architecture should head south on Mill Avenue to see two significant buildings. The **Arizona State University Art Museum** (51 E. 10th St., 480/965-2787, http://asuartmuseum.asu.edu, 11am-8pm Tues., 11am-5pm Wed.-Sat., free) is a Modernist concrete complex that is perfectly suited to its desert home, drawing inspiration from Native American architecture and creating brilliant subterranean spaces that highlight the desert's stark contrasts of light and shadow. The museum has a modest collection that features contemporary works as well as a host of often-daring rotating exhibitions.

Just south of the museum, you'll find **Gammage Auditorium** (1200 S. Forest Ave., 480/965-5062, www.asugammage.com), the last public commission of Frank Lloyd Wright, which now hosts Broadway shows and public events. Based on an old design for an opera house in Baghdad, Iraq, Wright modified the concept for its new home on the edge of ASU's campus. He said, "I believe this is the site. The structure should be circular in design, and yes, with outstretched arms,

saying 'Welcome to ASU!'" Those arms became flying buttresses that serve as pedestrian ramps and echo the building's interlocking-circle motif. Both Wright and ASU president Grady Gammage, who is credited with landing the commission, died before its completion in 1964.

Arizona Museum of Natural History

One of the Valley's best-kept secrets, the **Arizona Museum of Natural History** (53 N. MacDonald, 480/644-2230, www.azmnh.org, 10am-5pm Tues.-Fri., 11am-5pm Sat., 1pm-5pm Sun., $12 adults, $7 children ages 3-12) appeals to kids—dinosaurs!—and even adults who aren't "museum people." Formerly known as the Mesa Southwest Museum, it explores the region's natural and cultural history with plenty of hands-on, interactive, sound-and-light, try-this-on excitement. Pan for "gold," visit a territorial jail, and scope out the three-story Dinosaur Mountain, complete with a simulated flash flood and mechanical monsters. Those who revel in the nerdy joy of museums will love the in-depth exhibits on prehistoric Native American life and the assembled mammoth and mastodon fossils. The museum also cares for **Mesa Grande**

Gammage Auditorium at Arizona State University

Cultural Park, which preserves a series of classical-period ruins that housed as many as 2,000 Hohokam people from approximately AD 300 to 1450. See azmnh.org for seasonal hours and admission prices.

AHWATUKEE AND SOUTH PHOENIX

Southern Phoenix and its affluent bedroom community of Ahwatukee (pronounced "ah-wuh-TOO-kee") are home—primarily—to a sea of stucco housing developments. But if you know where to go, exploring this area can be worth your time.

★ South Mountain Park and Preserve

The City of Phoenix loves to boast about **South Mountain Park and Preserve** (10919 S. Central Ave., 602/262-7393, www.phoenix.gov/parks/trails/locations/south-mountain, 5am-11pm daily, free) and with good reason. It's one of the largest municipally operated parks in the country—and perhaps the world—with more than 16,000 acres. This is where many Valley residents escape from the city to hike, bike, horseback ride, and picnic. Don't expect large grassy meadows or shady forested hideaways,

though. This is bona fide Sonoran Desert, preserving hardy creosote bushes, palo verde trees, and dozens of varieties of cactus. You may even come across a few critters, like jackrabbits and huge chuckwalla lizards (many of the snakes, scorpions, and coyotes that also live in the park come out a night when it's much cooler, but you should still keep an eye out for them). The park also protects hundreds of petroglyphs and pictographs, rock art created by the Hohokam and other indigenous tribes. These small drawings, carved or painted onto stones, depict people, animals, and geometric patterns; anthropologists theorize that they may have been a means of recording history, part of religious ceremonies, or even ancient street signs or border markings.

If working up a sweat exploring more than 50 miles of trails on foot or by bike isn't your thing, there are a few scenic drives, including a five-mile winding road that snakes its way up the mountain to the popular Dobbins Lookout at the summit, where the panoramic views reveal Phoenix's sprawling suburban growth. Keep in mind, however, that the fourth Sunday of each month is the "Silent Sunday," during which the roads are closed to motorized vehicles. For more information about

South Mountain Park and Preserve

What Are Those Red Lights in South Phoenix?

Scan the Valley's horizon at night and you can't help but notice a cluster of red, twinkling lights in South Phoenix. These blinking spires mark the **South Mountain Antenna Farm,** a city beacon of 30-plus towers that beam radio and television transmissions from the mountaintop. The antennas provide more than music, news, and sports, though, as the red lights serve as an important navigational marker for pilots flying into nearby Sky Harbor Airport. They also seem to be a magnet for residents who drive to the top of South Mountain at night, for a panoramic view of the Valley bathed in shimmering lights from the highest vantage point.

the park's wildlife or where to find rock art, visit the **South Mountain Environmental Education Center** (10409 S. Central Ave., 623/334-7880, 8am-2pm Wed.-Sat. and the fourth Sunday of every month).

Mystery Castle

"*Life* Visits a Mystery Castle," proclaimed the cover of *Life* magazine in 1948, featuring a teenage Mary Lou Gulley on a spiral staircase that overlooked the eccentric house built by her father, Boyce Luther Gulley. The name **Mystery Castle** (800 E. Mineral Rd., 602/268-1581, www.mymysterycastle.com, 11am-3:30pm Thurs.-Sun. Oct.-May, $10 adults, $5 children ages 5-12) stuck. In 1930 Boyce had abandoned his wife and daughter in Seattle, moving to the dry climate of Phoenix after being diagnosed with tuberculosis. Inspired by his daughter, who cried when her sandcastles were washed away by the tide and asked her father to build her one in the desert large enough to live in, he built Mystery Castle from a hodgepodge of found objects: rocks, adobe, glass, auto parts, even petroglyphs. When Boyce died in 1945, Mary Lou and her mother moved into the eccentric castle, and Mary Lou was still welcoming visitors into her home up until her death in 2010. Today, you can tour the 18 rooms, furnished with quirky pieces designed by Boyce as well a sofa designed by Frank Lloyd Wright. To reach Mystery Castle, head south on 7th Street, past Baseline Road, and make a left where the road dead-ends at South Mountain.

Rawhide Western Town

Rawhide Western Town (5700 W. North Loop Rd., 480/502-5600, www.rawhide.com, 5pm-10pm Fri., noon-10pm Sat., noon-8pm Sun., free) delivers 1880s, Old West-themed family fun. Check out the stunt shows or try your luck on the mechanical bull. Of course, there are easier rides in town, such as the desert train or stagecoach tours guided by a trained mule team. It's all a little hokey, but having an "old-time" photo taken or browsing the candies at Sweet Sally's Candy Store is still a lot of fun, especially for kids. Although admission to the park is free, each attraction or show requires a $4.95 ticket, or you can buy an all-day Town Pass for $14.95. During April and May, visitors can experience an old-fashioned cowboy experience under the stars ($12-16), which includes dinner, live music, dancing at the outdoor stage, and access to a cash bar.

WEST VALLEY

The West Valley isn't particularly known as a tourist attraction, so don't expect the drive to this area of town to be especially thrilling. It's a suburban life in the West Valley—mostly dominated by neighborhoods and strip malls. Still, there are a few places definitely worth visiting.

Deer Valley Petroglyph Preserve

Long before the Valley's urban sprawl began creeping into Northwest Phoenix, ancient

Native Americans made it their home. These indigenous people literally left their mark on the landscape, carving more than 1,500 petroglyphs onto the basalt boulder formations in the Hedgpeth Hills. This impressive concentration of rock art is a fascinating and revealing look at the civilization that once thrived here, and the petroglyphs—geometric and anthropomorphic drawings carved onto rock—give a peek into their stories, religious rites, and hunting practices. The **Deer Valley Petroglyph Preserve** (3711 W. Deer Valley Rd., 623/582-8007, https://shesc.asu.edu/dvpp, hours vary per season, $7 adults, $3 children ages 6-12) is more than archaeological site, though; the 47-acre park also serves as a nature preserve for native wildlife and an ethnobotanical garden for the hardy crops that have been cultivated in Arizona for thousands of years. Visitors may want to bring a pair of binoculars or rent some at the center to view the more distant petroglyphs.

Challenger Space Center

Science fiction and outer space lovers can't resist a tour of the **Challenger Space Center** (21170 N. 83rd Ave., 623/322-2001, www.azchallenger.org, 10am-4pm Mon.-Sat., $8 adults, $6 children ages 3-12). The museum is teeming with space memorabilia and artifacts including meteorites, an interactive video display of the solar system, and an Atlantis Space Shuttle model. The real draw here is the simulated space mission exercises for families or groups that act out comet rendezvous, voyages to Mars, and moon landings all played out on models of a flight deck, mission control, and the International Space Station. Check the website for upcoming mission events.

Entertainment and Events

Frequently overshadowed by Scottsdale's over-the-top trendy clubs, Phoenix's nightlife caters to an entirely different culture. Artists, writers, and musicians are known to frequent the club and bar scene downtown and with the light rail making for easy access without fear of a DUI, a robust nightlife has emerged. Live music, DJ nights, and dive-bar dance floors are what Phoenix is known for. There's also a healthy amount of low-key, tasteful bars that are well suited for intelligent conversations that joyfully disintegrate as the booze flows. If you're in town on the first or third Friday of the month, you may want to consider joining art-lovers and the post-hipster crowd at the art walks in downtown's Roosevelt Historic District.

NIGHTLIFE
Downtown
BARS AND PUBS

In an area where going out and drinking among critically fashionable artists can be intimidating, **Chambers on First** (705 N. 1st St., 602/296-5043, www.chambersphx.com, 11am-2am Mon.-Fri., 10am-2am Sat.-Sun.) caters to a more regular crowd craving tall beers, pub fare, and whiskey. Formerly known as "The Turf," new owners gave the place a much-needed makeover but were smart enough to keep the big booths and dark, cool decor that make the place cozy and friendly. They've also got a revolving roster of wine events, live music, and other happenings.

For a longtime favorite located in the thick of downtown, head to **Seamus McCaffrey's Irish Pub and Restaurant** (18 W. Monroe St., 602/253-6081, www.seamusmccaffreys.com, 10am-2am daily). Next to the historic Hotel San Carlos, the place gets pretty crazy for happy hour (4pm-7pm Mon.-Fri.) when all the suits who work downtown are looking to blow off some steam. On a busy weekend night, you'll be up close with a rowdy crowd excited to wrap their hands around a cold beer chosen from one of the best selections

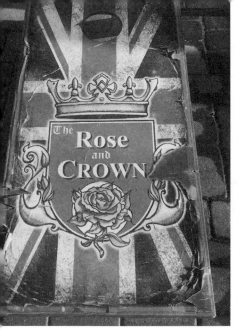

The Rose & Crown

of imported draught beers and ales in town. And whiskey lovers will be in heaven with a bonkers selection of premium single malt and blended scotch whiskies.

Killing time before a game at Chase Field? Grab a pint or a classic gin and tonic at **The Rose & Crown** (628 E. Adams St., 602/256-0223, www.theroseandcrownaz.com, 11am-2am Mon.-Sat., 10am-2am Sun.) in Heritage Square. The converted historic home has a full bar, imports galore from the British Isles, and an excellent patio and lawn for enjoying the weather when it's warm outside. The pool table, darts, and pop art paintings of Queen Elizabeth II and Winston Churchill add some fun British style to the turn-of-the-20th-century bungalow.

Take the magic memories you have of childhood games of skeeball, add fond family memories of board-game night, throw in the nostalgia of drunken evenings playing darts at a dive bar, then mix it all together with a hip scene and you have **Valley Bar** (130 N. Central Ave., 602/368-3121, www.

valleybarphx.com, 4pm-2am Mon.-Fri., 6pm-2am Sat.-Sun.). This place is quite possibly the site of the most fun you will have on a night out. One side of the venue is filled with darts, skeeball, arcade games, billiards, and booths housing small groups playing board games and cards. The other side of the place is a live music and dance club. Wandering between the two—along with two separate bars to provide plenty of free-flowing drinks—guarantees a whole ton of fun. Plus, there's a kitchen open late night with really tasty food.

And yet another bar for nostalgic gamer geeks, **Cobra Arcade Bar** (801 N. 2nd St., Ste. 100, 602/595-5873, cobraarcadebar.com, 4pm-2am Mon.-Sat., noon-2am Sun.) put it best on their website, "We like to drink and play games. Join us." Clever, right? Even more clever are the drink names like "1up," "Invader," and "Ryuken." Grab a libation and play more than 40 vintage arcade games. There are 14 beers on tap and not enough hours in the day.

Step into **Bikini Lounge** (1502 Grand Ave., 602/252-0472, www.thebikinilounge.com, 3pm-2am daily) and you'll suddenly appreciate how Phoenix history can be grungy and oddly inspiring all at once. The authentic tiki dive bar is a relic from the 1940s, complete with the hokey decor. The place has collected some dust over the decades but somehow has survived the ages and been rediscovered by a young bunch for the 21st century. It has an eclectic crowd, including gravely voiced regulars, ultra-fashionable hipsters, and anyone in between. With regular DJ nights and a palpable "anything goes" vibe, it's a must-visit for a memorable night out.

Okay, it probably seems like every bar in downtown Phoenix has a gimmick, but they just do it so well! **FilmBar** (815 N. 2nd St., 602/595-9187, www.thefilmbarphx.com, 5pm-midnight Mon.-Thurs., 5pm-2am Fri., 1pm-2am Sat., 1pm-midnight Sun.) is no exception. It's a lively, raucous bar that could easily be a destination on its own. The kicker is that it features a small movie theater and shows both contemporary films and classics (like

Showgirls). Indie movies, local films, and even live bands have all packed the theater with an eager audience. The theater's bar is usually packed, too, with folks looking to get boozy over a glass or two of beer and wine, grabbing a delicious tamale to eat, and dancing to spins by local DJs.

LOUNGES AND WINE BARS

Like all good speakeasies, **SideBar** (1514 N. 7th Ave., 602/254-1646, www.sidebarphx. com, 4pm-2am Mon.-Thurs., 3pm-2am Fri.-Sun.) can be tough to find. Enter through the side door on 7th Avenue and climb the stairs to the swanky, loft-like space, where you'll find a stylish mix of exposed-brick walls, funky lights, and flat-screen TVs playing obscure, long-forgotten films. The laid-back vibe appeals to many city residents, and it's not uncommon to see a meeting of up-and-coming politicos next to a couple on a date or a group of friends celebrating a birthday. The large lineup of specialty cocktails, dozens of beers, and 40-plus wines should appeal to most. There's even absinthe—treat it with respect or you'll be sorry.

The sleek and contemporary **Hanny's** (40 N. 1st St., 602/252-2285, www.hannys. net, 11am-1:30am Mon.-Fri., 5pm-1:30am Sat.-Sun.) emerged from the shell of an old Phoenix department store. When it opened in 1947 as an upscale men's store, the building was praised for bringing the clean lines of Modernism to downtown Phoenix. A three-year renovation has preserved much of the building's original character and given it a glossy update with chocolate-brown leather banquettes, taupe walls, and small votive candles that flicker on the white marble tables. The classic cocktails are an excellent complement, and its "abandoned" elevator shaft and maze-like bathrooms are fun additions. It works really well and now Hanny's is no-brainer for any night out.

Bitter & Twisted Cocktail Parlour (1 W. Jefferson St., 602/340-1924, www.bitterandtwistedaz.com, 4pm-2am Tues.-Sat.) has quickly become a go-to place for the 30-ish crowd of young, cool people looking to blow off a little steam. The chic bar is located inside the historic Luhrs Tower, which was the Prohibition headquarters for Arizona back in the 1930s. The menu features expertly executed cocktails and fun dishes like grilled cheese bites and burgers with crispy ramen buns. This a great place to grab a table with a group of close friends.

Before the city's empty dirt lots were populated with modern architecture filled with young professionals, there was **Carly's Bistro** (128 E. Roosevelt St., 602/262-2759, www. carlysbistro.com, 10:30am-midnight Mon.-Thurs., 10:30am-2am Fri., 10am-2am Sat., 10am-midnight Sun.), which used to be the only place along Roosevelt where local artists and musicians could grab a drink. Other eateries and bars have come and gone, but Carly's remains a neighborhood favorite. Serving cocktails, beer, and wine as well as a really delicious menu of fresh and healthy fare, the atmosphere is casual, cozy, and very friendly.

LIVE MUSIC

Among the lively shops and art galleries on Roosevelt Row is **The Lost Leaf** (914 N. 5th St., 602/258-0014, www.thelostleaf.org, 5pm-2am Mon.-Fri., noon-2am Sat.-Sun.), which is a regular hangout for local artists and musicians, thanks in part to its low-key vibe and regularly rotating series of local artwork. The small, converted bungalow maintains much of the house's original character, including its hardwood floors, exposed brick walls, and former kitchen, which now serves as a bar with an overwhelming selection of beers, wines, and sakes. Most nights, The Lost Leaf features live music by local and indie bands. Its intimate setting always makes for a good spot for conversation.

Local, regional, and national acts can be seen at **Last Exit Live** (717 S. Central Ave., 602/271-7000, www.lastexitlive.com, hours vary). Its easy-to-miss exterior in South Phoenix's ghost-like warehouse district may not seem like much, but inside you'll find a friendly, casual atmosphere that's all about the

Geordie's at the Wrigley Mansion

A Valley landmark, the Wrigley Mansion sits atop a small hill in Central Phoenix's Biltmore neighborhood, like a Spanish Colonial citadel safeguarding the suburban houses and golf courses. Chewing-gum magnate William Wrigley Jr. built the 24-room, 16,000-square-foot mansion in 1931 as a winter "cottage" and gave it to his wife, Ada, for a 50th wedding anniversary present. The couple only stayed a month or two each year, as the mansion was the smallest of the family's five homes.

Long gone are the days when the Wrigley family wintered at the house while they managed their real-estate empire, which included California's Catalina Island and the Arizona Biltmore Resort. And although the mansion's pristine desert view has evolved into a sprawling cityscape since they departed, it retains much of its original 1930s' appeal, thanks to a $2 million renovation that was completed in 2003. This added dining space and a bar as well as restoring everything from hand-carved doors to an elegant rotunda ceiling. Even the 17 bathrooms, which reflect the Art Deco tastes of the era, were carefully restored, reviving the chartreuse, turquoise, black, and royal-blue tiles that were made in the Wrigley family kiln.

Today, the "cottage" hosts events, tours, and dinners. The 2003 additions, including a two-story patio and balcony, have been converted into an intimate lounge and restaurant, **Geordie's at the Wrigley Mansion** (2501 E. Telawa Trail, 602/955-4079, lunch 11am-3pm Tues.-Sat., dinner 5pm-9pm Tues.-Sat., lounge 3pm-close Tues.-Sat., brunch Sun. 10am-2pm) is named after the mansion's last owner, the late heir to the Spam fortune, George "Geordie" Hormel, and it serves as an observation deck with picture windows offering unobstructed views of the city lights at night. Due to neighborhood zoning restrictions, the Wrigley Mansion must operate as a private club (membership was set at a whopping $15 in 2015, with the money going to charity) but non-members can enjoy a guided tour, drinks, or Sunday brunch.

music. The sound can be loud, and the quarters cramped—which is perfect for a live show.

No one will argue that the very best mid-sized live venue in Phoenix (and possibly in Arizona) is **Crescent Ballroom** (308 N. 2nd Ave., 602/716-2222, www.crescentphx.com, 11am-midnight Mon.-Wed., 11am-2am Thurs.-Fri., 5pm-2am Sat., 5pm-midnight Sun.). Any night is a great night at Crescent, even if you're not going to catch a show. The venue is split into two parts: a charming indoor-outdoor bar area that entertains with the occasional small band (or solo musician or DJ) and a big room where you might catch artists such as Father John Misty or even off-beat comedy acts like Neil Hamburger. Crescent throws the best shows and parties in town, but also makes for a great, low-key weeknight out with their tasty menu of chips, salsa, burritos, and tortas. For smaller bands and dance nights, its sister venue, **Valley Bar,** picks up the slack.

Phoenix can't exactly claim to be known for a great jazz scene but at **The Nash** (110 E. Roosevelt St., 602/795-0464, www.thenash.org, hours vary) jazz lovers unite for some pretty spectacular shows. In fact, the club was named after jazz MVP drummer, Lewis Nash and was recognized by *Downbeat Magazine* as one of the top jazz venues in the United States. It's all here: classic, contemporary, students, pros, and touring artists. With beer and wine served at the bar, The Nash provides a sure-fire great night out.

GAY AND LESBIAN

Bliss ReBAR (901 N. 4th St., 602/795-1792, blissrebar.com, 11am-midnight Mon.-Thurs., 11am-2am Fri., 10am-2am Sat.-Sun.) is a lovely Roosevelt Row neighborhood joint that serves lunch, happy hour, dinner, weekend brunch, and drinks until late in the night. The vibe is generally laid back as patrons enjoy tasty bites with their drinks day and night. If you want to jazz it up, head there for the Sunday Phunday Fun with make your own mimosas,

$4 bloody Marys, a live DJ in the afternoon, and karaoke at night.

Central Phoenix
BARS AND PUBS

It all started here. This location of **The Vig** (4041 N. 40th St., 602/553-7227, www.thevig. us, 11am-2am Mon.-Fri., 10am-2am Sat.-Sun.) was the very first and is still the favorite in the Valley. It has become the place to go for folks who want Desert Modernist design with their cocktails and European beer. The restaurant and bar are always busy, although it's The Vig's backyard that has made it such a hotspot. On weekends, a DJ spins tunes on the large, shady patio and friends battle it out on the bocce ball court. Despite all of the polish, this "modern tavern" is pretty relaxed and the perfect place to start your evening or to finish it off with a nightcap.

Shady's Fine Ales & Cocktails (2701 E. Indian School Rd., 602/956-8998, 11am-2am daily) is the kind of place where you start your night and, before you know it, you're also ending your night there because there's no reason to leave. The cramped quarters, pool table, and well-stocked jukebox creates a jolly energy that forces elbow rubbing and spurs conversation. The patio teems with a laid-back crowd that's eager to chat and Shady's consistently wins the accolade of best neighborhood bar in local publications.

George & Dragon (4240 N. Central Ave., 602/241-0018, www.georgeanddragon.com, 11am-2am daily) is a long-term staple for pub lovers; it's casual, easy, and when it's busy, has a great "anything goes" vibe. It received a total makeover from the reality show *Bar Rescue,* giving it a British feel with stone walls, fireplaces, and Union Flags to match its impressive selection of English, Welsh, and Scottish beers. In fact, the GnD promises the largest selection of imported draught beer and scotch in the Phoenix area. So grab yourself a Tetley's and an order of bangers and mash—you could do worse—as the irascible but lovable staff will surely tell you.

When the local teams are winning, Phoenix is a sports town, and there's no better place to catch a big game with two hundred of your closest friends than **Half Moon Sports Grill** (2121 E. Highland Ave., 602/977-2700, www.halfmoonsportsgrill.com, 11am-2am daily). Thanks to big screens galore throughout the restaurant, bar, and patio, you'll find plenty of opportunities to follow a host of games and tournaments. The ambience and food are decidedly more upscale than your traditional sports bar, although the selection of beer is up to the test of most connoisseurs. And why the name Half Moon? You'll figure out the cheeky reference when you get there.

Rosie McCaffrey's Irish Pub (906 E. Camelback Rd., 602/241-1916, www.rosiemccaffreys.com, 11am-2am daily) is big, loud, and always a lot of fun—perfect for a Friday night out. Yes, it can get too crowded and the bands too loud, but with Smithwick's on tap and Jameson at the ready, it's an easy cross to bear. Grab a booth in the back or a table out front if you'd like a quieter place to chat.

Attention: Phoenix has the most perfect dive bar and it's called **The Swizzle Inn** (5835 N. 16th St., 602/277-7775, 10am-2am daily). It has everything you want in a dive bar. Cheap, strong drinks? Check. A dartboard and pool table? Check. A jukebox, a sassy bartender, and a group of colorful regulars who welcome newbies? Check, check, *and* check. This hole-in-the-wall bar feels like a neighborhood hangout because it is just that. Rumor has it that people have lived at the Swiz for an entire weekend, sustaining themselves on the potluck dishes and ever-flowing cocktails. As the sign says, "swizzle in and swagger out."

After a hike up neighboring Piestewa Peak, a little time on **Aunt Chilada's** patio (7330 N. Dreamy Draw Dr., 602/944-1286, www.auntchiladas.com, 11am-1am daily) with a margarita or three could be just the cure for sore muscles. The old hacienda-style restaurant has three bars, and there's a lively calendar featuring live music and bocce ball tournaments.

Phoenix has a habit of dusting off unassuming dive bars and transforming them into really happening dance clubs. After **Rips Ales & Cocktails** (3045 N. 16th St., 602/266-0015, http://ripsbar.weebly.com, 6am-2am daily) received its cultural makeover, it's become a regular destination with the party crowd—and specifically the post-hipster, artsy scene. The bar staff make very decent cocktails, the place has got darts and billiards, and the dance floor goes off on weekend nights.

LOUNGES AND WINE BARS

Dark, sleek, and sexy, the **MercBar** (2525 E. Camelback Rd., 602/508-9449, www.mercbar.com, 5pm-12:30am Mon.-Tues., 5pm-1am Wed.-Thurs., 5pm-1:45am Fri.-Sat., 7pm-12:30am Sun.) is Phoenix's finest watering hole, a chic, modern lounge that exudes quiet elegance. Softly lit lanterns and flickering candles reflect off the bar's polished copper tables, creating a warm glow and the ambience of a hidden Manhattan speakeasy—although this bar is tucked into the Esplanade Center at 24th Street and Camelback. You'll find well-heeled and sophisticated locals sipping glasses of vintage champagne and aged Scotch whisky. All in all, the mix of expensive cocktails and seen-and-be-seen preening is a whole lot of fun.

In-the-know Phoenicians have made the **Clarendon Rooftop SkyDeck** (401 W. Clarendon Ave., 602/252-736, https://goclarendoncom/rooftop-deck, 6am-10pm daily) one of their favorite hangouts, particularly at sunset when the city seems to glow and the sky is streaked with oranges and reds. The vast outdoor lounge, which is perched on the eastern rooftop of The Clarendon Hotel, features a view of the Phoenix skyline that few watering holes are able to top.

Love this name: The **Linger Longer Lounge** (6522 N. 16th St., 602/264-4549, www.lingerlongeraz.com, 4pm-2am Mon.-Sat., 11am-2am Sun.). Luckily, the experience lives up to its name and this neighborhood bar is fast becoming a local favorite with folks who want a casual place with good food, quality drinks, and reasonable prices. Oh, and a whole room dedicated to games! Yes, shuffleboard, darts, and skeeball are all available for patrons to play as they sip a well-mixed cocktail, tap beer, or glass of wine. There's a regular rotation of DJs and hear this: Happy hour ALL DAY on Sundays.

LIVE MUSIC

This is a place with some character—and quite a few characters. **Char's Has the Blues** (4631 N. 7th Ave., 602/230-0205, www.charshastheblues.com, 8pm-1am Sun.-Thurs., 7:30pm-1am Fri.-Sat.) also plays live funk, soul, and jazz seven nights a week. Head inside the small converted cottage, grab yourself a drink at the bar, and find your way to the softly lit dance floor. Oh, and be sure to call ahead so you know when to catch the stylish funk of Soul Power, the best R&B and soul cover band this side of Detroit.

For top blues acts and killer live music, head to **The Rhythm Room** (1019 E. Indian School Rd., 602/265-4842, www.rhythmroom.com, hours vary). This dark, intimate club highlights some of the best jazz, bluegrass, and roots musicians, as well as touring bands. It's been a mainstay for live music in Phoenix for decades and has one of the best dance floors in town. Add a host of food trucks on weekend nights and you have a serious winner here.

The Rebel Lounge (2303 E. Indian School Rd., 602/296-7013, www.therebellounge.com, hours vary) is housed in a building that was once home to a much-loved music venue called The Mason Jar; it has elevated the site since those days and Valley residents are happy to see that this venue is popular once more. The Rebel Lounge is a great place to catch a live music show; it specializes in regional and national rock plus up-and-coming indie bands and great DJ events such as Emo Night. The interior is perfect for live shows, with a dark, enclosed, cave-like feel, a long bar, and a no-fuss room with plenty of standing space.

GAY AND LESBIAN

Kobalt (3110 N. Central Ave., Ste. 125, 602/264-5307, www.kobaltbarphoenix.com, 11am-2am Mon.-Fri., 10am-2am Sat.-Sun.) at Park Central Mall is a trendy destination for Valley gays and lesbians. Quite laidback, the lounge has a pretty outdoor patio and features themed nights ranging from trivia and movies to an ultra-popular karaoke most nights of the week. It may also be the only bar in town with a Tuesday "endless" happy hour.

You don't have to be a real cowgirl to enjoy a little two-steppin' at **Cash Inn Country** (2140 E. McDowell Rd., 602/244-9943, www.cashinncountry.net, 4pm-1am Tues.-Thurs., 4pm-2am Fri., noon-2am Sat., noon-1am Sun.). Phoenix's "down-home lesbian country nightclub" offers free line-dancing lessons every Tuesday at 7:30pm and Wednesday night karaoke make this ladies' saloon a fun place to grab a cheap beer. The rest of the week you'll find ice-cream socials, paint nights, and other fun themes. And if you're not into country, don't worry—the music and crowd is more diverse than the name might indicate.

Men who'd like to give their cowboy boots a workout should head to **Charlie's** (727 W. Camelback Rd., 602/265-0224, www.charliesphoenix.com, 2pm-2am Mon.-Thurs., 2pm-4am Fri., noon-4am Sat., noon-2am Sun.). Although one might call it a cowboy bar, all walks of life are welcome to this lively club. With regular shows hosted by the lovable and hilarious Pussy LeHoot and patio events like foam parties, it's no wonder the place is considered one of the best gay bars in town.

Tempe and the East Valley
BARS AND PUBS

Casey Moore's Oyster House (850 S. Ash Ave., 480/968-9935, www.caseymoores.com, 11am-2am daily) is a Tempe mainstay, where college students and professors share an enormous patio with hipsters and hippies. The old creaky house-turned-restaurant is rumored to be haunted, and you may just see a ghost in one of the upstairs bedrooms, which have been converted into small dining rooms for private parties. Still, the real action is outside or in the bar, where you can get one of two-dozen beers on tap and a cheap cocktail. The fresh oysters and appetizers aren't half bad, either.

Graduates of neighboring Arizona State University make a point of visiting **Four Peaks Brewing Company** (1340 E. 8th St., 480/303-9967, www.fourpeaks.com, 11am-1am Mon.-Thurs., 11am-2am Fri.-Sat., 10am-1am Sun.) when they return to their old stomping grounds in Tempe. The popular brewpub is a bit of a legend and has many delicious ales, stouts, and pilsners that were served way before the microbrewery movement hit the country. The Four Peaks amber Kilt Lifter Scottish-style ale is drunk at restaurants and bars throughout the Valley, and the refreshing Hefeweizen, Hop Knot IPA, and seasonal brews are just as tasty (don't miss the Pumpkin Porter in the fall). Be forewarned: There is no air-conditioning, so make sure you sample the brews when the weather is pleasant.

Tops Liquors in Tempe pioneered the appreciation of small-time breweries for decades before the craft-beer movement took hold of the nation, so when the family-owned business opened up their own bar next door, **Taste of Tops** (403 W. University Dr., 480/967-2520, www.topsliquors.com/tasteoftops, 3pm-midnight Mon.-Thurs., midnight-2am Fri.-Sat., 3pm-10pm Sun.), their loyal customers immediately put it on their short list of bars to visit. The bar features 30 rotation craft taps, 600 bottles and cans of craft beer, 20 by-the-glass wines, and growlers to fill and take home. The small bar is pleasant, relaxed, and friendly and patrons are allowed to enjoy take-out meals from other establishments. As if that weren't awesome enough, a few board games are available, just to make sure it's the best beer bar in the whole wide world.

On a weekend night, follow the sound of the energetic live band into **Rúla Búla** (401 S. Mill Ave., 480/929-9500, www.rulabula.com, 11am-2am daily). This lively Irish pub oozes Gaelic charm and honors the building's roots as an former saddler's shop with plenty of tools, woods, and old engravings of horses. You'll feel right at home among the friendly regulars at the large oak bar imported from Ireland, or you may want to grab a table outside on the inviting patio. If you can tear yourself away from the comprehensive beer list, treat yourself to the Guinness and chocolate brownie or whiskey-spiked bread pudding that will have you thanking St. Patrick himself.

LIVE MUSIC

If you're a 20-30 something with a hipster, punk, or rockabilly vibe and you're looking for a free live music show on any night of the week, **Yucca Tap Room** (29 W. Southern Ave., 480/967-4777, www.yuccatap.com, 6am-2am daily) is your place. It happens to be a lot of peoples' place, too, as it enjoys a steady stream of Valley residents eager to dance and get soused for cheap. And it's been doing this for over 40 years. Open at 6am every day, it doubles as a lovable daytime dive that welcomes all walks of life. The addition of a lounge has been a big hit, as patrons can escape the live music and enjoy softer tunes by DJs as well as a better selection of beer and a food menu.

CASINOS

While newcomers to Arizona once tried to strike it rich in the mines, today visitors can go for big payouts at the Gila River Indian Community's three casinos south of Phoenix. **Wild Horse Pass Casino** (5040 W. Wild Horse Pass Blvd., 800/946-4452, www.wingilariver.com) is the closest casino to the city and the largest. In addition to live poker, blackjack, and 875 slot machines, it offers live entertainment such as Pat Benatar and Ziggy Marley. **Lone Butte Casino** (1077 W. Kyrene Rd., 800/946-4452, www.wingilariver.com) in Chandler features over 800 slot machines and 24 Las Vegas-style table games, including blackjack and Pai Gow. Southwest of downtown Phoenix and near Laveen, you can try your luck at **Vee Quiva Casino** (15091 S. Komatke Ln., 800/946-4452, www.wingilariver.com), which has slots, bingo, table games, and a 16-table poker room.

All the casinos are open 24/7.

COMEDY

When it's 115°F outside, the only thing you can do is laugh. Join the locals at the constantly air-conditioned **Tempe Improv** (930 E. University Dr., 480/921-9877, www.tempeimprov.com), the Valley's long-time outpost of the national comedy-club chain. Most weekends you can catch touring comedians as well as standup masters like Ralphie May, Wayne Brady, and Pauly Shore. With the addition of CityScape's **Stand Up Live** (50 W.

Stand Up Live

Jefferson St., Ste. 200, 480/719-6100, www.standuplive.com), comedy nerds have another stage to see their favorite national acts like Mo' Nique, Dave Attell, and Marc Maron.

PERFORMING ARTS

The Valley has a slew of venues for catching a play, concert, or dance performance. **Phoenix Symphony Hall** (75 N. 2nd St., 602/495-1117, www.phoenixconventioncenter.com/symphony-hall) is home to three of the city's most respected cultural institutions. For a dose of Verdi and Puccini, the **Arizona Opera** (602/266-7464, www.azopera.com) produces lavish spectacles ranging from traditional to the occasionally experimental. The **Phoenix Symphony** (602/495-1999, www.phoenixsymphony.org) performs classics, chamber orchestra, and symphony pops throughout the year. **Ballet Arizona** (602/381-0184, www.balletaz.org) also takes to the stage with a year-round schedule of performances including *The Nutcracker* during the holiday season.

The **Herberger Theater** (222 E. Monroe St., 602/254-7399, www.herbergertheater.org) stages a host of performances by Valley drama and dance groups.

The ornate **Orpheum Theatre** (203 W. Adams St., 602/495-7139, www.phoenixconventioncenter.com/orpheum-theatre), which hosts a range of musical, theatrical, and dance performances, is wowing audiences after a massive $14 million renovation restored the historic theater's Baroque architectural details. Its auditorium creates the illusion of sitting in a Spanish courtyard, complete with a ceiling that changes from a blue sky with floating clouds to a golden sunset and a starry firmament.

Nearby, Broadway shows, comedy acts, and concerts by Lil Wayne, Flight of the Conchords, and Chris Rock take the stage at **Comerica Theatre** (400 W. Washington St., 602/379-2800, www.comericatheatre.com).

Celebrity Theatre (440 N. 32nd St., 602/267-1600, www.celebritytheatre.com) is one of the best venues to catch a show in Phoenix. Its in-the-round stage and small theater guarantee that no seat is farther than 75 feet from the stage. Performers have included Chicago, Brian Wilson, Chris Isaak, Louis C. K., and Dwight Yoakam.

In the East Valley, the modern **Tempe Center for the Arts** (700 W. Rio Salado Pkwy., 480/350-2822, www.tempe.gov/TCA) overlooks Tempe Town Lake, and its two theaters stage performances by local arts and children's organizations.

The Frank Lloyd Wright-designed **Gammage Auditorium** (1200 S. Forest Ave., 480/965-5062, www.asugammage.com) regularly hosts touring Broadway musicals and plays as well as concerts and lectures.

Further east, the boldly designed **Mesa Arts Center** (1 E. Main St., 480/644-6500, www.mesaartscenter.com) has four theaters for visiting acts and regional arts groups like the **Southwest Shakespeare Company** (480/435-6868, www.swshakespeare.org).

FESTIVALS AND EVENTS
January
In the first few days of the year (or sometimes late December) Phoenix kicks things off with the **Fiesta Bowl** (1 Cardinals Way, 480/350-0900, www.fiestabowl.org) at the University of Phoenix Stadium in Glendale. The big game, which is part of the Bowl Championship Series, is preceded by the **Fiesta Bowl Parade** in Central Phoenix, with dozens of floats, bands, cheerleaders, balloons, and equestrian groups.

A few weeks later in mid-January, the **Arizona Rock 'N' Roll Marathon** (800/311-1255, www.runrocknroll.com) runs through Phoenix, Scottsdale, and Tempe. Now one of the most popular races in the country, the event also stars more than 30 bands performing along the route.

February
In mid-February, book lovers converge on the **VNSA Book Sale** (1826 W. McDowell Rd., 602/265-6805, www.vnsabooksale.org)

The Westgate Entertainment District

In the West Valley, the **Westgate Entertainment District** (6751 N. Sunset Blvd., 623/385-7502, www.westgateaz.com, 11am-9pm Mon.-Sat., 11am-6pm Sun.) is an outdoor entertainment mall featuring a movie theater, tons of restaurants, and bars. It's all about food, sports, and big events, and is home to the Gila River Arena, where the Phoenix Coyotes hockey team plays, as well as the University of Phoenix Stadium, where the Arizona Cardinals football team plays. Don't miss the WaterDance Plaza, which houses a $6 million "dancing water attraction" inspired by the Bellagio in Las Vegas and where live music shows are often hosted.

at the Arizona State Fairground, featuring more than half a million used, rare, and out-of-print books.

Also in February, Lord and Ladies (and enthusiastic thespians) flock to the **Annual Arizona Renaissance Festival and Artisan Marketplace** (12601 E. Hwy. 60, 520/463-2600, www.royalfaires.com/arizona) as it descends upon Gold Canyon in the far East Valley, for two months of ye olde-fashioned fun. Enjoy raucous jousting tournaments, rides, live shows, and giant turkey legs fit for Henry VIII.

March

The **Heard Museum Guild Indian Fair & Market** (2301 N. Central Ave., 602/252-8840, www.heard.org) in March is the state's largest festival of Native American arts and crafts, with more than 600 nationally successful artists. An estimated 15,000 serious collectors and curious browsers attend the annual event, where they are able to purchase original artwork and enjoy authentic food and entertainment.

In late March (sometimes early April), Mesa hosts the **Great Arizona Beer Festival** (2330 W. Rio Salado Pkwy., 480/774-8300, www.azbeer.com), where beer drinkers unite to taste the creations of about 50 local, national, and international breweries.

For some quirky fun, head out to Chandler in the middle of the month for the **Ostrich Festival** (2250 S. McQueen Rd., 480/588-8497, www.ostrichfestival.com), which

features live races, a carnival, and lots of food and entertainment.

If that sounds good, you'll also love **Wiener Mania** (1501 W. Bell Rd., 602/942-1101, www.turfparadise.com), hosted in Phoenix in mid-March, where Valley residents unleash their beloved dachshunds to compete on the racetrack.

April

Hollywood comes to town in April for the **Phoenix Film Festival** (7000 E. Mayo

a dancer at the Heard Museum Guild Indian Fair & Market

Blvd., 480/513-3195, www.phoenixfilmfestival.com). You can check out soon-to-be released features as well as documentaries, shorts, independents, and foreign films. Past attendees include Ed Burns, Peter Fonda, director John Waters, and the ever-connected Kevin Bacon.

Tempe stays busy during April with the **Tempe Festival of the Arts** (Mill Ave. and University Dr., 480/355-6075, www.tempefestivalofthearts.com) transforms Mill Avenue into a pedestrian-only zone lined with artists' booths, food stalls, and concert stages.

May

As the temperatures start to rise, families make the drive to Schnepf Farms in Queen Creek for the annual **Peach Festival** (24810 S. Rittenhouse Rd., 480/513-3195, www.schnepffarms.com), where you can pick a box of peaches fresh from the orchard. Peach pies, cinnamon rolls, and pancakes are also available to sample as well as hay rides, live music, and a carousel for youngsters.

June

The weather is great year-round inside the Phoenix Convention Center where **Phoenix Comicon** (www.phoenixcomicon.com) is held every June. This annual conglomeration of nerd culture (and proud of it!) is a four-day celebration of multi-genre entertainment like sci-fi, fantasy, and superhero. The yearly celebrity roster is huge and includes "con" megastars like Ralph Macchio, Sean Astin, and Gates McFadden. The convention includes meet and greets, cosplay, shopping, parties, and gaming.

October

Events tend to grind to a screeching halt when the temperatures climb into triple digits during summer, but they start up again with a bang in October at the **Arizona State Fair** (1826 W. McDowell Rd., 602/252-6771, azstatefair.com). The multi-week carnival combines rides, deep-fried food, big-name concerts, and farm-animal exhibitions for a bit of classic Americana.

At the end of the month, the Valley's Latino community—along with everyone else—celebrates **Dia de los Muertos,** or Day of the Dead. The Mesa Arts Center hosts a weekend festival with foods, a market, and entertainment and the Burton Barr Central Library hosts art shows and events to celebrate.

November-December

By mid-November, most of the Valley is gearing up for elaborate holiday events like **Las Noches de las Luminarias** at the Desert Botanical Garden (1201 N. Galvin Pkwy., 480/941-1225, www.dbg.org). These celebrations are a Southwestern tradition that sees thousands of flickering luminarias laid out in the desert garden, creating a spectacular sight.

ZooLights (455 N. Galvin Pkwy., 602/273-1341, www.phoenixzoo.org) has also become a family tradition and delights kids with elaborate light displays, carousel rides, and hot cocoa at the Phoenix Zoo.

In the West Valley, **Glendale Glitters** (58th Ave. and Glendale Ave., 623/930-2000, www.glendaleaz.com) dazzles visitors in the city's historic district with 1.5 million twinkling lights and holiday entertainment, a petting zoo, children's snow field, and food.

Shopping

Phoenix helped pioneer the outdoor mall when the upscale Biltmore Fashion Park opened in the 1960s, and the retail landmark is still one of the city's few pedestrian-friendly enclaves. Shoppers who are looking for funky mom-and-pop stores and vintage boutiques should head downtown or to Central Phoenix, which offers some surprisingly affordable retail options. Mill Avenue's shops in Tempe attract students from the neighboring Arizona State University.

DOWNTOWN
Shopping Districts and Centers
CITYSCAPE

In 2010, downtown Phoenix got a big boost when **CityScape** (1 E. Washington St., 602/772-300, www.cityscapephoenix.com, 9am-8pm daily) opened up a large complex of

kid-friendly CityScape

apartments, office space, retails shops, restaurants, bars, and hotel. Since then, the mall has been a successful addition to the townscape and is frequently visited by locals and travelers alike. CityScape is made of four buildings, walkways, and outdoor courtyards that stretch from 1st Avenue to 1st Street between Washington and Jefferson Streets. It has a healthy mix of shops and restaurants like the popular bowling alley Lucky Strike, big retailers including Urban Outfitters, chain restaurants like Five Guys, and live music bars such as Copper Blues. Catch a comedy show at Stand Up Live and in the winter months, enjoy ice-skating on an outdoor rink. With Hotel Palomar on the premises, you could theoretically spend all your time at CityScape—although we don't recommend that, because it's within walking distance of so many attractions including Chase Field, Comerica Theatre, and the Phoenix Convention Center.

ARIZONA CENTER

The outdoor **Arizona Center** (400 E. Van Buren St., 602/271-4000, www.arizonacenter. com, 10am-9pm Mon.-Sat., 11am-5pm Sun.) is a pleasant mix of restaurants, bars, and shops surrounded by downtown Phoenix's office towers. There's even a 24-screen multiplex movie theater—perfect for escaping the heat—and a Grid Bike Share Station. Sadly, residents often overlook its best feature: a small, shady garden with benches, waterfalls, and a tranquil pond. It's a nice place to enjoy a picnic lunch or catch a few rays.

★ ROOSEVELT ROW

The small collection of independent shops, galleries, and restaurants that make up **Roosevelt Row** (602/829-5259, www.rooseveltrow.org) has tried to do the impossible: Transform downtown Phoenix into a vibrant, pedestrian-friendly neighborhood. And since the turn of the 21st century, their Herculean efforts appear to be working.

Every Saturday, the **Open Air Market at the Phoenix Public Market** (721 N. Central Ave., www.phxpublicmarket/openair.com, 8am-noon Sat. May-Sept., 8am-1pm Sat. Oct-Apr.) pops up near Central Avenue and McKinley Street, made up of local farmers and artisans selling organic produce and homemade goods. Some of the best art in Phoenix is on display along Roosevelt Row, where vibrant, colorful murals cover almost every exterior wall.

The monthly **First Fridays Art Walk** (www.artlinkphoenix.com, 6pm-10pm) fills Roosevelt Street and Grand Avenue between 15th Avenue and 7th Street, with people darting in and out of the neighborhood's small galleries, artists' studios, and live/work spaces that have sprung up. The event has been so popular that there is now a **Third Friday Art Walk,** a similar but smaller art walk on the third Friday of the month.

Some of the smaller shops come and go, but the collective, artist-run space **Eye Lounge** (419 E. Roosevelt St., 602/430-1490, www.eyelounge.com, 6pm-9pm Fri., 1pm-5pm Sat., 11am-3pm Sun.) promotes the works of local emerging artists, making it an excellent opportunity to invest in a piece on the ground floor.

There are a few independent stores of note on Roosevelt, including **Made Art Boutique** (922 N. 5th St., 602/256-6233, www.madephx.com, 11am-7pm Mon.-Sat., 11am-4pm Sun.), which sells fun books, T-shirts, jewelry, and artwork.

Vintage-clothing lovers in the area swooned when **Antique Sugar** (801 N. 2nd St., Ste. 104, 602/277-5765, 11am-7pm Mon.-Sat., 11am-5pm Sun.) moved to Roosevelt Row in 2015. The store boasts over 2,000 square feet of racks and hangers filled with "sweet vintage threads."

Every city needs a humble record store that's jam-packed with vinyl and authentic memorabilia; **Revolver Records** (918 N 2nd St., 602/795-4980, www.revolveraz.com,

noon-8pm Mon.-Thurs., 11am-10pm Fri.-Sat., noon-5pm Sun.) is that place, with a glorious, slightly musty vibe of digging through a neighbor's record collection for a great find. Revolver specializes in used LPs but also sells used and vintage electronics as well as a variety of CDs, DVDs, and books.

Clothing

Bunky Boutique (1437 N. 1st St., 602/252-1323, www.bunkyboutique.com, 10am-6pm Mon.-Sat., 10am-5pm Sun.) has become a Phoenix retail darling, with an eclectic selection of men's, women's, and children's clothing and accessories. Well-known labels and independent designers are represented and the store's almost modular architecture shares space with indie coffee shop Giant Coffee. Owner Rachel Malloy is charming as can be and has a real eye for lightweight cotton wear in a Southwest style that is absolutely perfect for Phoenix.

CENTRAL PHOENIX
Shopping Districts and Centers
BILTMORE FASHION PARK

Biltmore Fashion Park (24th St. and Camelback Rd., 602/955-8400, www.shopbiltmore.com, 10am-8pm Mon.-Sat., noon-6pm Sun.) is much more than a mall. Since opening in 1963, the open-air shopping center has become a sort of public square in Phoenix's posh Biltmore neighborhood, attracting many of the city's residents (and their dogs) to its upscale shops, landscaped courtyards, and popular restaurants. **Macy's** and **Pottery Barn** anchor the western end of the complex. Next door, **Saks Fifth Avenue** overlooks a grassy lawn, attracting well-heeled clients who visit the store's mini-boutiques dedicated to Chanel, Gucci, Louis Vuitton, and Prada. Under the Biltmore's shaded canopies you'll find other big-name brands like Escada, Ralph Lauren, Apple, and an Elizabeth Arden Red Door Spa. A controversial remodel has transformed the much-beloved midcentury landmark's design, although it did add a new

Central Phoenix

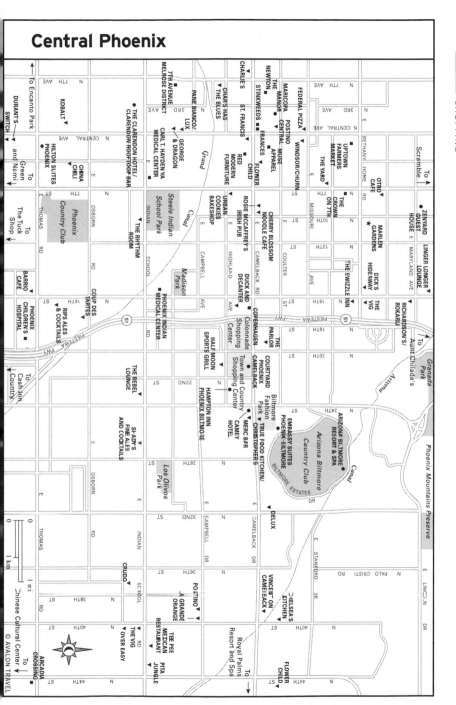

© AVALON TRAVEL

underground pedestrian walkway connecting the center to restaurants, a movie theater, and The Camby Hotel on the opposite side of Camelback Road.

MELROSE DISTRICT

The **Melrose District** on 7th Avenue has become the city's thrift-store haven. Among the half-dozen antiques stores, **Zinnias at Melrose** (724 W. Indian School Rd., 602/264-4166, www.zinniasatmelrose.com, 10am-5pm Sun.-Tues., 10am-6pm Wed.-Sat.) is one of the best, featuring a huge warehouse of furniture, collectibles, and bric-a-brac galore. Another favorite is **Retro Ranch** (4303 N. 7th Ave., 602/297-1971, www.retroranch.net, 11am-6pm Tues.-Sun.). If your Pinterest board is filled with home decor boards that showcase sparsely decorated, midcentury inspired rooms, go to **Twigs and Twine** (4427 N. 7th Ave., 602/625-5527, www.twigsandtwine.com, 10am-5:30pm Thurs.-Mon.), where that aesthetic becomes a reality. The store specializes in vintage furniture that is professionally refinished and midcentury inspired pieces.

COFCO CHINESE CULTURAL CENTER

The **COFCO Chinese Cultural Center** (668 N. 44th St., 602/273-7268, www.phxchinatown.com) is an outdoor strip mall with graceful pagodas, traditional arches, and small gardens. Stroll the grounds and visit the small shops, like **Golden Gifts** (602/275-1311, 10am-7pm Mon.-Sat., 10am-6pm Sun.) and the **Chinese Herbal Shop** (602/244-9885, 10am-7pm daily), and make some time to pop into the mammoth **Super L Ranch Market** (602/225-2288, 10:30am-8pm daily), which features rows of imported goods, fresh produce, and a restaurant known for its duck dishes.

THE NEWTON

When the masterminds behind Changing Hands Bookstore in Tempe and MADE Art Boutique in downtown Phoenix set their sights on the uptown/Camelback Corridor area for a new development, the whole city buzzed. With an overhaul of an old Phoenix restaurant came the establishment of a mixed-use building housing retail shops, a restaurant, and event space called **The Newton** (300 W. Camelback Rd., www.thenewtonphx.com). The second location of **Changing Hands Bookstore** (602/274-0067, www.changinghands.com, 9am-10pm Mon.-Fri., 9am-10pm Sat., 9am-8pm Sun.) draws literary types as well as families with small children who love the kid's area and the story-time events. Sharing an open wall with the store is **First Draft Book Bar** (602/274-0067, www.changinghands.com/firstdraftbar, 9am-10pm Mon.-Sat., 9am-8pm Sun.), where visitors can enjoy a coffee, beer on tap, wine, and snacks. Neighboring **Southwest Gardener** (602/279-9510, southwestgardener.com, 10am-6pm Mon.-Fri., 10am-5pm Sat., 11am-4pm Sun.) is a great stop for picking up desert garden decorations, wind chimes, birdhouses, and ceramics.

CROWN ON SEVENTH

Yet another transformation of old to new in North Central Phoenix is **Crown on Seventh** (5813 N. 7th St., www.crownon7.com), which is still up and coming. The revitalization includes restaurants and shops, which are slowly filling up 18,000 square feet of retail space around a lush courtyard garden. The beautiful **White House Design Studio Urban Boutique** (602/595-1149, www.whitehouseflowers.com, 10am-8pm Sat.) is the perfect place to pick up a small gift for a shower or wedding with candles, housewares, and stunning fresh flower arrangements. Nearby, ultra-chic **The Root Salon** (602/277-4072, www.therootsalon.com, 10am-6pm daily) mainly deals with hair and beauty but carries local-made, handcrafted accessories and handbags that are Southwestern in style yet contemporary and always on trend.

Clothing

A few modern, independent shops are clustered around Camelback Road and Central

Avenue, like **Frances** (10 W. Camelback Rd., 602/279-5467, www.francesvintage.com, 10am-6pm Mon.-Sat., noon-5pm Sun.), where shoppers will find an eclectic mix of goods reflecting the boutique's vintage-inspired aesthetic, like embroidered blouses, wallets, retro paper goods, soy candles, and fun gifts for kids and adults. Similarly, **Muse Apparel** (100 E. Camelback Rd., 602/749-8880, www.shopatmuse.com, 10am-7pm Mon.-Sun.) caters to an upscale crowd and features a curated selection of contemporary designers.

Home Furnishings

The Danish Modern aesthetic is a natural fit for a city filled with midcentury modern architecture. When **Copenhagen** (1701 E. Camelback Rd., 602/266-8060, www.copenhagenliving.com, 8am-6pm Mon.-Sat., noon-5pm Sun.) opened in the 1970s, homeowners and business owners looking for unique pieces to punch up their style relied on this store to provide. Business has been so good that it has since opened multiple locations in the state and across the Southwest. The minimalist designs are beautiful and, at the very least, call for an inspiring browse in the 45,000 square feet of showroom—assuming you can resist the urge to pick something up.

Red Modern Furniture (201 E. Camelback Rd., 602/256-9620, https://red-modernfurniture.com, 10am-5pm Mon.-Fri., by appointment Sat.-Sun., summer hours may vary) is the place to go for original vintage pieces by Eero Saarinen, Arne Jacobsen, Knoll, Henredon, Giò Ponti, and Charles and Ray Eames. This hidden gem is a resource for some of the nation's top interior designers and collectors, and the displays are always changing and ever thrilling to design junkies.

Music

Video killed the radio star, and the Internet is slowly killing the music shop. Fortunately, **Stinkweeds** (12 W. Camelback Rd., 602/248-9461, www.stinkweeds.com, 11am-8pm Mon.-Sat., noon-6pm Sun.) keeps hope alive for Valley music lovers as one of the city's last independent record shops, specializing in up-and-coming bands, imports, and music from independent labels. Both new and used records are for sale.

NORTH PHOENIX
Shopping Districts and Centers
DESERT RIDGE MARKETPLACE

Decidedly more casual than some of the upscale shopping places listed, **Desert Ridge Marketplace** (21001 N. Tatum Blvd., 480/513-7586, www.shopdesertridge.com, 11am-9pm Mon.-Sat., 11am-6pm Sun.) offers 1.2 million (yes, million) square feet of retail space. You could spend an entire day at this outdoor mall and never get bored. Sure, most retailers are chains but with so much space, it's like *all of them* are there. Barnes & Noble, Hot Topic, Old Navy, DSW, Pier 1 Imports, and Sunglass Hut are just a small sample of stores available. Food options include Island Fine Burgers & Drinks, California Pizza Kitchen, Macaroni Grill, and Rocky Mountain Chocolate Factory. A splash pad is open for the kids in the hot weather months, the AMC movie theater features 18 screens, and Dave & Buster's guarantees a raucous time playing interactive video games.

THE OUTLETS AT ANTHEM

On the northern edge of town, a bargain hunter's paradise unfolds in the desert for those who still seek such opportunities in real life rather than online. **The Outlets at Anthem** (4250 W. Anthem Way, 623/465-9500, www.outletsanthem.com, 10am-8pm Mon.-Sat., 10am-7pm Sun.) is home to more than 60 designer-brand stores loaded with merchandise at significantly reduced prices. You'll find Banana Republic, Michael Kors, J. Crew, and Calvin Klein duds marked down by up to 70 percent. A food court with just about anything you're looking for will keep you full enough to search out every last deal.

NORTERRA

In the great tradition of massive outdoor malls that require driving from store to store rather than walking, **Norterra** (2460 W. Happy Valley Rd., 623/582-9599, www.norterrashopping.com, 10am-8pm Mon.-Thurs., 10am-9pm Fri.-Sat., 11am-6pm Sun.) serves the retail needs of the north Phoenix crowd. Here's the short list: Charming Charlie, Victoria's Secret, Sunglass Hut, Bath & Body Works, Massage Envy, BevMo!, Elevate Coffee Co., Fractured Prune Doughnuts, Mellow Mushroom, Pita Jungle, and a 14-screen movie theater are what's in store for patrons. Norterra is also the location of monthly events such as live music or family movies for $1.

TEMPE AND THE EAST VALLEY
Shopping Districts and Centers
MILL AVENUE

Mill Avenue has always been a busy street thanks to its proximity to Arizona State University. Although it became a little too popular for its own good in the 1990s, when high rents chased out mom-and-pop shops and bars, it's now back on its feet with a charming collection of small shops, eateries, and coffee shops. The big national chain that still remains is **Urban Outfitters** but you can also shop at smaller, unique places like DIVAZ Boutique. If clothes aren't your thing, there's **Candy Addict, Churchill's Fine Cigars,** and **The Henna Shoppe** (just a few examples) to keep you entertained.

TEMPE MARKETPLACE

A couple of miles east of Mill Avenue, you'll find the sprawling **Tempe Marketplace** (2000 E. Rio Salado Pkwy., 480/966-9338, www.tempemarketplace.com, 11am-9pm Mon.-Sat., 11am-6pm Sun.). The mega-complex of chain retailers boasts a lot of names you'll recognize from the mall, like Gap, Nordstrom Rack, and Barnes & Noble, as well as a movie theater and dozens of restaurants and bars. Its light shows, outdoor fireplaces, and unique water features make it a great place to hang out at night, especially for the robust calendar of live concerts.

Mill Avenue

GUADALUPE

Driving into the one-square-mile town of **Guadalupe** is an unforgettable experience. It's home to a historic community founded by Yaqui Indians who settled in the area in the early 20th century. Today, the roads are delightfully rich with Yaqui, Latino, and distinctly Southwest culture. The family-owned **Guadalupe Farmers Market** (9210 S. Avenida del Yaqui, 480/730-1945, 8am-9pm Mon.-Fri., 9am-7pm Sat., 10am-5pm Sun.) sells locally grown fruits and vegetables as well as Latin American specialties like fresh tortillas, tamales, roasted chilies, and homemade salsas and jams. There's also a large selection of dried spices and Arizona honey that make terrific gifts. Shoppers may want to make time to stop into the **Mercado Mexico** (8212 S. Avenida del Yaqui, 480/831-5925), which is an incredible store selling quality imported products from south of the border, like ceramics and paper gifts that are often sold in higher-end shops for way higher prices. If you have cash in hand and can speak Spanish, the owners may knock a few bucks off your total.

Bookstores

One of the stores that fled Mill Avenue, **Changing Hands Tempe** (6428 S. McClintock Dr., 480/730-0205, 10am-9pm Mon.-Fri., 9am-9pm Sat., 10am-6pm Sun.) features 12,000 square feet of new and used books, specializing in contemporary fiction. Known for its regular events, the store's impressive roster of signings includes David Sedaris, Jimmy Carter, Hillary Clinton, and Elizabeth Gilbert. Collectors can find rare first editions like Harper Lee's *To Kill a Mockingbird* as well as signed copies of Jonathan Franzen's *The Corrections* and Nick Hornby's *About a Boy.*

Vintage Clothing

When it comes to vintage and used clothing, Tempe has a few spots worth checking out. Of course it goes without saying that **Buffalo Exchange** (227 W. University Dr., 480/968-2557, www.buffaloexchange.com, 10am-9pm Mon.-Sat., 11am-7pm Sun.) sells an eclectic mix of new and (mostly) vintage threads.

Speaking of vintage, on the Tempe/Scottsdale border sits a true gem of a vintage shop. **Blue Jean Buyer** (1810 N. Scottsdale Rd., 480/947-8245, 11am-6pm Tues.-Fri., noon-5pm Sat.) is super well-known for selling an unbelievably cool collection of vintage denim. Jeans, cutoffs, jackets—especially of the Levi variety—are in abundance here as well as a one-of-a-kind gathering of boots, vintage band T-shirts, and Native American jewelry.

WEST VALLEY
Shopping Districts and Centers
HISTORIC DOWNTOWN GLENDALE

The cute **Historic Downtown Glendale** has become a mecca for Arizona antique hunters and pickers, thanks to its two shopping districts of Old Towne (Glendale Ave. and 58th Ave.) and Caitlin Court (Myrtle Ave. and 58th Ave.). This pedestrian-friendly neighborhood features old bungalows with white picket fences and shady trees that have been converted into small specialty shops, like **Country Maiden** (7146 N. 58th Ave., 623/930-7303, www.thecountrymaiden.com, 10am-4pm Mon.-Sat.) and **The Cottage Garden** (7142 N. 58th Ave., 623/847-3232, 10am-5pm Tues.-Sat.).

Sports and Recreation

Few cities in the world offer such a rich selection of activities for outdoor lovers. Phoenix and the city's surrounding suburbs will seem like paradise for diehard golfers, hikers, and bikers. And don't let the summer heat stop you from taking advantage of the city's incredible landscapes. Many Phoenicians set their alarm clocks early in the summer, when cool morning temperatures make a round of golf or jog along the canals downright pleasant.

AIR ADVENTURES AND BALLOONING

Act out all your *Top Gun* fantasies at **Fighter Combat International** (5865 S. Sossaman Rd., Mesa, 480/279-1881, www.fightercombat.com), where you can tempt both gravity and death by flying a plane on a virtual combat mission. Even beginners learn to take the stick during in-the-air training in air-combat tactics, lead-and-follow drills, and weapons training. As they say, "only the bullets aren't real." Prices range from $725 for a two-to-three-hour adventure up to the thousands for a multiday experience.

Hot Air Expeditions (702 W. Deer Valley Rd., 480/502-6999, www.hotairexpeditions.com) flies its balloons about 400 feet above the desert floor, low enough to spot critters like jackrabbits, roadrunners, and coyotes. But the best part may come after landing: A red-carpet treat that includes champagne breakfast or dinner catered by award-winning Arizona chef Vincent Guerithault's restaurant, Vincent's on Camelback. The company is FAA-certified and offers free hotel transfers. The 60-90 minute trips cost $179 per adult.

A Valley favorite, **Aerogelic Ballooning** (2501 W. Happy Valley Rd., 602/478-1797, www.aerogelicballooning.com) focuses on basic flights that soak up the beauty over the Sonoran Desert outside Phoenix. More special experiences include Dawn Patrol flights, which start half an hour before sunrise to show the city's lights as they wink out for the day, or a night flight that is decidedly more thrilling as you soar through the dark skies lit by moonlight and stars. Packages range between $169-799.

DESERT AND JEEP TOURS

You can't go wrong with the company **Carefree Adventures** (40222 Spur Cross Rd., 480/488-2466, www.carefreeadventures.com). Although they are headquartered in Cave Creek, AZ, they serve the Phoenix area by guiding guests on archeological, gold mine, and Jeep tours through the Four Peaks area. Tours and costs vary but average at $100 per adult and $50 per child.

Phoenix Tours (212/852-4822, www.phoenixtours.us) leads Jeep and van tours of the Apache Trail in the Superstition Mountains, a daylong Sedona trip, and trips to the Grand Canyon. Drivers pick up at individual hotels and drive out to the desert, where guides cover the history and ecology of the tour area. Prices are around $75-700 depending on the trip.

BIKING AND JOGGING

Phoenix's 181 miles of canals give it some of the most extensive biking and running-trail systems anywhere. One of the best paths in town is along the gravel bank of the **Arizona Canal** (ww.srpnet.com/water/canals) between Scottsdale Road and Central Avenue. The full distance is just over 11 miles, but luckily, the best parts are at either end. From Scottsdale Road to 56th Street is particularly appealing, with a tour of the attractive Scottsdale Waterfront living and shopping area and the stunning Arcadia Falls where the canal waters cascade over a dramatic drop by a viewing pavilion. The stretch between 16th Street and 40th Street enjoys views of the nearby Phoenix Mountains and the Biltmore Hotel.

Desert Hiking Safety

It happens every year. Someone comes to Phoenix, hikes on a hot day, and dies. We're talking about fit kids in their 20s who could probably survive incredible physical challenges. But dehydration and heat stroke are not to be taken lightly, and they tragically kill many people each year. Here are a few tips to keep you safe.

- **Do not plan multi-hour, daytime hikes in full sun from late May to early September.** Period. Plan for trails under three miles long at dawn or dusk only. It will still be hot, so bring plenty of water.

- **Bring water and more water no matter what time of year it is.** On a temperate day, you can expect to drink about one liter for every two miles. When it's a hot day, you'll be shocked at how much water you need to keep your body moving and your mind working. Water is your best defense against heat stroke, which can lead to such severe disorientation that many die within a tragically short distance of a house or a road.

- **Know where you are going.** The trail systems in our parks are usually well maintained and sufficiently labeled but with so many trails that lead to extremely remote desert areas, it's easy to get lost out there. Park maps are usually posted or available at city trailheads, so be sure you make a thorough consultation before you head out. Better yet, print off a trail map from www.phoenix.gov/parks/trails/.

- **Dress appropriately.** Wear shoes with good tread and laces with workout or trail-appropriate clothing. It's not a bad idea to have a first-aid kit in a pack along with some snacks and all that water you packed (right?).

- **Hike with a friend, if possible.** Two heads are better than one in many scenarios and if something were to happen on the trail, it's good to be with someone who has your back.

- **Don't rely on your cell phone!** It's a great backup for rescue and trail map apps but it's just one drop away from being non-functional. A paper map and a compass are your best bets always.

- **Tell someone where you are going.** Once you have it all figured out, send a quick text to a trusted friend or tell the front desk at your hotel of your hiking plans for the day. If you happen to get lost out there or have an accident, this will be critical in securing a rescue.

One of the best introductions to mountain biking in the Sonoran Desert is the **Desert Classic** trail at South Mountain Park. The nine-mile (one-way) trail (find the trailhead at 9904 S. 48th St., near Guadalupe Road, www.phoenix.gov/parks/trails/locations/south-mountain) runs the gamut of terrain from steep-sided washes to single-track speedways and even a few rocky, technical climbs without becoming impossible for bikers with intermediate skills. Anyone looking for more of a challenge can take a right on the **National Trail**—where the rocky, steep descents make for one of the toughest rides in the state—to make a loop back to the parking area. Be sure to reference a good map (available online at www.phoenix.gov/parks/trails/locations/south-mountain/trail-descriptions-and-map) and bring it with you, because the trail system is tricky in these parts.

Ample mountain biking is available in the Phoenix Mountains along the **Charles M. Christiansen Memorial Trail 100** (www.phoenix.gov/parks/trails/locations). The best access points are at the North Mountain Visitor Center (12950 N. 7th St.) and Dreamy Draw Recreation Area (2421 E. Northern Ave.), where you can hop right on for an excellent mix of flat stretches, straining uphill battles, and incredible scenery.

Roadies will find it nearly impossible to get a traffic-free pedaling fix in Phoenix, but one

A Nation of Preservation

Phoenix loves to brag about its hiking. You'll find this vulgar display of pride is warranted, however, when you tour the grand **Phoenix Mountains Preserve** (www.phoenix.gov/parkssite). The preserve was only a few scattered parks until the early 1960s, when a group of passionate citizens started advocating for greater efforts to preserve the mountains and surrounding foothills. Their mission led to the protection of approximately 7,000 acres, which serve today as the city's much-loved resource for hiking, biking, and horseback riding.

The preservation of the Phoenix Mountains paved the way (get it?) for the city to continue this fine tradition. As wild desert gets bulldozed to accommodate the rapidly growing suburbs, the city continues to set aside huge swaths of land for hiking, biking, and, most importantly, for wildlife to flourish. Today, the city enjoys more than 41,000 acres of desert parks and preserves with 200 miles of trails. Protected areas **Deem Hills Recreation Area** (51st Ave. and Deem Hills Pkwy, 602/495-6939, www.phoenix.gov/parks/trails/locations/deem-hills, open sunrise to sunset) and **Sonoran Preserve** (1600 E. Sonoran Desert Dr., 602/262-7901, www.phoenix.gov/parks/trails/locations/sonoran-preserve, open sunrise to sunset) in the North Valley are the newest kids on the block with more in development.

of the city's rare paved hill climbs is on **Valle Vista Road** on the south side of Camelback Mountain. The best approach is from the south, either on Arcadia Drive or 56th Street, because the streets link up to form a loop back to wherever you parked your car or to the light-rail stop at 44th Street and Washington.

HIKING AND ROCK CLIMBING

Phoenix is lucky enough to have mountains peppered along its valley floor. And Phoenix residents are lucky enough to enjoy a legacy of setting aside land preserves that provide ample opportunity for hiking in the incredible Sonoran Desert. The best part? You can usually find a trailhead within a 20-minute drive, no matter where you're staying in Phoenix. It's pretty freakin' awesome. For detailed maps and information about each preserve visit, www.phoenix.gov/parkssite.

The **Phoenix Parks and Recreation** department helps to organize small hikes and outdoor programs with two major events: The **National Trail Trek** (www.phoenix.gov/parks/trails/special-events/national-trail-trek) in late January, when hikers convene and travel across the 15.5-mile National Trail in South Mountain, and the **Phoenix Summit**

Challenge (www.phoenix.gov/parks/trails/special-events/summit) during which superhikers climb four to seven summits in one day sometime in November.

The steep canyons and rock spires that shape the mountains around Phoenix are a playground for rock climbers, but the sandstone terrain is often treacherous. Guide outfit **360 Adventures** (602/795-1877, www.360-adventures.com) offers instruction and equipment for beginners and the lay of the land for experts. Prices for half-day and full-day rock-climbing or canyoneering trips range between $250-450 per person, depending on the activity and size of the group. The company also offers biking, hiking, air, ground, and water tours of local wilderness preserves and areas.

Phoenix Mountains Preserve

The **Phoenix Mountains Preserve** (www.phoenix.gov/parkssite) is the main hiking hub for centrally located locals and visitors. With over 50 miles of trails, you could fill an entire vacation exploring these foothills, ridgelines, and peaks.

You can take your pick from the many trails at your disposal, but for the grand tour of the preserve, consider the **Charles M. Christiansen Memorial Trail 100.** Set aside a full day for this trek, which will lead you from one end of the park to the other, totaling about 11 miles. You'll see all the major summits (Shaw Butte, North Mountain, and Piestewa Peak) without having to climb any of them (woohoo!). This trail is also a good jumping-off point to explore canyons and washes that feel like they're far from the surrounding city. Find information on the flora and fauna and get maps at the **North Mountain Visitor Center** (12950 N. 7th St., 602343-5125, www.northmountainvisitorcenter, 8am-1pm Mon.-Thurs., 8am-3pm Fri.-Sun.).

★ PIESTEWA PEAK

No trip to Phoenix would be complete without climbing **Piestewa Peak.** The short but challenging Summit Trail rises just over 1,200 feet in 1.2 miles and is the toughest summit trail in the Phoenix Mountains Preserve. The peak offers panoramic views of the city stretched out for miles in every direction, and when the wind carries the scent of creosote and citrus blossoms up from the Valley below, it can be hard to begin the clamber back down. On weekend mornings, the trail becomes a mountainside promenade as throngs of tanned, fit hikers and runners (and those who wish to be so) make even panting by the side of the trail interesting. But it is on the quieter weekdays when jackrabbits, Gila monsters, geckos, and the occasional rattlesnake or coyote come out to sun themselves among the cacti and desert trees that pepper the hillsides. To reach the trailhead, turn east onto Squaw Peak Drive from Lincoln Drive between 22nd and 24th streets.

Camelback Mountain

Perhaps the most famous hike in the Valley, summiting **Camelback Mountain** at 2,704 feet is a job best done by the physically fit. It's a heck of a climb up the rocky terrain, gaining a whopping 1,200 feet in just 1.3 mile (one way) along the **Echo Canyon Summit Trail.** Starting at the "camel's head" at the **Echo Canyon Recreation Area** (4925 W. McDonald Dr., 602/261-8318, www.phoenix.gov/parks/trails/locations/camelback-mountainphoenix.gov), be sure to meet this adventure in good weather and pack plenty of

the summit at Piestewa Peak

water. In recent years, visitors have attempted the trail on hot summer days without enough to drink and have met a tragic end. But if you're careful and capable, you won't be disappointed with the workout or the unobstructed view of the entire city from the summit. The sights on the way up aren't too shabby, either, with dramatic sandstone rock formations that literally glow in the sun. Other options from this trailhead include the half-mile **Bobby's Rock Trail,** which leads to an area popular with rock climbers.

The less popular **Cholla Trail** (6131 E. Cholla Lane) climbs up the "camel's hump" from the backside to the summit. Some might claim it's more manageable than the Echo Canyon route but it's still quite a haul as you enjoy a peek into the Eden-like Phoenician Resort. The trailhead starts on Cholla Lane; note that parking is limited to parallel street parking only.

Papago Park

Hiking "quickies" seldom lead to anything interesting, let alone iconic, but the **Hole-in-the-Rock Trail** in **Papago Park** is the exception. The easy trail is only 835 feet long and leads up to a tunnel-like hole in the sandstone. The entrancing views of downtown Phoenix make this one of the best places anywhere to watch a colorful Southwestern sunset. Get there by turning off the Galvin Parkway onto the Papago Park and Phoenix Zoo road. The trail begins from a picnic area on the northern end of the Ranger Office Loop road. Across Galvin Parkway, on the west side of the road, sits another trailhead that leads to an easy, wheelchair-accessible hike that offers multiple trails traveling between two massive sandstone buttes visible from across the Valley.

South Mountain Park and Preserve

The other must-hike destination is **South Mountain Park and Preserve** (www. phoenix.gov/parks/trails/locations/south-mountain). 16,000 acres of three mountain ranges filled with *arroyos* (dry creeks), washes,

canyons, and flats crisscrossed by 51 miles of hiking trails make this one of the largest municipal parks in the United States. It's so large that simply telling someone you're hiking South Mountain could mean a lot of different things. So, to narrow it down for you, try the two-mile **Kiwanis Trail** hike that travels through a lush canyon before hooking up with the National Trail to a stone structure on a ridge. This trail can be found from the main trailhead accessed from Central Avenue, south of Dobbins Road. If you're looking for more mileage the **Mormon Trail to Hidden Valley** is a stunning, 3.6-mile hike up a steep hill and then through a flatland on top of the mountain. It's scenic, rocky, and offers a fun wiggle through Fat Man's Pass, an opening through two massive boulders. This trailhead is located at the south end of 24th Street, south of Baseline Road. And if you want to be super ambitious, go for the **National Trail,** which travels South Mountain Park end to end in 15.5 miles of incredible trail that you'll remember for life. It's essential to check online for map details and information about road closures, which may affect access to trails.

North Phoenix

With the popularity and cultural identity that the Phoenix Mountains and South Mountain preserves have provided, the city of Phoenix is thinking ahead with developing new areas. Enter **Deem Hills Recreation Area,** a newly developed preserve located in the north Phoenix area. Try the 4-mile Circumference and Ridgeline Loop on the east side of the park, which offers sweeping views of the Arizona Canal cutting through the north valley. The trailhead is located on the east side of a gorgeous park and playground on 51st Avenue and Deem Hills Parkway. The other new kid on the block in north Phoenix is the **Sonoran Preserve.** The Dixie Mountain Loop is a favorite hike with almost 6 miles through a beautiful area of the desert filled with wildflowers in spring. The trail offers a few summit spurs along the way and passes by a rusty old truck in a wash that makes for some awesome photos.

Aqua Vitae

Summer in the Sonoran Desert means hot, sunny days and warm nights. To combat the super-high temperatures, Phoenicians find relief in the region's most valuable resource: water.

- **Pools:** Arizona without swimming pools is like New York City without hot-dog carts. Take a peek out the window of your airplane as you near the airport and you'll see a blue-spotted landscape created by countless backyard swimming pools. Most hotels and resorts have at least one pool, although the most elegant has to be the main pool at **The Phoenician** (6000 E. Camelback Rd., 480/941-8200, www.thephoenician.com), which is lined with mother-of-pearl tiles.

- **Misters:** Where would Phoenix patios be without the mister? You'll see them producing a fine mist of water at houses, restaurants, and bars throughout the city. These simple machines produce water droplets as fine as the diameter of a human hair, and when they make contact with the dry desert air, the droplets "flash evaporate," resulting in a dip in temperature by several degrees—and all with just a slight increase in noticeable humidity. During a summer evening as the sun goes down and a breeze picks up, it can get downright chilly…like down to 81°F!

- **Lakes:** Thanks to a series of dams around the Valley, there are seven large lakes within an easy drive of Phoenix. The most convenient body of water, though, has to be **Tempe Town Lake** (620 N. Mill Ave., 480/350-5200, www.tempe.gov/lake, free). Created by dams along the Salt River, the manmade lake is a popular gathering spot for festivals, joggers, and rowing clubs. But don't expect to swim in this lake. Instead, you can rent a pontoon or surrey (boats4rent. com/tempe-az).

- **Splash Pads:** For Phoenix parents, splash pads become a way of life during the summer when the insufferable temperatures make outdoor play miserable. Many can be found in city parks or shopping centers. Check out the one in the courtyard at **CityScape** (1 E. Washington St., 602/772-300, 9am-8pm daily, free), or the one at the **Tempe Marketplace** (2000 E. Rio Salado Pkwy, 480/966-9338, www.tempemarketplace.com, 7am-11pm daily, free), located near Barnes & Noble.

- **Water Parks:** In summer, nothing beats the heat like gliding down a slide into a clear pool of water. There are a half-dozen water parks throughout the Valley, including a few at the larger resorts, but only **Wet 'n' Wild** (4243 W. Pinnacle Peak Rd., 623/201-2000, http://phoenix.mywetnwild.com, $4.99 general admission) can claim the title of "Arizona's largest." The Glendale retreat opened in summer 2009 with $30 million worth of slides, rides, and splish-splashin' good times.

- **Rivers:** Many Phoenicians regularly make the 20-minute commute northeast of the Valley to the mountain-fed Salt River. Tubers can float past majestic sandstone cliffs, spiraling hawks, wading blue herons, and towering saguaro cacti—as well as beer-soaked partiers on the river and jacked-up trucks blasting classic rock on the shore. It's an inimitable experience and tour company **Salt River Recreation** (480/984-3305, www.saltrivertubing.com) will rent you a tube and give you a ride to and from the river for $17 a person.

- **Fountains:** Head out to the aptly named suburb of Fountain Hills to see the Valley's answer to Old Faithful, **The Fountain,** a 560-foot-tall jet of water. One of the world's tallest fountains, the slender column rises to 330 feet most days in the center of **Fountain Park** (12925 N. Saguaro Blvd., 480/816-5100, www.fh.az.gov) for 15 minutes at the top of every hour (9am to 9pm). On special occasions, the town turns on all three pumps to send it soaring to its maximum height of 56 stories. The park also has a great playground for children. Take Shea Boulevard 15 minutes east from central Scottsdale and turn north on Saguaro Boulevard.

GOLF

Welcome to the Southwest's golf capital. Phoenix and neighboring Scottsdale lure professionals and amateurs alike with one of the finest collections of courses in the world. Its championship greens dot the city, and residents practically live on the links—some literally, thanks to dozens of golf-course communities. Arizona State University graduates Phil Mickelson, Billy Mayfair, and Grace Park refined their skills here, while Tom Lehman and Annika Sorenstam were compelled to move here by the constant sunshine and top-notch fairways.

Scottsdale's luxury desert courses may be better known, but Phoenix offers quality for a good price. Here you'll find a broad mix of traditional and desert courses as well as some unique landmarks. Many courses close their lawns for a few weeks in the fall and spring for re-seeding between seasons, so be sure to call ahead and ask when you make a tee time. Like hotel and resort rates, greens fees tumble as the heat rises, with even the best courses charging a fraction of their winter prices in the summer. Call ahead for current fees.

One of the best golf experiences in the state features courses designed by two legends. **Wildfire Golf Club** (5350 E. Marriott Dr., 480/473-0205, www.wildfiregolf.com) at the JW Marriott Desert Ridge Resort & Spa showcases two 18-hole desert courses designed by giants Arnold Palmer and Nick Faldo. The scenic Palmer Signature Course has expansive fairways and rolling greens, while the Faldo Championship Course treats golfers to large bent-grass greens, tee boxes, and a bewildering 108 deep pot bunkers. If you'd prefer to hit a few balls and take in the views of the McDowell Mountains, however, grab a bucket at the practice green, complete with bunkers and pitching areas.

A little bit closer to town, **Lookout Mountain Golf Club** (11111 N. 7th St., 602/866-7500, www.tapatiocliffshilton.com) at the Pointe Hilton Tapatio Cliffs Resort is a par-71, 18-hole championship course that wraps around North Mountain Park and the Lookout Mountain Preserve, giving golfers a chance to appreciate the occasional Sonoran Desert rabbit or coyote along with their birdies and eagles. The medium-length course should appeal to most skill levels, although the back nine features a few challenging target holes. The well-regarded golf academy is a good place to grab a few lessons if you're new to the game, and the Lookout Mountain Golf Pro Shop has been named one of the top 100 golf shops in the country.

Looking for a green with a view? **Papago Golf Course** (5595 E. Moreland St., 602/275-8428, www.papagogolfcourse.net) has become one of the most loved slices of turf in the Valley since opening in 1963. Golf course architect William Francis "Billy" Bell, whose roster of 100-plus courses includes Torrey Pines in San Diego, designed it to highlight the so-close-you-can-touch-it views of the red-hued Papago Buttes, Camelback Mountain, and downtown Phoenix. And the course is now better than ever, having re-opened after a $5.8 million renovation that reshaped and added bunkers, reseeded the lawns, restored its lakes, and trimmed mature trees along the fairways. This city-owned course is one of Phoenix's best golfing bargains.

Arizona State University boasts one of the finest collegiate golf programs in the country, so it's small surprise that their home course in Tempe should earn 4.5 stars from *Golf Digest*. The challenging **ASU Karsten Golf Club** (1125 E. Rio Salado Pkwy., 480/921-8070, www.asukarsten.com) may force you to use every club in your bag, but with four sets of tees, you don't have to be PGA-bound to make par—or at least have fun. Designer Pete Dye incorporated his trademark mounding and inspired pot bunkers, as well as lakes, rolling hills, and well-protected greens. The Scottish links-style course books well in advance, so be sure to call early for a tee time.

If you're bored of seeing cacti lining the fairways, try **Raven Golf Club** (3636 E. Baseline Rd., 602/243-3636, www.raven-phx.com). This traditional course features thousands of mature trees, including large African sumacs and towering pine trees. You'll find water hazards, strategically placed bunkers, and a few challenging target holes. Raven regularly earns nods for its incomparable service and it's also the home of Martin Chuck's Tour Striker Golf Academy, which offers golf schools and private coaching.

The **Legacy Golf Club** (6808 S. 32nd St., 602/305-5550, www.golflegacyresort.com) in South Phoenix was named the number-one public course in the city by ESPN.com. Old structures from the 7,500-acre ranch of Dwight Heard—founder of the Heard Museum—now line the 18-hole desert golf course, where you'll find manicured greens and views of South Mountain and the downtown Phoenix skyline. Golf school, lessons, and junior programs are available through the Golf Academy.

On the west side of Phoenix, hit up **Verrado Golf Club** (4242 N. Golf Dr., 623/388-3000, www.verradogolfclub.com), which is fast becoming a well-known course for its incredible scenery as the greens kiss the foothills of the rugged White Tank Mountains. Over 7,000 yards, the vast elevation changes create a variety of contrasting challenges. It all builds to a memorable finish at the 18th hole, which has been described as a "hard core par 4."

San Marcos Golf Resort (100 N. Dakota St., 480/963-3358, www.sanmarcosgolfresort.com), opened in 1913, is part of the Crowne Plaza Resort Phoenix. Many say this is where Arizona's reputation as a mecca for golfers began, as it was the state's first course with grass greens. Over the years, presidents and celebrities have played its wide, forgiving fairways, and more than a few have found their balls in its numerous bunkers. The Chandler landmark is good value and should be considered if you're staying in the East Valley.

By the time you lose your second ball, you'll ask yourself where so much damn water came from in the middle of the desert. Chandler's **Ocotillo Golf Resort** (3751 S. Clubhouse Dr.,

480/917-6660, www.ocotillogolf.com) is one of the state's most individual courses as 24 of its 27 holes feature water hazards—from small lakes and cascading waterfalls to a few island holes. Still, the challenging course is beautiful, and many say it's one of the best manicured in the city. Games are reasonably priced for most of the year.

Okay, this is so worth the drive. Take Highway 60 well beyond Mesa and Gilbert to **Gold Canyon Golf Resort** (6100 S. Kings Ranch Rd., 480/982-9090, www.gcgr.com), a spectacular course tucked into the Superstition Mountains. *Sports Illustrated* named it one of the country's most underrated courses, thanks to nosebleed elevation changes, mountain views, and lush, green fairways lined by pristine desert. Its Dinosaur Mountain Course snakes through mountain passes while the Sidewinder wraps around the foothills. You'll pay a bit for all of this scenery, but why not splurge?

HORSEBACK RIDING

The easiest place to set up an equine adventure is at **Ponderosa Stables & South Mountain Stables** (10215 S. Central Ave., 602/286-1261, http://arizona-horses.com) in South Mountain Park. The experienced trail guides lead rides almost everywhere through the 16,000-acre park, as well as special sunrise and sunset rides that include breakfast or dinner seven days a week, all year long. Trail rides start at $40 a person for one hour and can change depending on the size of the group. Morning reservations are recommended, especially for summer days when the temperature can top 104°F.

On the west side of the city, climb into the saddle at **White Tank Stables** (20300 W. Olive Ave., 623/692-9498, www.potagoldadventures.com). Staff members lead one- and two-hour rides deep into the wilderness of the White Tank Mountains, with the two-hour tour dipping into a canyon that opens up into a stunning meadow. Guided rides start at $40 per person for an hour.

Spring Training

If you're a baseball fan, then you've probably planned out your ideal vacation. No, not Hawaii, South America, or Mount Everest. Baseball fans just want to jump in the car and make the drive from coast to coast, taking in a game at every Major League Baseball ballpark. The alternative is to spend a week in the Valley of the Sun during **spring training** (www.cactusleague.com).

For baseball fans, it's an annual rite—as quintessential as peanuts and Cracker Jacks. Beginning in February and March, 15 Major League Baseball teams descend upon Arizona, allowing fans to catch a game—or two—every day until early April. There really isn't a bad ballpark in the Cactus League. Each place has its own unique qualities. The key is to pick out a couple of teams you want to see and then plan accordingly. Remember to get there early, because most of the big-name players leave the game after a couple of innings, but that's also when you'll see the stars of tomorrow.

The **Los Angeles Dodgers** and **Chicago White Sox** share **Camelback Ranch** (10710 W. Camelback Rd., 623/877-8585, web.camelbackranchbaseball.com) stadium in Glendale. The park is about 10 miles west of Phoenix, right across Highway 101 (Loop 101) from the Westgate City Center and University of Phoenix Stadium. Outside, you'll find a nice lake to walk around, and be sure to check out the replicas of Dodger Stadium and U.S. Cellular Field.

Take the 101 to the I-10 east, and you're likely to spot more than a few Ohio license plates. The **Cincinnati Reds** and **Cleveland Indians** just moved to the new **Goodyear Ballpark** (1933 S. Ballpark Way, 623/882-3120, www.goodyearbp.com) in Goodyear, a town 20 miles southwest of Phoenix that's named after the Ohio-based tire company. You can enjoy a view of the Sierra Estrella and White Tank Mountains from some seats in the ballpark.

Follow the smell of bratwurst a few minutes east on the I-10. The **Milwaukee Brewers** are the only tenant at **Maryvale Stadium** (3600 N. 51st Ave., 602/534-5500, www.phoenix.gov/parks), built in 1998. It's in one of Phoenix's older neighborhoods, but the park itself is one of the most serene in the Cactus League. Tickets are usually available, and even if the game is out-of-hand, be sure to stick around for the popular sausage race.

Continue on I-10 toward Tucson and you will be able to see right field in **Tempe Diablo Stadium** (2200 W. Alameda Dr., 480/350-5205, www.tempe.gov/city-hall/community-services/community-recreation-centers/diablo-stadium) from the freeway. The stadium has hosted spring training games since the 1960s, and it underwent a $20 million renovation in 2006. The **Los Angeles Angels of Anaheim** consistently lead the Cactus League in attendance. This is a popular pastime for Arizona State University students.

Keep heading east on Highway 202 (Loop 202), and you'll come across **Hohokam Stadium** (1235 N. Center St., 480/644-4451, mesaaz.gov) where the **Oakland As** made a celebrated return. In the heart of Mesa, the stadium has undergone a major renovation that updated the place (originally built in 1977) with state-of-the-art features like an HD scoreboard display and new seating areas.

Still in Mesa, you'll find the toughest ticket in the Cactus League at **Sloan Park** (2230 W. Rio Salado Pkwy., 480/668-0500, http://mlb.mlb.com/chc/mesa) is the spring training home of the **Chicago Cubs,** the team that earns a fanatical following despite a less-than-stellar World Series record. Also, it's the best place in the Cactus League to get autographs and pictures with the players.

Heading back west on Highway 202 (Loop 202), stop off smack dab in the middle of Scottsdale, home of the **San Francisco Giants.** There is a really cool picture on the press box wall from

when the Red Sox used to train at the old stadium in the 1950s, when it was in the middle of a farm. There's really never a bad time to take in a game at **Scottsdale Stadium** (7408 E. Osborn Rd., 480/312-2856, www.scottsdaleaz.gov/scottsdale-stadium), with all the dinner and entertainment options now right outside the park.

Back on the west side, exit Highway 101 at Bell Road. The **Seattle Mariners** and **San Diego Padres** play a couple blocks to the south at **Peoria Sports Complex** (16101 N. 83rd Ave., 623/773-8700, peoriasportscomplex.com). Many consider the park the best in the Cactus League. Every seat feels like it's right on top of the action, and you don't feel crammed if it's a sellout crowd. It also features the best lawn seating in the city.

Head north on Bell Road and you'll end up in Surprise, home of the **Texas Rangers** and **Kansas City Royals. Surprise Recreation Campus** (15960 N. Bullard Ave., 623/222-2222, www.surpriseaz.gov/2679/Recreation-Campus) is a hike from Phoenix but it's the best place to bring a family. There's plenty of room to play catch and tailgate in the parking lot. It's also a great park to walk around while the game is going on because you can always see the action.

How funny that while Phoenix hosts the country's teams, our own team would hoof it to Tucson, away from their home stadium in Phoenix, for their spring training. Not so anymore. As of 2011, the **Arizona Diamondbacks**—along with the **Colorado Rockies**—moved to **Salt River Fields at Talking Stick** (7555 N. Pima Rd., 480-270-5000, www.saltriverfields.com). The facility claims to be the biggest Major League Baseball spring training stadium in the country and the views of the surrounding mountains are unbeatable.

Contributed by Mark McClune, host/reporter, FOX Sports Arizona

Auto Racing Classes

Drivers in Phoenix sometimes seem like they're trying out for a spot on a Grand Prix racing team, but Bob Bondurant is the real thing. The former racer for Carol Shelby and Team Ferrari coaches thousands of students every year at the **Bondurant Racing School** (20000 S. Maricopa Rd., 800/842-7223, www.bondurant.com), his custom-designed, 60-acre facility near Phoenix's Firebird International Raceway. Single-day courses are designed to impart skills ranging from introductory racing techniques to highway survival. Multiday courses cover all kinds of training, including military and security hazard-avoidance strategies and general high-performance driving experiences. Fees start at $500 and rise to well over $5,000.

A similar, although less intensive experience can be had at **Racing Adventures** (8776 E. Shea #106-117, 888/572-7223, www.racingadventures.com), which typically takes its laps at Arizona Motorsports Park (15402 W. Camelback Rd.). You can sign up for high-performance driving school with a Porsche, Cobra, or other car options. The Exotic supercar lapping experiences are one-day programs and you can take your pick from an Aston Martin, Ferrari, Corvette, Lamborghini, and others. Fees range from $325 to $1,400.

TUBING AND WATER PARKS

Tubing in the Salt River northeast of Phoenix is a fascinating combination of relaxing and trashy. On the two- to four-hour trips, tubers float along the banks of the lower Salt River, experiencing an interesting mix of wildlife and some raucous partiers. The tour company **Salt River Recreation** (9200 North Bush Hwy., 480/984-3305, www.saltrivertubing.com, $17) will rent you a tube and give you a ride to and from the parking lot. Take Highway 202 (Loop 202) to Power Road in east Mesa and drive seven miles north to a four-way stop sign.

As might be expected in a town where summertime temperatures regularly top 104°F, metro Phoenix has a wealth of water parks. Most parks offer discounted prices for seniors, toddlers, and children under a specified height and the three biggest all feature the requisite water slides, wave pools, and tubing areas, but each has a slightly different focus. The claim to fame of **Big Surf** (1500 N. McClintock Dr., 480/994-2297, www.bigsurffun.com, $29.95 general admission) is a wave pool big enough to allow actual surfing, as featured in the 1987 movie *North Shore*. **Mesa Golfland-Sunsplash** (155 W. Hampton Ave., 480/834-8319, www.golfland.com/mesa, $29.99 general admission) in Mesa has a dozen different water slides but a less powerful wave pool. And the newest destination, **Wet 'n' Wild** (4243 W. Pinnacle Peak Rd., 623/201-2000, www.wetnwildphoenix.com, $34.99 general admission) opened in summer 2009 with $30 million worth of slides and whitewater rafting rides in Glendale.

SPECTATOR SPORTS
Auto Racing

Half a dozen times a year, the roar of NASCAR comes to the **Phoenix International Raceway** (7602 S. Avondale Blvd., Avondale, 623/463-5400, www.phoenixraceway.com). The facility was renovated in 2008 and sports several bars and restaurants, including the new Speed Cantina, but its upscale makeover didn't break with stock-car tradition. Fans still camp on the grounds all weekend in an RV while watching dozens of high-speed racecars turn left really, really quickly.

Baseball

The **Arizona Diamondbacks** won a World Series in 2001—just four years after the team was formed during Major League Baseball's 1997 expansion—and Phoenicians have loved them ever since. In typical Arizona style, **Chase Field** (401 E. Jefferson St., Phoenix,

602/462-6500, http://arizona.diamondbacks. mlb.com) in downtown Phoenix has a retractable roof that can be opened on balmy spring and fall days or closed during the heat of summer. There's also a pool in right field. Really. Single-game tickets can be had for as little as $12, but prices rise quickly to as much as $250 for box seats. Scalping is legal in Arizona, so check websites and the streets around the field (prices often drop once the game starts) to find deals.

The crack of the bat also comes earlier to Arizona than most other places thanks to the Cactus League. A dozen teams arrive in late February and stay through March (or the first week of April) at their **spring training** (www. cactusleague.com) homes in metro Phoenix, including the Chicago Cubs, Chicago White Sox, Cleveland Indians, Kansas City Royals, Los Angeles Angels of Anaheim, Los Angeles Dodgers, Milwaukee Brewers, Oakland Athletics, San Diego Padres, San Francisco Giants, Seattle Mariners, and Texas Rangers. Two more—the Arizona Diamondbacks and Colorado Rockies—joined the Phoenix roster in 2011. Games are often more casual than in "The Show," and the small fields give fans a chance to get a close look at superstars and up-and-comers both.

Basketball

Next door to Chase Field sits **Talking Stick Resort Arena** (201 E. Jefferson St., 602/379-2000, www.talkingstickresortarena.com), the home of both Phoenix's professional basketball teams: The **Phoenix Suns** (602/379-7900, www.nba.com/suns) and the **Phoenix Mercury** (602/252-9622, mercury.wnba. com). Tickets for the Suns can vary quite a bit but usually start around $40 for nosebleed seats and go up to $500 or more for courtside. Phoenix Mercury tickets typically start around $30.

Football

The **Arizona Cardinals** (602/379-0102, www.azcardinals.com) spent years in the National Football League's rankings cellar before making their first Super Bowl appearance ever in 2009. They put up a good fight, but many long-suffering fans would say it's typical of the team to lose their lead—and the game—at the last minute. However, the team's home at **University of Phoenix Stadium** (1 Cardinals Dr.) in Glendale is spectacular. The round shape of the building is designed to mimic the Sonoran Desert's native barrel cactus, and it features a retractable roof as well as a retractable field that can slide out to catch the sunshine. Tickets cost around $100.

Horseracing

For an entertaining time watching races with thoroughbred horses winning, placing, and showing, head to **Turf Paradise** (1501 W. Bell Rd., 602/942-1101, www.turfparadise.com). The course is open October through May and races generally start shortly after noon or at 1pm in the spring, but the track is open 9am-7pm daily for horse workouts and simulcast races from tracks around the country. The 1,000-seat clubhouse is air-conditioned and serves food and cocktails for just a $5 admission. Special events include wiener dog, zebra, and camel races that are truly unforgettable. The place could use a remodel but it sure makes for a fun day out.

Ice Hockey

To experience a temporary cold snap during Phoenix's not-so-frosty winters, either make for the mountains north and east of town or go to Gila River Arena (9400 W. Maryland Ave., Glendale, www.gilariverarena.com) to cheer on the town's National Hockey League team, the **Arizona Coyotes** (480/563-7825, http://coyotes.nhl.com).

SPAS

While Scottsdale might be better known for its world-class spas, Phoenix has much to offer in the art of luxuriating. Buffing and pampering abound in the capital city, and while old-school resorts have been making their guests look and feel great for decades, some new hotspots are attracting spa-goers to their spacious surroundings and ever-expanding lists of amenities.

A tried-and-true classic, the **Arizona Biltmore Spa** (2400 E. Missouri Ave., 602/381-7656, www.arizonabiltmore.com/spa-biltmore, 8am-6pm Sun.-Wed., 8am-7pm Thurs.-Sat.) is located in the grounds of the famed **Arizona Biltmore, a Waldorf Astoria Resort,** for which Frank Lloyd Wright served as the consulting architect. It specializes in massage and body and skin care treatments, but also offers guests the use of a full-service salon, fitness center, bicycles, and six cushioned tennis courts. Oh, and a dry sauna, wet steam room, whirlpool, and power shower. The spa offers a variety of packages like turquoise sage stone massage, intentional apothecary body polish, and grape stem cell solutions facials that minister to physical, mental, and spiritual health. Prices for massage options range between $140-230, depending on method and time. Guests may enjoy outdoor retreat areas in the gardens and choose from a wealth of classes, including yoga, aqua aerobics, sculpting, and power step.

Alvadora Spa at the **Royal Palms Resort & Spa** (5200 E. Camelback Rd., 602/977-6400, www.royalpalmshotel.com, 8:30am-7pm daily) exudes a Mediterranean charm and has consistently landed on local and national "best of" lists for over a decade. It serves up classic treatments that settle in the $100-220 price range such as hot stone, reflexology, and watsu massages (water therapies); skin treatments; and signature citrus treatments, including the Citrus Grove Facial, Orange Blossom Body Buff, and Simply Citrus mani-pedis. Hair and make-up sessions are also available and, as with anything at the Royal Palms Resort, you can expect a fabulous experience top to bottom.

The water-inspired **Revive Spa** at the **JW Marriott Desert Ridge Resort & Spa** (5350 E. Marriott Dr., 480/293-3700, www.spa.jwdesertridgeresort.com, 8am-7:30pm daily) is 28,000 square feet and 41 treatment rooms of bliss. It's got all the regulars: massages, facials, manicures, and pedicures as well as a few unique items like "Body Rituals", body scrubs, and a turquoise cocoon. The fitness options are pretty great with personal training, tai chi, meditation, yoga, cycling, and aqua fitness on offer. For more aqua activity, take a dip in the lap pool lined by tall palm trees for privacy. There are separate relaxation rooms for men and women and an outdoor co-ed lounge to unwind in the fresh air. Services range from about $150-250, depending on the treatment.

In Chandler, just south of Phoenix, **Aji Spa** at the **Sheraton Grand at Wild Horse Pass** (5594 W. Wild Horse Pass Blvd., Chandler, 602/225-0100, www.wildhorsepassresort.com/chandler-spa, 7am-7pm daily) offers authentic Native American treatments that are inspired by tribal elders from the local Gila River Indian Community's Pima and Maricopa tribes. Try the Sacred Prickly Pear Body Treatment, Burden Basket Meditation, or Gila River Rock Massage, in which a therapeutic treatment incorporates energy anatomy and ancient techniques to create a relaxed atmosphere conducive to spiritual healing. In addition to more traditional massages and treatments, Aji Spa also hosts tennis, personal training, and private fitness classes.

Food

For years, Phoenix suffered from a dearth of quality, innovative restaurants, as most of the city's groundbreaking restaurateurs and chefs preferred to set up shop in Scottsdale. Happily, the times have changed and a host of culinary mavericks have transformed the city's dining scene.

DOWNTOWN
American

The Tuck Shop (2245 N. 12th St., 602/354-2980, www.tuckinphx.com, 5pm-10pm Tues.-Sat., $9-32) is still one of Phoenix's best-kept secrets. It seems like only in-the-know foodies frequent this Desert Modernist remodel of a 1950s-era building in the Coronado neighborhood. The casually chic establishment serves up comfort food, and the small plates are quite simply phenomenal. Bring some friends and order up a medley of dishes, like the chorizo-stuffed medjool dates with melted gruyère, mac 'n' cheese with house-cured bacon and lobster, or the beet crudo ravioli. The hand-crafted cocktails are just as thoughtful; try the No. 7 cocktail with gin, ginger, lime juice, and agave nectar topped with a slice of cucumber.

★ **Durant's** (2611 N. Central Ave., 602/264-5967, www.durantsaz.com, 11am-10pm Mon.-Thurs., 11am-11pm Fri., 5pm-11pm Sat., 4pm-10pm Sun., $31-60) is a classic in every sense of the word. From its ever-so-dry martinis to its deep-red decor, the steakhouse is a bona fide local landmark that has changed little since then-newlyweds Marilyn Monroe and Joe DiMaggio dined there in 1954. Enter like locals through the kitchen in the back, and take a peek at the thick steaks and oysters Rockefeller before heading into the dining room. The food is excellent and the vibe is old school Hollywood—unlike any other restaurant in town. Don't be surprised if you bump into a familiar face—it is a favorite haunt of Arizona politicos.

Next door, Phoenix urbanites flock to the LGBT-friendly **Switch** (2603 N. Central Ave., 602/264-2295, www.switchofarizona.com, 11am-10pm Mon.-Thurs., 11am-11pm Fri., 10am-11pm Sat., 10am-10pm Sun., $10-22), a restaurant bar on the north tip of what's considered downtown. The blue-on-blue decor and hip music provide a background for an absolutely massive menu of burgers, sandwiches, and full entrées. Switch caters to a younger crowd, though it's packed at lunch with downtown workers of all ages. You can sit at the community bar, on the patio, or in the lounge-like dining room; be sure to head there for a tasty weekend brunch from 10am-3pm.

For a nostalgic lunch stop, **MacAlpine's Soda Fountain** (2303 N. 7th St., 602/262-5545, 11am-7pm Sun.-Thurs., 11am-8pm Fri.-Sat., $7-11) offers a truly vintage experience. The location is a genuine, original soda fountain that's been in operation for more than 70 years. While the sandwiches and soups are pretty basic, it's the old fashioned malts and sundaes served at the bar that make for a real charming experience. It's connected to an antique shop that is fun to browse after you eat.

A refurbished bungalow now serves as the home of **The Main Ingredient Ale House & Café** (2337 N. 7th St., 602/843-6246, www.tmialehouse.com, 11am-11pm Mon.-Thurs., 11am-midnight Fri.-Sat., 11am-9pm Sun., $7-10). This is a lovely little neighborhood spot to eat a fresh, tasty (and cheap) meal while enjoying a glass of wine or cold beer. With beers on tap from local and Southwestern breweries, specialty cocktails, and a very manageable wine list, the vibe is casual and relaxed. And you can't go wrong with the griddled cheese sandwich made with havarti, muenster, and cheddar on sourdough. I mean, come on.

It's tough to describe exactly what **The Duce** (525 South Central Ave., 602/866-3823, theducephoenix.com, kitchen hours 4pm-midnight Tues.-Wed., 11am-midnight Thurs.,

11am-1am Fri.-Sat., 10am-10pm Sun., $3-19) is because there's a whole lot going on. It's a jazz club bar, a drug store soda fountain, a surplus store, and an old-time gym complete with boxing ring—all within a giant warehouse. We'll focus on the airstream-camper-turned kitchen that churns out salads, sliders, and breakfast all day made from local produce. It's a charming and funky place with good food and, if you're in the mood, a cocktail. Or a beer. Or a round of ping-pong. Or an ice cream. You get the idea.

For soul food, **Mrs. White's Golden Rule Cafe** (808 E. Jefferson St., 602/262-9256, 10:30am-7pm Mon.-Sat., $7-15) has been a legendary, one-of-a-kind, hole-in-the-wall establishment for decades. From Food Network to Phoenix Magazine, the place consistently lands on top restaurants lists. The fried chicken is light, moist, and crispy and is the clear favorite on a menu that also features pork chops, chicken fried steak, catfish, oxtails, and peach cobbler that's to die for. They even have a pretty darn good vegetable plate.

The Arrogant Butcher (2 E. Jefferson St., Ste. 150, 602/324-8502, www.foxrc.com/restaurants/the-arrogant-butcher/, 11am-9pm Mon.-Thurs., 11am-10pm Fri., noon-10pm Sat., 3pm-9pm Sun., $7-23) is a well-loved and popular restaurant located in the heart of downtown at CityScape, the area's newest shopping and leisure center. Lunch offers a huge menu of salads, sandwiches, and entrées like the BBQ Baby Back Ribs. Sandwiches are diverse, including a Chinese chicken salon, smoked pork Cubano, and turkey pastrami. The dinner menu is just as large but with a little more sophistication and entrées that include crab-stuffed chicken and sweet potato tortellini or a meat and cheese combo plate served with cherry marmalade and housemade mustard. As far as the booze goes, there's a fabulous variety of beers, wines, and signature cocktails.

Another CityScape favorite is **Blue Hound Kitchen & Cocktails** (2 E. Jefferson St., 602/258-0231, www.bluehoundkitchen.com, 11am-6pm Mon.-Thurs., 11am-11pm Fri., 11am-3pm, 5pm-11pm Sat., 11am-3pm, 5pm-10pm Sun., $7-15) located in Hotel Palomar. Bring friends and be ready for small dishes designed for sharing so you can order a variety. Appetizers, fish, meats, vegetables, and brick-oven flatbreads are the categories from which you can choose. Although that may seem a little ho-hum, the flavors are expertly delivered in dishes like the corn grit fries with smoked bacon and white cheddar, or crispy cauliflower doused in chili vinaigrette and served with a fried egg. The food is as inventive and delicious as their cocktail list and the ingredients are sustainable, local, and free-range so you can indulge guilt-free.

Although many hit **Hanny's** (40 N. 1st St., 602/252-2285, www.hannys.net, 11am-1:30am Mon.-Fri., 5pm-1:30am Sat.-Sun. $8-25) late at night for the atmosphere in the bar, it's also an excellent spot to grab a booth and enjoy a great dinner with friends. It's an ultra-chic bar and restaurant housed in a midcentury building that used to be a high-end men's department store of the same name. The menu includes really delicious pizza, shareable appetizers, steak, sandwiches, and salad prepared as American cuisine with an Italian influence. Hit it for lunch on a weekday or dinner before the bar crowd starts rolling in (usually around 9pm). Brought to Phoenix by the same owners as AZ88 in Scottsdale, it's been a huge win for downtown Phoenix. The vibe is cool, the food is delicious, and, much like its Scottsdale counterpart, you shouldn't miss an opportunity to visit the restrooms upstairs. Yes, you read that right.

The convenience of fast food meets the health-food movement at **GrabbaGreen** (50 W. Jefferson St., Ste. 120, 602/734-9200, grabbagreen.com, 7am-8pm Mon.-Sat., 9am-3pm Sun., $7-10) at CityScape, where you can get a quick bite to eat that is super healthy, fresh, and tasty. Organic ingredients, delicious flavors, and meals packed with good stuff like quinoa, avocado, kale, chia, and mint dominate the menu. The grain bowl and green bowls (aka rice/noodle and salad) are a favorite with the downtown crowd, as is the $7 healthy smoothie that you can choose from the menu or mix yourself.

Asian

Hey, guess where **Squid Ink** (2 E. Jefferson St., Ste. 108, 602/258-0510, squidinkshop.com, 11am-10pm Sun.-Thurs., 11am-midnight Fri.-Sat., $5-25) is located? If you said CityScape, you are correct! This contemporary sushi restaurant mixes tradition with new styles like seared tuna tataki with tuna, avocado, daikon sprouts, and honey-jalapeño sauce. The house rolls are inventive as well, with ingredients like spicy aioli and cilantro used in some rolls. But sushi isn't all there is—you can order a rice bowl, noodle bowl, soup, or salad and, if you're in the mood, go ahead and spring for the Kobe burger. You won't be sorry.

Although the outside may look dubious, **New Garden Cafe** (823 S. Central Ave., 602/254-9110, www.newgardencafe.com, 11am-9:30pm Mon-Tues. & Thurs., 11am-10pm Fri., noon-10pm Sat., noon-9:30pm Sun., $7-10) has been serving authentic, hole-in-the-wall-style Chinese food since 1942. Still family owned, the menu has endured with pork, chicken, shrimp, beef varieties of foo young, chop suey, chow mein, fried rice, and lo mein. Of course, there's a whole list of combination platters to choose from as well. Loyal customers have enjoyed this humble establishment for years and with the super low prices, it's more than worth it.

Breakfast and Lunch

Wallet-friendly ★ **Matt's Big Breakfast** (825 N. 1st St., 602/254-1074, www.mattsbigbreakfast.com, 6:30am-2:30pm daily, $6-11) is Phoenix's best breakfast joint, hands down, and one of three locations. Famously featured on Food Network's *Diners, Drive-ins, and Dives*, the diner is bright and sunny, and its pleasant orange motif, vintage barstools, and 1950s' decor are the perfect backdrop for griddlecakes and homemade hash browns. Owners Matt and Erenia insist on quality, off-the-farm ingredients, which means the orange juice is squeezed each morning and the fresh

eggs come from local chickens. There may be a short wait at this popular restaurant, but you won't mind once you sit down for the salami scramble or sample the lunchtime offerings. P.S.: Order something with hash browns. They are killer.

Back in the day, you really had to be clued in to know about ★ **Lo-Lo's Chicken and Waffles** (1220 S. Central Ave., 602/340-1304, www.loloschickenandwaffles.com, 9am-10pm Mon.-Thurs., 8am-11pm Sat., 8am-6pm Sun., $8-14). It was well known to those who love soul food but once everyone else found out about it, the craze took over. Today, it's a franchise operation with multiple locations in the Valley (including one at Sky Harbor International Airport) and across the Southwest but don't let that sway you from visiting its original location. Lo-Lo is the nickname for owner Larry White, whose grandmother owned Mrs. White's Golden Rule Café. He perfected his recipe of flaky waffles and crispy fried chicken in her kitchen, opened his restaurant, and gained a ravenous following for his menu of soul food that is prepared fresh, from scratch, every day. The all-day breakfast options include heart-stopping omelets, pancakes, French toast, and grits. The lunch and dinner menu serves up burgers, fried green beans, and fried green tomatoes. And everyone loves to order their dishes with a jar of "drank."

The short menu at **America's Taco Shop** (2041 N. 7th St., 602/682-5627, www.americastacoshop.com, 11am-8pm Mon.-Sat., $3-8) revolves around its carne asada—a marinated, flame-broiled beef that you can get wrapped in tacos and burritos or topped on tostadas, quesadillas, and fluffy tortas. Non-meat eaters can enjoy the veggie quesadilla or bean and cheese burrito, although whatever you get, you'll want an order of the rich and creamy flan. The bright, converted bungalow is a terrific breakfast or lunch spot and was so insanely successful that America's Taco Shop has become a popular franchise with multiple locations across the Valley. If you've grown tired of the greasy tacos and refried

Gourmet on the Runway

Land in Terminal 4 at Phoenix's Sky Harbor International Airport and you'll find the very best concentration of the trendiest restaurants the Valley has to offer. Gone are the days when airport food was plagued by generic cafés or, worse, national and regional chains that specialize in mediocrity. No, sir! Here in Phoenix we offer the best of the best as soon as you set foot in our city.

Want more details? The restaurants listed here have full descriptions for their other locations in the Food sections and, rest assured, there are no duds on this list. That said, expect that some establishments will have abbreviated menus.

- **America's Taco Shop:** Grab-n-go Mexican Food, pretty spectacular carne asada (Pre-Security).

- **Chelsea's Kitchen:** Southwest-inspired, contemporary American fare (Pre-Security).

- **Lola Coffee:** Get your caffeine fix from a real barista, open 24 hours a day (Pre-Security).

- **Lo-Lo's Chicken & Waffles:** Scratch-made soul food (Pre-Security).

- **Barrio Café:** Food Network-recognized gourmet Mexican food (Post-Security, Gates D1-D8).

- **Cartel Coffee:** Really serious coffee expertly prepared (Post-Security, Gates C11-C20).

- **Delux:** Delicious, melt-in-mouth burgers (Post-Security, Gates A17-A30).

- **Four Peaks Brewery:** Deliciously prepared bar fare with tasty local brews (Post-Security, Gates A17-A30).

- **La Grande Orange:** Trendy pizzas with fresh, local ingredients (Post-Security, Gates D1-D8).

- **Matt's Big Breakfast:** American breakfast favorites made fresh (Post-Security, Gates B1-B14).

- **Olive & Ivy:** Unique Mediterranean-inspired American fusion (Post-Security, Gates A1-A14).

- **Sweet Republic:** Artisan ice cream (Post-Security, Gates B1-B14).

- **Tammie Coe Cakes:** Decadent baked goods, beautifully decorated (Post-Security, Gates A17-A30).

beans many American restaurants pass off as authentic Mexican food, give this charming shop a try.

Coffee

Okay, get ready. **Cartel Coffee Lab** (1 N. 1st St., 480/621-6381, www.cartelcoffeelab.com, 7am-11am Mon.-Fri.) is some serious, cutting-edge coffee business. Here's the deal: they take coffee seriously. Very seriously. And they do it with some serious style. So if you know what aeropress coffee is and you want to be served by a beautiful barista with braided hair and funky eyeglasses, this is your place. If you feel intimidated, don't be. The service is friendly and they'll gladly walk you through your options or just serve you a simple cup of coffee, prepared with care.

If trendy urban coffee joints get your juices flowing on a Sunday morning, **Lola Coffee** (1001 N. 3rd Ave., 602/252-2265, www.lola-coffeebar.com, 7am-7pm daily) is your kind of place. The café is usually full of boisterous, good-looking caffeine addicts. Its plush couches and big family-style table are more suited to conversation than to serious work. You won't find a lot of food options at Lola, but the coffee is seriously good and the homemade pastries are a treat. If the weather is sunny, enjoy a seat outside and watch the light-rail cars quietly roll downtown.

Desserts

Tammie Coe Cakes (610 E. Roosevelt, Ste. 145, 602/253-0829, www.tammiecoecakes. com, 6:30am-6pm Mon.-Fri., 10am-6pm Sat., 7am-1pm Sun.) had brides and sugar addicts clamoring for artfully sculpted confections back when no one had heard of fondant icing. This little street-side shop along Roosevelt Row is the perfect place to satisfy that sweet tooth with an Ooey Gooey Cupcake, frosted brownie, or the famous sugar cookie. These treats are crazy delicious.

Italian

It was no surprise when chef Chris Bianco won the James Beard Award in 2003 for his wood-fired pizzas. Since then, ★ **Pizzeria Bianco** (623 E. Adams St., 602/258-8300, www.pizzeriabianco.com, 11am-9pm Mon.-Thurs., 11am-10pm Fri.-Sat., $10-18) has become a culinary legend in Phoenix. Jerry

Pizzeria Bianco

Seinfeld, Oprah, and Martha Stewart are fans, and *Esquire* magazine named his thin-crust pies the best pizza in the country. A Slow Food Movement champion, Bianco uses only the freshest ingredients, including herbs cultivated next to the former 1929 machine shop where he set up the pizzeria. As for the menu, the sausage-topped Wiseguy and classic Margherita with fresh mozzarella are impeccable. Aficionados covet the Rosa, a so-so-good-I-want-it-now combination of red onion, parmigiano reggiano, rosemary, and Arizona pistachios. And although the pizza may be the most popular choice on the menu, the roasted antipasto and fresh salads are well worth the infamous wait—that used be a guaranteed two- or even three-hour experience before they expanded their hours. Best advice: Embrace the wait and enjoy a glass of wine or a beer next door at **Bar Bianco** or go there during non-peak hours.

In the tradition of great wood-fired pizza joints in Phoenix, **Pomo Pizzeria Napoletana** (705 N. 1st St., 602/795-2555, www.pomopizzeria.com, 11am-2pm, 5pm-10pm Tues.-Thurs., 11am-2pm, 5pm-11pm Fri.-Sat., 11am-2pm, 5pm-10pm Sun., $11-16) is sure to please. This hot, bumpin' joint is one of the many recommended stops in the Roosevelt Row area and prepares delicious pizza in the Napoli, Italy, style. Slow-rising sourdough is from a Pomo family recipe with flour imported from Naples. The pizzas are cooked in a hand-built, wood-burning oven and it's really, really good. Take your pick from 22 pizzas that all feature super-fresh vegetables, Italian meats, and cheeses.

Some people will tell you to go to **Cibo Urban Pizzeria** (603 N. 5th Ave., 602/441-2697, www.cibophoenix.com, 11am-9pm Mon., 11am-10pm Tues.-Thurs., 10am-11pm Sat.-Fri., 5pm-9pm Sun., $8-17) for the best pizza in town. And this author would not disagree. The salads, antipasto, and wood-fired pizzas feature subtle flavor pairings with ultra-fresh ingredients like premium prosciutto and parmigiano reggiano cheese. It's all simply prepared and often topped with a light drizzle of olive oil. There are more than a dozen pizzas from which to choose—the Diavola with tomato sauce, mozzarella, and spicy salami offers a bit of a kick. Dine outside on one of the best patios in Phoenix or inside the charming 1913-era bungalow. Either way, be sure to save room for a chocolate crepe—so good. P.S. it's pronounced "CHEE-boh."

Mexican and Southwest

★ **Barrio Café** (2814 N. 16th St., 602/636-0240, www.barriocafe.com, 11am-10pm Tues.-Thurs., 11am-10:30pm Fri.-Sat., 11am-9pm Sun., $11-30) will have you saying *hola*. Chef Silvana Salcido Esparza serves up a culinary tour of the country's best dishes. Start with the pomegranate-seed guacamole, prepared tableside, and survey the small restaurant's award-winning menu. Consider the *cochinita pibil,* an overnight-roasted pork marinated in *achiote rojo* (sour orange), or the amazing *pollo poblano*, tender chicken breast with roasted poblano peppers, caramelized onions, and *queso fresco* in a tomatillo buerre blanc. The weekend brunch between 11am and 3pm is also a treat.

Los Dos Molinos (8646 S Central Ave., 602/243-9113, www.losdosmolinosphoenix.com, 11am-9pm Tues.-Thurs., 11am-10pm Fri.-Sat., $14-18) is located in what's considered south central Phoenix—just south of downtown along Central Avenue. It's been a Valley favorite for decades and serves up traditional Mexican fare in the classic Sonoran style. Yes, the plates of burros, enchiladas, tostadas, and tacos are served with steaming sides of rice and beans, slathered in melted cheese, all while overflowing the sides of the plate. It's known to be on the spicy side so be prepared.

It doesn't look like much from the outside, but once you step into **San Carlos Bay Seafood Restaurant** (1901 E. McDowell Rd., 602/340-0892, 9am-9pm daily, $12-15), you'll think you've landed in a small café on the Sonoran coast of Mexico. Start with a cold beer and the Seven Seas cocktail, a buffet of tasty ocean creatures. The spicy seafood stews are extraordinary, but you won't want to miss filling up on fresh tortillas topped with garlic shrimp.

Jamaican

★ **The Breadfruit & Rum Bar** (108 E. Pierce St., 602/267-1266, www.thebreadfruit.com, 5pm to 10pm Mon.-Thurs., 5pm-11pm Fri.-Sat., cocktails until midnight at the bar, $10-22) has "jet-fresh" seafood and a casual island vibe that will make you suddenly feel like you aren't hopelessly landlocked by hundreds of miles of dry dirt. Award-winning and critically acclaimed, the delicious menu features contemporary presentations of Jamaican standards like jerk chicken and roasted plantains alongside lesser-known favorites like the beer-curried prawns. The attached Rum Bar is an absolute must-visit, with over 150 types of rum that will convert any drinker into a rum fanatic. After a scrumptious meal, relaxation and conversation are highly encouraged on the back patio, where patrons puff on cigars and sip tasting flights of premium-aged rums.

CENTRAL AND NORTH CENTRAL PHOENIX
American

★ **Postino Central** (5144 N. Central Ave., 602/274-5144, www.postinowinecafe.com, 11am-11pm Mon.-Thurs., 11am-midnight Fri., 9am-midnight Sat., 9am-10pm Sun., $7-10) has been a go-to destination since it opened in 2009. It was the second location in what has now become a valley-wide series of Postino restaurants—the original location being in the Arcadia neighborhood (3939 E. Campbell Ave., 602/852-3939, 11am-11pm Mon.-Thurs., 11am-midnight Fri., 9am-midnight Sat., 9am-10pm Sun., $7-10). Serving delicious and affordable sandwiches, salads, and mix-and-match bruschettas like the outstanding tomato jam with fresh sheep's milk cheese or prosciutto with figs and mascarpone. Postino provides a lovely ambience with floor-to-ceiling windows and alfresco dining on the patio. A wide selection of wine and beer complements a casual-yet-notable menu. You really can't go wrong here, folks, and the weekend brunch is to die for.

Really cool people in the Arcadia neighborhood flock to **La Grande Orange Pizzeria** (4410 N. 40th St., 602/840-7777, www.lagrandeorangepizzeria.com, 4pm-close Mon.-Thurs., 11am-close Fri.-Sun., $9-15) for pizzas, burgers, and sandwiches. This neighborhood delight is one of a group of restaurant concepts that make the corner of Campbell Avenue and 40th Street a madhouse on Saturdays and Sundays and a must-visit for any traveling foodie. The pizzas are the menu favorite and if you want to try a little of everything, come with a group and order multiple dishes. Just make sure to include the Gladiator with house-made sausage, pepperoni, and cheese. After your feast, stop by the pizzeria's grocery for gifts ranging from wine to pet products and potted plants.

Chelsea's Kitchen (5040 N. 40th St., 602/957-2555, www.chelseaskitchenaz.com, 11am-10pm Mon.-Sat., 9:30am-9pm Sun., $9-34) starts with a great patio and builds from there. The sleek interior manages to be both lively and private, especially in the tall leather booths, but the canal-side outdoor space is the showstopper. Gorgeous views of the sunset and the city make it easy to linger over a pitcher of Chelsea's signature white sangria or a plateful of grilled swordfish tacos. Alternatively go for the wood-fired rotisserie chicken or the Howie burger with havarti cheese and caramelized red onion. Whatever you choose, Chelsea's delivers in a very stylish package.

Chef Cullen Campbell has an almost cult-like following, and with his restaurant ★ **Crudo** (3603 E. Indian School Rd., 602/358-8666, www.crudoaz.com, 5pm-10pm Tues.-Sat., $35-55), his fans have a place to reaffirm their love. "Crudo" means raw in Italian, so get ready for Italian-style sashimi. If you're squeamish, don't freak out. The menu is categorized by crudo, cooked, mozzarella, and grilled with dishes that are all cut, compiled, layered and presented in a minimalist style. The preparation is perfection, the flavors are phenomenal, and the varieties are inventive. Listen: Crudo octopus with glacier lettuce and pickled spring garlic; ricotta with walnut sauce and honey; brisket fingerlings with radicchio collatura and bone marrow as an additional extra.

If you knew the wonders of sweet-potato fries before all of your friends, **Delux** (3146 E. Camelback Rd., 602/522-2288, www.deluxburger.com, 11am-2am daily, $4-15) is the burger joint for you. This hip spot dishes up fanciful versions of burgers, hot dogs, and sandwiches that are actually worth the price. Try the burger topped with blue and gruyère cheese, organic arugula, caramelized onion, and bacon on a handcrafted demi-baguette for a red-meat treat. Don't forget the side of fries, either. They're served in a miniature shopping cart and come in regular and sweet potato varieties. The restaurant looks like it could double as a nightclub and thankfully it keeps nightclub hours, too. It's open until 2am in a town where late-night dining options are all too rare. Now get this: They also have a sushi menu.

True Food Kitchen (2502 E. Camelback Rd., Ste. 135, 602/774-3488, www.truefoodkitchen.com, 11am-9pm Mon.-Thurs., 11am-10pm Fri., 10am-10pm Sat., 10am-9pm Sun., $8-24) is an innovative collaboration between holistic-health guru Dr. Andrew Weil and Arizona's über-restaurateur Sam Fox. The fresh, flavorful menu incorporates many health-conscious, eco-friendly movements that have transformed the way many people eat. Chefs use healthy fats like olive oil, prepare spaghetti squash, and serve sustainable seafood dishes. Much of the organic, seasonal produce is locally grown, and the chicken and turkey are certified hormone- and antibiotic-free. And with a revolving, seasonal pizza menu and steak tacos topped with avocado and tomatillo salsa, meals are as tasty as they are nutritious.

Sharing a location with Richardson's, the **Rokerij** (6335 N. 16th St., 602/287-8900, richardsons.com/rokerij, 11am-1am Mon.-Fri., 8am-1am Sat.-Sun., $11-43) has quickly become a staple for fine food. Before dinner, go downstairs to the basement bar; it's a perfect sanctuary on a hot summer day. In winter, a fireplace transforms the room into a cozy cocktail den. It's a favorite location for happy hour (3pm-6pm and 9pm-close daily) when glasses of wine and margaritas are just $5, and the $6 small-plate menu features tasty bites like the chipotle ribs, Sriracha chicken skewers, and bacon-wrapped shrimp. The menu shares a few New Mexican items from Richardson's with steakhouse options like the prime rib or chicken schnitzel. Oh, and just a head's up, it's pronounced, "ROW-ker-ee."

St. Francis (111 E. Camelback Rd., 602/200-8111, stfrancisaz.com, 11am-10pm Mon.-Thurs., 11am-11pm Fri., 9am-11pm Sat., 9am-9pm Sun., $10-30) is a go-to restaurant in the Camelback Corridor. With a polished modern design, the two-story restaurant has a clever layout with intimate corners, exposed booths, a tiny bar, and a peaceful patio. The menu is fresh, fresh, fresh, with contemporary American dishes like kale Caesar salad, whole roasted sweet potato, roasted chicken, and wood-fired flatbreads. The brunch menu is a popular favorite and the happy hour (3pm-6pm daily) has a fabulous menu of $2 beers, $5 glasses of wine, and tasty bites for cheap.

It's rare to find a restaurant that strikes the perfect balance of hip and comfortable; welcoming and modern; casual and juuuust a little bit fancy. **Windsor** (5223 N. Central Ave., 602/279-1111, windsoraz.com, 11am-11pm Mon.-Thurs., 11am-midnight Fri., 9am-midnight Sat., 9am-10pm Sun., $9-20) is a fabulous neighborhood restaurant and bar that's the obvious choice for an evening out. The dishes are superbly prepared and the menu features the best veggie burger in town. Meat eaters will be very pleased with the delicious New Orleans-style pork ribs. The bar creates Prohibition-style cocktails that are super tasty and has a darn good beer and wine menu. The patio is beautiful and has the coolest wall covering we've ever seen: every inch of the wall in the walkway is covered with cassette tapes.

Okay, so this place called **The Yard** (5832

Windsor has an incredible wall covered in cassette tapes.

N. 7th St.) has three restaurants that are enclosed in an open-air patio filled with tons of lawn games like cornhole, shuffleboard, and ping-pong—and during any sports season, the games are blasted on big-screen televisions. It may sound like a crazy mess, but somehow it works. It's a popular venue for all types. Take your pick from **Little Cleo's Seafood Legend** (602/680-4044, www.foxrc.com, 4pm-10pm Mon.-Thurs., 4pm-11pm Fri.-Sat., $5-55), which serves almost every seafood dish created in America; **Barrio Urbano** (602/287-9000, www.barriourbanophx.com, 9am-close daily), which serves upscale Mexican food; and **Culinary Dropout** (602/680-4040, www.culinarydropout.com, 11am-11pm Mon.-Thurs., 11am-1am Fri., 10am-1pm Sat., 10am-10pm Sun., $7-26), which serves contemporary American cuisine and bar snacks. Note that the main patio with all the games is for Culinary Dropout customers, although there's no rule against letting the kids play while you dine at the other establishments.

Asian

Family-owned, fresh, clean, authentic, unassuming location, and a big gold door—that's the recipe for a fabulous restaurant and ★ **Reign of Thai** (12032 N. Cave Creek Rd., 602/328-9000, reignofthai.com, 11:30am-3pm, 5pm-9pm Tues.-Fri., noon-3pm, 5pm-9pm Sat., noon-3pm, 5pm-8:30pm Sun., $5-26) delivers all the ingredients. Word is catching on with the business crowd, who frequents the place for its lunchtime buffet special. Otherwise, you can catch Asian food fanatics enjoying *rad na, pad see yaw,* and pad Thai.

Cherry Blossom Noodle Café (914 E. Camelback Rd., 602/248-9090, www.cherryblossom-az.com, 11am-9:30pm Sun.-Thurs., 11am-10:30pm Fri.-Sat., $6-20) is a go-to for all the noodles from Asian to Italian. But it's the Asian noodle dishes that stand out, including the udon noodles and *yakisoba*. With a few Italian items—as well as salads, sushi, tofu, and homemade soups—there's a lot to choose from. The *hakata* ramen with barbecue pork is a Tokyo-worthy dish that newbies to Japanese cuisine will find quite approachable.

Like any quality Asian restaurant, the exterior of **China Chili** (302 E. Flower St., 602/266-4463, www.chinachilirestaurant.com, 11am-9pm Mon. Thurs., 11am-10pm Fri., noon-10pm Sat., 4:30pm-9pm Sun., $11-30) isn't much to write about. But the clean and delicious Chinese food restaurant has been a favorite for years. It's what you have come to expect from a Chinese restaurant with a humungous menu featuring kung pao chicken and chow mein. A much-loved dish is the Peking duck served with Chinese pancakes, scallions, and plum sauce. The menu has asterisks indicating that if you love spicy food, you have an excellent selection here.

Breakfast, Lunch, and Snacks

Stopping in to **Scramble** (9832 N. 7th St., 602/374-2294, www.azscramble.com, 6am-2pm daily, $5-12) for breakfast or lunch feels like visiting an impossibly good school cafeteria, only smarter. Diners walk up to the counter to order morning mainstays such as buttermilk pancakes, eggs Benedict, and omelets, as well as a few surprises such as "brizzas"—a Scramble creation that puts eggs, bacon, chorizo, and other breakfast toppings on pizzas. The modern self-serve space is bright, airy, and everything you wish your school had been.

La Grande Orange Grocery (4410 N. 40th St., 602/840-7777, www.lagrandeorangegrocery.com, 6:30am-10pm daily, $5-11) is one of those magical neighborhood joints where young and old, couples and families, big groups of friends, and quiet newspaper readers can all sit down and enjoy themselves. The small grocery store is housed in the same building as La Grande Orange Pizzeria and has a counter service kitchen as well as a breakfast and coffee bar. Drop in early in the morning and try out the Commuter Sandwich, served on LGO's signature English muffins. Later in the day, pop in to grab a tasty guacamole B.L.T. or a quick salad. The hip market also offers a fun selection of gifts and wine, and its coffee bar is among the best in the city. There is gelato happy hour from 3pm-5pm each day, so take a seat on the shady patio for first-rate people watching.

Even non-morning people like starting their day at **Over Easy** (4730 E. Indian School Rd., 602/468-3447, https:// eatatovereasy.com, 6:30am-1pm Mon.-Fri., 6:30am-2pm Sat.-Sun., $4-16). The sunny yellow interior and bright patio provide a pleasant setting for eggs, waffles, and big, fluffy pancakes. Got a sweet tooth? The brioche French toast topped with caramelized banana and pecans is divine, as is the iced coffee with cinnamon, cardamom, sweetened condensed milk, and mint. Or heck, if you really have no shame, order the chocolate chip, M&M's, or Reese's pancakes.

Duck and Decanter (1651 E. Camelback Rd., 602/274-5429, www.duckanddecanter.com, 7am-7pm Mon.-Wed., 7am-9pm Thurs.-Fri., 8am-7pm Sat.-Sun., $5-8) is a Camelback classic. The popular brown-bag lunch put this gourmet sandwich shop on Phoenix's culinary map in the 1970s. Since then, the wine bar, assortment of European beers, and well-stocked deli and cheese shop have earned it a loyal following—not to mention the reasonable prices, which mean weekly trips for many. The mile-high sandwiches come with a choice of 17 breads and each is expertly prepared with fresh ingredients. You can get your food to go, but you should join the neighborhood regulars on the large, shaded patio. You'll also find European imports and Arizona-made products like cactus candies in the culinary shop.

Although its older sibling, **Pizzeria Bianco,** gets most of the attention, ★ **Pane Bianco** (4404 N. Central Ave., 602/234-2100, www.pizzeriabianco.com, 11am-8pm Mon.-Thurs., 11am-9pm Fri.-Sat., 11am-3pm Sun., $7-12) is just as worthy of high praise and a slew of accolades. Bianco's genius is his simplicity, and the choice for lunch is limited to a perfect four sandwiches and four salads. The *soppressata* with aged provolone and winter relish is the standout, but everything here is exemplary. The location recently expanded to include a dinner menu that serves the chef's signature high-quality antipasti, big plates, and his famous pizzas. Bianco is a strong supporter of local growers and his food reflects this sensibility with its incredible freshness and delicious taste.

A mix of house-roasted coffee, tempting baked goods, and midcentury modernist furniture attracts the local hipsterati and those looking for a good cuppa joe alike to **Lux** (4400 N. Central Ave., 602/327-1396, www.luxcoffee.com, 6am-midnight Sun.-Thurs., 6am-2am Fri.-Sat.,). Baristas pride themselves on remembering names and drink orders after just a couple of visits, and regulars just keep coming back. Repeated visits often reveal the same groups of designer-types meeting clients, blogging from their laptops, or discussing the Pantone color of the year. Now also serving beer and wine, the vibe loosens up as the booze starts to flow.

Farmers Markets

Welcome to the best Farmers Market in the city and maybe even the state. **Uptown Farmers Market** (5757 N. Central Ave., 602/859-5648, www.uptownmarketaz.com, 8am-noon Wed. & Sat.) features everything you want in a farmers market: excellent produce, fresh dairy products, delicious bread, homemade hummus, delectable pastries, a bounce house for the kids, food trucks for immediate hunger needs, and a sea of water bowls for dogs. With over 70 vendors, all those things we just listed barely scratch the surface. They've got artisan cutting boards, pottery, popsicles, pickled vegetables, local honey, handcrafted soaps, tamales, essential oils…okay, okay, we'll stop. Oh, and live music and…

French

Dining spots don't get much more romantic than **Coup des Tartes** (1725 E. Osborn Rd., 602/212-1082, www.nicetartes.com, 11am-2pm Tues.-Fri., 4pm-9pm Tues.-Thurs., 4pm-10pm Fri., 5pm-10pm Sat., 10am-3pm Sun., $12-34). This delightful French bistro has a snug interior that's pitch-perfect for first dates, anniversaries, and all manner of intimate meals—especially ones that involve an engagement ring. The menu changes regularly but almost always includes classic treatments of lamb, duck, and fish. If summer chicken is on the menu, don't hesitate; its mix of herbs and citrus is the perfect pick-me-up for hot summer days. Two other don'ts: Don't skimp on appetizers and don't skimp on desserts. The cheese plate and house-made tarts are good enough to make you and your date swoon.

Christopher's & Crush Lounge (2502 E. Camelback Rd., 602/522-2344, www.christophersaz.com, 11am-9pm Mon.-Tues., 11am-10pm Wed.-Sat., noon-8pm Sun., $9-38) is a sleek little spot at the Biltmore Fashion Park—appropriate for James Beard Award-winning chef Christopher Gross. The French bistro-inspired menu includes his cult favorites—red bell pepper soup, goat cheese salad, roasted foie gras, specialty pizzas—but he's debuted a more casual side at the restaurant's **Crush Lounge,** where you get half off the menu during happy hour (3pm-6pm).

Chef Vincent Guerithault and his eponymous **Vincent's on Camelback** (3930 E. Camelback Rd., 602/224-0225, www.vincentsoncamelback.com, 5pm-10pm Tues.-Sat., $31-60) are local classics. The James Beard Award winner combines Southwestern ingredients with French technique and his elegant restaurant is perennially popular for its signature appetizers—duck tamale with Anaheim chili and raisins—and creative entrées like wild boar loin with parsnip puree and habanero sauce. This is a favorite restaurant in town among foodies and attracts a mature crowd.

Italian

The Parlor (1916 E. Camelback Rd., 602/248-2480, theparlor.us, 11am-10pm Mon.-Thurs., 11am-11pm Fri.-Sat., 11am-9pm Sun., $8-16), a stylish pizzeria in the Camelback Corridor, won Phoenicians over quickly when it opened in 2009. A glamorous makeover has preserved a few retro details from the building's previous life as the Salon de Venus, although its updated look—with polished-concrete floors and recycled-wood tables—has made the restaurant a hit, especially the popular bar (sample the refreshing basil gimlet). The kitchen serves Italian favorites, including a pappardelle bolognese with meat sauce, shaved pecorino, and rosemary oil as well as a delicious selection of salads—particularly the Caesar salad served with white anchovies. Most people order one of the wood-fired pizzas, like the Pesto or the Smokey, which is topped with ricotta, olive tapenade, arugula, and smoked prosciutto.

Pizza! More pizza! Get some great pizza at **Federal Pizza** (5210 N. Central Ave., 602/795-2520, www.federalpizza.com, 11am-11pm Mon.-Thurs., 11am-midnight Fri.-Sat., 11am-10pm Sun., $9-16), a really popular pizza joint with an interior like a midcentury dream come true. Here you can try tasty pizzas like the At Last made with broccolini, roasted corn, goat cheese, and Calabrian chilies (super good) or the Brussels Sprout, sprinkled with pancetta and manchego (super yum). Okay,

now here's the best part: They have a drive thru. And you can get growlers of craft beers in the drive thru. Super heck yeah!

One of the best pizza restaurants in Phoenix sits in a very, very odd area of town. **Pizza a Metro** (2336 W. Thomas Rd., 602/262-9999, www.pizzametrohome.com, 11am-9pm Mon.-Fri., 11am-9:30pm Sat., $11-34) defines hole-in-the-wall—it shares a wall with a sketchy convenience store. Don't let that discourage you. The wood-fired pizzas are simply delicious, the fresh pasta is absolutely killer, and they make one of the best Caesar salads in the state. Be prepared: The teeny, tiny restaurant can get quite cozy.

Mediterranean and Middle Eastern

It's all about ambience at **T. Cooks** (5200 E. Camelback Rd., 602/808-0766, www.tcooksphoenix.com, breakfast 6:30am-10:30am Mon.-Sat., 6:30am-10am Sun., lunch 11am-2pm Mon.-Sat., dinner 5:30pm-10pm daily, $9-48), a romantic hideaway at the Royal Palms Resort. The intimate Spanish Colonial dining room is complemented by the menu, which features Southwest-meets-Mediterranean seasonal dishes, fresh fish, and fire-roasted meats. The pan-fried frog legs served with espelette and house-made andouille sausage is just one of the bold culinary creations on the menu. Phoenicians regularly gather here for breakfast, devouring Provençal French toast, Mediterranean eggs Benedict, brown butter pancakes, and mimosas.

Mexican and Southwest

Once you discover ★ **Richardson's** (6335 N. 16th St., 602/265-5886, www.richardson-snm.com, 8am-11pm Mon.-Wed., 8am-midnight Thurs.-Sat., 8am-11pm Sun., $10-45), you'll be a convert to New Mexico's own Southwestern cuisine: roasted chilies, gooey melted cheese, and smoky, grilled meats. You could easily make an entire meal of a small salad and the jumbo shrimp quesadilla with red pepper sauce and cheese, or the must-try relleno platter, a spicy mass of pork, cheese, smoked turkey or beef best served with red and green sauce. And then there's the garlic shrimp pasta dish with the most decadent garlic cream sauce you'll ever taste, the NY Steak, the wood-oven pizzas, blackened scallops... it's all crazy delicious. And there's a whole brunch menu with equally mouth-watering menu items.

On a related note and in a nearby plaza, the compact **Dick's Hideaway** (6008 N. 16th St., 602/241-1881, www.richardsonsnm.com, 7am-midnight Sun.-Wed., 7am-1am Thurs.-Sat., $10-45) offers the same menu, but in a dark, rustic setting that feels a bit like a modern saloon. Intensely popular, the tiny bar area gets pretty cramped. Pull up a stool at the polished copper bar, order a drink from the extensive beer and wine list, and watch the rotisserie chickens spin over an open flame.

Hmmm, what can we say about **Tee Pee Mexican Restaurant** (4144 E. Indian School Rd., 602/956-0178, www.teepeemexicanfood.com, 11am-9pm Sun.-Wed., 11am-10pm Thurs.-Sat., $6-14)? Yes, former President George W. Bush ate there in 2004 and Phoenicians have been coming to this hole-in-the-wall for almost 50 years, but we can't say it's the best in town. Still, it has a loyal following for those who enjoy that midcentury, greasy spoon interpretation of the cuisine. If that's your style, go for the chili rellenos, which come to the table as an intimidating mountain of cheese and chili peppers. The menu is affordable and diverse, but be prepared for tight quarters—the original orange booths are separated by a single divider, which means you'll get to know your neighbor. In case you're curious, President Bush dined on two enchiladas, rice, and beans.

The casual, hip vibe and deliciously simple menu that's the perfect mash-up of American meets Mexican street food has made **Otro Café** (6035 N. 7th St., 602/266-0831, www.otrocafe.com, 11am-9pm Mon., 11am-10pm Tues.-Fri., 8am-10pm Sat., 8am-9pm Sun., $4-22) a popular choice for locals. Start with the made-to-order guacamole and *elote callejero*, grilled corn on the cob with fresh *cotija* cheese

Richardson's

and smoked paprika. You'll also want to sample the small homemade tacos, which range from seasonal veggies to *achiote*-marinated shrimp and slow-roasted pork belly. A delicious breakfast is served all day and the *huevos rancheros* are particularly tasty.

One of the best things about being a border state is the quality of the Mexican food. **Via Delosantos Mexican Café** (9120 N. Central Ave., 602/997-6239, 10:30am-8:30pm Sun.-Thurs., 10:30am-10:30pm Fri., 10:30am-9:30pm Sat., $11-30) is no exception. The café is known for its mom-and-pop atmosphere and its inexpensive margaritas (which start at $3) and boasts a huge selection of tequilas. But it is the food that keeps the patrons coming back. Beloved for its low prices and tasty Sonoran-style Mexican dishes, this Sunnyslope eatery is frequented for its well-marinated chicken enchiladas and the deep-fried perfection of its *machaca* chimichangas.

Dessert

For whatever reason, this area of town has a lot of little sweet spots. For ice-cream lovers, **Sweet Republic** (6054 N. 16th St., 602/535-5990, www.sweetrepublic.com, noon-10pm

Sun.-Thurs., noon-11pm Fri.-Sat.) is like Baskin Robbins on drugs—in a good way. The original flavors are handcrafted and laid out under glass for sampling before buying. Patrons enjoy their scoops at small tables just like a traditional ice-cream shop.

Speaking of ice cream, another place people freak out for it is **Churn** (5223 N. Central Ave., 602/279-8024, www.churnaz.com, 11am-11pm Mon.-Fri., 9am-11pm Sat.). This bright-white tiled ice-cream shop is a favorite stop for folks eating at the neighboring restaurants (Windsor, Federal Pizza, Postino) and it's no wonder. The interior is downright charming and the back patio is the perfect place to enjoy a cone. Try the pretzel cone with any of their daily rotating flavors like caramel cashew, whiskey toffee almond, or peaches 'n' honey.

Urban Cookies (4711 N. 7th St., 602/451-4335, www.urbancookies.com, 11am-11pm Mon.-Fri., 9am-11pm Sat.) makes delicious cookies, yes. But it's really known for its award-winning cupcakes. Ahem, its Food Network *Cupcake Wars* award-winning cupcakes, that is. Honestly, everything on the menu is great. They've also got donuts, dessert bars, cakes, and breads.

Vegetarian and Vegan

Vegans can rejoice and carnivores can relax at **Green** (2022 N. 7th St., 602/258-1870, www.greenvegetarian.com, 11am-9pm Mon.-Sat., $6-10). The casual restaurant features 100 percent vegan comfort food such as burgers, burritos, po' boys, and rice bowls made with mock meat and vegan cheeses. If this sounds more like a diet than a meal, close your eyes and take a bite. The spicy Buffalo wings, Chicago cheesesteak, and big "WAC" are tasty enough to please even the most hard-core meat eater.

After, hop next door to **Nami** (2014 N. 7th St., 602/258-6264, www.tsoynami.com, 7am-9:30pm Mon.-Sat., 9am-2pm Sun., $3-5) for all-vegan desserts including a staple in these parts, the tSoynami, which is sort of like a Dairy Queen Blizzard but made with organic soy-based ice cream. If you're on the east side, head for Nami's Tempe location (2240

N. Scottsdale Rd., 480/941-9003, 11am-9pm Mon.-Sat., $6-10).

Okay, there is meat served at this restaurant but with so many vegetarian and vegan options on the menu, we're putting it in this category. The contemporary American-with-Asian-influence **Flower Child Uptown** (100 E. Camelback Rd., 602/212-0180, www.iamaflowerchild.com, 11am-9pm daily, $8-13) is big with the health-food crowd seeking ultra-fresh vegetables to stock their salads, quinoa bowls, and whole-grain wraps. Each menu item can be made with your choice of protein: chicken, salmon, steak, or tofu. Everything on the menu is tasty and filling in that I-have-so-much-energy-from-this-healthy-meal way and the super-casual vibe works really well with the ordering at the counter. So well in fact that many eat here after a hike or yoga class. Sound good but don't want to drive to Central? There's also **Flower Child Arcadia** in the Arcadia neighborhood (5013 N. 44th St., 602/429-6222, 11am-9pm Mon.-Sun. daily, $3-5).

AHWATUKEE AND SOUTH PHOENIX
Breakfast and Lunch

The Farm at South Mountain (6106 S. 32nd St., www.thefarmatsouthmountain.com) is a slice of classic Arizona—and sadly, its rural, agricultural setting is nearing extinction in Phoenix. Fortunately for residents and visitors, though, the farm's restaurants still showcase the city's former rustic beauty. Students, families, the Scottsdale brunching set, and about every other human who has been there raves about the **Morning Glory Café** (602/276-8804, 8am-11am Tues.-Fri., 8am-1pm Sat.-Sun., closed summers, $8-13). The open-air restaurant isn't fancy, but the farm-fresh food is spectacular: *huevos rancheros*, ham omelet, and brioche French toast with sautéed bananas topped with candied pecans. Also on the property, **The Farm Kitchen** (602/276-7288, 10am-3pm daily, closed summers, $9-12) features soups, salads, and sandwiches for a lunchtime picnic. Families flock to the picnic tables and enjoy lunch sitting under the old pecan trees. It's the perfect way to recharge after a hike up South Mountain. Head south of Southern on 32nd Street, and pull into the charming farmstead's gravel driveway.

The other post-hike recommendation in the South Mountain area is **Hillside** (4740 E. Warner Rd., 480/705-7768, www.hillsidespot.com, 6:30am-9pm daily, $11-30). It offers craft beers, wines, local produce and vendors, and a menu that serves breakfast, lunch, and dinner. It's a casual yet chic place with what might be the best pancakes in town drizzled with whipped butter and syrup. Omelets, sandwiches, salads, *elote,* burritos—all good.

Mexican and Southwest

★ **Kai** (5594 W. Wild Horse Pass Blvd., 602/385-5726, www.wildhorsepassresort.com/kai, 5:30pm-9pm Tues.-Thurs., 5:30pm-9:30pm Fri.-Sat., $24-55), which means "seed" in the Pima language, taps into the Native American influence on Arizona culture and cuisine. Named as a AAA Five Diamond/Forbes Five Star restaurant and one of Open Table's 10 Best Restaurants in America for 2015, this restaurant at the Sheraton Grand at Wild Horse Pass Resort hits high marks with an innovative menu that consists of indigenous ingredients produced on the Gila River Indian Community's land. The Life of Fowl with Saguaro-lacquered quail breast and a nest of yucca straws, for instance, is a uniquely Arizona experience. Give the 13-course tasting menu a try if you're feeling adventurous, not to mention hungry. The restaurant is rather formal—which in Arizona means no jeans or shorts. Also, be sure to make reservations for this destination restaurant.

There are scores of great places to grab good tacos and enchiladas in the Valley, but ★ **Carolina's** (1202 E. Mohave St., 602/252-1503, www.carolinasmex.com, 7am-7:30pm Mon.-Fri., 7am-6pm Sat., $4-8) is among the very best, with fresh, made-from-scratch Mexican food. The less-than-stellar neighborhood and dumpy building is as authentic as you can get. We lovingly call the decor "humble" because the care that is given to the homemade tortillas, guacamole, and salsa is what makes the place feel like a palace. To experience chef Carolina Valenzuela's original recipes, order one of the hearty combination platters, which include tamales, *machaca,* flautas, and tostadas.

Steakhouse

Cowpokes crave **Rustler's Rooste** (8383 S. 48th St., 602/431-6474, www.rustlersrooste.com, 5pm-10pm Mon.-Fri., 4pm-10pm Sat.-Sun., $15-27). This giant barnlike restaurant is perched on an outlook in the South Mountain range and offers splendid views of Phoenix. The giant live steer corralled at the entrance foreshadows hefty servings of steak, ribs, and corn on the cob. Although it's a bit touristy and overpriced, the energetic vibe can tempt the most urban epicurean to pick up a country twang and salivate for good ole chuckhouse grub. Oh, and the best part? You can avoid the stairs and instead opt for a two-story slide that whizzes eaters (okay, mostly kids) between floors. The restaurant is full of gimmicks, but the great atmosphere and live music are pure fun.

TEMPE AND THE EAST VALLEY
American

House of Tricks (114 E. 7th St., 480/968-1114, www.houseoftricks.com, 11am-10pm Mon.-Sat., $11-36) has long been known as one of Tempe's best restaurants. Tucked behind big, shady trees, the 1920s' cottage offers casual charms and sophisticated New American dishes with French, Asian, and Southwestern flavors. Enjoy a glass of wine in the outdoor Garden Bar or opt for a cozy dinner inside. The eclectic, seasonal menu features bold menu items like the Green Chili Chorizo Oysters with sweet corn and honey glaze, or the seared jalapeño and goat's cheese grits. The entrées feature your pick of carefully prepared meats that are seared, crusted, glazed, and roasted to perfection.

★ **Four Peaks Brewing Company** (1340

E. 8th St., 480/303-9967, www.fourpeaks.com, 11am-1am Mon.-Thurs., 11am-2am Fri.-Sat., 10am-1am Sun. $10-14) is a regular on "best of" lists for tasty bar food and locally brewed ales. Set in an 1892 red-brick, mission-style building just off the beaten path in Tempe, the brewery shows off its floor-to-ceiling steel casks in the back and a chalkboard with the day's brews in the front, including alcohol-content percentage. Savor the Kilt Lifter, a frequent medalist at the Great American Beer Festival, for its flavor and provocative moniker. When hunger strikes, try the pub's Southwest burger topped with chilies and jalapeño dressing, or indulge your deep-fried fantasies with the 8th Street Ale Chicken Strips, the only chicken tenders you can order without feeling like you have an immature palate.

ASU staff and students have been lured pretty much forever by the smell of cooking burgers at **The Chuckbox** (202 E. University Dr., 480/968-4712, www.thechuckbox.com, 10:30am-11pm Mon.-Sat., 10:30am-8pm Sun., $5-9). The magic happens over an open flame, which comes as no surprise. Flipping burgers for over 35 years, The Chuckbox has landed on too many "best of" lists for us to list here. The menu is simple: choose the amount of burger you want, then choose the toppings. Not into the burger thing? They have chicken sandwiches and wings, too. Wash them down with a beer and you have yourself the perfect American lunch.

British

Tempe residents flock to **Cornish Pasty Company** (960 W. University Dr., 480/894-6261, www.cornishpastyco.com, 11am-midnight daily, $7-10) for delicious Cornwall-inspired pasties from southwest England—savory meats and vegetables cooked within a pastry shell. Hot pocket jokes aside, these things are deliciously filling and were first mentioned in medieval times before becoming popular in Cornwall in the 17th century as they could be eaten one-handed by miners. A pasty is like a British burrito and with options including lamb and mint,

made with lamb, potatoes, rutabaga, onion, and fresh mint, they are just as tasty. The variety is endless and at Cornish Pasty Company, they serve everything from super meaty to breakfast to vegetarian. And obviously we aren't the only ones to make the pasty-burrito connection—there's a Mexican pasty on the menu, too.

Asian

For tasty, accessible Vietnamese and pan-Asian cuisine, **Cyclo Vietnamese Cuisine** (1919 W. Chandler Blvd., 480/963-4490, www.azseats.com/cyclo, 11am-2:30pm, 5pm-9pm Tues.-Thurs., 11am-2:30pm, 5pm-10pm Fri.-Sat., $6-12) can't be beat. The decor is surprisingly stylish for the strip-mall setting—imagine the riotous colors of Saigon let loose in an IKEA—and the owner, Justina, is a hoot. The food is also first class. The *goi du du* (green papaya salad), *canh ga* (spicy chicken wings), and *pho xe lua* (beef noodle soup) never disappoint, especially if they're paired with a Vietnamese coffee brewed into a glass of condensed milk at the table. And just for the record, the name (pronounced "SEE-klo") is the Vietnamese word for a three-wheeled pedicab.

RA Sushi (411 S. Mill Ave., 480/303-9800, www.rasushi.com, 11am-midnight Sun.-Thurs., 11am-1am Fri.-Sat., $5-19) is often the first place in Tempe that people tried sushi back in the 1990s. Add a backbeat that wafts through the dining room and a distinct energy supplied by a Mill Avenue address and proximity to ASU, and dinner at RA is akin to an entire night on the town. The bar is always packed with revelers, and the sushi bar and dining tables serve up solid sushi, sashimi, noodles, and tempura. The drinks are nothing to sneeze at, either, featuring a bunch of beers and an array of sakes as well as an extensive cocktail list. If this all sounds great to you but you don't want to head to Tempe, there are now RAs across the city and country.

Farmers Markets

One of the toughest challenges for farmers

markets in the Valley is our hot weather in the summer. Not a problem for **Tempe Farmers Market** (805 S. Farmer Ave., 480/557-9970, www.tempefarmersmarket.com, 8am-11pm daily), which sells all local, all healthy foods in an air-conditioned store.

Italian

Tucked away from the main drag on Mill Avenue, **Caffe Boa** (398 S. Mill Ave., 480/968-9112, www.cafeboa.com, 11am-10pm Sun.-Wed., 11am-11pm Thurs.-Sat., $12-36) is a longtime favorite. The stylish restaurant's exposed brick walls, dark hardwood floors, and elegant, modern light fixtures are chic, but the overall mood is quite casual. Boa's seasonal menu can swing from a light organic wild arugula, grape tomato, and lemon olive oil dressing in the summer to braised meats and rich sauces in the winter. The handmade pastas and raviolis with a revolving roster of fillings and sauces are always winners.

After the bars close, plop down with the pepperoni and cheese from **Slices** (11 E. 6th St., 480/966-4681, www.slicespizzajoint. com, 11am-10pm Mon.-Thurs., 11am-3am Fri.-Sat., 11am-8pm Sun., $3-5) and you'll be in heaven. There's nothing swank about this small, New York-style, grab-a-big-slice-and-fold-it pizza joint, which prepares a changing lineup of pies, including chicken parmesan, potato and bacon, chipotle veggie, and the salty Greek combination of olive, feta cheese, and onion. Order a slice (or two) at the counter and fine-tune with a quick shake of crushed red pepper, garlic powder, or oregano. Hungry college students swarm to this crowded shop off Mill Avenue, especially late at night.

Mexican

Housed in Tempe's old train station, **Macayo's Depot Cantina** (300 S. Ash Ave., 480/966-6677, www.macayo.com, 11am-11pm Mon.-Wed., 10am-midnight Thurs.-Fri., 9am-midnight Sat., 9am-11pm Sun., $6-17) is a festive Mexican restaurant just west of Mill Avenue's main drag. It's a convenient lunch or dinner option for visitors to the popular shopping district or neighboring Tempe Town Lake and Papago Park. Lunch specials feature shredded beef tacos, tamales, and chicken chimichangas, although Macayo's fajitas and spicy Baja specialties are certainly worth a taste. The large, colorful restaurant is best known for its crowded happy hours from 3:30pm to 6:30pm, particularly on Fridays, when college students and office workers are anxious to jumpstart their weekends on the open-air patio.

Middle Eastern

The first **Pita Jungle** (4 E. University Dr., 480/804-0234, www.pitajungle.com, 10:30am-10pm daily, $6-15) in Tempe opened in a funky strip mall near the Arizona State University campus with a goal of attracting the burgeoning market of healthful eaters. And it did. In 20 years, the eatery expanded to 19 restaurants (and counting) across the state and in California. Having moved closer to Mill Avenue, the contemporary decor blends seamlessly with the eatery's healthy menu of hummus, baba ghanoush, and feta- and olive-topped lavash pizzas, and regulars swear by the chicken shawarma. The restaurant is well suited for mixed company—that is, vegetarians and carnivores—because it offers multiple meatless options, including two types of veggie burgers, as well as a selection of beef, chicken, and lamb dishes.

Accommodations

Thanks to a growing downtown and convention center, Phoenix offers several hotel options. You'll likely want to choose one of downtown's high-rise towers (which offer convenient light-rail access) or one of the popular and quintessentially Arizona resorts in the Camelback Corridor. The resorts tend to be pricier than their hotel brethren, but they offer a mini-oasis of manicured grounds, multiple swimming pools, and adjacent golf courses. Their lavish amenities are well worth a few extra dollars a night. In summer, rates at all Phoenix hotels are dramatically discounted, with half off or more.

DOWNTOWN
$50-100

To be perfectly frank, hotels at this price range in downtown Phoenix can be seedy. That said, the best choice is **Rodeway Inn Downtown Phoenix** (402 W. Van Buren St., 602/254-7247, www.choicehotels.com, $60-100 d). Clean, updated, and run by Choice Hotels International, it's got all the amenities you would want, like high-speed internet, continental breakfast, and flat-screen television; it's also pet friendly.

Another option is the **Super 8 Phoenix Downtown** (965 E. Van Buren St., 602/252-6823, www.super8.com, $70-100 d). There's mixed reviews as far as cleanliness goes, but the staff is friendly and it's a legit place with free internet, breakfast, laundry facilities, and an outdoor pool.

The Ramada **Phoenix Midtown** (212 W. Osborn Rd., 602/595-4444, www.ramada.com, $70-120 d) is a bit north but has a light-rail station just a block away, so it makes a convenient stay for business travelers planning to spend a lot of time downtown. The rooms are clean and the service is good, although there's not much else to this hotel. It will meet your basic needs and you can often score a decent-sized room for under $100.

$100-250

Bombshells Mae West and Marilyn Monroe slept here. So did Ingrid Bergman, Humphrey Bogart, and Cary Grant. The **Hotel San Carlos** (202 N. Central Ave., 602/253-4121, www.hotelsancarlos.com, $145-180 d) is a Valley landmark that gives guests a taste of old Phoenix. When the Italian Renaissance-style hotel opened in 1928, it featured luxury amenities like elevators and air-conditioning, a first in Phoenix. Today, guests will find the idiosyncrasies of a historic hotel: tiny bathrooms, quaint rooms, thin walls, and even a few ghosts. If you're into the whole spooky vintage hotel thing, you'll find it delightfully charming. If not, best to book somewhere else.

If you prefer fresh and modern over historic and quirky, try the new **Sheraton Grand Phoenix** (340 N. 3rd St., 602/262-2500, www.sheratonphoenixdowntown.com, $170-300 d). The $350 million hotel was part of a massive revitalization of Copper Square, which includes the Phoenix Convention Center. It's just a straightforward place to stay with contemporary rooms styled with neutral furnishings, warm dark woods, and modern touches like flat panel televisions. You'll find a small outdoor pool and on-site fitness center at this 1,000-room, 31-story hotel, the largest in Arizona.

If you're looking for the best hotel downtown, go ahead and book at ★ **Hotel Palomar Phoenix** (2 E. Jefferson St., 602/253-6633, www.hotelpalomar-phoenix.com, $170-300 d). Located at the popular CityScape, you walk out of your hotel and into many options for shopping, restaurants, and bars. If you're drifting further, hop onto one of the hotel bicycles available for guests. But you can choose to stay on the premises, too, as it is a frequent destination for locals wanting to enjoy a contemporary, classy afternoon or evening in the heart of downtown. Lounge around the third-floor outdoor pool and grab a drink from the LUSTRE Rooftop Bar as you listen to live entertainment, or join other hotel guests at the daily wine reception from 5pm-6pm. And you get free Wi-Fi, which, oddly enough, is a rarity at these downtown hotels (sheesh).

A close runner-up to the title of best hotel downtown would have to be **The Westin Phoenix Downtown** (333 N. Central Ave., 602/429-3500, www.westinphoenixdowntown.com, $150-450 d). Sleek, modern, clean, and accommodating, you really can't go wrong with your stay here. Located at the heart of all the action and, of course, near a light-rail stop, it has everything you want and need. It's considered a boutique hotel with just 242 rooms, but each are spacious and beautifully decorated in minimalist neutrals with a pop of red. Take a dip in the ultra-stylish, heated, saltwater terrace pool with a commanding view of the city. Speaking of views, you'll surely have a nice one from your hotel room window.

Phoenix has a nasty habit of bulldozing its best architecture. Thankfully, in the gorgeous Art Deco building housing the ★ **Hilton Garden Inn Phoenix Downtown** (15 E. Monroe St., 602/343-6000, www.hilton.com, $150-400 d) this is not the case. In fact, the building was beautifully restored and opened in late 2015, so you know this place has some fresh furniture and bed linen. Speaking of decor, they nailed the vibe by going with a highly polished, updated midcentury aesthetic mixed with original elements like marble elevator facades with intricately carved brass doors. Complimentary Wi-Fi is offered throughout the hotel (yay!) and if you can, request a corner room for spectacular views. Staff members are professional and incredibly helpful and this hotel promises to soon be on the short list of recommended places to stay downtown.

A more-than-decent option downtown is the **Renaissance Phoenix Downtown Hotel** (50 E. Adams St., 602/333-0000, www.marriott.com, $180-300 d), an older hotel with a contemporary makeover. It's terrific

Hotel Palomar Phoenix

for business travelers looking for clean rooms, large bathrooms, and great service.

Next door, the **Hyatt Regency Phoenix** (122 N. 2nd St., 602/252-1234, www.phoenix.hyatt.com, $225-300 d) offers a less expensive stay with the advantages of the downtown location. You get what you pay for here—the hotel is clean but showing its age. Consider having a drink at its funky, revolving restaurant, The Compass Arizona Grill—although the food is overpriced and not exactly amazing, you won't find a better way to take in the city.

Situated just north of downtown and about 10 minutes from the airport, the **Hilton Suites Phoenix** (10 E. Thomas Rd., 602/222-1111, www.hilton.com, $90-180 d) is a no-frills selection for business travelers looking for value and convenience. The handy light-rail stop just outside the front door makes commuting to the convention center and downtown's restaurants easy, although guests can also take advantage of the complimentary shuttle service. The hotel's 11-story atrium provides a light-filled retreat complete with a pleasant garden and small pond. The rooms are large and clean and the price is decent.

CENTRAL PHOENIX
$50-100

Near Piestewa Peak and Highway 51, **Best Western Inn Suites** (1615 E. Northern Ave., 602/997-6285, http://phoenix.innsuites.com, $80-125 d) offers excellent value. Budget travelers and families will appreciate the in-room refrigerator, microwave, and complimentary breakfast buffet each morning, not to mention the large swimming pool and hot tub in the central courtyard. Still not convinced? It's a short walk to the Dreamy Draw Recreation Area in the Phoenix Mountains with ample hiking and biking.

ZenYard Guest House (830 E. Maryland Ave., 602/845-0830, www.zenyard.com, $60-110 d) is an eccentric alternative to the city's plethora of chain hotels and resorts. The offbeat bed-and-breakfast is tucked into a North Central Phoenix neighborhood, and it offers a private, solar-powered heated pool. The mid-20th-century ranch house has been decorated with small Asian touches and there are five suites from which to choose.

$100-250

Looking for a little L. A. style in Central Phoenix? ★ **The Clarendon Hotel and Spa** (401 W. Clarendon Ave., 602/252-7363, http://goclarendon.com, $160-240 d) is a unique boutique alternative to the mid-price chains that permeate the area. The property initially attracted a lot of business and celebrity guests like the Black Eyed Peas, AC/DC, and The Rolling Stones, and after years of some serious hipster partying, the rooms could use a little sprucing. But it's still a one-of-a-kind hotel with most rooms opening onto its star attraction, a hip courtyard pool and 50-person Jacuzzi with striped tile, two-story glass water walls, and lounge-y cabana furniture. At night, the pool's floor twinkles with 1,000 illuminated starry lights and the rooftop bar transforms into an open-air lounge popular with locals in search of strong cocktails and impressive views of the downtown skyline.

Bed-and-breakfasts are a rare breed in Phoenix, although **Maricopa Manor Bed and Breakfast Inn** (15 W. Pasadena Ave., 602/264-9200, www.maricopamanor.com, $150-220 d) happily picks up the slack. Its six unique suites are enhanced by gas fireplaces and French doors that open onto charming, palm tree-lined courtyards. The 1928 Arts and Crafts-style bungalow creates an inviting space in which to relax between hikes and shopping expeditions, thanks to small touches like potted plants and colorful flowers around its pool and sundeck. For a little Southwestern flavor, try to reserve the sunflower-yellow Siesta Suite, which features carved Mexican Colonial furniture, hand-painted Talavera tiles, and a small sunroom with a twin daybed for a third guest. In the morning, breakfast is delivered to guest rooms in picnic baskets, allowing a leisurely meal on your private patio.

The **Embassy Suites Phoenix-Biltmore** (2630 E. Camelback Rd., 602/955-3992, www.embassysuites.com, $180-240 d) is conveniently situated next door to Biltmore Fashion Park's shops and restaurants. This Camelback Corridor hotel is a relatively inexpensive option, complete with complimentary made-to-order breakfasts. The rooms could use an overhaul but the pleasant atrium and round outdoor pool are popular with families and business travelers.

Conveniently situated near the Biltmore neighborhood, **Courtyard Phoenix Camelback** (2101 E. Camelback Rd., 602/955-5200, www.marriott.com, $160-260 d) is within easy reach of numerous restaurants and shops at Town and Country Shopping Center and Biltmore Fashion Park. The four-story, midlevel hotel offers clean rooms with many overlooking a landscaped pool and courtyard. It also offers a few amenities that offset the less-than-economical price: complimentary Wi-Fi and a pullout sofa for an extra sleeping space.

Hampton Inn Phoenix-Biltmore (2310 E. Highland Ave., 800/956-5221, www.hamptonphoenixbiltmore.com, $100-160 d) may seem to be just another middle-of-the-road type of place but by comparison to the other chain hotels in this price range, it's probably the best of the bunch. The place is spotless, modern, and the customer service is excellent. Complimentary hot breakfast, outdoor pool, fitness center, hotel shuttle, and free Wi-Fi are just a few of the amenities. And it's just a quick walk to Biltmore Fashion Park's restaurants and shops. For the excellent price and location, it gets the job done and gets it done well.

Over $250

The ★ **Camby Hotel** (2401 E. Camelback Rd., 602/468-0700, www.thecamby.com, $230-400 d) is still making its mark on the Phoenix hotel scene and had big shoes to fill, being the former location of the Ritz-Carlton. With an entirely new vibe, the target market here is 30/40-somethings who enjoy posh getaways and funky decor like, say, a horned cow skull light fixture that projects the word "Moo" onto the wall. It is a stunning remodel with the high polish of midcentury modern basics accented by splashes of turquoise and other Southwest elements. Looks aside, you can expect a luxurious stay in the heart of Camelback Corridor. Many rooms overlook neighboring Biltmore Fashion Park with Piestewa Peak in the distance. With 11 floors, 263 rooms, and 15 suites, guests have the opportunity to enjoy the luxurious cotton

bedding, hotel art that's surprisingly memorable, Sunday morning yoga, two restaurants, a rooftop pool and bar, and an on-site spa.

Resorts

Tucked into an upscale residential neighborhood, the 1929 ★ **Arizona Biltmore** (2400 E. Missouri Ave., 602/955-6600, www.arizonabiltmore.com, $260-700 d) is a Phoenix landmark. The Art Deco gem elegantly blends geometric forms and Southwest touches and is a credit to its architect Albert Chase McArthur, who was a student of Frank Lloyd Wright. The Biltmore has attracted presidents, old Hollywood movie stars, and former guests of the Wrigley family, whose winter home sits atop a hill neighboring the property. Even composer Irving Berlin was an occasional guest, penning "White Christmas" while sitting poolside. For those who are not content to lounge by one of the resort's eight pools or hit the links at the two adjacent PGA golf courses, the Biltmore offers a full docket of activities that range from wine-tasting and "dive-in" movies to kids' cooking classes and live music.

Unlike Scottsdale's large, sprawling resorts, the romantic ★ **Royal Palms Resort & Spa** (5200 E. Camelback Rd., 602/840-3610, www.royalpalmshotel.com, $300-700

Royal Palms Resort & Spa

d) is understated, elegant, and intimate. The Mediterranean-style hideaway features stone courtyards with potted flowers and tiled fountains, and its casitas and villas are decorated with Spanish Colonial furniture, rich colors, and Old World accents. It's the ultimate couples' getaway spot. You won't find better ambience in the city, nor is it easy to top the Alvadora Spa and T. Cook's restaurant. Best of all, the former private estate sits at the base of Camelback Mountain, an easy 10-minute drive on Camelback Road to the Biltmore neighborhood or Old Town Scottsdale.

The mountainside **Pointe Hilton Squaw Peak Resort** (7677 N. 16th St., 602/997-2626, www.squawpeakhilton.com, $150-400 d) is a decent vacation destination for families, especially in the summer when the property becomes an aquatic oasis. Kids will revel in the Hole-in-the-Wall River Ranch's four acres of multiple pools, waterfall-fed lagoon, half-mile lazy river for tubing, and a 130-foot slide. There's also a hands-on Coyote Camp and transport to the nearby Lookout Mountain golf course. The spa and tennis courts aren't bad, either. And thanks to 430 one-room suites and 133 two-bedroom casitas, the resort can accommodate big parties or large broods. It's about time for a renovation, though, as many of the rooms are showing some wear.

The **Pointe Hilton Tapatio Cliffs Resort** (11111 N. 7th St., 602/866-7500, www.tapatiocliffshilton.com, $100-250 d) is also a great budget option. A summer 2016 renovation to the guest suites has given a bit of polish to the North Central Phoenix property—which is a good thing because the rooms could use it. Not like you'll spend much time there. The Falls Water Village features multiple pools, streams, waterfalls, private cabanas, and a 138-foot slide. Not to be outdone, the restaurants are just as pleasurable, especially the sleek Different Pointe of View, which wows diners with a "mile-high" view of Phoenix. And best of all, the sprawling mountainside resort has hiking right outside its backyard as the property backs up to the Phoenix Mountains Preserve. You can hop on Trail 100 and walk or bike for miles with beautiful views of the city. You can also play golf to your heart's content at the Lookout Mountain course, located next door.

SOUTH PHOENIX
Resorts

It can be hard to get a sense of Arizona's native culture when you spend your days poolside or on the golf course. Fortunately, the **Sheraton Grand at Wild Horse Pass** (5594 W. Wild Horse Pass Blvd., 602/225-0100, www.wildhorsepassresort.com, $200-700 d) incorporates much of the Sonoran Desert's indigenous culture and wildlife into its design, while still providing a luxurious spa and AAA Five Diamond/Forbes Five Star restaurant. Built on the Gila River Indian Community, the resort reflects the architecture, art, and history of the Pima and Maricopa tribes, and is named after the wild horses that still roam the community's land south of Phoenix. Although it's a 10-minute drive from Chandler and 25 minutes from downtown Phoenix, you'll find plenty to do, like play golf, ride horses, or visit the neighboring casino. The boat rides and indoor boulder formation can feel a little Disney-like at times, but the setting is gorgeous.

Arizona Grand Resort (8000 S. Arizona Grand Pkwy., 602/438-9000, www.arizonagrandresort.com, $150-700 d) is a family-friendly 744-suite property that has all the amenities found at most resorts—a championship golf course, spa, fitness classes—but it's the Oasis Water Park that has kids and adults buzzing. Many spend days at a time braving the ocean-like wave pool, tubing the lazy river, or plunging down the eight-story water slide. At the end of the day, the spacious suites provide plenty of room for the whole gang—although Mom and Dad may want to grab a drink in the new lobby, which overlooks the golf course's rolling hills.

NORTH PHOENIX
Resorts

Everything about the ★ **JW Marriott**

Phoenix Desert Ridge Resort & Spa (5350 E. Marriott Dr., 480/293-5000, www.marriott. com, $275-550 d) is enormous, from the soaring lobby and 869 rooms to its seven restaurants and Revive Spa. It carries its size well, with clean, modern lines that give a nod to the Southwest's indigenous architecture. There are also subtle Western details, like leather couches, light-colored stone, and delicate ironwork. The massive meeting space frequently hosts multiple conferences and trade shows at once, but you're just as likely to see leisure travelers and families at the pools (complete with lazy river and waterslides) or on the two championship golf courses designed by Arnold Palmer and Nick Faldo.

TEMPE AND THE EAST VALLEY
$100-250

Formerly the shoddy Twin Palms, ★ **Graduate Tempe** (225 E. Apache Blvd., 480/967-9431, www.graduatetempe.com, $100-240 d) has received a much-loved makeover. The chic decor is funky, artsy, and current. It's got two quality restaurants on site, a rooftop bar with excellent views, and a pool and Jacuzzi open 24 hours. Of course, expect to be sharing the halls with a sometimes-raucous college crowd, but it's so conveniently situated across the street from Arizona State University's campus and Gammage Auditorium that you probably won't care.

The W Hotel's younger, funkier sibling, **Aloft** (951 E. Playa Del Norte Dr., 480/621-3300, www.alofttempe.com, $120-160 d) packs a bit of style into its Tempe Town Lake location. The loft-inspired space plays up its urban appeal with light woods, exposed ducts, and is proudly the only LEED-certified hotel in Arizona—in other words, it's green—with recycling process, eco-friendly cleaning products, storm-water management systems, and optional housekeeping. Guests check in through the SPG App for Apple Watch and the app unlocks your door. The rooms are bright and airy, and even the walk-in showers, loaded with Bliss Spa products, benefit from natural light. The outdoor pool, sleek gym, WXYZ bar, and small lounge with a hot-pink pool table add to the slick L. A. vibe.

There's nothing worse than being stuck in a bland, vanilla box when you travel. Thankfully, the **DoubleTree by Hilton Hotel Phoenix Tempe** (2100 S. Priest Dr., 480/967-1441, www.fdoubletree3.hilton.com, $100-150 d) is an unexpected bit of character in the midlevel price range. The Frank Lloyd Wright-inspired resort is nicely maintained and its 270 rooms are up to date. Thankfully, the public spaces retain much of their vintage character, with stacked concrete blocks, warm woods, and stained-glass accents. Guests can soak up the sun at the pool, which is surrounded by green lawns and tall palm trees.

Tempe Mission Palms Hotel (60 E. 5th St., 480/894-1400, www.missionpalms.com, $160-290 d) is a solid choice if you're in town to catch a game at Sun Devil Stadium. You can't beat the hotel's Mill Avenue location, which houses dozens of bars and restaurants just outside the front door. The hotel itself is both dated and updated, as in there are some new niceties mixed with a few leftovers from yesteryear although its rooftop terrace pool and tennis court are great places to hang out and survey Tempe and the adjacent ASU campus.

Resorts

Perched on a desert hilltop, **Phoenix Marriott Tempe at The Buttes** (2000 W. Westcourt Way, 602/225-9000, www.marriott. com, $135-220 d) burrows into its rugged locale, incorporating rock formations right into lobby walls and its pools. It's hard to forget that you're in the middle of the desert and a big city here, as the small resort offers spectacular views of the Valley, especially from its beautifully designed Top of the Rock restaurant. The I-10 freeway runs along the base of the mountain, which can detract from the skyline at rush hour, but thanks to its elevated height, you won't hear a thing.

An East Valley landmark, the **Crowne Plaza Resort Phoenix** (1 San Marcos Pl.,

480/812-0900, www.ihg.com, $120-270 d) has been welcoming guests since Dr. A. J. Chandler opened the hotel in his namesake town in 1913. Chandler's friend, Frank Lloyd Wright helped oversee the construction of the California Mission-style resort, and he was just one of a succession of celebrities to spend time at the San Carlos, including President Herbert Hoover, Fred Astaire, Joan Crawford, and Bing Crosby. Today, the resort has lost a bit of its luster but its beautiful lobby and large rooms are a good value. Plus, you can still enjoy the historic San Marcos golf course, which was the first in the state with grass greens.

Gold Canyon Golf Resort (6100 S. Kings Ranch Rd., 480/982-9090, www.gcgr.com, $180-275 d) isn't for everyone, but diehard golfers and travelers hoping to retreat into the desert will love this secluded property in the East Valley community of Gold Canyon, which is about 50 minutes from the airport. Surrounded by the rugged Superstition Mountains, the resort's white adobe-style buildings gleam in the Sonoran Desert setting, and the expansive views of the cacti and palo verde trees that dot the landscape would cost three times as much in North Scottsdale. There's a spa, ample hiking nearby, pool swimming, and golf, golf, golf…and golf. The real highlight is Gold Canyon's two championship desert courses, consistently named as the best courses in Arizona.

WEST VALLEY
Resorts

For a taste of old Arizona, try the **Wigwam Golf Resort & Spa** (300 Wigwam Blvd., 623/935-3811, www.wigwamarizona.com, $170-425 d) in the West Valley community of Litchfield Park. The Wigwam began as a winter guest ranch in 1929 for Goodyear tire executives and their families. Today, it's a 331-suite resort with three 18-hole championship golf courses, nine tennis courts, four swimming pools, and an Elizabeth Arden Red Door Spa. The elegant Southwestern property—lushly landscaped with green lawns and slender palm trees—features casita-style rooms decorated with wooden furnishings, Mexican ceramic tile, slate floors, and copper and leather fixtures.

Information and Services

TOURIST INFORMATION

The **Greater Phoenix Visitors Bureau** (602/254-6500, www.visitphoenix.com) is a great place to start for additional information about the Valley of the Sun. Its **Downtown Phoenix Visitor Information Center** (125 N. 2nd St., Ste. 120) is conveniently located in the Phoenix Convention Center.

LIBRARIES

The **Phoenix Public Library** has 16 branches across the city, including the **Burton Barr Central Library** (1221 N. Central Ave., 602/262-4636, www.phoenixpubliclibrary. org, 9am-5pm Mon., 9am-9pm Tues.-Thurs., 9am-5pm Fri.-Sat., 1m-5pm Sun.). You'll find computer terminals and an array of resources. The newer branches are almost as architecturally interesting as Burton Barr and worth a mini-tour, particularly **Agave** (23550 N. 36th Ave), **Desert Broom** (29710 N. Cave Creek Rd.), **Palo Verde** (4402 N. 51st Ave.), and **Juniper** (1825 W. Union Hills Dr.). Call the main number (602/262-4636) or visit the website (www.phoenixpubliclibrary.org) for opening hours at individual libraries.

HOSPITALS AND EMERGENCY SERVICES

In an emergency, dial 911 for immediate assistance. **St. Joseph's Hospital and Medical Center** (350 W. Thomas Rd., 602/406-3000, www.stjosephs-phx.org) is Phoenix's premier hospital and home of the Barrow Neurological

Institute as well as a Level 1 trauma center. Nearby, **Phoenix Children's Hospital** (1919 E. Thomas Rd., 602/933-1000, www. phoenixchildrens.org) is one of the 10 largest children's hospitals in the country, offering a host of pediatric specialties, including neonatology, neurosciences, and Level 1 trauma. **Banner Health** (www.bannerhealth. com) operates more than two-dozen clinics and medical centers around the Valley, ranging from specialized services to general health care.

Transportation

GETTING THERE
Air
Phoenix Sky Harbor International Airport (3400 E. Sky Harbor Blvd., 602/273-3300, www.phxskyharbor.com) is a major regional hub for national and international flights. More than 15 carriers fly to Sky Harbor's terminals 2, 3, and 4, including Southwest Airlines, United Airlines, British Airways, and Hawaiian Airlines. Shuttles connect the three terminals, as well as parking lots, the Rental Car Center, and the light rail's 44th Street stop.

Phoenix-Mesa Gateway Airport (6033 S. Sossaman Rd., 480/988-7600, www.phx-mesagateway.org) in east Mesa serves as a small hub for regional carrier **Allegiant Air** (702/505-8888, www.allegiantair.com), with service to northern parts of the country. As the Valley continues to grow, the airport will likely relieve growing congestion at Sky Harbor.

GETTING AROUND
Car
RENTAL CARS
You'll need a vehicle to get around Phoenix, especially if you plan to explore the Valley of

Pedal to the Party

In its ever-persistent effort to become a destination city, Phoenix really amped up its game when the **Grid Bike Share** (http://gridbikes.com) program debuted, making 500 public bikes accessible at 50 locations 24/7. With parking often being so difficult downtown, Phoenicians are taking to bikes for their transportation needs from restaurant to music venue to a night of barhopping. For those who don't have their own set of wheels, the Grid Bike Share operation couldn't be more simple.

Here's how it works: Reserve a bike using the mobile app, website (app.socialbicycles.com) or at the bike using its keypad. You'll get a PIN code to unlock the bike. Take your ride around town using the PIN-operated bike lock to secure the bike to any bike rack. Once you're done, simply find a Grid Bike Share hub and lock the bike up. Feeling lazy? Just ditch the bike locked up to any regular bike rack for a small additional fee. The whole operation costs just $2 for the "out of hub fee" and $7 per hour after. Monthly or annual rates are also available and payment is set up when you register using the app.

the Sun's diverse attractions scattered around the city. Take the free shuttle from any of the terminals to the **Rental Car Center** (1805 E. Sky Harbor Circle, 602/683-3741). You'll find major companies, like **Budget** (602/261-5950, www.budget.com), **Hertz** (602/267-8822, www.hertz.com), and **Enterprise** (602/225-0588), which have convenient drop-off centers around Phoenix and Scottsdale. It can be hard to find a gas station near the airport's rental-car center, so be sure to fill up before returning your vehicle.

Limos, Shuttles, and Taxis

Join a shared-van ride to your resort or hotel with the reliable **SuperShuttle** (602/232-4610, www.supershuttle.com). Its bright blue vans are easy to spot at each of Sky Harbor's terminals.

Desert Knights Sedans & Limousines (480/348-0600, www.desertknights.com) provides rides in sedans, limos, vans, and luxury minibuses, which can be a practical option for families or groups.

You can grab a taxi at Sky Harbor with one of three contracted companies: **Apache Taxi** (480-557-7000), **AAA/Yellow Cab** (480-888-8888), and **Mayflower Cab** (602/955-1355). And if you want to hit the town at night, try **Discount Cab** (602/200-2000, www.discountcab.com), which also offers service via text (send address with city or zip code to 777222).

Phoenix rejoiced in summer 2016, when rideshare services like **Uber** and **Lyft** gained access to the airport's arrivals curb for passenger pickup.

Public Transportation

VALLEY METRO

The **Valley Metro** (602/253-5000, www.valleymetro.org) is a public-transportation network that connects the entire Phoenix metropolitan area. It opened in December 2008 and has proven to be popular with commuters, barhoppers, and visitors alike.

The **Light Rail** trains wend from 19th Avenue and Dunlap Road in Phoenix, through downtown and Tempe's Mill Avenue, before ending in downtown Mesa. It stops at many of the city's most popular attractions, including the Heard Museum and Phoenix Art Museum, the Phoenix Convention Center, Sky Harbor Airport, and Sun Devil Stadium in Tempe. Trains run every 10 to 20 minutes daily. Start and end times vary depending on the location of each stop but you can usually catch a train starting around 4am and ending around 1am from Monday to Thursday. Hours are extended on Friday and Saturday to 2am and reduced on Sunday (check the full schedule online). Fares start at $2 for a one-ride trip, or it's $4 for an all-day pass.

There are also **buses** that run throughout the city. Visit the website for a comprehensive schedule, map, and fares.

Apache Trail and Superstition Mountains

Teddy Roosevelt took a tour through this area along the Apache Trail in 1911 and he compared it to the striking beauty of Yellowstone or Yosemite. Today, you can take a tour that's little changed from what Teddy experienced back in the day. Parts of this loop are still rugged, unpaved, rarely traveled, and offering a bit of a thrill as your vehicle narrowly negotiates rough terrain along steep drop-offs.

Visitors can choose to take the daunting 100-mile loop as a hefty day trip or just venture in along the roads as far as they like, taking in the scenery, stopping for a hike, setting up for a night of camping, or boating at one of the three lakes along the way.

Apache Trail Scenic Loop

© AVALON TRAVEL

0
0
10 mi
10 km

Four Peaks Wilderness

Salome Wilderness

Sierra Ancha Wilderness

Tonto National Forest

Salt River Canyon Wilderness

Tonto National Forest

Pinal Mountains

White Canyon Wilderness

Superstition Wilderness

Superstition Mountains

Salt

Roosevelt Lake

Roosevelt Dam

ROOSEVELT LAKE MARINA

Roosevelt

TONTO NATIONAL MONUMENT

Apache Lake

Apache Dam

APACHE LAKE MARINA & RESORT

Horse Mesa Dam

APACHE TRAIL HISTORIC ROAD

FISH CREEK HILL

REAVIS SCHOOL

Iron Mountain

CANYON LAKE MARINA/LAKESIDE RESTAURANT & CANTINA

Canyon Lake

Mormon Flat Dam

Saguaro Lake

BOULDER CANYON TRAILHEAD

Tortilla Flat

Salt River

MAMMOTH STEAKHOUSE & SALOON

GOLDFIELD GHOST TOWN

SUPERSTITION MOUNTAIN MUSEUM

FIRST WATER TRAILHEAD

LOST DUTCHMAN STATE PARK

LOST GOLDMINE (HIEROGLYPHIC TRAILHEAD)

Weaver's Needle

PERALTA TRAILHEAD

GOLD CANYON GOLF RESORT & SPA

Gold Canyon

Apache Junction

ARIZONA RENAISSANCE FESTIVAL

BOYCE THOMPSON STATE PARK

Superior

Miami

Globe

BESH BA GOWAH

60

88

87

288

188

77

70

60

60

No matter how you choose to experience this area, any glimpse of the sharp, igneous rock spires and walls of the Superstition Mountains is downright inspiring.

APACHE TRAIL SCENIC LOOP

What we refer to as the Apache Trail Scenic Loop is a combination of roads that start in the far east city of Apache Junction. From Highway 60, you'll hop onto State Route 88 (aka Apache Trail) where the road climbs and curves deeper into the Superstition Wilderness. A rugged, unpaved road and three lakes (created by a series of dams along the Salt River) later, explorers then take Arizona 188 southeast through a very deserted area until reaching U.S. 60 near the towns of Globe, Miami, and Superior. From there, it's just a long drive back to the city.

The following describes this trip in the order that one would experience it as described above, starting with State Route 88. There's a lot to take in that could take well over a day so be choosy. But know this: It's an experience unlike any other, which mixes remote mountain passes with water sports and Old West legends. You'll love every minute of it.

Apache Junction

After exiting Highway 60 to Idaho Road (Exit 196), you have reached the city of Apache Junction. While it's considered a dusty old town way out on the outskirts of the Valley, there are quite a few things to do.

Consider the **Superstition Mountain Museum** (4087 N. Apache Trail Hwy. 88, 480/983-4888, www.superstitionmountainmuseum.org, 9am-4pm daily, $5), which is jam-packed with old-timey, Old West relics and photographs that tell the story of how the area was settled, unsettled, and settled again. Highlights include Boot Hill, where funny inscriptions are borrowed from other cemeteries across the west; a massive 20-stamp mill that crushes material looking for gold; and the very noticeable white Elvis Memorial Chapel,

which shows movies filmed at "Apacheland," a 1,800-acre movie set that closed in 2004.

Another fun stop is **Goldfield Ghost Town** (4650 Mammoth Mine Rd, 480/983-0333, goldfieldghosttown.com, 10am-5pm daily), where you can walk down Main Street to visit shops, historic buildings, and a museum. Panning for gold, a train ride, and an Old West gun fight are also in store. Maybe it's the remote backdrop, but for whatever reason, this is the least hokey of all the touristy Western towns. And the history is rich: the place was established in 1895 and boasted three saloons, a boarding house, general store, blacksmith, brewery, meat market, and a school. Head into **Mammoth Steakhouse & Saloon** (4650 N. Mammoth Mine Rd., 480/983-6402, goldfieldghosttown.com, 11am-9pm daily, $7-23) for burgers, steaks, and beer.

You can't write about things to do in Apache Junction without mentioning the **Annual Arizona Renaissance Festival & Artisan Marketplace** (12601 E. Highway 60, www.royalfaires.com), which takes place just south of town. Yes, the weekends of February through April of every year, Highway 60 is choked with lords and ladies patiently waiting in their sedans for entrance into the festival, which features jousts, people posing as statue fountains, and other off-beat entertainers working the circuit. Jewelry, clothing, carnival rides, and other vendors are abundant as well as food, food, food (don't leave without your own turkey leg).

Lost Dutchman State Park

You don't have to travel far to have a full-on outdoor experience at **Lost Dutchman State Park** (6109 N. Apache Trail Hwy. 88, 480/982-4485, https://azstateparks.com/Parks/LODU, $7 per vehicle) where hiking and biking, tent and RV camping is available for all to enjoy. Named after the legend of the Lost Dutchman who supposedly discovered a rich gold mine in the Superstition Mountains, the park now acts as a hiking hub for people wanting to explore the area. With its own network of

Lost Dutchman State Park

trails that connect to longer trails into the Superstition Mountains, you can pitch camp at one of its 134 campsites (complete with restrooms and showers) for a multi-day adventure of day hikes. The park also has trails specific for mountain biking, a Junior Ranger program, and many day-use picnic sites.

Canyon Lake

Next on this adventure is the first of three lakes created by a series of dams. Canyon Lake is reached after driving a hefty climb up winding roads and across a one-way bridge. The reveal is quite dramatic as you see the glittering blue waters among the rocks and cacti. It's pretty enough to drive through but a stop at **Canyon Lake Marina** (16802 N.E. Highway 88, 480-288-9233, www.canyonlakemarina. com) might just be in order. If you're up for a swim, consider the day use campground area with a beautiful beach and picnic area for $20 per car and up to six people (first come, first served). Explore the whole lake and inner waterways with a ride on **Dolly Steamboat** (dollysteamboat.com) where you'll no doubt see wildlife like bald eagles, big horn sheep, and waterfowl. The guided tours vary from the daytime scenic nature cruise to the twilight dinner cruise and the astronomy dinner

cruise with on-board telescopes. The fine folks who run the marina also offer overnight camping so you can enjoy a host of other activities such as jet skiing, hiking, fishing, and boat rentals. FYI, it's best to make a reservation in advance for overnight camping.

Thankfully, you won't have to pack in your own food for a visit to Canyon Lake because the **Lakeside Restaurant & Cantina** (480/288-8290, www.canyonlakerestaurant. com, 10:30am-5pm Mon.-Thurs., 10:30am-8pm Fri., 8am-8pm Sat., 8am-6pm Sun., $8-12) is happy to serve. While the food may be hit or miss, the view certainly is a big hit and sipping a cold cocktail at the bar overlooking the water is heavenly.

Tortilla Flat

Okay, so we've told you to go to a number of "Old West" towns in this book but this one may be the most credible of them all. Tucked way back in the mountains (milepost 213) sits **Tortilla Flat** (www.tortillaflataz.com), affectionately called "the town too tough to die." This small, grassy valley and the creek running through it were natural pit stops for ancient native peoples, Spanish explorers, and prospectors searching for gold, and it's an authentic piece of history that became a stagecoach stop in 1904. Today, six people (yes, six) live in Tortilla Flat, where a restaurant, ice-cream shop, saloon, country store, and gift shop treat passersby to a charming visit.

If you continue this drive, Tortilla Flat is the last stop on the paved portion of Apache Trail State Route 88. After milepost 220, the road is no longer paved and can get pretty rough and twisty. While many say a two-wheel drive car will make it, you'll feel much safer in a high-clearance, four-wheel drive vehicle.

Apache Lake

Welcome to lake number two (out of three) on your scenic loop. Just after passing through Tortilla Flat you'll see the beautiful waters of Apache Lake to the north. Soon, at milepost 229, you'll find the **Apache Lake Vista,** which is worth a stop if you're passing through.

For a more involved visit, turn off on Road 79 to the **Apache Lake Marina and Resort** (20909 E. Apache Trail 6, 928/467-2511, www.apachelake.com, $80-105 d), which might get a snicker or two at the use of "resort" to describe it. It's a humble place (which is to be expected, given the location) that is outdated and rather worn. Owners admit that the motel portion of the "resort" is a work in progress, so don't expect much. However, the onsite restaurant and bar, **Jack's Landing** ($8-17) isn't bad and serves sandwiches, burgers, and other American fare. The real bonus here is the 27 single space RV and camper hookups at $30-35 per day.

For campers, one of the best campsites in the state is at **Burnt Corral Recreation Site** (www.fs.usda.gov, $8 per vehicle, Tonto Pass required) where a whopping 82 units are available, with some located right on the lake's edge. It doesn't get much better than that.

Roosevelt Dam and Lake

Your reward for white-knuckling it through the rugged road along the tail end of the Apache Trail is **Roosevelt Dam and Lake.**

The popular area is accessed easily by taking Highway 188 so there's a little more life here than you've seen for the past ten miles. And life as we know it started here way back in 1911 with the completion of the Theodore Roosevelt Dam, creating what was then the largest man-made lake in the world. Now it's just the largest lake in Arizona but still attracts desert-weary vacationers wanting to boat, fish, camp, or hike near a body of water (how novel!). Be sure to pull off at the signs before reaching the lake to take in the view from the **Roosevelt Dam Overlook.**

The area is home to the **Roosevelt Lake Marina** (28085 AZ-188, 602/977-7170, www.rlmaz.com), which is the hub for all activities listed above. And just a few miles south of the marina, campers go crazy for the **Windy Hill Recreation Site** (www.fs.usda.gov, $8 per vehicle, Tonto Pass Required), which features 347 camp units with shade ramadas, water hydrants, playgrounds, hiking trails, and showers. The Tonto Pass costs $8 per day and is available for purchase at the Tonto National Forest offices (2324 E. McDowell Rd., 602/225-5295) and at a variety of retail outlets in the city or along routes that visitors use to reach recreation sites (look for signs at gas stations as you drive). Visit www.fs.usda.gov/detail/tonto/passes-permits for more information.

Tonto National Monument

Now that you finished the Apache Trail State Route 88 portion of the tour and have successfully turned onto Highway 188 heading southeast (right?!), your next stop is **Tonto National Monument** (26260 N. Arizona Hwy. 188, 928/467-2241, www.nps.gov/tont, 8am-5pm daily, $5 per person). For folks interested in ancient history, this place is really spectacular. The monument protects two well-preserved cliff dwellings where the Salado people lived around 700 years ago. Back then, the Salt River ran wild and the area was rich with natural resources, bustling with people and agriculture. This is just one example of the various peoples who have lived and traveled in the Tonto Basin over the centuries.

The **Lower Cliff Dwelling** is accessible from 8am to 4pm and is a one-mile walk that takes about an hour. To see the 40-room **Upper Cliff Dwelling,** guided tours are available (make reservations in advance) for a three-mile hike that has some steep inclines and is suited to people in good shape with hiking gear. If you're interested in this site and don't want to do the whole Apache Trail Scenic Loop, simply take U.S. 60 toward Globe and turn left on State Highway 188. Continue 25 miles and Tonto National Monument will be on your left.

Globe, Miami, and Superior

Welcome back to civilization! Once you've cleared Highway 188, you slam into the good old U.S. 60. If you have surly teenagers with you, you'll probably just head back to town, but if you're still looking to kill some time, stop off at one of these three towns for some sightseeing, shopping, and eating.

Hang a left from Highway 188 to reach Globe, a tiny historic city that has attracted a population of artists and dusty desert rats. Big surprise, it was a mining town established at the turn of the 20th century and named after a globe shaped piece of pure silver discovered in the area. While Globe and Miami are often simply referred to as "Globe-Miami" since they are so closely located along the U.S. 60, to hit Miami from Highway 188, you'll turn right heading southwest into town. The area still relies mostly on copper mining and ranching as its economic base but loves to offer hospitality to travelers.

SIGHTS

During your visit, take a trip to **Besh Ba Gowah Archaeological Park** (1000 S. Jesse Haynes Rd., 928/425-0320, www.globeaz. gove/visitors/besh-ba-gowah, 9am-4:30pm daily, $5 per adult, free children ages 12 and under), which features the nearly 800-year-old ruins of a Salado Indian pueblo, an ethno-botanical garden showing how native plants were used in the ancient peoples' daily lives, and a museum. If you're swinging by in December, check out the **Annual Festival of Lights,** during which 2200 glowing luminaries are placed along the ruin walls.

Another popular stop is the **Cobre Valley Center for the Arts** (101 N. Broad St., 928/425-0884, globearts.org, 10am-5pm Mon.-Sat., noon-4pm Sun.) housed in the former Gila County Courthouse, where the work of local and regional artists are presented on the main gallery floor; the old courtroom houses a community theater.

FOOD AND ACCOMMODATIONS

Hungry? There's a smattering of decent Sonoran Mexican food restaurants in Globe that are all pretty decent, so don't be fooled by the humble **Los Robertos** (1666 E Ash St., 928/425-3221, 7am-9pm daily, $3-10). Many say it's the best Mexican food around, serving what one would expect from a Sonoran menu like tacos, burritos, enchiladas, rice, and beans. If you're craving something else, try **Nurd Berger Café** (420 S. Hill St., 480/316-0882, 10:30am-8pm Mon.-Sat., $6-13), which has a sleek, contemporary vibe rare in these parts. The simple menu features super tasty burgers and there are steak and chicken sandwiches, too.

Tired? We've got two really excellent places to tell you about. **The Noftsger Hill Inn** (425 North St., 928/425-2260, www.noftsgerhillinn.com, $90-135 d) is found in a converted elementary school. Classrooms-turned-guest rooms provide ample space, each with a sitting area and private bath. Some even have a fireplace. And the chalkboards in every room that act as guest books are beyond charming. The second recommendation for this area is, without a doubt, the **Dream Manor Inn** (1 Dream Manor Dr., 928/425-2754, www.dreammanorinn.com, $80-200 d). This boutique resort is downright perfect from soup to nuts. With 20 rooms, each expertly decorated in a modern classic style, the resort offers sweeping views from its location perched on a hill. With swimming pool, putting green, waterfalls, walking paths, and free Wi-Fi, there's no better place to stay.

Boyce Thompson Arboretum State Park

If you enjoyed a tour through Desert Botanical Gardens in Phoenix and want more, more, and more plants to peruse, head to the **Boyce Thompson Arboretum** (37615 U.S. Highway 60, 520/689-2811, www.azstateparks.com, 8am-4pm daily, summer hours vary, $10 per adult, $5 per child ages 5-12, free for children ages 4 and younger) which offers a grand tour of 3,000 desert plants in an outdoor museum that's over 1,000 acres huge. More than 300 species of birds, mammals, reptiles, and amphibians also live in the grounds and its 1.25-mile main trail promises dramatic scenery courtesy of the Picket Post Mountain nearby. Guided walking tours are organized by the nearby University of Arizona and include many themes focusing on trees, butterflies, and edible-medicinal desert plants (check ag.arizona.edu/bta for upcoming events).

HIKING THE SUPERSTITION MOUNTAINS

The title of this section is almost laughable if you know how ginormous the Superstition Wilderness happens to be (just about 160,000 acres, no biggie). Still, hard-core hikers in the Valley make it a lifetime goal to get the lay of the land via a well-maintained trail system. Follow these suggestions for the best day hikes accessible from trailheads close to the city.

Northwest

The most popular hike in the Superstition Mountains is, by far, **Siphon Draw Trail to the Flatiron.** Taken in its entirety, the six-mile trail climbs a massive 2,750 feet to the top of a huge rock formation visible from miles away. The trail begins innocently with a two-mile hike across a field (that is covered with wildflowers in spring, btw) until it runs smack into the mountain. From there is a grueling down-on-all-fours crawl up a drainage path to the top, with a few vertical scrambles along the way. Only attempt this if you're in good shape with good shoes and a good pair of gloves. Oh, and be sure to start good and early—this one is going to take at least six hours. The trailhead is located at the Siphon Draw Trailhead in **Lost Dutchman State Park** (6109 N. Apache Trail Hwy. 88, 480/982-4485, azstateparks.com/Parks/LODU, $7 per vehicle). For an easier hike, simply follow the Siphon Draw Trail for about two miles in and turn around once the heavy climbing begins.

Next on your Superstitions hiking bucket list is the **Black Mesa Loop,** which is an all-day, nine-mile adventure crossing washes, thick riparian areas, and a cholla cactus forest. Not for the faint of heart, this hike will take about five hours and requires trail-reading and map skills. From the First Water Trailhead, hang a left from the main trail entrance to follow the Second Water Trail. You'll do a bit of climbing for about two miles, then turn right to follow the Black Mesa Trail heading southeast. At three miles total, you're deep in the cholla forest and most likely won't see another soul for quite a while. Continue on for another two miles and (that's five miles total) turn right to follow Dutchman's Trail heading west. Just keep hoofing it along Dutchman's Trail, which curves northwest and neatly delivers you back to the trailhead. Sound complicated? Get yourself a good map (plug: there's a great trail map and description in MOON Take a Hike Phoenix). To get to the trailhead, follow S.R. 88 past Lost Dutchman State Park and turn right on First Water Road, which is unpaved but doable in most vehicles. The trail is located in Tonto National Forest, so no passes or fees are necessary.

Park at **Canyon Lake Marina** (16802 N.E. Highway 88, 480/288-9233, www.

canyonlakemarina.com) and cross the road to access **Boulder Canyon Trail.** This hike's a straight shot up a short hill and down into the canyon. We recommend going four miles in until you reach the junction with Second Water Trail, where you'll turn around. Once on the return trip, gear up for the brutal 460-foot climb back up the canyon. Out and back this hike will run you eight miles total and is a great training ground if you're planning to hike the Grand Canyon.

South

The Superstition Mountains are decidedly less accessible from the U.S. 60 but offer some of the most expansive views of the wilderness and the Valley below. The ever-popular **Hieroglyphic Trail** is pure delight and easy to follow at just three miles total. You'll follow the trail, which starts in a quiet neighborhood in Kings Ranch, over a very subtle incline until you enter a canyon that is totally covered in petroglyphs (ancient rock carvings) depicting wildlife, spirals, and other curious designs. The area also features tanks—deep pools of water carved into rock from harsh rainfall—that can be fun for a swim after the water has been refreshed by rainfall. Find the trailhead off the U.S. 60 heading north onto King's Ranch Road and following the signs to Cloud View Avenue.

Okay, the second most popular trail in all of the Superstition Mountains is the **Peralta Trail.** This beauty of a 4.5-mile,

up-and-back trek skirts along the walls of Peralta Canyon and ends at Fremont Saddle with a punch-me-in-the-face amazing view of Weaver's Needle, a volcanic rock plug that juts an astonishing 4,553 feet into the air—seemingly out of nowhere. Getting to the trailhead is easy; take the U.S. 60 to Peralta Road and follow it for just over seven miles to the Peralta trailhead. The road becomes a graded dirt road but most cars will travel it without issue.

GETTING THERE AND AROUND

To experience the Apache Trail Scenic Loop from central Phoenix, take U.S. 60 east to Idaho Road (Exit 196) and go north to Apache Trail State Route 88. Follow this northeast through the Superstitions and take note that the trail is unpaved shortly after hitting Tortilla Flat. Follow the narrow, dirt road to Highway 188 at Roosevelt Lake. Take Highway 188 southwest toward Globe and Miami, then take the U.S. 60 southwest back to the Valley.

If you're not wild about DIY-ing the drive, leave it to someone else and join an excursion by one of the many outdoor companies offering tours. Operating out of Goldfield Ghost Town, **Apache Trail Tours** (4650 N. Mammoth Mine Rd., 480/982-7661, www. apachetrailtours.com) is an obvious choice offering multiple adventures throughout the area starting around $80 for a 2-hour tour.

Scottsdale

Sights 120

Entertainment and Events 126

Shopping...................... 134

Sports and Recreation 140

Food 148

Accommodations.............. 159

Information and Services 165

Transportation................. 165

Vicinity of Scottsdale 167

Look for ★ to find recommended
sights, activities, dining, and lodging.

Highlights

★ **Old Town Scottsdale:** Take a walking tour of this bustling area, which includes museums, restaurants, bars, galleries, and Scottsdale City Hall (page 120).

★ **Scottsdale Museum of Contemporary Art:** This intimate museum of modern art, architecture, and design stands out in the capital of cowboy art. The permanent *Knight Rise* installation, which distorts your perception of Arizona's wide blue sky, is one of the most peaceful places in the world (page 123).

★ **Taliesin West:** Frank Lloyd Wright's winter home blends the architect's trademark techniques and design motifs with the desert landscape. The National Landmark is still a working architecture school (page 125).

★ **Nightlife:** Scottsdale's downtown transforms from a shoppers' paradise to a bumpin', grindin' mass of bronzed bodies when the sun goes down. The city's sizzling bars, lounges, and clubs are famous—and occasionally infamous—for their posh crowds and steep prices (page 127).

★ **Art Galleries:** Scottsdale's downtown arts district showcases a wide range from Southwestern pieces to avant-garde works (page 138).

★ **Golf:** The city's sprawling courses tee up some of the best golf in the world. The lush fairways contrast beautifully with the natural, rocky desert landscape (page 142).

★ **Hiking the McDowell Mountains:** The

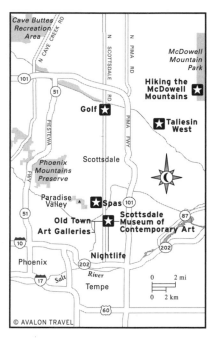

massive range of the McDowell Mountains dominates the north region of Scottsdale. Luckily, the whole area can be explored via a spider's web of trails that lead through every peak, ridge, and wash (page 144).

★ **Spas:** Scottsdale's opulent spas impress even the most jaded. Revel in the outdoor showers, Native American-inspired treatments, healing mineral pools, and chic decor (page 146).

Unlike Phoenix's other suburban communities, Scottsdale easily stands on its own. As the glamorous, overindulged sibling to Phoenix, Scottsdale demands the spotlight, luring residents and visitors to its resorts, restaurants, clubs, five-star spas, and eclectic boutiques.

Despite its flashy exterior (and occasionally hedonistic impulses), Scottsdale is still firmly rooted in its decades-old slogan as "The West's Most Western Town." The city is bordered to the east by mountains and the agricultural land of the Salt River Pima-Maricopa Indian Community, which has kept the city's sprawling tendencies in check. It's still one of the few spaces in metropolitan Phoenix where you can truly feel like you are living in the desert—perhaps the city's greatest luxury.

ORIENTATION

Scottsdale sits in the northeast of the Valley of the Sun and is divided into three areas. The compact, southern part of the city, downtown, is where you'll find Old Town and the arts districts of 5th Avenue and Marshall Way as well as the city's best shops and nightlife venues.

The area is bordered by the college town of Tempe to the south and by Phoenix to the west.

The central part of Scottsdale extends east, featuring an indistinguishable sprawl of housing developments and strip malls called the Shea Corridor. You'll also find the community of Paradise Valley, the Valley's answer to Beverly Hills and home to big-name celebrities and five-star resorts.

Within the last couple of decades, the northern half of the city has become one of the most sought-after areas in the region and has begun to creep into formerly pristine desert and the relatively isolated arts communities of Cave Creek and Carefree. Fortunately, developers have taken an enlightened approach to the city's growth, sparing much of the area's indigenous wildlife.

Previous: Kierland Golf Club; *Knight Rise* installation by James Turrell at the SMoCA. **Above:** sign for Old Town Scottsdale.

Scottsdale and Vicinity

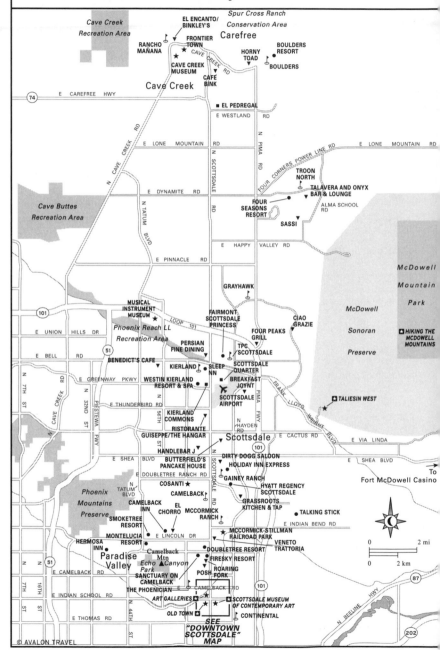

Cave Creek Recreation Area

Spur Cross Ranch Conservation Area

Carefree

EL ENCANTO/ BINKLEY'S

RANCHO MAÑANA

FRONTIER TOWN

HORNY TOAD

BOULDERS RESORT

CAVE CREEK MUSEUM

CAVE CREEK RD

BOULDERS

CAFÉ BINK

Cave Creek

74

E CAREFREE HWY

EL PEDREGAL

E WESTLAND RD

E LONE MOUNTAIN RD

N CAVE CREEK RD

N SCOTTSDALE RD

N PIMA RD

FOUR CORNERS POWER LINE RD

E LONE MOUNTAIN RD

Cave Buttes Recreation Area

N TATUM BLVD

E DYNAMITE RD

TROON NORTH

TALAVERA AND ONYX BAR & LOUNGE

ALMA SCHOOL RD

FOUR SEASONS RESORT

SASSI

E PINNACLE RD

E HAPPY VALLEY RD

McDowell Mountain Park

GRAYHAWK

101

MUSICAL INSTRUMENT MUSEUM

LOOP 101

McDowell

Sonoran

Preserve

HIKING THE McDOWELL MOUNTAINS

Phoenix Reach LL Recreation Area

FAIRMONT SCOTTSDALE PRINCESS

CIAO GRAZIE

E UNION HILLS DR

FOUR PEAKS GRILL

51

PERSIAN FINE DINING

TPC SCOTTSDALE

E BELL RD

BENEDICT'S CAFE

SCOTTSDALE QUARTER

KIERLAND

SLEEP INN

SCOTTSDALE QUARTER

N 7TH ST

N CAVE CREEK RD

E GREENWAY PKWY

WESTIN KIERLAND RESORT & SPA

BREAKFAST JOYNT

N 32ND ST

N 56TH ST

E THUNDERBIRD RD

SCOTTSDALE AIRPORT

PIESTEWA FWY

KIERLAND COMMONS

N HAYDEN RD

PIMA RD

RISTORANTE GUISEPPE/THE HANGAR

Scottsdale

E CACTUS RD

E VIA LINDA

TALIESIN WEST

FRANK LLOYD WRIGHT BLVD

HANDLEBAR J

101

E SHEA BLVD

BUTTERFIELD'S PANCAKE HOUSE

DIRTY DOGG SALOON

HOLIDAY INN EXPRESS

E SHEA BLVD

E DOUBLETREE RANCH RD

GAINEY RANCH

To Fort McDowell Casino

Phoenix Mountains Preserve

N TATUM BLVD

COSANTI

CAMELBACK

HYATT REGENCY SCOTTSDALE

N SCOTTSDALE RD

CAMELBACK INN

EL CHORRO

McCORMICK RANCH

GRASSROOTS KITCHEN & TAP

TALKING STICK

SMOKETREE RESORT

E LINCOLN DR

E INDIAN BEND RD

0   2 mi

MONTELUCIA RESORT

HERMOSA INN

Camelback Mtn

Echo Canyon Park

McCORMICK-STILLMAN RAILROAD PARK

VENETO TRATTORIA

0   2 km

Paradise Valley

51

E CAMELBACK RD

SANCTUARY ON CAMELBACK

DOUBLETREE RESORT

FIRESKY RESORT

POSH

ROARING FORK

87

N 7TH ST

N 16TH ST

N 44TH ST

E INDIAN SCHOOL RD

THE PHOENICIAN

ART GALLERIES

E CAMELBACK RD

101

E THOMAS RD

OLD TOWN

SCOTTSDALE MUSEUM OF CONTEMPORARY ART

CONTINENTAL

N BEELINE HWY

202

SEE "DOWNTOWN SCOTTSDALE" MAP

PLANNING YOUR TIME

Don't rush your time in Scottsdale. Relax and relish a make-believe word where life really does consist of endless days soaking up sunshine, sipping tequila, and dining alfresco at topnotch restaurants that forgo the formality of suits and ties. After all, this is the city that invented resort casual—both in terms of attire and attitude.

Half the fun of Scottsdale is knowing you don't have to be anywhere or doing anything. You could easily spend a week enjoying days by the pool, playing rounds of golf, browsing in galleries, and getting pampered at one of the city's five-star spas.

If you only have a weekend, though, be sure to see Frank Lloyd Wright's winter home, Taliesin West, before witnessing the clash of civilizations in Old Town. The eclectic mix of expensive galleries, trendy clubs, yuppie biker bars, and boutiques selling Western and Native American kitsch creates some the best people-watching this side of the Rocky Mountains. Bars and restaurants literally slide away their glass walls from November through April, giving you a front row seat to the street-side spectacle.

Visiting during the summer's triple-digit heat will force you to change your plans—both in terms of what you do and when you do it. But that's not a bad thing. Take a cue from the natives—both wildlife and residents—who switch to a more nocturnal schedule from May well into October. Wake at dawn to take advantage of an early tee time or a sunrise hike at one of Scottsdale's craggy peaks. Then spend your afternoons in one of the city's air-conditioned malls, like Scottsdale Fashion Square. You can also hit up the resort pool for a wicked party featuring limitless day drinking while local DJs spin. When late afternoon arrives, make like a lizard and find some shade for a nap (the thermometer hits its hottest point around 4pm).

Come out to play in the evening when the sun dips below the horizon and the desert's beige tones and blue sky give way to a rich burst of color. The Technicolor sunsets are just a preview of the evening's lime-green margaritas, vibrant Southwestern cuisine, and flashy lounges and clubs. And as the temperature drops 20 degrees throughout the night, let the warm, weightless air convince you that living in the desert can be heaven.

HISTORY

The city of Scottsdale may look new, but its roots date back to the ancient Hohokam civilization, which first inhabited the Salt River Valley circa 300 BC until the Hohokam mysteriously abandoned their villages in the 16th century. Their canals served as a foundation for the Pima Indian village known as Vasai Svasoni, or "rotting hay." Although it wasn't the most appealing name, the area proved to be an enduring home for the Pima, who still live in the Salt River Pima-Indian Community, which borders Scottsdale's city limits.

In 1888, U.S. Army chaplain Winfield Scott bought 640 acres of rocky, desert land northeast of Phoenix. At $2.50 an acre, the purchase may be the Valley's best land deal on record. Scott saw the cheap desert land and its still-functioning canals as rife with opportunity, as well an ideal climate to recover from wounds he had sustained in the Civil War.

Scott and his wife, Helen, became the first of a succession of New Yorkers who would abandon the East Coast's cold, gray winters—and tell their friends about it. Scott used his oratory gifts to convince other families to move to his fledgling community of Orangedale. You can still see the olive trees Scott planted to mark the border of his original 40-acre orange grove down the center of 2nd Street and Civic Center Boulevard (across from the Scottsdale Center for the Performing Arts and Scottsdale Stadium). The citrus trees didn't prove to be as hardy, dying in a drought in the late 1890s.

During the next few decades, the small community attracted cowboys, ranchers, and miners, as well as Native Americans looking to trade goods and tuberculosis patients seeking the dry desert air to recover from their respiratory ailments.

The mild winter climate and stark landscape even lured famed architect Frank Lloyd Wright, who was in Phoenix to consult on the design of the Arizona Biltmore Resort. Wright was so taken by the Sonoran Desert that he established his "winter camp," Taliesin West, at the base of the McDowell Mountains in 1937. The rocky desert site would serve as a constant source of inspiration until his death in 1959.

Following World War II, airmen who had trained at Scottsdale Airfield returned to the city, bringing their families and green lawns from the Midwest. The growing community, which was officially incorporated in 1951, attracted burgeoning high-tech corporations, like Motorola in 1956. Bill Keane, Scottsdale's answer to *Peanuts* creator Charles Schultz, reflected the postwar suburban boom in his comic strip, *Family Circus.*

Scottsdale became the first city in the nation to enact a sign ordinance in 1969, which restricted the size and height of billboards—a controversial measure that was even challenged at the U.S. Supreme Court.

New resorts and the availability of air-conditioning only increased Scottsdale's popularity. City leaders annexed huge swaths of land in the north, areas once roamed only by ranchers and wildlife. Developers happily created large master-planned communities with amenities like parks and golf courses, attracting retirees and young families. The skyrocketing home prices, new business parks, and chichi art galleries and shopping centers earned the increasingly affluent city the nickname "Snottsdale" by residents of neighboring communities.

Since the 1950s, Scottsdale has grown from 2,000 residents to nearly a quarter of a million. It seems the country's "Most Livable City," as it was deemed by the United States Conference of Mayors in 1993, has become one of its most desired.

Sights

Scottsdale's biggest attraction is the city's unapologetic resort lifestyle. You'll want to spend your time like the locals: shopping, eating and drinking, browsing art galleries, hitting the links, and hiking some of the region's most interesting desert mountains. Indulge at one of the world-class spas, and make time to visit Frank Lloyd Wright's winter home, Taliesin West.

DOWNTOWN

Downtown Scottsdale is one of the few places in The Valley that doesn't require a car to navigate. In fact, driving a car in this area can be a bit of a hassle, so park that thing, get out, and take a walk to discover beautiful public spaces and museums speckled throughout the bars, shopping, and restaurants the area is known for.

★ Old Town Scottsdale

Old Town Scottsdale really is one of the most adorably Western places in the United States. There's no better place to begin a tour of "The West's Most Western Town." This touristy hodgepodge of restaurants, bars, and Old West-themed boutiques is a little cheesy to a cynic, so our advice is to not be a cynic and embrace the cowboy vibe. You'll find some historic sites along with the kitschy shopping and art. And even if you're not a big shopper, the live music courtesy of singing cowboys on horseback and Native American performers makes for an entertaining "only in Arizona" experience.

Start at the beautifully landscaped **Scottsdale Civic Center Mall,** a 21-acre park ringed by chic hotels and restaurants, hole-in-the-wall bars, arts venues, and the

Downtown Scottsdale

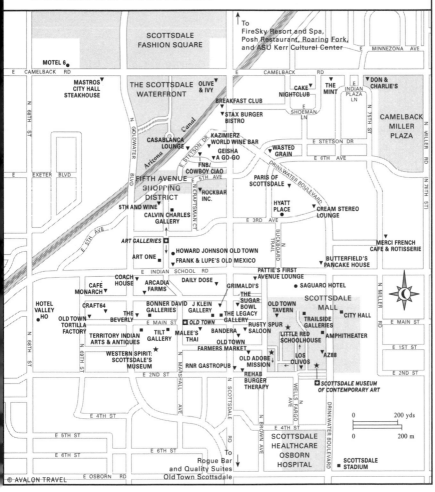

city hall and library. The walkways, shaded by mesquite trees and cool fountains attract visitors and residents year-round. You're likely to see friends playing chess in the sunken garden or young girls posing for pictures in elaborate white dresses for their *quinceañeras* (a Mexican coming-of-age ceremony held on a girl's 15th birthday).

Head east to the outdoor **amphitheater,** a popular site for festivals and outdoor concerts. You can see pop artist Robert Indiana's iconic *Love* sculpture on the lawn, along with a host of other public artworks.

On the far eastern end of the plaza, you'll see the Scottsdale **City Hall** (3939 N. Drinkwater Blvd., 480/312-3111, www.scottsdaleaz.gov), designed by native Arizonan architect Benny Gonzales, whose mid-20th-century modern interpretation of traditional Southwest design transformed the region's architecture.

Across from the statue of Winfield and

the Scottsdale City Hall

Helen Scott on the western end of the mall, you'll find the **Little Red Schoolhouse** (7333 E. Scottsdale Mall, 480/945-4499, www.scottsdalemuseum.org, 10am-5pm Wed.-Sat., noon-4pm Sun., closed July-Aug., free), the original 1909 Scottsdale Grammar School that now houses the Scottsdale Historical Society. Inside, artifacts from the Scotts' home and a collection of historic photographs illustrate the city's modest beginnings as a territorial farming community.

From here, keep heading west and you'll find the real Old West stuff along the pedestrian-friendly streets that surround Scottsdale Road (the area spans north to south from Indian School to Osborn Road, and east to west from Goldwater Boulevard to Drinkwater Boulevard—ish). Poke around, mosey, and stroll through the sidewalks filled with tiny shops, bars, restaurants, and galleries complete with Old West facades on some of the store fronts.

Western Spirit: Scottsdale's Museum of the West

One of the newest museums to grace Scottsdale is **Western Spirit: Scottsdale's Museum of the West** (3830 N. Marshall Way, 480/686-9539, www.scottsdalemuseumwest.org, 9:30am-5pm Tues.-Wed., Fri.-Sat., 9:30am-9pn Thurs., 11am-5pm Sun., $13 per adult, $8 per child, children 5 and under free), which opened in January 2015. This beautiful, modern building is located in the heart of downtown and tells the story of how the West was settled through historic artifacts, fine art, film, and docent tours. Gaze upon an incredible collection of over 800 saddles, guns, poker chips, and sheriff badges or learn the story of the early American West through paintings, pottery, and photography. There are four ongoing exhibitions to enjoy as well as a smart roster of rotating shows that span art, history, and other visual storytelling.

Old Adobe Mission

Established originally as Our Lady of Perpetual Help, Scottsdale's first Catholic church was built in 1933 by Mexican and Yaqui Indian families who settled in the area. Today, the **Old Adobe Mission** (3821 N. Brown Ave., 480/947-4331, www.olphaz.org, 10am-4pm daily Oct.-May, free admission) is being restored to its former glory and is still in use as a spiritual center. The brilliant white facade and domed bell tower of the Spanish Colonial Revival church were designed to resemble the Mission of San Xavier del Bac,

the Old Adobe Mission

south of Tucson. Peek inside to see the building's original adobe bricks through a small cutaway in the plaster on the north wall. The bricks—which were made by blending local soil, straw, and water, then molded and baked in the sun—allow the walls to "breathe," moderating the church's temperature in both summer and winter.

★ Scottsdale Museum of Contemporary Art

On the southern end of the Scottsdale Civic Center Mall, next to the Scottsdale Center for the Performing Arts, you'll see the city's best piece of contemporary architecture. The **Scottsdale Museum of Contemporary Art** (7374 E. 2nd St., 480/874-4666, www. smoca.org, noon-5pm Tues.-Wed., noon-9pm Thurs.-Sat., noon-5pm Sun., $7 adults, $5 students, children 15 or younger free, admission free Thurs. and after 5 pm Fri.-Sat.) specializes in contemporary art, architecture, and design, providing a refuge for avant-garde art lovers in the land of cowboy paintings. Take a walk around the building before heading in. The "eggplant gray" stucco is meant to evoke the McDowell Mountains to the east, while the shimmering steel facade reflects the frequently blue Arizona sky.

Inside, Will Bruder, the Desert Modernist architect behind Phoenix's Burton Barr Central Library, deftly converted four theaters of an old cinema into a series of flexible galleries. The ever-changing lineup of exhibitions highlights today's movements in the art world and is the best in the Valley. The museum is small, which is preferable for viewing the mind-bending, challenging works on display. Whatever you do, do not miss the permanent outdoor installation *Knight Rise,* a James Turrell "Skyspace"—an oval-shaped concrete room with a single opening in the ceiling. Gaze through an oculus in the ceiling, similar to Rome's Pantheon, as the smooth, gray walls distort your perception of sky, focusing your attention on the changing colors from the morning's bright blues and evening's deep purples to gathering gray clouds on a stormy day. It's one of the most peaceful places in the city. *Knight Rise* is a public art piece and can be viewed free of charge (just check in with the front desk first) but visiting the interior of the museum is highly recommended.

CENTRAL SCOTTSDALE AND PARADISE VALLEY

Central Scottsdale and Paradise Valley may not have the concentration of attractions that

Downtown Scottsdale has, but that's exactly what makes it a worthwhile destination. The sprawling properties and parks that populate the area exist in the beautiful foothills of Camelback Mountain.

Cosanti

Architect Paolo Soleri moved from Italy in 1947 to Scottsdale for a fellowship with Frank Lloyd Wright at Taliesin West. More than a half century later, he has emerged as one of the region's most innovative architects, with an organic style that focuses on his philosophy, "arcology" (architecture and ecology). In other words, he pushed for this whole sustainability movement before it got trendy. **Cosanti** (6433 E. Doubletree Ranch Rd., 480/948-6145, www.cosanti.com, 9am-5pm Mon.-Sat., 11am-5pm Sun., free) served as Soleri's gallery, studio, and home, and reflects many of his theories on environmentally responsible design. The visionary architect and local darling passed away in 2013 at the age of 94. His property remains and includes his original subterranean "Earth House," outdoor studios, and living spaces set amid terraced courtyards and shaded paths.

Much of Soleri's Arcosanti (page 229), an experimental artists' community 70 miles north of Phoenix, is funded by the sale of his "windbells," available for purchase at Cosanti. These metal-and-ceramic wind chimes, which range in price from under $5 to upwards of $1,000, are designed and forged at Cosanti's on-site foundry and ceramics studio. If you're lucky, you may catch a viewing of artists pouring the molten hot metal as a part of the bronze casting process.

McCormick-Stillman Railroad Park

Children and train buffs love **McCormick-Stillman Railroad Park** (7301 E. Indian Bend Rd., 480/312-2312, www.therailroad-park.com, open daily, closed Thanksgiving and Christmas, free), a popular city park near Paradise Valley that began as the personal ranch of Anne and Fowler McCormick, who was a grandson of John D. Rockefeller. Today, visitors can ride a scale reproduction of a Colorado narrow-gauge railroad that was donated by Anne's son, Guy Stillman (rumor has it Walt Disney tried to buy it for one of his parks) and the train carries passengers on a one-mile loop around the whole park.

The park has an air of Old Americana meets Old West to it, with a general store selling hand-dipped ice cream and an adobe-style

windbells at Cosanti

Taliesin West

cacti among the newly-built houses and shopping centers here. But the best example of embracing the landscape through architecture came long before the current developments: Taliesin West.

★ Taliesin West

A literal hothouse for design, Frank Lloyd Wright's winter home **Taliesin West** (12345 Taliesin Dr., 480/860-2700, www.franklloydwright.org, 8:30am-5:30pm daily, tours range from $26-75) is the perfect synthesis of architecture and the desert.

Wright's use of local sand, gravel, and stone (what he called "desert masonry") creates the impression that the complex emerged out of the ground. He masterfully incorporated the environment by integrating indoor and outdoor spaces, diffusing harsh sunlight through canvas ceilings, and creating asymmetrical lines evocative of the surrounding mountains. The effect is simply stunning.

In 1927, Wright first came to Phoenix from his Wisconsin home, Taliesin, to serve as a consultant on the building of Arizona Biltmore. He was so captivated by the desert landscape and light that in 1937 he used the money from his Falling Water commission to purchase 600 acres of land in the foothills of the McDowell Mountains.

Wright's original "winter camp" evolved into a small cooperative community, where his architecture school apprentices helped with the building of Taliesin West and lived on-site in communal sleeping spaces. They were expected to study, help with chores, and even perform in the Cabaret Theater and Music Pavilion, as Wright thought his students should be well-rounded.

Some students chose to live in tents around the property, where they could experiment with their own designs and building techniques. This practice grew into a more formalized program of "apprentice shelters" that continues today, with older structures eventually being razed to make room for the designs of new students.

Today, this National Historic Landmark

playground. The beautifully restored carousel and shaded ramadas make it a popular spot for parties, concerts, and events throughout the year.

Antique engines and train cars dot the property, including a Pullman car that was used by every president from Herbert Hoover to Dwight Eisenhower. Be sure to check out the "Merci Train," one of 49 boxcars donated by France to thank Americans for their aid after World War II. The cars were originally loaded with personal belongings that ranged from wooden shoes and toys to wedding dresses and war medals from dead soldiers. Admission to the park is free, with $2 tickets required to ride the train, carousel, or to visit the museum exhibition. The train and carousel schedules vary per month. Check the website for detailed information on hours.

NORTH SCOTTSDALE

North Scottsdale has a reputation for new real estate that embraces the desert in its natural beauty. You'll see more desert landscaping and

Public Art Tour

Among all cities in the greater Valley, none support the arts as much as Scottsdale. Known for its galleries and museums, the city also has a robust and exciting public art program with permanent and temporary installations throughout the city. To see what's on deck during your visit, check out Scottsdale Public Art (scottsdalepublicart.org) for upcoming temporary art and events. Otherwise, look at the map online and treat yourself to a self-guided tour of the 90+ (wow!) permanent pieces around town.

You don't even have to leave your car for this one: Drive by the rusted steel fish of the **Tributary Wall** on Goldwater Boulevard between Indian School and Camelback Roads. It is a tribute to the nearby Arizona Canal and water, the desert community's most important resource.

The Doors, a two-story collection of three wooden doors on the southwest corner of Scottsdale and Camelback Roads, doesn't seem like much. But walk inside the piece and you'll find a mirrored audio installation that muffles traffic and provides a "sound massage."

Google image search "Scottsdale Engagement Photos" and you will undoubtedly see photos of love-struck couples kissing in front of Robert Indiana's **LOVE.** Located on the lawn of the Civic Center mall, this huge, red text sculpture provides an optimistic message and upbeat backdrop for a selfie.

Also located in the Civic Center Mall is **Atmosphere and Environments XIII (Windows to the West)** by the famous Louise Nevelson. The curious arrangement of geometric shapes and cut outs on a multi-dimensional metal wall dates back to 1973 and was the first public art piece in Scottsdale.

For a dramatic interactive experience, head to the southeast corner of Marshall Way and Indian School Road where **Horseshoe Falls** by Michael Maglich creates a literal haze. The towering pillars set into a concrete seat wall are stacked horseshoes whose spirit of grit and strength is softened by a dense fog that periodically invades the space from a bed of river rock.

Have you heard of James Turrell's **Knight Rise** installation? We've only mentioned it, oh, maybe ten times in this book and that's because we really, really want you to go. The oval-shaped concrete room is called a "Skyspace" and invites viewers to enter an elliptical, minimal enclosure with a single opening in the ceiling. And then? Magic. Feel your blood pressure and pulse lower as you observe the sky, the quiet, and your inner self.

serves as the headquarters of the Frank Lloyd Wright Foundation and the Frank Lloyd Wright School of Architecture. Guided tours, which vary throughout the year, are required to explore the property and range from a two-hour apprentice shelter tour to the popular 90-minute insights tour ($32), which showcases Wright's private living quarters and the canvas-roofed office where he designed many of his masterpieces, including the Guggenheim Museum and Tempe's Gammage Auditorium. Discounts are available for students, seniors, and large groups. Call ahead or visit the website for details.

Entertainment and Events

Scottsdale may not be the city that never sleeps but it sure goes to bed partied out. Its pleasure-loving residents and visitors happily fill their days with weeklong culinary events and international film festivals while their evenings simmer with energy at performing-arts venues before coming to a full boil at the dozens of nightclubs and lounges that lure the Valley's self-indulgent party set, as well athletes and pop stars who regularly serve as tabloid fodder.

That's not to say you won't find less style-conscious venues where you can have fun.

The Old West's saloons and gambling halls manage to live on. Cowboy bars still attract boot-wearing regulars to their live shows and honky-tonk dance floors, and casinos at the neighboring Native Indian communities now offer glittery slot machines along with old-fashioned poker.

★ NIGHTLIFE

With the exception of Las Vegas, no other city in the Southwest offers a nightlife with as much glitz as Scottsdale. The see-and-be-seen bars, thumping clubs, and trendy lounges are primarily located downtown. Put on your clubbing finest, as you'll be given the once-over by your fellow patrons (and probably a few bouncers). This is where the Gucci-loving set comes to preen and play—or bump and grind after enough drinks.

Downtown
BARS AND PUBS

AZ88 (7353 Scottsdale Mall, 480/994-5576, www.az88.com, 11:30am-1:30am daily) is a great place to eat, drink, and be seen. With its killer comfort food and first-class martinis, the perennial Scottsdale favorite attracts older couples on their way to a show, as well as trendy scenesters who descend on the bar and mod patio. It's a true staple of Scottsdale and you can't go wrong with a quick stop during your night out. Try the classic French 75 martini or Pimm's Cup and scope out the chic glass-and-white-wall decor, which provides a minimalist backdrop for the over-the-top and always changing art installations. Oh, and be sure to use the restroom. No, seriously—each stall is covered from floor to ceiling in mirrors, making a private experience hilariously revealing.

The neighboring **Old Town Tavern** (7320 E. Scottsdale Mall, 480/945-2882, www.old-towntavernaz.com, 10am-midnight Sun.-Thurs., 10am-2am Fri.-Sat.) is a more laid-back option. This comfortable hideaway, tucked into the grassy lawn of the Scottsdale Mall, is a great place to treat yourself to a late-afternoon drink. The crowd is mixed, with young hot things looking to "pre-game" it before a wild night out as well as cougars and silver foxes seeking another chance at the nightlife. There's live music daily and the cozy fireplaces on its two patios are perfect for cooler evenings. And with $3 beers and cheap cocktails, you'd barely know you're in Old Town.

Day drinkers, listen up! **RnR Gastropub** (3737 N. Scottsdale Rd., 480/945-3353, www.rnrscottsdale.com, 11am-midnight Mon.-Thurs., 11am-2am Fri., 8am-2pm Sat., 8am-midnight Sun.) is a two-story, 5,500 square foot mecca of drinking, eating, game watching, and indoor-outdoor seating that easily makes the clock zip through an afternoon. With a second-story patio perched right on Scottsdale Road, it's way too easy to let life pass you by as you sip drink after drink. The food menu features a huge line-up of American contemporary classics serving breakfast, lunch, and dinner. If you want to save the big spending for your next night out, the daily drink or food specials are great options.

Dark wood floors, brick walls, tufted leather boots, and tin ceiling tiles set the tone for **The Beverly** (7018 E. Main St., 480/889-5580,

the patio at AZ88

Party Drive

Boy, this bar and club section is long, eh?

There's good reason for that. Scottsdale—along with its luxurious daytime activities like golf, hiking, and spa-going—has a very fine and respectable tradition of partying until you pass out or find yourself watching the sunrise from a swimming pool in your underwear.

Some of the best nights out in the country can be had in Scottsdale. And as you navigate the roads of downtown on a Saturday night, you'll see packs of young folks skipping, hopping, and stumbling down the streets in search of the next happening bar or club. Singles flock to the scene to peacock their shiny cars, which match their shiny, bronzed bodies.

Speaking of cars, if you're planning to get wild (and we highly encourage you to do so, because, you know, YOLO—you only live once), it's best to leave the driving to someone who isn't imbibing. Not only is it the right thing to do, but Arizona DUI laws are extremely strict, with just one offense having the potential to land you ten days in jail, a court order to perform community restitution, and fees.

Luckily, if you're staying downtown, driving is rarely necessary since the area is so packed with clubs that barhopping on foot is totally an option. But if you're wearing your five-inch heels (get it, girrrrl!), you may opt for a cab company like **Discount Cab** (602/200-2000, www.discountcab. com), **Camelback Cab Company** (480/939-3366, www.camelbackcab.com), or Uber. If you're staying in Central or North Scottsdale where there are less venues within walking distance, check with your hotel or resort for shuttle services. Either way, catching a ride is your best bet.

www.thebeverly.us, 4pm-midnight Mon.-Thurs., 4pm-2am Fri.-Sat.), a sophisticated bar that may as well be the scene for those old-timey illustrations during the intro song for Cheers. To match the vibe, whiskey is the pride and joy here, with a selection of over 100 options that your well-versed bartender or server can help navigate. Of course, you can enjoy any other libation you desire as well as satisfy any late night hunger pangs with sliders, flatbreads and other snacks.

Wannabe rock stars who may be a little shy will love the private karaoke rooms at **Geisha A Go-Go** (7150 E. 6th Ave., 480/699-0055, www.geishaagogo.com, 3pm-10:30pm Mon.-Thurs., 3pm-1am Fri.-Sun.), a rock 'n' roll Japanese bistro. Order Japanese beer or sushi in the dark, wood-paneled bar or at the restaurant, where the music blasts among portraits of Jimi Hendrix and Jim Morrison. Couples and groups up to 20 people can rent the rooms by the hour (rates starting at $50 per hour for a six-person room during peak hours), and reservations are recommended.

The chic **Olive & Ivy** (7135 E. Camelback Rd., 480/751-2200, www.foxrc.com/

restaurants.com, 10am-10pm Sun.-Thurs., 11am-11pm Fri, 10am-11pm Sat.) is a great place to see Scottsdale's professional set at play. The upscale Mediterranean restaurant offers decent food, but its posh decor and large outdoor lounge overlooking the Scottsdale Waterfront's Arizona Canal have made it a place to mingle. The people-watching hits its prime at the dinner hour, when a steady stream of styled 30- and 40-somethings sidle up to the bar for Grey Goose martinis.

Yes, there is a cool dive bar in the heart of trendy Scottsdale. Duck into **Coach House** (7011 E. Indian School Rd., 480/990-3433, www.coachhousescottsdale.com, 6am-2am daily) from Halloween through New Year's Eve to witness a holiday-drinking miracle: thousands of Christmas lights covering the walls and ceiling of this tiny old wooden house. The bar is a popular destination year-round, though, attracting an impressively diverse mix of barhoppers, club goers, and old regulars. Make a new friend over darts or pinball, or grab a seat on the patio.

Let's say you've never been to a spa, tanning bed, or golf course in your life. First, what are you doing in Scottsdale? Second, you should just head to **TT Roadhouse** (2915 N. 68th St., 480/947-8723, www.ttroadhouse. com, 11:30am-2am daily) a neighborhood dive bar that serves locals who don't partake in the shiny parts of Scottsdale. Head in and relax as you slam back a cheap beer while skate videos play on the televisions. Darts, pool, and a jukebox are all that patrons need for a good time. Oh, and whiskey shots—many whiskey shots.

LOUNGES AND WINE BARS

If you're looking for great wine and a more adult crowd, **Kazimierz World Wine Bar** (7137 E. Stetson Dr., 480/946-3004, www. kazbar.net, 6pm-2am daily) provides an unpretentious retreat for friends or a romantic date. Serious wine lovers will appreciate the listing of over 2,000 wines from around the world, which has earned regular recognition from *Wine Spectator* magazine for its depth and value. Curl up on one of the plush sofas, take in the nightly live music, and pair a glass from the wine list (it's *only* 79 pages long) with one of the delicious flatbreads. Be forewarned, though; "Kazbar" isn't easy to find: "Like all good speakeasies, the entrance is hidden in the rear."

Wine lovers unite! **5th and Wine** (7051 E. 5th Ave., 480/699-8001, www.5thandwine. com, 11am-9pm Sun.-Mon., 11am-10pm Tues.-Thurs., 11am-11pm Fri.-Sat.) is a great stop after shopping and art gazing to grab a bite, sip wine (or beer or a martini), and gaze upon the glorious horse fountain on the pedestrian-friendly intersection of 5th Avenue and Marshall Way. Snack on bruschetta, calamari, salads, and panini sandwiches to fuel the remainder of your night out in downtown.

DANCE CLUBS AND LIVE MUSIC

Often referred to as a dive bar, **Pattie's First Avenue Lounge** (7220 E. 1st Ave., 480/990-0103, 9pm-1am Thurs., 7am-2am Mon.-Fri., 9am-2am Sat., 10am-2am Sun.) turns from dive in the day to dance club in the night. The

place has been around forever and acts as a much-needed respite in downtown from the tucked-and-toned crowds at other clubs. This place is for the people of Scottsdale who want to have a great night on the cheap. On weekend nights, DJs spin and the place is packed. The patio bar also has games for folks stopping by during the quieter hours.

If you want some live, loud, rock music, head to **Rockbar Inc.** (4245 N. Craftsman Ct., 480/331-9190, www.rockbarinc.com, 3pm-2am Mon.-Fri., noon-2am Sat.-Sun.) right in the heart of downtown. The two-story venue features live bands making the walls vibrate on the ground floor, with a more relaxed hang out on the rooftop patio. It's a departure from the glitz and a welcome one at that, with national acts that range from rockabilly to soul to straight-up rock 'n' roll.

The Mint Ultra Lounge (7373 E. Camelback Rd., 480/970-5000, www.themintaz.com, 9pm-2am Thurs.-Sat.) is 7,000 square feet of Scottsdale club that has over taken a former bank (the original vault door still remains). Any other history is wiped clean by the contemporary decor, which is sleek, clean, and packed with a party crowd dressed (and sometimes barely dressed) to impress. This club features a huge patio, 30-foot bar, LED light installations, a killer dance floor, and a rotating line-up of DJs playing house and pop music. For a seriously swank night, make reservations for a private room.

Paris of Scottsdale (4280 N. Drinkwater Blvd., 602/418-6969, www.parisofscottsdale. com, 10pm-2am Fri.-Sat.) is what Scottsdale is known for when it comes to the party scene. The speakers blast spins by nationally known DJs as well as EDM, hip hop, reggaeton, and salsa. As with all the fancy clubs, bottle service and VIP treatment can be yours. As far as attire goes, dress to party—expect to see tight dresses and flashy outfits.

Probably one of the more mixed-age and welcoming live-music venues in Scottsdale is **Wasted Grain** (7295 E. Stetson Dr., 480/970-0500, www.wastedgrain.com, 3pm-2am

Wed.-Sun.), which basically means you can have a great night enjoying music with a crowd that's down to earth. The large club features a lounge, three bars, a dance floor, and open concert areas. They've also got a full menu filled with flatbreads, sandwiches, and wraps plus a few funky treats like Poutine, fried pickles, and tableside S'mores that you roast yourself.

The place is called **Cake Scottsdale** (4426 N. Saddlebag Trail, 480/939-1559, www.cakenightclub.com/scottdsdale, 10:30pm-2am Wed., Fri.-Sun.), and the female staff members are called "cake girls." And you might need to call to cancel your morning plans after a night out here. This small club is a bit crammed when it gets busy, but that only makes for a delicious manic energy. Young, hot people flock to this place, so throw on your sexiest outfit and book a table or try to get the nod from the bouncers if you're feeling good. Either way, once you pass through the doors, be ready for an epic party.

The Casablanca Lounge (7134 E. Stetson Dr., 480/970-7888, www.thecasablancalounge. com, 5pm-12am Wed.-Thurs., 7pm-2am Fri.-Sat.) is slightly different than other dance clubs in Scottsdale in that it's got the classy feel of a lounge but still offers up a dance floor to cut a rug. Folks looking to grind on the dance floor with clubbers should pass this one over. Everyone else will love it, though, and there's still a fair amount of fun mingling to be had. Loosen up with a cocktail or two at one of the tables or enjoy a cigar on the beautiful patio overlooking the waterfront canal. With a rotation of live music and DJs, there's ample opportunity to join the crowd on the dance floor. And if you get hungry, there's a menu of tasty bites to enjoy.

Okay, so what if you're not into the whole shiny, plastic vibe of Scottsdale, but you still want to dance? Head to **The Rogue Bar** (423 N. Scottsdale Rd., 480/947-3580, www.theroguebar.com, 6am-2am daily), where the angsty side of Scottsdale likes to party. This trendy dive bar and live music venue on the south end of town attracts artsy club kids and punked-out burnouts to its small dance floor, where local DJs spin the likes of The Cure, Pat Benatar, and The Smiths. Grab a Pabst Blue Ribbon or a Stella Artois at the bar and scope out one of the booths for some serious people watching.

COWBOY BARS AND SALOONS

If you're barhopping in Old Town, do not miss a stop at "Scottsdale's Last Real Cowboy Saloon," the **Rusty Spur Saloon** (7245 E.

the Rusty Spur Saloon

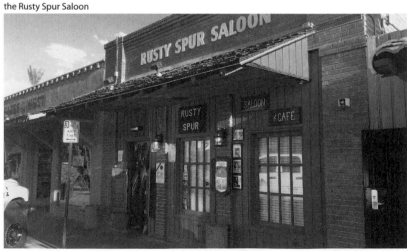

Main St., 480/425-7787, www.rustyspursaloon.com, 10am-1am Sun.-Thurs., 10am-2am Fri.-Sat.). This place is a hoot. Truly. The saloon has been open for 60 years and is housed in an old bank (the former vault is now filled with booze). Local cowboys and bikers have a true love for the small, crowded bar and all patrons are welcome to grab a drink and do a little shake or scoot to the nightly live music.

Central Scottsdale and Paradise Valley
BARS AND PUBS
Scottsdale Beer Company (7419 E. Shea Blvd., 480/219-1844, www.scottsdalebeercompany.com, 11am-11pm Mon.-Thurs., 11am-midnight Fri., 10am-midnight Sat., 10am-11pm Sun.) is one of the latest on the radar of local breweries—a popular genre that is growing fast in Arizona. IPAs, ales, blondes, and beers, beers, beers dominate the drinks menu—both from their brewery and other local beer makers like Four Peaks Brewery. Order up a burger, "Sam'ich," or their bacon-wrapped meatloaf to fill that belly right up.

LOUNGES AND WINE BARS
Enjoy a drink at **Jade Bar** (5700 E. McDonald Dr., 480/948-2100, www.sanctuaryoncamelback.com, 11am-midnight Sun.-Thurs., 11am-1am Fri.-Sat.) early in the evening, when you can catch Mummy Mountain bathed in a desert sunset. This chic, modern bar at Paradise Valley's **Sanctuary on Camelback Mountain Resort & Spa** is a stylish alternative to the gaudy lounges of Old Town. Try one of the signature cocktails like the Grapefruit Basil, a blend of vodka, basil leaves, and fresh grapefruit juice.

COWBOY BARS AND SALOONS
Hang your hat, along with the hundred others that dangle from the rafters, at **Handlebar-J Restaurant and Saloon** (7116 Becker Lane, 480/948-0110, www.handlebarj.com, 4pm-2am Tues.-Sun.). The country-and-western bar offers live music every night, and its outdoor bar can't be beaten. Even if you're not a fan of country music, you can't help but have a great time with the locals who pack the dance floor—Loretta Lynn and Lyle Lovett have been known to pop in. Handlebar-J offers country-dance lessons Tuesday and Thursday evenings.

You have to instantly love a place with a name like **The Dirty Dogg Saloon** (10409 N. Scottsdale Rd., 480/368-8095, www.thedirtydogsaloon.com, 3pm-2am Mon.-Sat.). Yes, this dive is popular with the biker crowd, but laid-back enough to welcome all walks of life. Expect loud rock music and girls dancing on the bar as you throw back a beer and hit the pool table.

North Scottsdale
BARS AND PUBS
You would think that all the booze in Scottsdale gets sucked up by Old Town, but some has been spared for North Scottsdale at **The Hangar** (13610 N. Scottsdale Rd., 480/951-8897, www.hangarfoodandspirits.com, 11am-10pm Sun.-Tues., 11am-midnight Wed.-Thurs., 11am-2am Fri.-Sat.). This sports bar serves grub, alcohol, and the big games to the crowd who hangs (get it?) near the Scottsdale Airport. Dog-friendly patio, off-track betting, burgers, tacos, and wings make for a leisurely Scottsdale outing.

DANCE CLUBS AND LIVE MUSIC
Downtown doesn't hold the premium on dance clubs. **Degree 270** (9800 E. Indian Bend Rd., 480/270-5539, www.talkingstickresort.com/degree270, 8pm-2am Fri.-Sat.) at Talking Stick Resort serves up stellar dance parties to the North Scottsdale crowd. Located on the 14th floor of the resort and with a large patio, you can enjoy the scenery as you get down to sounds mixed up by a revolving list of DJs every weekend. Of course, like any good club (attached to a casino, no less) VIP table reservations are an option with each table located for a specific view of the city, the pools, or the dance floor.

CASINOS

It seems like the decadence offered with high-end restaurants, spas, and a bumpin' nightlife should be enough for anyone to blow off a decent amount of steam. But, get this, a trip to Scottsdale means you can also gamble! Thanks to two neighboring Native American communities, Scottsdale is within easy access of three big casinos, all of which offer gaming 24 hours a day, seven days a week.

Operated by the Salt River Pima-Maricopa Indian Community, **Casino Arizona** (Highway 101 and McKellips Rd., 524 N. 92nd St., www.casinoarizona.com, 480/850-7777) has almost a thousand slot machines, in addition to nearly 50 table games (including a $1,000 blackjack limit) and plenty of Keno. For a break from the din of the casino, the 250-seat theater regularly books tribute bands of classic music acts like Iron Maidens, an all-girl Iron Maiden tribute band.

The **Casino at Talking Stick Resort** (9800 E. Talking Stick Way, 480/850-777, www.talkingstickresort.com) is run by the same people as Casino Arizona and is home to the state's largest poker room, the Arena Poker Room. Daily, weekly, monthly, and an annual tournament for a one-million-dollar prize pool make it a favorite place to play among serious players of Texas Hold 'Em, Omaha, and Seven Card Stud. But it's not all about poker. At this beautiful casino and resort, there are 50 table games, 800 slot machines, and Keno. Get nuts!

The **Fort McDowell Casino** (10424 N. Fort McDowell Rd., 800/843-3678, www.fortmcdowellcasino.com), operated by the Fort McDowell Yavapai Nation, is a little bit further out of town. Take Shea Boulevard 20 minutes east to State Route 87 (Beeline Highway) toward the town of Fountain Hills, and turn left on Fort McDowell Road. Slots, live bingo, Blackjack, and $5 to $60 poker tournaments (and a no limit Texas Hold 'Em tournament) throughout the week should keep any gambler busy.

PERFORMING ARTS

The **Scottsdale Center for the Performing Arts** (7380 E. 2nd St., 480/994-8587, www.scottsdaleperformingarts.org) showcases a host of live events, from theater and comedy to music and dancing. The SCA's white Modernist pavilion and its stages have featured a diverse roster of touring acts, like Etta James, Dave Brubeck, the Kronos Quartet, and David Sedaris. Larger shows are held at its **Virginia G. Piper Theater,** but you'll also find touring acts and local performers at **Stage 2,** while the **Dayton Fowler Grafman Atrium** hosts fashion and art events.

The open-air, outdoor **Scottsdale Civic Center Amphitheater** (75th St. and Main St., 480/994-2787, www.scottsdaleperformingarts.org), just outside SCA on Scottsdale Mall's grassy lawn, provides a lovely setting for concerts. Hosting up to 1,800 people on the sloped ground, families and couple bust out the picnic blankets for the popular "Sunday A'Fair" events starting in January.

Built in 1959, the **ASU Kerr Cultural Center** (6110 N. Scottsdale Rd., 480/596-2660, www.asukerr.com) has served as an important venue for emerging musicians, artists, and writers. Today, Kerr's beautifully maintained adobe studio provides an intimate setting for jazz, choral, and chamber-music performances.

FESTIVALS AND EVENTS

Thanks to the near-perfect weather in winter and spring, it's easy to catch a fun outdoor festival well into April. Bring your sunblock, floppy hat, and sunglasses because you'll easily spend a few hours traipsing in the glorious sun.

January

The **Barrett-Jackson Collector Car Auction** (16601 N. Pima Rd., 480/421-6694, www.barrett-jackson.com) kicks off the social calendar with an impressive showcase of luxury and historic vehicles. The weeklong event at the WestWorld of Scottsdale complex

The Greatest Show on Grass

The **Waste Management Phoenix Open** (www.wmphoenixopen.com) is the biggest party in town—and the largest event on the PGA Tour, luring more than a half million people to the famous TPC Scottsdale golf course over the span of a week.

The infamous annual event, usually held in late January or early February, is not your traditional, polite-applause tournament. In fact, it's more like a nightclub on the fairway. You're as likely to see seniors with scorecards as 20-somethings in tube tops and heels, barhopping from beer gardens to VIP skyboxes. The plentiful bars and young crowds fuel a raucous party atmosphere, so much so that Tiger Woods, who sunk a legendary hole-in-one on the 16th hole, vowed not to return.

TPC Scottsdale's Stadium Course was specifically designed to accommodate an "unlimited number of people." And by the final day, that can mean as many as 50,000 fans gathered around the 18th hole to watch pros like Phil Mickelson and Vijay Singh sink a tournament-winning putt.

Golf is only part of the draw, though, with half the crowd arriving when the sun sets and the putting is over. These latecomers flock to the Birds Nest, a party tent where big-name bands entertain thousands of drinking carousers.

The Thunderbirds, a group of the Valley's leading businessmen, have hosted the event since 1939, making it one of the oldest events on the PGA tour. It's the philanthropic group's biggest fundraiser, netting millions of dollars for Arizona charities. Admission begins at $25 per day, although there are additional fees for skyboxes and entrance to the after-hours Birds Nest.

in North Scottsdale is one of the largest and best-attended auto auctions in the world.

The annual **Celebration of Fine Art** (southeast corner of Hayden Rd. and Loop 101, 480/443-7695, www.celebrateart.com) runs January through March, when big white tents dot the desert. Some 100 artists set up their studios, allowing browsers and buyers to peruse an extensive collection of Western and contemporary paintings, sculptures, glass, ceramics, and jewelry.

The **Waste Management Phoenix Open** (www.wmphoenixopen.com), usually held in late January or early February, is the largest event on the PGA tour, attracting more than half a million visitors to TPC Scottsdale over the course of a week.

February

A bit of old Arizona that manages to survive, **Parada del Sol Rodeo** (various venues, www.paradadelsol.org) reminds

Scottsdale residents in late February that despite the BMWs and designer sunglasses, this is still the Wild West. The event usually has a slightly different mix of events each year, which can include Pony Express rides, dances, and live country music. The highlights are the professional rodeos and the Parada del Sol Parade and Trails End Festival, which has been a tradition for over 60 years.

Also in February, the 60-year-old **Scottsdale Arabian Horse Show** (16601 N. Pima Rd., 480/515-1500, www.scottsdaleshow.com) gathers upwards of 2,000 Arabian horses and their handlers at WestWorld for 11 days of shows, competitions, demonstrations, seminars, and shopping.

March

The three-day **Scottsdale Arts Festival** (7380 E. 2nd Street, 480/874-4697, www.scottsdaleartsfestival.org) in March gathers up to 175 jury-selected artists and close to 30,000 visitors to the Scottsdale Civic Center Mall

for entertainment, artist demonstrations, live music and exhibitions galore.

April

This city is a foodie mecca, so it's little wonder that April's **Scottsdale Culinary Festival Weekend** (Scottsdale Civic Center Mall, 7380 E. 2nd St., 480/945-7193, www.scottsdalefest.org) entices tens of thousands of people to eat, drink, and party. Taste the hard work of local restaurants and national celebrity chefs, get crafty with interactive art projects, listen to live music on multiple stages, or dine at one of the dozen events around town. The event coordinators put on smaller, similar food events throughout the year.

October

The **Scottsdale International Film Festival** (480/499-8587, www.scottsdalefilmfestival.com) draws cinema-loving crowds every October to Valley theaters with a global assortment of dramas, comedies, and documentaries.

Shopping

Scottsdale loves to shop. Luxury brands, cool boutiques, Native American crafts and jewelry, authentic cowboy boots and hats— this city has it all. Scottsdale is also home to a nationally known art market, with galleries featuring traditional Southwestern pieces as well as cutting-edge, contemporary installations that blend painting, sculpture, glass, and ceramics.

Spend some time browsing downtown shops and galleries to find those "only in Arizona" souvenirs. If you're in need of an air-conditioned getaway in the summer, the colossal Scottsdale Fashion Square has nearly 200 stores and eateries to keep your credit cards busy. The majority of the city's retail options are found at malls and open-air shopping centers along Scottsdale Road.

SHOPPING CENTERS AND DISTRICTS
Old Town and the Arts Districts

Park your car at the old hitching posts and make your way down the covered sidewalks. Next to the Scottsdale Civic Center Mall, **Bischoff's Gallery** (3925 N. Brown Ave., 480/946-6155, www.bischoffsouthwestart.com, 9am-5:30pm daily) is a terrific place to pick up Southwestern and Native American artworks. Paintings by well-known and award-winning Southwestern artists dominate the gallery and shop that features books, pottery, rugs, Hopi kachina dolls, intricately beaded leather goods, Pima baskets, and rustic antique armoires and trunks. The store's brick walls and high ceilings originally housed a bank, which explains why Bischoff's doesn't feel as touristy as some of the other shopping options in Old Town. Pick up a few postcards and head out to the charming shaded courtyard to jot down a few notes to friends.

The larger **Bischoff's Shades of the West** (7247 E. Main St., 480/945-3289, 9am-9pm Mon.-Fri., 9am-8pm Sat., 9am-7pm Sun.) offers "everything needed to transform a bunkhouse into a Southwestern palace," from Mexican glasses and blankets to bronze hardware.

You can smell the leather when you walk through the door of **Saba's** (7254 E. Main St., 480/949-7404, www.sabas.com, 10am-7pm Mon.-Fri., 10am-6pm Sat., 11am-5pm Sun.). "Arizona's Original Western Store" has grown considerably (eight locations!) since David Saba opened his first trading post in 1927, and you'll still find the Saba family selling belt buckles and hats to real cowboys and old friends almost every day. The rows and rows of cowboy boots are both overwhelming and inspiring. Pick up a pair or five, because it's impossible to choose the best one from such a fabulous selection. Check out the Western apparel, too, since you'll need some new threads to go with those boots. Additional locations include another in downtown (3965 N. Brown Ave., 480/947-7664, same hours) and North Scottsdale (7231 E. Shea Blvd., 480/948-9201, same hours).

It seems like you can't turn a corner in Old Town without bumping into one of the **Gilbert Ortega Galleries,** mammoth emporiums filled with Navajo rugs, Southwestern furniture, turquoise jewelry, equestrian art, and even headdresses, in a range of prices. The best of the bunch is the **Gilbert Ortega Gallery** (3925 N. Scottsdale Rd., 480/990-1808, 10am-6pm Sun.-Wed., 10am-9pm Thurs., 10am-7pm Fri.-Sat.). If you're looking for the perfect Southwest souvenir, you'll find something here.

Civil War buffs and Old West admirers should stop in at **Guidon Books** (7109 E. 2nd St., 480/945-8811, www.guidon.com, 10am-5pm Mon.-Sat.). Having been in business over 50 years and with a move to a larger location, the bookstore is filled with new and out-of-print specialty titles about Western America and the Civil War. Peruse the shelves, where you'll find categories that range from women of the West and union generals to Indian crafts and mountain men. Proprietor Shelly Dudley will happily steer you towards the subject matter you desire.

The Poisoned Pen (4014 N. Goldwater Blvd., 480/947-2974, www.poisonedpen.com, 10am-7pm Mon.-Fri., 10am-6pm Sat., noon-5pm Sun.) got its start in 1989 as a store specializing in mystery and thriller books. Fast-forward to today and the Poisoned Pen has expanded its first-rate titles to include general fiction, signed first editions, and most other genres. The place is well respected locally and nationally among book lovers, and hosts over 200 author events a year.

Scottsdale Fashion Square

Shoppers, welcome to your temple. The nearly two-million-square-foot **Scottsdale Fashion Square** (Camelback Rd. and

Scottsdale Fashion Square

Scottsdale Rd., 480/941-2140, www.fashion-square.com, 10am-9pm Mon.-Sat., 11am-6pm Sun.) is one of the country's best shopping centers. For decades, the mall has been a draw for travelers across the country and is the absolute stand out retail resource in Arizona.

High-end department stores like Nordstrom, Neiman Marcus, and a Barneys New York anchor the vast air-conditioned megamall, and the impressive list of luxe boutiques should send any fashionista's heart racing: Burberry, Kate Spade, Gucci, Louis Vuitton, Tiffany and Co., Cartier, and Bottega Veneta, just to name a few. Shoppers will also find the usual mall standbys like Banana Republic and Anthropologie, along with Harkins Theatres, where you can catch a flick in a reclining seat and order a drink from the bar.

Even if you're not into the high-end labels, the mall has separate stores solely dedicated to one brand, so you can peruse the entire collection of each product line. There's Clarks and Crocs shoe stores, 7 for all Mankind clothes, a Disney store, a store selling Fossil watches, a store called The Art of Shaving, a Tesla store (yes, you read that correctly), and endless others. Oh, and if you have kids in tow, head to the Build-a-Bear Workshop, where they get to choose outfits and accessories for a customized teddy bear.

Scottsdale Waterfront

Located across the street from Scottsdale Fashion Square, the pedestrian-popular **Scottsdale Waterfront** (7135 E. Camelback Rd., www.scottsdalewaterfrontshopping.com, 480/247-8071) was smart enough to take advantage of the city's canal system to develop residences, restaurants, and shops overlooking the flowing waters. While the best views are reserved for the high-rise homeowners, shoppers are welcome to dine, drink, and damage their wallets with the retail shops nearby and then take a stroll on walkways and bridges along the water.

Scottsdale Waterfront is best experienced during one of the many events that take place along the Arizona Canal. Art and food festivals liven up the area when the weather is good (check the mall website for upcoming events). On any other day, it still promises a fine outing to poke around well-known retailers like Urban Outfitters, which carries trendy clothing for college-aged 20-something kids, or VOM FASS, with its offerings of cask-aged vinegars, oils, wines, and spirits.

It's the dining, however, that keeps people

Scottsdale Waterfront

Strip Search

At some point, travelers to Phoenix and Scottsdale will visit the ubiquitous strip centers that line streetscapes across the Valley. Like many cities in the West, Phoenix came of age after the birth of the automobile and, as a result, the city's postwar building boom created a city tailor-made to serve the automobile.

Despite their bland facades, strip centers are frequently home to some of the city's most noteworthy small businesses, from ethnic restaurants to yoga studios and vintage shops. **Hilton Village** (6015 N. Scottsdale Rd., www.hiltonvillage.com), near Paradise Valley, for example, features popular restaurants, trendy boutiques, and salons. Stop by **Bink's Kitchen + Bar** (6107 N. Scottsdale Rd., 480/664-9238, www.binkleysrestaurantgroup.com, 11am-9:30pm Mon.-Thurs., 11am-10pm Fri., 10am-10pm Sat., 10am-9pm Sun., $9-38) for brunch if you're there on a weekend.

noon-6pm Sun.) opened, so did the H&M store. And that's how all women aged 20-35 learned about this mall. H&M still remains, but there's a whole lot else going on there, too. It is surely the go-to destination for North Scottsdale visitors wanting to drop some serious coin on new threads, a delicious meal, and even a movie if the mood strikes.

The indoor and outdoor, pedestrian-friendly shopping center has trendy retailers like lululemon athletica, Calvin Klein, Warby Parker, Pottery Barn, L'Occitane, and Paris Optique. Grab a super healthy bite to eat at True Food Kitchen, which specializes in organic, farm to table dishes with plenty of vegetarian and vegan options, or opt for sushi at the adventurous Stingray Sushi, featuring traditional sushi as well as unique rolls that might even feature jalapeños.

Want to catch a movie? Head to iPic Theaters, which is like a bar, restaurant, living room, house party, and movie theater rolled into one. Settle into a squishy seat and sip wine or beer as you order from a full-service menu. The on-site Salt Lounge even has a dance floor if you're up for a party after the show.

Kierland Commons

The perfectly manicured **Kierland Commons** (15205 N. Kierland Blvd., 480/348-1577, www.kierlandcommons.com, 10am-9pm Mon.-Sat., noon-6pm Sun.) was the first mall in the Valley to kick off the "urban village" concept, offering residential opportunities among shops, restaurants, and bars. It's like Arizona's version of a "real" city without the hassle of outdated infrastructure. Park street side and stroll the complex's sidewalks, small gardens, and water fountains, where you'll see children playing on warm afternoons.

Restaurants, bars, and big-name chains like J. Crew and Michael Kors set up shop on the ground floor, while residents live upstairs in steel-and-glass condos. If you're in need of poolside garb, this place has you covered with Tommy Bahama, Everything But

coming back to the Scottsdale Waterfront. **Olive & Ivy** (480/751-2200, www.foxrc.com/restaurants.com, 10am-10pm Sun.-Thurs., 11am-11pm Fri, 10am-11pm Sat.) has become an established stop for many locals who love dining on its huge, shady patio or mixing it up at the bar. The restaurant serves Mediterranean-inspired cuisine or quick bites, and bottles of wine are available to go at its attached market. **Wildfish** (480/994-4040, www.wildfishseafoodgrille.com, 4pm-10pm Sun.-Wed., 11am-8pm Thurs., 4pm-11pm Fri.-Sat.) serves (surprise!) seafood as well as steaks but it's the happy hour in the lounge (4pm-7pm Tues.-Sat., all night Sun.-Mon.) with $10 appetizers alongside $6 cocktails and glasses of wine that boasts prices unheard of in Scottsdale.

Scottsdale Quarter

When the **Scottsdale Quarter** (15037 N. Scottsdale Rd., 480/270-8123, www.scottsdalequarter.com, 10am-9pm Mon.-Sat.,

Water, and Solstice Sunglasses. Restaurants include the local favorite Postino WineCafe, with arguably the best bruschetta in town; and Snooze and A.M. Eatery for the breakfast crowd; or Teavana for a cup of loose-leaf tea created by the master teaologists—if you dig it, take the tea accessories home to recreate the experience.

★ ART GALLERIES

Scottsdale's art galleries are among the city's biggest attractions and an important center of commerce. Traditionally, Western and Native American art dominated the scene, but now a host of contemporary galleries showcase some of the art world's biggest names as well as emerging talent.

Most of the city's galleries are clustered in the Marshall Way and Main Street arts districts, located just west of Scottsdale Road in Downtown. It's not too hard to find attractive pieces to take home, although prices are expensive at the larger, more established galleries. Also, you can expect shorter hours at galleries in the summer, so be sure to call ahead for times.

The best way to become a part of the art scene—at least for an evening—is to join the weekly Thursday night **Scottsdale ArtWalk** (www.scottsdalegalleries.com). Socialize with artists, collectors, curators, and Valley residents 6:30pm-9:30pm, when almost all downtown galleries open their doors for the popular event.

Contemporary

The paintings and sculpture at **J Klein Gallery** (7136 E. Main St., 480/941-3442, www.mainstreetartgalleries.com, 10am-5pm Mon.-Wed., Fri.-Sat., 10am-9pm Thurs., noon-5pm Sun.) are inspired by nature and boast the variety and beauty one discovers in the outdoors. With three main artists showcasing their work, the gallery has both variety and consistency. Jim Klein's paintings are easy to spot with bright, colorful nature scenes that straddle figurative and abstract. Dan Ostermiller's bronze sculptures capture uncanny realism of animals both exotic and common, and Jeff Berryman transforms traditional Western imagery into surrealistic dreamscapes.

Photographic galleries are not uncommon but the contemporary work at **tilt gallery** (7077 E. Main St., 602/716-5667, www.tiltgallery.com, 10am-5pm Mon.-Sat., noon-4:30pm Sun.) is truly memorable. It specializes in works that employ historic formats and alternative processes with imagery that speaks to modern sensibilities and the spectacular monthly exhibitions are thoughtfully curated, offering an experience of photography that is innovative, fresh, and beautiful.

Bonner David Galleries (7040 E. Main St., 480/941-8500, www.bonnerdavid.com, 10am-5:30pm Tues.-Fri., 10am-6pm Sat.,) is a bit of a two-for-one deal among the Scottsdale art galleries. For those seeking to be challenged, hit up the Contemporary Gallery with current wall art and sculpture. Those who enjoy safer, mostly figurative works, should head to the Traditional Gallery. The two spaces are located side by side, with a relaxed and comfortable vibe.

If you don't have the deep pockets to invest in a piece of art, this unpretentious gallery highlights the works of emerging talent. **Art One** (4130 N. Marshall Way, 480/946-5076, www.artonegalleryinc.com, 10am-5:30pm Mon.-Sat., 11am-4pm Sun., 7pm-9pm Thurs.) showcases reasonably priced paintings and sculpture by young, up-and-coming artists, including local students. The regularly changing lineup can be a fun way to dip your toes into the art world.

The polished concrete floors, high ceilings, and natural light make **Calvin Charles Gallery** (4201 N. Marshall Way, 480/421-1818, www.calvincharlesgallery.com, 10am-6pm Mon.-Wed., Fri.-Sat., 10am-9pm Thurs., by appointment Sun.) a terrific spot to view contemporary works by mid-career and emerging artists. Collectors will find modern works from China, Vietnam, and Japan as well as Europe and the Americas. The rooftop sculpture terrace offers a nice view of Camelback

Mountain and the revolving exhibitions make each visit a unique experience.

Cowboy, Native American, and Southwestern

With more than 100 nationally known artists, **The Legacy Gallery** (7178 Main St., 480/945-1113, www.legacygallery.com, 10am-5:30pm Mon.-Sat., 11am-5pm Sun., and 7-9pm Thurs.) is one of Scottsdale's largest Southwestern art galleries. With three locations in the U.S. (the others being in Wyoming and Montana), the owners have a premium on imagery of life in the great West. Survey the Native American portraits, Western landscapes, romantic pastels, and life-size bronze sculptures. You may even be tempted to take one home.

Wolves. Cowboys. Livestock. Landscapes. Native Americans. This is what you can expect to see in the paintings and bronze sculpture at **Trailside Galleries** (7340 E. Main St., 480/945-7751, www.trailsidegalleries.com, 10am-5pm Mon.-Sat.). Most of the works here are very traditional and focus on representational works ranging from realism to subdued impressionism (but even that might be a stretch). There are occasional contemporary pieces to round out the collection but the imagery still focuses on Western themes. The works are beautiful and classic and could make a very fine memento of your trip out West.

Turquoise lovers, get in line for **Territorial Indian Arts & Antiques** (7077 E. Main St., 480/945-5432, www.territorialindianarts.com, 10am-4pm Mon.-Sat.). This stunning gallery and store has an incredible collection of Native American jewelry, pottery, textiles, and baskets both contemporary and antique. Be ready to plunk down several hundred (or thousand) dollars for an incredible piece because it's the real deal here.

The bronze sculptures by artist Dave McGary at **Expressions Gallery** (7077 E. Main St., 480/424-7412, www.expressions-galleries.com, 10am-5pm Mon.-Sat., 7pm-9pm Thurs.) are like the fine-art version of the Uncanny Valley—they are so realistic, it can be a little unsettling. Unsettling or not, the skill is incredible as you gaze upon the most lifelike expressions and stances of Native American figures ranging from fierce warriors to fearless chiefs and small children. The gallery also offers a beautiful collection of Southwestern-inspired paintings.

Art One

Sports and Recreation

Scottsdale isn't all glitz and glamour. Its spectacular desert setting makes it an ideal place to get some dirt under your shoes by exploring nature first-hand. The Sonoran Desert may only get an average of seven inches of rain per year, but it is teeming with life—life that has to duke it out in harsh conditions. The extraordinarily unique plants and animals make it one of the most diverse ecosystems on Earth.

You've probably been lured to Scottsdale by the city's sweeping desert landscapes and color-saturated sunsets, but the best way to truly appreciate this unique locale is by experiencing it firsthand—whether on a bike, on a raft, or on the links.

Of course, be sure to drink lots of water and be hyper-cautious about outdoor activities in the summer (it's best to stick to dawn or dusk for non-swimming activities). Many visitors are caught off-guard by the heat and dehydrating arid climate.

ADVENTURE TOURS

Stellar Adventures (602/402-0584, www. stellaradventures.com) offers a variety of ways to get out in the desert and get dirty, from ATV Adventures (up to $175 rental) and Blazer tours ($100 adult, $80 child) of mining ghost towns and ancient Native American ruins to Hummer tours ($185) that show off the rock-hopping, wall-climbing, hole-busting capabilities of these military vehicles.

For the next step in Jeep safaris, try driving your own TOMCAR ATV off-road vehicle with **Desert Wolf Tours** (47801 N. Black Canyon Hwy., New River, 877/613-9653, desertwolftours.com, from $159). The off-road vehicles are fun on their own but the folks at Desert Wolf punch it up by providing half-day guided adventures over rocky roads and through desert washes, bringing new meaning to the word "convoy." If that's not enough of a thrill ride for you, sign up for the ELITE Combat Simulator (from $450) for a day's

adventure as a member of a simulated special-operations unit for a day complete with tactical gear and advanced non-lethal training weapons.

BALLOONING

There are few better ways to get a new perspective on the desert than by gliding silently above it in a hot-air balloon. On calm days, the sky might be dotted with dozens of colorful balloons, but inside the basket the world feels like it's all yours.

A Balloon Experience by Hot Air Expeditions (702 W. Deer Valley Rd., 480/502-6999, www.hotairexpeditions.com) flies its balloons up to 5,000 feet above the desert floor and then low enough to see critters like jackrabbits, roadrunners, and coyotes. But the best part might come after landing: A welcome that includes either a champagne breakfast or evening hors d'oeuvres catered by award-winning chef Vincent Guerithault's restaurant, Vincent on Camelback, awaits ($179). The company is FAA-certified and offers hotel transfers.

The rides with **Arizona Hot Air Balloons** (480/282-8686, www.arizonahotairballoons. com) are sure to please any traveler, especially those who don't self-describe as "morning people". The company offers afternoon flights November through March as well as their year-round morning flights. Shared basket prices run at $155 per person or you can rent the ride for a private experience for two people at $425 on the weekend ($325 for a weekday).

SEGWAY

Yes, you read that section headline right. Segway tours are available via **Scottsdale Segway Tours** (14821 N. Hiawatha Hood Rd., Fort McDowell, 1-800-755-0935, www. advoutwest.com, $85). With charismatic tour leader Cowboy Wayne as your guide, you'll benefit from his 30 years of experience

McDowell Mountain Regional Park is great for biking.

leading tours in the desert. With a lesson and two-hour trip in the Fort McDowell off-road tour, you can experience a long-distance hike without the usual physical effort. It should be memorable—especially if you run over a rattlesnake as you silently glide through the trails.

BIKING
Mountain Biking

When it comes to mountain biking in this area, it all happens in North Scottsdale, where the fabulous McDowell Mountains provide endless miles and hours of recreation for some serious two-wheelin'. This pristine swath of mountain desert land is managed by two entities: The **McDowell Mountain Regional Park** (www.maricopa.gov/parks/mcdowell) and the **McDowell Sonoran Preserve** (www.scottsdaleaz.gov/preserve), which features newly developed trails and recreation areas run by the City of Scottsdale.

Some of the finest mountain-biking trails in the U.S. snake their way up the rocky peaks

and through the desert washes in and around Scottsdale. The **Pemberton Trail** is one of the best. Located just north of Scottsdale on the northeast end of the McDowell Mountains range is the **McDowell Mountain Regional Park** (www.maricopa.gov/parks/mcdowell); this 15.3-mile loop shoots riders up and down rolling hills along a trail that alternatively narrows to single-track and widens to open speed-runs. It's easy enough for novice riders to navigate but varied enough to keep even the hard-core adventurer interested.

Working our way west across the McDowell Mountains, the next recommended biking adventure starts at the Gateway Trailhead in the **McDowell Sonoran Preserve** on Thompson Peak parkway, just north of Bell Road. Grab a map and hop on the trail system here, starting with the Gateway Loop, Windgate Pass, and Bell Pass Trails for a super hard-core 14 miles up and over some challenging terrain that will definitely cause you to hop off in a few areas for some good ol'-fashioned hiking. This one's for experienced bikers only and although it's well signed all the way (thank you, City of Scottsdale), be sure to grab a free map at the trailhead and take a moment to study up.

For beginners looking for low mileage but practice on slightly challenging terrain, the 4.5-mile Gateway Loop is an excellent option. From the same start as the Gateway Trailhead, grab a map and follow the trails to the Gateway Loop for the shorter, less-insane option of that ride.

For an experience with an expert, try a guided mountain bike tour of the McDowell Mountains and Sonoran Desert with **Arizona Outback Adventures** (16447 N. 91st St., Suite 101, 480/345-2881, www.aoa-adventures. com). With bike rentals and options to accommodate all skill levels, let these guys take you on the ultimate tour. Half-day mountain biking tours start at $125 per person, with discounts for groups of four or more.

Road Biking

Road bikers shouldn't feel left out, either.

Speeding along **Pima Road to Bartlett Lake** (start anywhere north of Frank Lloyd Wright Boulevard) is popular with the skinny-tire crowd. The ride passes through spectacular high desert and quite a few tiny neighborhoods, but the full distance from Frank Lloyd Wright to the dam (following Cave Creek Road to Bartlett Dam Road) is about 60 miles. Park farther north along Pima for a quicker out-and-back.

Finally, a biking option that's not in North Scottsdale! Check out the **Indian Bend Wash Greenbelt** (www.scottsdaleaz.gov/parks/greenbelt), a flood-control project that doubles as a beautiful, 11-mile stretch of grass and walking or biking path extending from Shea Boulevard just past McDowell Road. Along the way, you'll find public art, libraries, skate parks, nature areas, and golf courses.

Other good tips can be found at local bike shops, including **Rage Cycles** (6411 E. Thomas Rd., 480/968-8116, www.ragecycles.com, Mon.-Fri. 10am-7pm, Sat. 10am-5pm, Sun. 11am-4pm) and the **Phoenix Metro Bicycle Club** (www.pmbcaz.org), an online community that schedules regular group rides.

★ GOLF

Golf may have been born in Scotland, but it has been transformed into a way of life in Scottsdale. The natural rocky terrain and lack of rainfall may seem like an odd match for acre after acre of thirsty greens, yet Scottsdale's residents and visitors will tell you that the region's year-round sunny skies and expansive landscape are far too tempting to let a little thing like water get in the way.

It's only half a joke, as water is a real concern for these courses. Laws limit the amount of water that can be used, and this challenge has pushed the creativity of designers further, with new courses showcasing the stunning contrast between verdant green fairways and golden desert washes.

The city's 50-ish courses span the gamut from municipal executive greens to PGA tournament stops. And although you'll find far more affordable options in Phoenix and its suburbs, none of them will match Scottsdale's premier courses.

Like hotel and resort rates, greens fees tumble as the heat rises, with even the best courses charging a fraction of their winter prices in the summer. Call ahead for current fees.

Camelback Golf Club (7847 N. Mockingbird Ln., 480/596-7050, www.camelbackgolf.com) tees up 36 holes of championship golf. Try the par-72 Padre Course, which is known for its challenging water holes, including the infamous 18th. The Ambiente Course is known for its elevation changes and rolling fairways, making even the most experienced golfers puzzle over the best strategy. After a hard game, pop into the terrific golf shop to cool off.

Who says you can't find a decent and affordable golf course in Scottsdale? The executive-style **Continental Golf Course** (7920 E. Osborn Rd., 480/941-1585, www.continentalgc.com) is a fun, par-60 course just a few blocks from Old Town. The long tees and narrow greens give the Continental a little character. Play the full 18 holes or hit the executive nine before your kids get up. Call the pro shop to ask about any specials deal.

McCormick Ranch Golf Club (7505 E. McCormick Pkwy., 480/948-0260, www.mccormickranchgolf.com) is another reasonably affordable option, conveniently located near downtown Scottsdale and Paradise Valley. *Golf Illustrated* named its Palm Course's ninth hole as one of the top water holes in the country, and its practice facility has one of the Southwest's largest putting greens. Best of all, parents can bring their children to the Junior Golf Academy to learn golf rules and etiquette, as well as technique and strategy.

It's hard to believe this 27-hole, luxury golf sanctuary sits in the middle of the Phoenix and Scottsdale metropolitan area. **The Phoenician** (6000 E. Camelback Rd., 480/423-2430, www.thephoenician.com) has nine-hole offerings that sprawl below the red-hued Camelback Mountain, and the backdrop couldn't be better. The course is a fantastic splurge and a popular choice for golfers of all skill levels, thanks in part to its slightly shorter fairways.

Who doesn't want to play like the pros—or at least play the golf course of the pros? **TPC Scottsdale** (17020 N. Hayden Rd., 480/585-4334, www.tpc.com/scottsdale) lives up to its hype as one of the country's best courses. Tee off at the Stadium Course (home of the Waste Management Phoenix Open), designed by Tom Weiskopf and Jay Morrish, or head out to the Champions Course. Even if your game's a little off, you'll be rewarded with spectacular views of the McDowell Mountains. Plus, you can't beat the thrill of sinking a putt on the 16th-hole "stadium" green. Private instruction and two-, three-, and five-day classes at the Tour Academy are available for any Phil Mickelsons in the making.

Never one to be outdone, **Kierland Golf Club** (15636 N. Clubgate Dr., 480/922-9283, www.kierlandgolf.com) brings a lot of high-tech fun to the links, as it was the first course in Arizona to roll out the Segway GT (Golf Transporter), which carries a golfer and bag around the 27-hole course. Surf the turf on the club's golfboards or ride the course on golf bikes for a new twist. Oh, and let's not forget the golf carts with built-in misting systems for those brutal summer temperatures. But

Kierland doesn't let the toys get in the way of its challenging desert course, which offers up a legit day of golf. If you'd like some help with your technique, the LaBauve Golf Academy and Foremax Training System pumps up anyone's golf game.

For a younger crowd, check out **Grayhawk Golf Club** (8620 E. Thompson Peak Pkwy., 480/502-1800, www.grayhawkgolf.com) in North Scottsdale. This 36-hole desert club features two courses that are among the best in the Valley, the "Talon" and the Tom Fazio-designed "Raptor." Before you meet your challenge on the courses, hit the "Rock and Range" practice facility for a rockin' warm-up as you jam out to classic tunes by the likes of Lynyrd Skynyrd, Van Morrison, and Boston.

Troon North Golf Club (10320 E. Dynamite Blvd., 480/585-7700, www.troonnorthgolf.com) and its three courses have emerged as the pinnacle of desert golf course design (appropriately located in the shadow of Pinnacle Peak) and just enjoyed a total revamp by its original designer and British Open Champion, Tom Weiskopf. Rolling greens meander seamlessly through the natural ravines and unspoiled terrain. It will almost convince you that lush, perfectly manicured grounds grow naturally in this arid climate.

The golf course at The Phoenician has a spectacular view of Camelback Mountain.

The state-of-the-art 18-hole Monument and Pinnacle courses and the nine-hole executive Monument Express attract serious players and North Scottsdale's most affluent residents.

National magazines regularly rank the 36-hole **Boulders Golf Club** (34631 N. Tom Darlington Rd., 480/488-9009, www.theboulders.com) as one of the best golf resorts in the country. It's a real desert course so don't be surprised to see rabbits, coyotes, or javelina scurrying across the fairway as you tee off. The scenic South Course is a highlight of the property, with its greens nestled along the resort's signature rock formations. A bonus is a spa program offering recreation and relaxation that begins on the driving range with margaritas, chips, and salsa, followed by three days of instruction, fitness programs, healthy cuisine, and spa relaxation.

HIKING AND ROCK CLIMBING
★ McDowell Mountains

Tom's Thumb

Hiking has become one of the most popular outdoor activities in Scottsdale and the Valley. Locals like to consider themselves as living in a hiking city on par with Portland, Oregon, or Denver, Colorado. Once you experience the McDowell Mountains, you'll probably agree. The range is shared by two interlocking trail systems managed by the **McDowell Mountain Regional Park** (16300 McDowell Mountain Park Dr., 480/471-0173, www.maricopa.gov/parks/mcdowell, $6 per vehicle) and the **McDowell Sonoran Preserve** (7447 E. Indian School Rd., Suite 300, 480/312-7013, www.scottsdaleaz.gov/preserve, free)

Hikers, climbers, bikers, and horseback riders of all skill levels can trek through the McDowell Mountains on the northeastern edge of Scottsdale. The protected park serves as a wildlife corridor for the Tonto National Forest, making it an important habitat for a host of desert plants and animals. In fact, this book author once saw a desert tortoise cross the hiking trail—a very rare sight since the animal is on the endangered species list.

The McDowell Sonoran Preserve, alongside the City of Scottsdale, manages the majority of the area's trails, with the preserve split into two major areas: North and South. The Northern Region is an extensive network of trails that extend far enough north to reach the Tonto National Forest border. These trails are best accessed by the **Brown's Ranch Trailhead** (30301 N. Alma School Pkwy.), which has moderate trails but can also be the starting point for a hefty journey.

The Southern Region of the park is vastly more popular and offers trails that are decidedly more challenging. Get started at **McDowell Gateway Trailhead** (1833 N. Thompson Peak Pkwy.), which is the largest of the trailheads and has restrooms, water, interpretive signage, shade ramadas, and the wheelchair-accessible **Bajada Nature Trail.** The **Lost Dog Wash Trailhead** (12601 N. 124th St.) is a fairly easy five miles (up and back) to an overlook of Taliesin West.

On the east end of the preserve sits the **Sunrise Trailhead** (12101 N. 145th Way), which satisfies hikers looking for a more challenging climb to sweeping views of the entire Valley along the Sunrise Trail (approximately four miles up and back). And finally, the not-to-be-missed hefty, hard-core hike up to a massive hunk of rock called Tom's Thumb from the **Tom's Thumb Trailhead** (23015 N. 128th St.) is approximately five miles of intense climbing in some of the most incredible desert you'll ever encounter.

Paper maps are free at all the trailheads so be sure to grab one—you'll need it! If you'd like to enjoy the desert in an all-inclusive way, check out the guided hikes provided by the **McDowell Sonoran Conservancy** (7729 E. Greenway Rd., Suite 100, mcdowellsonoran. org, 480/998-7971).

McDowell Mountain Regional Park manages the eastern-most end of the trail system in the McDowell Mountains and operates an area largely comprised of foothills and flat desert land. The most popular hiking trail here is the **Pemberton Trail,** which is a mostly-flat loop that stretches just over 15 miles. Hikers can opt to cut the loop in half by combining Pemberton with the Tonto Trail for nine miles of hiking along flat (but super-gorgeous) desert terrain.

HORSEBACK RIDING

There's nothing like the desert to get visions of cowboys dancing in your head, and **Windwalker Expeditions, Inc.** (888/785-3382, www.windwalkerexpeditions.com, $165) can help you live out any Zane Grey (or even Billy Crystal, *City Slickers*-style) fantasies with trail rides atop Arabian or quarter horses. Beginners can even get lessons on the trail. For experienced riders, the company also organizes multiday pack trips through the backcountry lasting anywhere from 2 to 10 days.

Wanna push the herd? Maybe flank and brand a calf? Or perhaps do a little pickin' and singin' after a long day on the range? Well, have I got the place for you, cowhand. **Arizona Cowboy College** (30208 N. 152nd St., 480/471-3151, www.cowboycollege.com) offers honest-to-goodness, "no frills" lessons

in cowboying. From one-day sessions on horseback riding and roping ($450) to the comprehensive one-week course ($2,250), you'll have the experience of a lifetime learning how Arizona's pioneers won the Wild West.

RAFTING

Grab a paddle with **Desert Voyagers Guided River Tours** (16447 N. 91st St., Suite 101, 480/998-7238, www.desertvoyagers.com, $130 per person) and meander along the banks of the lower Salt River on a gentle rafting trip, where you'll spot a surprising mix of wildlife, including beavers, egrets, wild horses, and the most-active bald eagle nesting areas in Arizona. Alternatively opt for the kayaking excursions, which offer a more intimate journey and a few thrills more appropriate for older kids and adults ($160 per person).

See the Sonoran Desert from an unexpected perspective. Float down the Salt River with **Arizona Rafting By Wilderness Aware** (7360 E. Acoma Dr., Suite 4, 800/231-7238, www.saltriverraftingarizona.com) for a more intensive experience. The start point for these rafting trips is quite a drive from Scottsdale and experiences range from a half-day white water rafting trip ($79 per adult, $66 per child) to the five-day 51-mile wilderness adventure by raft ($919 per adult, $763 per child) that includes camping on sandy beaches, leisurely floating, and thrilling rapids.

SPECTATOR SPORTS

You'll find most of the Valley's sports action in Phoenix, but every March the Boys of Spring descend upon Scottsdale for the Cactus League spring training series and the whole city goes wild. Baseball fans can catch the San Francisco Giants at **Scottsdale Stadium** (7408 E. Osborn Rd., 480/312-2586, www. scottsdaleaz.gov/scottsdale-stadium), battling one of 14 other MLB teams on the field, including the Chicago Cubs, Seattle Mariners, Los Angeles Dodgers, and hometown Arizona Diamondbacks. You can also grab a hot dog and a game at the downtown stadium during the Arizona Fall League in October.

★ SPAS

Scottsdale is one of the spa capitals of the world, boasting some of the largest and most lavish facilities that you'll find anywhere. Whether you're in the mood for a deep-tissue massage or Native American-inspired treatments, you'll find the perfect spa in Scottsdale to get scrubbed, rubbed, and buffed.

Although there are a host of day spas throughout the city, none offer the amenities of the big resorts (nor do you really save any money). Many locals book a facial or massage at a resort so that they can spend the entire day taking advantage of the spa's pool, fitness classes, on-site gym, and amenities including steam rooms and saunas. It's a great way to experience a five-star resort without paying to stay there. Basic hour-long massages are affordable and multi-treatment packages are available.

The Centre for Well-Being at **The Phoenician Scottsdale** (6000 E. Camelback Rd., 480/243-2452, www.thephoenician.com, 8am-7:30pm daily) takes a holistic approach to spa-ing. In addition to the usual whirlpools, saunas, and showers, the Centre also features a meditation atrium. Massages and treatments utilize plants and minerals indigenous to the Southwest, like the Native American-inspired Well-Being Stone Ritual ($160) and the hydrating Desert Serenity Scrub, Wrap, and Massage ($260). For a New Age experience, a "circle of intuitive guides" offers personalized meditation, astrology, hypnotherapy, and tarot-card reading.

Younger spa-goers looking for hipper crowds and some poolside excitement may want to check out the **VH Spa** at the **Hotel Valley Ho** (6850 E. Main St., 480/248-2000, www.hotelvalleyho.com, 8am-8:15pm daily). Although a bit small, the mod decor, froufrou treatments, and poolside parties will appeal to 20-somethings looking to splurge. Massages here start at $125.

The Moroccan-inspired **Joya Spa** at the **Omni Scottsdale Resort & Spa at Montelucia** (4949 E. Lincoln Dr., 480/627-3020, www.omnihotels.com/hotels/Scottsdale-montelucia, 8:30am-7pm daily) has set the bar in Scottsdale for an over-the-top spa experience. You'll want to spend the day (and evening) at this sprawling complex to take advantage of the hammam-style bathing facilities, which include a warming room, sauna, steam room, cold deluge shower, and

Joya Spa

whirlpool. In between treatments, enjoy the rooftop pool terrace with views of Camelback Mountain and the Whisper Lounge, a serene place to relax with friends on cushy daybeds, surrounded by candles and soft music. For a real spend, try one of the suites, which feature private terraces and outdoor showers and copper tubs. Massages here start at $149.

A favorite of locals, the **Spa at Camelback Inn** (5402 E. Lincoln Dr., 480/596-7040, www.camelbackspa.com, 6:15am-7:30pm daily) offers the most amenity bang for your spa buck with saunas, steam rooms, whirlpools, cold plunge pools, and exercise classes, just to name a few. The soothing massages (starting at $160) feature techniques like hot stone, Shiatsu, Swedish, and aromatherapy. Treat that face with an anti-aging, hydrating, or active organics facial (starting at $160), then take care of your insides with healthy dishes from Sprouts, the spa restaurant, as you relax in a poolside cabana overlooking Camelback Mountain.

You would think that with a climate ready-made for reveling in the outdoors, more spas would take their amenities outside. **Spa Avania** at the **Hyatt Regency Scottsdale Resort & Spa at Gainey Ranch** (7500 E. Doubletree Ranch Rd., 480/483-5558, www.scottsdale.hyatt.com, 8:30am-8pm daily) has created a seamless indoor and outdoor facility. Glass walls slide open onto terraces with outdoor showers, comfy lounge chairs, and hot and cold plunge pools. The facility incorporates elegant stonework, garden treatment rooms, and a co-ed French-Celtic mineral pool and lotus pond. Avania's "science of time" philosophy takes a holistic approach to relaxation, syncing treatments to the body's natural biorhythms and incorporating herbal medicine and traditional Thai therapies into treatments. Massages here start at $165. Be sure to hit the Salt Room for an immune system boost and detox.

If you like chic design with your Swedish massage, **Sanctuary Spa** at **Sanctuary Camelback Mountain Resort & Spa** (5700 E. McDonald Dr., 888/722-6230, www.

sanctuaryoncamelback.com, 7am-8:30pm daily) won't disappoint. Design buffs will appreciate the stylish transformation of this 1960s "tennis ranch" into a Modernist Zen retreat, complete with men's and women's relaxation lounges overlooking a meditation garden and reflecting pond. The Asian-inspired treatments, which start at $175, are available in one of 12 indoor and outdoor treatment rooms. The heated Watsu massage pool, private outdoor suites, and location on the side of Camelback Mountain make this spa an extraordinary destination.

One of the finest spas in the world, **Well & Being Spa** at the **Fairmont Scottsdale Princess** (7575 E. Princess Dr., 480/585-2732, www.fairmont.com/scottsdale/spa, 6am-9pm daily) pays homage to the Arizona landscape with indigenous stone and native architectural details. The men's and women's areas provide a welcome bit of privacy to enjoy the Swedish dry sauna, wet steam room, hot whirlpool, cold plunge pool, Swiss shower, and eucalyptus inhalation room. Make a trip through the grotto waterfall for an outdoor waterfall massage then head up to the rooftop adults-only pool and cabanas. Try one of the signature body scrubs and wraps like the 120-minute Havasupai Falls Rejuvenation ($329), which includes an essential oil-infused salt scrub, herbal foaming salt bath, jojoba body butter massage, hot riverbed stone treatment, and herbal-infused oil stream.

The intimate **Spa at the Four Seasons Resort Scottsdale at Troon North** (10600 E. Crescent Moon Dr., 480/513-5145, www.fourseasons.com/Scottsdale, 6am-9pm daily) doesn't offer the sprawling (and sometimes overwhelming) amenities of its competitors, but its desert-inspired treatments make it a worthwhile option. Try the Jojoba and Prickly Pear Body Polish or Cocoa Mole Energizing Wrap.

The 33,000-square-foot **Spa at the Boulders Resort** (34631 N. Tom Darlington Dr., 480/595-3500, www.theboulders.com, 8am-8pm daily) offers a fascinating mix of Japanese bathing customs and Native

American traditions, set against Carefree's craggy desert landscape. Lounge in the traditional Japanese *o'furo* bath before heading outside to the swimming pool and meditative labyrinth, which overlook the resort's namesake boulder formation. If you're intrigued by ancient healing traditions, book the Lotus Blossoming Chakra Massage ($230) as a part of the Global Shaman Experiences offered, during which you'll be treated to a chakra-aligning rub down with seven oils "attuned to the energies of the seven chakras." The spa also offers rock-climbing clinics ($135) if you like a little adventure with your pampering.

Food

Scottsdale is known for the luxurious life and their food is no different. If you like to call yourself a foodie, then you probably already know that Scottsdale is a mecca for great eating. First-time visitors will discover outposts of New York's best-known chefs, as well as homegrown talents who infuse their cooking with the indigenous flavors of the Southwest. Get ready for a culinary adventure. And although some of the best restaurants can be a little pricey, it's well worth loosening the purse strings for a culinary treat.

DOWNTOWN
American
If you make one culinary splurge in Scottsdale, make ★ **Cowboy Ciao** (7133 E. Stetson Dr., 480/946-3111, www.cowboy-ciao.com, 11:30am-2:30pm, 5pm-10pm daily, $15-38) your stop. The Stetson Chop Salad is the stuff of gastronomic legend in the Valley, and the quote on the menu says it all: "I love that chopped salad so much that I put it on my screen saver!" The Exotic Mushroom Pan Fry and Niman Ranch Bone-In Pork Chop are almost as good. In fact, it seems like executive chef Lester Gonzalez has done everything he can think of to offer guests bold flavors and unpredictable combinations of fresh ingredients at reasonable prices. And few restaurants can compete with Cowboy Ciao's wine list or their accolades. The restaurant has consistently made "best of" lists in local publications like *Phoenix Magazine* and in print as distant as *The Times of London*.

Since its opening in 2009, **FnB** (7125 E. 5th Ave., Ste. 31, 480/284-4777, www.fnbrestaurant.com, 11am-2pm, 5pm-10pm Tues.-Sat., 1pm-5pm, 5pm-9pm Sun., $8-37) continues to be a favorite stop for locals and visitors seeking a delicious and thoughtful dining experience. The restaurant features a seasonal, local menu that changes with what's available from local farmers (imagine that!), offering interesting dishes with decidedly global influences, ranging from Mediterranean to Southwestern. Start with one of the fresh salads and sample from the hearty, roasted meats or fresh seafood. Wine lovers will not be disappointed by the extensive wine list of exclusively Arizona wines as well as a "Plan B" menu with wines handpicked from other regions. To end the meal, don't miss a chance to indulge in the innovative desserts.

The burger options are abundant at **Stax Burger Bistro** (4400 N. Scottsdale Rd., 480/946-4222, www.staxburgerbistro.com, 11am-9pm Sun.-Thurs., 11am-10pm Fri.-Sat., $5-12.50), which serves up mini-hamburgers in a host of mix-and-match options. Select your patty (or patties)—beef, lamb, buffalo, veggie, and others—then top it with your choice of bun, cheese, and condiments, including crispy bacon, fresh guacamole, and fancy aiolis. For the uninspired, there's an extensive menu of recommendations, including the "exotic" order that depends on the hunting season. Oh, don't forget to order a hearty side like the Mack N' Jack.

Let's make this easy. Don't ask questions. Just go to ★ **Café Monarch** (6934 E. 1st Ave., 480/970-7682, www.cafemonarch.com,

5:30pm-8:30pm Tues.-Thurs., 5pm-9:30pm Fri.-Sat., 5:30pm-7:30pm Sun., $65-80). Of all the culinary experiences in town, none is so intimate as a dinner at Café Monarch. This restaurant has one chef who conjures a four-course prix fixe menu that changes each week depending on what the market has to offer. Reservations are recommended for this experience but don't be intimidated—Chef Gus Lewkowicz is sweet as can be and the New American cuisine is simply to die for. So go. You won't regret it.

Welcome to the new frontier of haute dining. **Posh** (7167 E. Rancho Vista Dr., Ste. 111, 480/663-7674, www.poshscottsdale.com, 5pm-9pm Tues., 5pm-close Wed.-Sat., $65-175) pioneers into unchartered culinary territory with its seasonal "improvised" cuisine. Translation: There is no menu. Instead, you fill out a sheet that lists tastes, preferences, allergies, number of courses, and requests for wine pairings. The restaurant's chefs take over from there, preparing an innovative lineup of genre-breaking dishes with ingredients like monkfish liver, kangaroo, and geoduck (just as examples—the options change based on availability and chef's whimsy). Everyone in your party gets something different, which means an epic meal that's as memorable as it is surprising. Try to grab a seat at the bar that overlooks the open kitchen. For a set menu, pop in on a Tuesday night when the place turns into **Posh Ramen Shop** and serves Japanese street food from 5pm-9pm; this lower-priced culinary experience sets you back just $12 per Ramen bowl.

Salt Cellar (550 N. Hayden Rd., 480/947-1963, www.saltcellarrestaurant.com, 5pm-11pm Sun.-Thurs., 5pm-midnight Fri.-Sat., $23-80) is the place to go for a break from the desert. Enter through the blue-and-white shack and descend the antique wooden staircase leading underground to the dining area. Lobster is the house specialty, complemented by a wide variety of sea creatures that include mussels, oysters, scallops, monkfish, ahi, trout, and many more. Fresh seafood is flown in daily and dishes are prepared in a traditional, old-school way so the menu is easy to navigate. Take the plunge and try the baked lobster stuffed with scallops and crabmeat, or go with the basic and appreciate the waiters' expert cracking abilities. This subterranean venue is the perfect place for a date, as it maintains a casual vibe with tasty cuisine and a bar that opens 4pm-1am daily.

Just south of downtown Scottsdale, **Pig & Pickle** (2922 N. Hayden Rd., 480/990-1407, www.pigandpickle.com, 4pm-10pm Tues.-Wed., 11am-3pm Thurs.-Sat., 10am-2pm, 4pm-10pm Sun., $7-24) has been a welcome addition to the neighborhood. Its casual vibe is welcoming and warm, the staff is friendly and chatty, and the patrons are cheerful and breezy. And if you go, you will be full and happy. The lunch, dinner, late night, and Sunday brunch menus feature contemporary cuisine with clever names like the Apocalypse Sow (pork burger with bacon) or Dump Truck salad. And with original cocktails like the Red Headed Stepchild and the Funk-tional Drunk, you can't go wrong.

If you're in the mood, try **Rehab Burger Therapy** (7210 E. 2nd St., 480/621-5358, www.rehabburgertherapy.com, 11am-9pm Sun.-Tues., 11am-10pm Wed.-Thurs., 11am-11pm Fri.-Sat., $7-15). This place adopts a philosophy of kicking back and enjoying the good life—even if it's just for a moment. The beach-themed atmosphere helps put folks in the mood to hang out, enjoy some grub, and chat the afternoon away. Have some beer. Have some tequila. Have some wine. Order anything from wings to salads to pasta. Oh, and burgers. You have over 20 burgers to choose from!

Asian

Malee's Thai Bistro (7131 E. Main St., 480/947-6042, www.maleesonmain.com, 11am-9pm Mon.-Sat., noon-9pm Sun., $10-21) attracts a devoted following of diners who praise its comfy atmosphere, warm service, and reasonable prices. The Thai-inspired cuisine ranges from classic spring rolls, chow mein, and pad Thai to the "Tropical

Pineapple," a tasty mix of seafood and minced chicken in coconut curry sauce. Speaking of which, curry-lovers will find a decent selection of dishes—served as hot as requested and vegetarians will be pleased with many options.

Many claim that **Sushi J** (4320 N. Miller Rd., 480/946-3550, www.sushi-j.com, noon-3pm, 5:30pm-10pm Mon.-Thurs., noon-3pm, 5:30pm-10:30pm Fri., 5:30pm-10:30pm Sat., 5:30pm-10pm Sun., $10-18) has the freshest sushi in town. Located in an unassuming strip mall near Old Town, the casual eatery is great for a relaxed meal. The menu features all the standard rolls and sashimi with some funky specialty rolls like the Friday Night Fever or the Lord of Tuna. If you can't hang with the whole sushi thing, they've got you covered with entrées like the ginger calamari, chicken teriyaki, and sautéed white fish.

Breakfast and Lunch

You don't have to be one of the Scottsdale "ladies who lunch" to appreciate ★ **Arcadia Farms** (7014 E. 1st Ave., 480/941-5665, www.arcadiafarmscafe.com, 8am-3pm daily, $9-16). The charming, cottage setting provides a pleasant backdrop for breakfast, brunch, or lunch. Its fresh and organic omelets, sandwiches, and soups never disappoint, and the goat cheese salad with fresh raspberries is legendary—seriously.

The Breakfast Club (4400 N. Scottsdale Road, 480/222-2582, www.thebreakfastclub.us, 6am-3pm Mon.-Fri., 7am-3pm Sat.-Sun., $5-15) specializes in the most important meal of the day. The polished concrete floors and contemporary decor forgo the dowdy country-kitsch of most breakfast places but is still cozy and inviting. Try the Southwest-inspired breakfast burrito with eggs, black beans, chorizo, and pepper jack cheese. And when it comes to omelets, "The Bird"—turkey, avocado, mushrooms, and boursin cheese—is super yummy. Dishes are inexpensive and hearty but the people watching is the real treat, from older couples enjoying

lattes to 20-somethings hiding the shame of the previous evening behind sunglasses and messy hair.

Nursing a hangover? **Daily Dose** (4020 N. Scottsdale Rd., 480/994-3673, www.dailydosegrill.com, 7am-daily, $9-13) has just what you need. With a huge breakfast menu that includes all the standards (eggs, pancakes, French toast, waffles) *plus* protein bowls *plus* vegetarian options *plus* gluten free options *plus* a dish called the hangover sandwich *plus* cocktails for a hair of the dog—I mean, come on! Throw on a baseball cap, grab the sunglasses, and take a seat. Lunch is also available from 10:30am on in case you're in the mood for a burger and fries to settle that belly.

Dessert

If you have kids on this trip, take time to give them a treat and head to ★ **The Sugar Bowl** (4005 N. Scottsdale Rd., 480/946-0051, www.sugarbowlscottsdale.com, 11am-10pm Mon.-Thurs., 11am-midnight Fri.-Sat., 11am-10pm Sun.). Aptly named, The Sugar Bowl specializes in an old-time ice-cream shop experience, with two pages of dessert options on the menu. From the Creamed Walnut Fudge Sundae to the Gosh-Awful-Gooey Banana Split to fresh-fruit sherbets, creamy shakes and malts, it is a sugar overload in the best way. Serving Scottsdale for over 60 years, the nostalgia is thick. Lunch is also available with standard American classics if you're looking to make it a special outing with the kiddos.

Farmers Market

On Saturday mornings, a small parking lot at the corner of Brown and 1st Street transforms into the **Old Town Farmers Market** (3806 N. Brown Ave., www.oldtownfarmersmarket.com, 8am-1pm Sat., Oct.-June). Since its opening in 2010, this weekly market has become a staple of shopping for residents of the "dale." Hop from vendor to vendor and make a picnic from the seasonal specialties like local cheeses, fresh tamales, artisan breads, jams, and organic vegetables.

French

Merci French Café & Patisserie (7620 E. Indian School Rd., 480/947-2777, www.mercifrenchcafe.com, 9am-4pm Mon.-Tues., 9am-8pm Wed.-Sat., 9am-3pm Sun., $7-16) is an adorable little café tucked into a shopping center with a chain grocery store and a Subway. But don't let that sway you, as the place is charming and it serves delicious French breakfast and lunch. Bite into a crispy croissant or delicious quiche. The brie, club, or Croque Madame open-faced sandwiches are a perfect midday meal. There are a few American standards like burgers and a tuna melt plus plenty of French pastries to choose from to top off the meal.

Italian

DeFalco's Italian Eatery, Grocery & Deli (2334 N. Scottsdale Rd., 480/990-8660, www.deslcosdeli.com, 10am-9pm Mon.-Sat., 11am-9pm Sun., $5-17) is a family-owned, traditional Italian place with sauce recipes handed down through generations. The menu doesn't leave much to be desired with an all-inclusive line-up of hot sandwiches, cold sandwiches, salads, pizza, and pasta. The super-casual eatery is a great option if you're looking for tasty food on a budget. And, if you're so inclined after sampling the food, you can pick up olives, pasta, or wine at the adjoining market.

Mexican and Southwest

You can't help but love the **Old Town Tortilla Factory** (6910 E. Main St., 480/945-4567, www.oldtowntortillafactory.com, 4pm-9:30pm Sun.-Thurs., 4pm-10pm Fri.-Sat., $12-29). Enjoy one of the fantastic house margaritas on the large flagstone patio shaded by citrus and pecan trees, or choose from one of 120 premium tequilas in the gazebo bar. Move inside the 75-year-old adobe home to get cozy on a chilly day, although be aware that this restaurant is best experienced with tequila in hand plus a few snacks—a full meal is a bit pricey for what you get.

Rotisserie chicken—it's so simple but so good at **Bandera** (3821 N. Scottsdale Rd., 480/994-3524, www.banderarestaurants.com, 4pm-10pm Sun.-Thurs., 4pm-11pm Fri.-Sat., $15-43). This contemporary Western restaurant wood-fire-roasts its chickens all day and serves them along with ribs, steaks, and burgers. You'll absolutely devour the jalapeño cornbread served in a signature iron skillet before you try the tri-tip and enchilada platter with Mexican cucumber salad (akin to Greek). And this is the kind of place where you save room for dessert, like the banana cream pie or the homemade Oreo ice-cream sandwich with créme de cocoa and fresh whipped cream.

Frank and Lupe's (4121 N. Marshall Way, 480/990-9844, www.frankandlupes.com, 11am-10pm daily, $7-15) has been serving up delicious chicken enchiladas for more than 25 years. Every family has its favorite traditional, inexpensive Mexican food restaurant in town and this place is the go-to joint for many locals. It's hard to beat the casual atmosphere and colorful decor, not to mention the reasonable prices for the middle of downtown. Order a Mexican beer or house margarita and dig into the green corn tamales, shredded beef tacos, or Lupe's enchilada plate. Oh, and if the kids are with you, the place makes a mean cheese crisp.

Looking to try a different kind of Mexican cuisine? **Los Sombreros** (2534 N. Scottsdale Rd., 480/994-1799, www.lossombreros.com, 3:30pm-9pm Mon.-Thurs., 3pm-10pm Fri.-Sat., 3pm-9pm Sun., $10-25) serves up dishes from southern, central, and northern Mexico. The *queso fundido* with crab and crepes with *cajeta* and almond tequila are inspired, especially when paired with a margarita made with fresh lime juice. Dine outside on the homey patio to enjoy your meal even more.

★ **The Mission** (3815 N. Brown Ave., 480/636-5005, www.themissionaz.com, 11am-10pm Mon.-Thurs., 11am-11pm Fri., 10am-11pm Fri.-Sat., 10am-10pm Sun. $12-34) is a perfect Scottsdale combination of Latin flavors and chic style. You can't help but notice the restaurant's neighbor first: the domed Old Adobe Mission, which serves as the inspiration for the restaurant's modern-colonial

The Mission has great guacamole.

decor. Start with one of the house cocktails and the amazing *almejas al vapor,* steamed clams with rock shrimp, chorizo, and yucca. The grilled street corn, pork shoulder tacos, and diver scallops are delicious—but then again, so is everything on the menu. On the weekends, the kitchen offers a brunch menu with inspired morning boosts like the corn and crab pancakes or pollo a la brasa y waffles.

The Corral family started **Los Olivos** (7328 E. 2nd St., 480/946-2256, www.losolivosrestaurants.com, 11am-10pm Sun.-Thurs., 11am-11pm Fri.-Sat., $8-20) more than 60 years ago and named it for the old olive trees along 2nd Street. This affordable Old Town Scottsdale eatery holds a special place in many Scottsdalians' hearts and features the Sonoran-style Mexican food that Arizona natives grew up on. Enjoy your *machaca* and fajitas (served with homemade flour tortillas hot off the griddle) in the Gaudí-esque Blue Room, or go for the Mexican Flag dish filled with three enchiladas, accompanied by a traditional margarita with a salted rim.

★ **Roaring Fork** (4800 N. Scottsdale Rd., 480/947-0795, www.roaringfork.com, 4pm-10pm daily, $14-27) serves hearty American food with Southwestern influence and a bit of high-end flair. Appetizers range from tortilla soup and guacamole to plates of mussels and chorizo or the fondue pot with lamb chops. Order the Roaring Fork "Big Ass" Burger, sugar-cured duck breast with onion jam and sour cherry mustard, or grilled fish tacos. You're sure to find a nice pairing for the Western cuisine on the restaurant's bold wine list. Hit it up at Happy Hour for great prices on delicious snacks and house cocktails.

Pizza

Scottsdale is finally on board with the artisan wood-fired pizza craze at **Craft64** (6922 E. Main St., 480/946-0542, www.craft64.com, 11am-11pm daily, $10-19). This place will not disappoint folks who enjoy the finer kind of pizza—pizza that explodes with super-fresh flavor brought about by local ingredients, mozzarella made daily in house, and the slight char that a wood-fire oven produces so beautifully. You know what else is beautiful? The sparkling row of 35 tap handles featuring Arizona brewed beer. Not to mention one

Last, Last Call at 'Berto's

Be it Filiberto's, Juliobertos, Rolberto's, Raliberto's or any variant on the 'berto's name, a late-night splurge on the 24-hour drive-thru Mexican food offered at these fine establishments is a widely respected and well-loved rite of passage for partiers in Scottsdale and Phoenix. When you're well on the way to a heck of a hangover after a night out drinking and dancing, ask the cabbie or the Uber driver to take you to the closest 'berto's and they will know exactly what you're looking for: a late-night Mexican food fix that is cheap, greasy, and one of the best decisions you will ever make while under the influence.

The food is not fancy and the places are, well, delightfully urban. For just a few dollars you can snarf down super hefty portions of burritos, quesadillas, nachos, enchiladas, and any other Mexican food craving you may have. It's glorious. With different ownership of each fast-food restaurant, you'll find that even something basic like the bean and cheese burrito can vary from establishment to establishment. Therefore every person who lives in the Valley has their favorite 'berto's and it's not uncommon for friendly arguments to break out over which is the best. In fact, the 'berto's love runs so fierce that many who move away from the Valley insist on making a stop at their favorite 'berto's as soon as they get off the plane.

As you cruise through the streets of Scottsdale, keep an eye out for the iconic bright-yellow sign with cursive writing and (usually) an illustration of a taco. Scottsdale's **Filiberto's** are located on 7111 E. Thomas Rd., 7620 E. McKellips Rd., and 9150 E. Indian Bend Rd. We recommend asking your driver or anyone at the bar for their recommendation.

heck of a wine list available to drink at the table or to go. Heaven.

Grimaldi's Coal Brick-Oven Pizzeria (4000 N. Scottsdale Road, 480/994-1100, www.patsygrimaldis.com, 11am-10pm Sun.-Thurs., 11am-midnight Fri.-Sat., $9-25) brings a Brooklyn tradition to the Valley of the Sun with its coal-fired ovens and famous "secret recipe" dough. The simple menu offers salad starters, calzones, and pizzas accompanied by list of fresh toppings. Kids will love the quarter-sized slices of pepperoni, and the ricotta cheese is incredible. Be prepared to build up an appetite—its reputation for unique flavor draws large crowds to this casual and family-friendly spot.

Steakhouses

Don & Charlie's (7501 E. Camelback Rd., 480/990-0900, www.donandcharlies.com,

5pm-9:30pm Mon.-Sat., 5pm-9pm Sun., $10-44) woos sports-history and red-meat aficionados alike. The upscale eatery is adorned with rich, dark woods and enough sports memorabilia and autographs to make Bob Costas's head spin. The Ned Colletti's Chicken Schnitzels or the rib eyes are perfect accompaniments to a stiff cocktail from the full bar. Don't let the sports memorabilia fool you; Don & Charlie's is an old-Scottsdale gem, and the perfect place to fill your belly and lighten your wallet after a round of golf or a spring-training baseball game.

Mastro's City Hall Steakhouse (6991 E. Camelback Rd., 480/941-4700, www.mastrosrestaurants.com, 5pm-10pm Sun.-Thurs., 5pm-11pm Fri.-Sat., $35-70) serves all the classics you'd expect at a high-end steakhouse: lobster cocktails, oysters Rockefeller, and a host of filets, porterhouses, rib eyes, and chops. The side dishes—sautéed mushrooms, creamed spinach, Alaskan King Crab Black Truffle Gnocchi—are enough decadence for a meal in itself (although you wouldn't want to miss the entrées). The happening lounge (4pm-1am daily) attracts singles of all ages in the evenings.

CENTRAL SCOTTSDALE AND PARADISE VALLEY
Breakfast

It's tough to know where to begin at **Butterfield's Pancake House & Restaurant** (7388 E. Shea Blvd., 480/951-6002, www.butterfieldsrestaurant.com, 6am-3pm daily, $6-11). The menu is an epic breakfast journey, with a dozen kinds of pancakes, omelets that range from Denver to Mexicana, and enough egg dishes to shut down Denny's. That doesn't even count the French toast and crepes, Belgian waffles, oatmeal, or the oven-baked pancakes. Order a cup of coffee and take a deep breath. If you keep your head, it'll be worth it.

You always know you're at a quality place when the menu is small and manageable. At **Benedict's Cafe** (5555 E. Bell Rd., 602/992-3337, www.benedictscaterers.com, 8am-2pm

Sat.-Sun., $5-14) you can be assured that special attention is paid to each dish. Serving brunch only on the weekends, this catering company redefines classics like the, well, the eggs Benedict. Try the Florentine with tarragon biscuit sautéed spinach, and mushrooms or the California with sourdough, prosciutto, tomatoes, and avocado—both with poached eggs and hollandaise sauce, of course. If you're a no-can-do on the hollandaise, they offer other delicious items like the omelet, quiche, chorizo scramble, burrito, or the fabulous Croque Monsieur made with shaved ham, Granny Smith apples, fig jam, and a cheese Mornay sauce atop a croissant.

Italian

Veneto Trattoria Italiana (6137 N. Scottsdale Rd., 480/948-9928, www.venetotrattoria.com, 11:30am-2:30pm, 5pm-10pm Mon.-Sat., $18-28) specializes in cuisine inspired by the healthy living in the Mediterranean and Italian regions. Dine alfresco on the patio, and start with eggplant gratin or *baccala* (cod whipped with cheese spread atop polenta). The house signature dishes are taken straight from the streets (er... canals) of Venice like the calf liver served with onion and grilled polenta. For dessert, splurge and order the *affogato,* vanilla ice cream with white chocolate chips and a shot of Scotch-flavored espresso.

New American

They just don't make 'em anymore like **El Chorro** (5550 E. Lincoln Dr., 480/948-5170, www.elchorro.com, 5pm to close Mon.-Sat., 9am-2:30pm, 5:30pm-close Sun., $12-54). This Paradise Valley institution has been serving fresh fish, roasted chicken, beef stroganoff, and steaks since the 1930s. Come with that special someone to enjoy the stunning setting in the shadow of Camelback Mountain, order the "trailside specialty" Chateaubriand for two, and cap the evening with El Chorro's famous sticky buns, a 65-year-old house tradition.

The panorama shot of Mummy Mountain

at sunset is worth the reservation alone. From its perch atop Paradise Valley, ★ **elements** (5700 E. McDonald Dr., 480/607-2300, www.sanctuaryoncamelback.com/dining/elements, 7am-10:30am, 11am-2pm, 5:30pm-9:30pm Mon.-Thurs., 7am-10:30am, 11am-2pm, 5:30pm-10pm Fri.-Sat., 7am-2pm, 5:30pm-9:30pm Sun., $8-54) at Sanctuary Camelback Mountain Resort is a treat in many respects. The mod decor is stylish, and the views are stunning. However, it's the simple and natural menu by *Iron Chef*-winner Beau MacMillan, the friendliest chef you're likely to meet, that makes elements special. His innovative dishes change with the season but always maintain a farm-fresh American flavor with Asian accents. Serving breakfast, lunch, dinner, and brunch on Sundays, many visitors spend multiple meals at this Scottsdale favorite.

★ **LON's at the Hermosa Inn** (5532 N. Palo Cristi Rd., 602/955-7878, www.hermosainn.com/lons, 7am-10am, 11:30am-2pm, 5:30pm-10pm Mon.-Fri., 5:30pm-10pm Sat., 10am-2pm, 5:30pm-10pm Sun., $11-67) prides itself on being the most authentic hacienda in Arizona. Once the home of cowboy artist Lon Megargee, the elegant yet cozy adobe and wood-finished interior captures the allure of Old Arizona. Pan-roasted salmon with caper-raising butter sauce, roasted duck with blackberry jus, and truffle mac 'n' cheese round out the menu, which features ingredients organically grown on the inn's grounds. Dine on the patio for beautiful views of the desert, and save room for dessert—the cowboy candy bar with chili-spiced ganache is an experience.

Slow-food chef Chrysa Robertson's **Rancho Pinot** (6208 N. Scottsdale Rd., 480/367-8030, 5:30pm-9pm Mon.-Sat., www.ranchopinot.com, $18-33) is a master class in using fresh, seasonal food without a lot of hoopla or Scottsdale flash. You can't help but love the vegetarian antipasto and diver scallops on corn-bacon fritters—assuming it's the right season for those items. The menu is always subject to change because this place is the real deal for seasonal dining. The Southwest decor and artful recipes with experimental flavors make for a memorable night out.

Spanish

The tapas, wood-fired fare, and paellas set the tone for **Prado** (4949 E. Lincoln Dr., 480/627-3004, www.omnihotels.com/hotels/Scottsdale-montelucia/dining/prado, 7am-3pm, 5pm-11pm daily, $13-38) at the

LON's at the Hermosa Inn

Montelucia Resort. In keeping with the resort's Spanish and Mediterranean inspirations, the menu features paella of the day with ingredients varying according to the chef's whim as well as rich cheeses from Spain. The restaurant's wood-fired grilled meats, like the salmon, chicken, or lamb chops are perfect. But the place isn't all about meat and cheese—they include delicate preparations of roasted vegetables that are locally sourced. The high standards are present throughout the day with the restaurant serving breakfast, lunch, and dinner.

Steakhouse

Chef Laurent Tourondel's modern American steakhouse, **BLT Steak** (5402 E. Lincoln Dr., 480/905-7979, www.bltscottsdale.com, 6pm-9pm daily, $32-70) brings a bit of New York chic to the Camelback Inn. The beautifully streamlined interior decor seems to disappear when the lineup of certified Black Angus, USDA prime cuts, and Wagyu steaks arrive, not to mention side splurges like the smoked Gouda macaroni and cheese or the fontina-baked potatoes. Top it off with the Peanut Butter Chocolate Tart with Hazelnut Praline Ice Cream and waddle your way home. Worth it!

NORTH SCOTTSDALE
American

★ **Four Peaks Grill & Tap** (15745 N. Hayden Rd., 480/991-1795, www.fourpeaks.com, 11am-1am daily, $10-14) showcases its unique Tempe-brewed beers at this North Scottsdale location and continues to deliver all that a brewery should: excellent beer and tasty bar food. The curious can find a full listing of beers, with their alcohol contents, on the beer menu. The Kilt Lifter and 8th Street ales are local specialties, but serious hopheads will enjoy the Hop Knot IPA. If you happen to be in town during fall, you must try the Pumpkin Porter, which is so wildly popular it's a seasonal tradition for locals. If you're hungry, the Tap Room Tenderloin with beer-battered fries is especially good when upgraded from the hoagie to beer bread. And for those limiting their red meat intake, the veggie burger with spinach and roasted red pepper is one of the best in town.

Asian

For a little bit of modern Tokyo in the desert, try **Pure Sushi Bar & Dining** (20567 N. Hayden Rd., 480/355-0999, www.puresushibar.net, 11am-10pm Mon.-Thurs., 11am-11pm Fri.-Sat., 11am-9pm Sun., $12-28). The contemporary, clean decor provides the perfect setting for quality sushi. This is good stuff. The drink menu features sake from many regions of Japan, and the signature drinks, like the Thai Basil Lemonade with vodka, are light and refreshing. While the tuna and yellowtail nigiri shouldn't be missed, try a few of the house-specialty rolls, like WTF Roll. This twist on the traditional sushi roll is made with sea bass tempura, fresh jalapeños, avocado, and crab, with spicy mayo and eel sauce.

Breakfast and Lunch

Bright and airy, **The Breakfast Joynt** (20775 N. Pima Rd., 480/443-5324, www.thebreakfastjoynt.com, 7am-2:30pm daily, $7-10) serves up filling treats like Breakfast Fried Chicken, chocolate-chip waffles, and home-style biscuits with gravy. While you can get breakfast until close, their midday lunchtime menu features salads, burgers, classic Monte Cristos, and tuna melts as well as specialties like the Classic Triple Decker Turkey Club.

The hipster diner and market **Chloe's Corner** (15215 N. Kierland Blvd., 480/998-0202, www.chloescorneraz.com, 7am-6pm Mon.-Fri., 8am-6pm Sat., 8am-4pm Sun.) is a fun place to get a quick and inexpensive meal at Kierland Commons. Grab an egg sandwich and a 50-cent coffee in the morning, or plop down at the butcher-block counter when lunch rolls around for the chopped salad with turkey, blue cheese, and candied pecans. For a midafternoon treat, the pastries made in-house are delicious.

French

Why travel to Scottsdale to have French food? Well, taste the Onion Soup Gratinee at **Zinc Bistro** (15034 N. Scottsdale Rd., 480/603-0922, www.zincbistroaz.com, 11am-9pm daily, $12-42) and you'll know the answer (the answer is, because it's delicious). The Kierland Commons restaurant feels like a Parisian neighborhood favorite, right down to marble tables and wicker chairs. Grab a sidewalk table at lunch if you're up for a little people watching, or head for the candlelit garden patio for dinner if you'd like a more romantic setting to enjoy your bordeaux and filet mignon with foie gras.

Italian

North Italia (15024 N. Scottsdale Road, 480/948-2055, www.northitaliarestaurant.com, 11am-9:30pm Mon.-Thurs., 11am-10:30pm Fri.-Sat., 11:10am-9pm Sun., $12-34) at Kierland Commons offers a unique twist on northern Italian cuisine. The urban, loft-like design perfectly reflects the light, modern dishes and guests can enjoy traditional antipasti, ordering a variety from the small-plates menu, or sample the pizza of the day. Anyone arriving with an appetite should order the slow-cooked short rib with roasted vegetable and creamy white polenta or the Atlantic salmon with brown butter squash. The wine-savvy servers can suggest a bottle of vino to round out your meal.

The entire staff at family-owned **Ristorante Giuseppe** (13610 N. Scottsdale Rd., 480/991-4792, www.guiseppescottsdale.com, 11am-8:30pm Mon.-Fri., 5pm-9pm Sat., 5pm-8pm Sun., $8-16) makes you feel welcome. Start with the tasty garlic or pizza bread. Then move on to one of the delicious entrées—some are named after family members, one of whom will very likely be your server—Franco claims you'll dream about him after eating his namesake dish. Ordering one of their famous meatballs is a must. At the end of the night, you might end up enjoying a glass of wine with the server—it's just

that kind of place. The cash-only restaurant is BYOB, but there isn't a corkage fee.

★ **Sassi** (10455 E. Pinnacle Peak Pkwy., 480/502-9095, www.sassi.biz, 5pm-close Tues.-Sun., $20-40) means "stones" in Italian, a reference to its Pinnacle Peak location, but its food and service are anything but rocky. The southern Italian cuisine has been updated and re-imagined, earning praise from magazines and foodies alike. For antipasti try the 600-day-aged prosciutto di Parma or the Sicilian-style eggplant cakes with currants and pine nuts, and follow on with pastas ranging from hearty to subtle and delicate. Entrées include the veal chops and roasted duck breast with blood orange, fennel, and foie gras sauce. Aim to dine on the patio at sunset for the complete Sassi experience.

Latin American and Mexican

I can't say it more simply: **deseo** (6902 E. Greenway Pkwy., 480/624-1000, www.kierlandresort.com, 6pm-9pm daily, $12-35) is really good. The award-winning restaurant's survey of Nuevo Latino fare at The Westin Kierland Resort & Spa spans South American, Mexican, and Cuban cuisine. The impressive ceviche menu may convince first-timers to give the fresh seafood starter a try. Order a cocktail from the Muddle Bar, where fresh fruits and herbs are mashed together and given a little extra kick by an assortment of premium liquors. Then, dive into the churrasco-style Wagyu hanger steak, Mediterranean sea bass, and ripe plantains.

La Hacienda (7575 E. Princess Dr., 480/585-4848, www.fairmont.com/scottsdale/dining/la-hacienda, 5:30pm-9pm Sun.-Thurs., 5:30pm-10pm Fri.-Sat., $15-36) makes quite a big claim to being the best Mexican restaurant in Arizona, and many will agree. Located at the Fairmont Scottsdale Princess, the restaurant has teamed up with internationally acclaimed Chef Richard Sandoval, who is a pioneer in modern Mexican cuisine. The menu harnesses spectacular flavors by infusing traditional Mexican recipes with contemporary approaches to food. Oh, and there's an entire bar dedicated to serving tequila, with an artisan tasting each night from a collection of more than 200 varieties of tequila. Let the "Tequila God or Goddess" serve your pour on the weekends.

Mediterranean

Scottsdale is known for cutting edge, gastropub-like, new American experimental hotshot chefs. That's great and all, but sometimes you just want to taste something steeped in heavy tradition. Try **Persian Room** (17040 N. Scottsdale Rd., 480/614-1414, www.persianroom.com, 11am-9:30pm Sun.-Thurs., 11am-10:30pm Fri.-Sat., $13-30) for a flavorful Persian meal made with combinations of spices and seasonings developed over hundreds of years. The restaurant itself is lavishly decorated with gold and burgundy drapery, pillars, chandeliers, and horse statues (it's pretty awesome). Expect intense portions of charred-to-perfection kebab meats, skewered vegetables, and delicious stews served with saffron-flavored basmati rice.

New American

★ **Bink's Kitchen and Bar** (6107 N. Scottsdale Rd., 480/664-9238, www.binkleysrestaurantgroup.com, 11am-9:30pm Mon.-Thurs., 11am-10pm Fri., 10am-10pm Sat., 10am-9pm Sun., $9-38) is one of a few locations to the "parent" restaurant, Binkley's (see Cave Creek section), which may be the best restaurant in Arizona. At this outpost, the casual interior has an open patio where lunch, dinner, happy hour, and weekend brunch are served up. The focus is on super-fresh local ingredients packed with flavor and a changing menu to suit the season. Still, you can count on classic dishes with a culinary twist: Crispy Chicken Wings with apricot mostarda, Street Tacos with banana-leaf roasted pork, or the Five Spice Duck Breast with grilled grapes. Want to treat a large party to a unique dinner? Spring for the Pig's Head Special. It's a cooked pig's head with a whole host of sides that feeds up to six. Oink.

Next door, **Eddie V's Prime Seafood** (15323 N. Scottsdale Rd., 480/730-4800, www.eddiev.com, 4pm-10pm Sun.-Thurs., 4pm-11pm Fri.-Sat., $20-54) prepares the freshest catches of great seafood in town, with new deliveries of lobster, shrimp, and scallops arriving every morning. The place is known for its top-notch service and special touches like rose petals and cards to greet couples out to dinner on anniversaries. Go with Eddie V's oyster bar for the tower of chilled shellfish before trying out the Chilean sea bass, steamed "Hong Kong style." If seafood isn't your thing, no worries! There are plenty of premium hand-cut steaks decadently prepared for you to enjoy.

Grassroots Kitchen & Tap (8120 N. Hayden, 480/699-0699, www.grassrootsaz.com, 11am-9pm Mon.-Thurs., 11am-10pm Fri.-Sat., 11am-9pm Sun., $7-29) delivers contemporary dishes that are influenced by classic Southern cuisine. Soup, salads, and sandwiches are crowd pleasers for lunch and larger entrées are offered for dinner (or lunch, if you're down for that). Dishes come hot from the flames, like the barbecue brisket with jalapeño-cheddar grits, the spit-fired chicken, or the apple-cider brined pork chop. To top it off, guzzle down a craft beer or wine straight from the tap.

Pizza

Ciao Grazie (18835 N. Thompson Peak Pkwy., 480/685-3884, www.ciaograzie.us, 11am-9pm Sun.-Thurs., 11am-10pm Fri.-Sat., $12-23) is just a hop and skip away from the Gateway Trailhead in the McDowell Sonoran Preserve, so it gets our vote as a decent place to load up on carbs, cheese, and beer after a hefty hike (assuming you clean yourself up a bit first). The family-friendly restaurant is casual but nice and offers what one would expect from a contemporary pizza place menu: a caprese salad on the salad menu, a Margherita pizza on the pizza menu, and a few traditional entrées like chicken parmesan and lasagna.

Steakhouses

It seems celebrity chefs can't resist the

temptation to put their stamp on the Arizona steakhouse, and chef Michael Mina's chic-and-sleek ★ **Bourbon Steak** (7575 E. Princess Dr., 480/513-6002, www.michaelmina.net, 5:30pm-9:30pm Sun.-Thurs., 5:30pm-10pm Fri.-Sat., hours may vary seasonally, $35-85) at the Fairmont Scottsdale Princess is as over-the-top as they come. Try the elegantly prepared A5 Miyazaki steaks, garlic-charred prawns, and crisp salads, which are almost overshadowed by the stunning Desert Modernist architecture. If you can pry yourself away from stone-and-glass design, survey the extensive list of side dishes, including whipped potatoes made with duck-fat gravy, truffle mac 'n' cheese, and Brussels sprouts with Thai vinaigrette and peanuts. Order one of the classic, hand-crafted cocktails for the perfect complement to the meaty experience. It's pricey, but the ambience and re-imagined comfort foods are exquisite.

Talavera and Onyx Bar & Lounge (10600 E. Crescent Moon Dr., 480/513-5085, www.talavcrarestaurant.com, 5:30pm-9:30pm Tues.-Sun., $15-54) has views of Pinnacle Peak that will knock your socks off at sunset. And the food is pretty darn good, too. Upscale but unpretentious, the ambience is romantic, with a menu of New American plates heavy on the meat and seafood. Start with the Sunizona tomatoes served with fried feta and red onion, then move on to your entrée: Ahi Tuna Tartare, Lobster and Corn Bisque, and Press Coffee Rub Cervena Venison Rub are just a few of the unusual dinners to choose from. And for those who aren't so meaty, the vegan pappardelle with wild mushroom ragout and walnut gremolata is sure to please.

Located among the shops in the Scottsdale Quarter, **Dominick's Steakhouse** (15169 N. Scottsdale Rd., 480/272-7271, www.dominickssteakhouse.com, 5pm-9pm Sun.-Thurs., 5pm-10pm Fri.-Sat., $37-49) serves up high-end steaks to weary shoppers looking for a filling meal. At this place, however, diners dig in next to a giant image of an elephant swimming. Gotta love attempts at non-referential contemporary design! Luckily, the cuisine is just as memorable, with a menu that includes dishes like the delicious "PB&J" appetizer made with pâté and fig jam or the creamy double-baked truffle potato. Of course, this steak house has all the cuts of beef you might expect as well as seafood, salads, and other meats.

Accommodations

There is no shortage of great places in Scottsdale to make your temporary home, and you'll find a rather broad spectrum of options and prices. The city doesn't offer much in the way of historic hotels or bed-and-breakfasts, although you'll find many retro-cool and newly renovated 1960s properties, which were built when Scottsdale came of age as a resort destination.

If you'd like to experience the city's best shopping and nightlife without the hassle of a car, stay downtown, where most hotels offer a free shuttle within a three-mile radius. However, if you're looking to escape to a desert playground, you have to try one of the city's mega-resorts, which are an Arizona specialty. Enjoy mornings on the tee, afternoons in the pool, and evenings under the stars.

Fortunately, even the most luxurious resorts become affordable in the summer, when the temperatures soar into the triple digits and the prices in the hospitality industry plummet dramatically. It's a great time for locals, who take advantage of these hometown oases, spending a "staycation" at these four- and five-star resorts, which often offer spa and food vouchers. The price ranges listed in this section are merely averages, so don't consider a favorable place out of your price range until you give them a call or check their websites, because the prices can vary by hundreds of dollars per night's stay.

DOWNTOWN
$50-100

Finding an inexpensive hotel in Scottsdale is challenging, although not impossible, especially if you're not opposed to relying on a trusted chain. The good ol' **Motel 6 Scottsdale** (6848 E. Camelback Rd., 480/946-2280, www.motel6.com, $50-85 d) is downtown's cheapest hotel and its location next to Scottsdale Fashion Square cannot be beat.

Yet another tried-and-true chain, the **Quality Suites Old Town Scottsdale** (1635 N. Scottsdale Rd., 480/947-3711, www.choice-hotels.com, $70-85 d) may technically be in Tempe but if you're looking for something for under $100, you're going to have to make some concessions. That's not to say this hotel won't provide you with the basics like internet, pool, fitness center, and clean sheets. Bonus: It's pet friendly.

$100-250

If you're seeking a clean place that aims for merely "getting the job done," **Howard Johnson Old Town Scottsdale** (7110 E. Indian School Rd., 480/361-6001, www.hojo.com/hotels/Arizona/scottsdale, $125-200 d) will not disappoint you. This hotel is located in the heart of downtown and offers the basics with their abundant standard rooms featuring free internet, parking, flat-screen TVs, and breakfast. The rooms are nicely updated and there's a pool if you need to lounge.

The midcentury modern **Magnuson Hotel Papago Inn** (7017 E. McDowell Road, 480/947-7335, www.papagoinnscottsdale.com, $120-200 d) offers a bit of personality and rooms that overlook a grassy, flower-filled courtyard and swimming pool. Its location near Tempe, Papago Park, and the airport makes it a handy option if you plan to explore the rest of the Valley of the Sun.

★ **Hyatt Place** (7300 E. 3rd Ave., 480/423-9944, www.scottsdaleoldtown.place.

hyatt.com, $100-200 d) is also conveniently located within walking distance of Scottsdale Stadium and Old Town's shops, restaurants, and nightlife. The comfy, modern rooms feature free Wi-Fi and a 42-inch flat-screen TV. Downstairs, the convenient food counter prepares takeaway sandwiches and salads perfect for breakfast or a quick snack.

The budget-boutique **3 Palms** (7707 E. McDowell Rd., 480/941-1202, www.scottsdale-resort-hotels.com, $90-150 d) is a decent place to stay for a night or two if you don't want to shell out for a fancy place. The big perk: it's next door to El Dorado Park, which has a public golf course and disc (Frisbee) golf. The remodeled property, a 10-minute drive from Old Town, isn't perfect, but it's a terrific value. The large pool, rooftop sundeck, and fitness center cover the basic amenities and its location near Tempe attracts parents and friends visiting students at Arizona State University.

Over $250

Classic mid-20th-century modern architecture and a chic decor make ★ **Hotel Valley Ho** (6850 E. Main St., 480/248-2000, www.hotelvalleyho.com, $179-359 d) a swanky place to hang your fedora. The 2005 overhaul restored the 1956 property to its golden-age glory, when Hollywood celebrities like Tony Curtis and Janet Leigh lounged by the pool, and Robert Wagner and Natalie Wood held their wedding reception at the hotel. The translucent walls, Philippe Starck tubs, and hip bar attract a younger crowd, but the large patios, mod rooms, and ZuZu restaurant are fun for everyone.

Those who think of the desert as a colorless wasteland will think again once they see the **Saguaro Scottsdale**'s (4000 North Drinkwater Blvd., 480/308-1100, www.jdvhotels.com/saguaroscottsdale, $250-750 d) take on the Southwestern color palette. The Joie de Vivre hotel totally nailed it when they updated the decor in an explosion of color inspired by the Sonoran Desert. While the stay in this boutique hotel is, well, boutique (nothing

the pool at the Saguaro Scottsdale

super posh here), you can take advantage of the cabana-lined, heated swimming pools and a rotation of poolside DJs and live music. Ever watch that crazy cooking competition called *Iron Chef*? Now's your chance to have one of the winners cook for you. Enjoy a dinner of the award-winning modern Mexican cuisine available at the restaurant Distrito, manned by *Iron Chef* winner Jose Garces. Then kill some time and some stress at the Saguaro Spa, which features luxurious massages, body treatments, and facials.

CENTRAL SCOTTSDALE AND PARADISE VALLEY
$100-250

The family-owned **Smoke Tree Resort & Bungalows** (7101 E. Lincoln Dr., 480/948-7660, www.smoketreeresort.com, $125-200 d) is a quaint and private place to stay with a bed-and-breakfast vibe. Smoke Tree is the longest-running independent hotel in Paradise Valley, and it's no wonder. The charming, homey decor of the 26 remodeled private bungalows feels like you are staying in a friend's cozy

guesthouse or at an exclusive retreat. There are one- and two-bedroom villas, some with small, full-service kitchens. Don't be surprised by the not-so-great curb appeal to the entrance but the sense of privacy during your stay can offer a nice getaway.

For more amenities, consider the **DoubleTree Resort by Hilton Hotel** (5401 N. Scottsdale Rd., 480/947-5400, www.doubletree3.hilton.com, $125-250 d) sprawling over 22 acres. The two large pools, racquetball and tennis courts, health club with spa treatments, and putting green are fun for families and business travelers who would like a few distractions in between meetings. Although using the word "resort" is generous and the decor is a bit dated, the rooms are spacious and clean.

Ain't no shame in staying at the **Holiday Inn Express Scottsdale North** (7350 E. Gold Dust Ave., 480/991-1414, www.ihg.com/holidayinnexpress/hotels/us/en/scottsdale, $125-160 d) because the location is pretty killer for the price. Although the title of the hotel implies a North Scottsdale location, it's a bit inaccurate; it is located near Shea Boulevard and Scottsdale Road, which is very centrally located and offers a convenient drive to either downtown or North Scottsdale. As with any Holiday Inn Express, you can expect the simple, clean rooms for which the hotel chain is known.

Resorts

When **Camelback Inn** (5402 E. Lincoln Dr., 480/948-1700, www.camelbackinn.com, $375-425 d) first opened in 1936, wealthy travelers who arrived by train had to make a 12-mile journey across the desert to reach the hacienda-style resort. Fortunately, things are bit easier today, and thanks to a $50 million restoration, the five-star property has a new sheen of luxury. Celebrities from Jimmy Stewart and Bette Davis to Oprah Winfrey have decamped to this Paradise Valley institution. Guests can relax at the world-class spa or play golf at Camelback Golf Club's 36-hole course. Because of its age, the rooms have some quirks, but who doesn't want to "rough it" a bit in the Wild West?

The romantic **FireSky Resort & Spa** (4925 N. Scottsdale Rd., 480/945-7666, www.fireskyresort.com, $250-400 d) is a terrific home base just north of Scottsdale Fashion Square. The recently renovated property is an excellent value, offering friendly service and amenities similar to those at the five-star resorts up the road. Couples appreciate the gorgeous stonework, cathedral ceilings, lush grounds, and complimentary evening wine hour, while kids love being able to bring the family dog along for the vacation. Check out their promotions for discounts and special trip packages like "Girls Just Wanna Have Fun" or "Bros and Brews."

The charming ★ **Hermosa Inn** (5532 N. Palo Cristi Rd., 602/955-8614, www.hermosainn.com, $200-600 d) quietly exudes a taste of old Arizona. In the 1930s, cowboy artist Lon Megargee built an adobe home and studio on the land and to supplement his art income, ran the place as a guest ranch. Today,

the intimate boutique hotel features 34 hacienda-style rooms and casitas. After a $2 million renovation, locals and guests rave about time spent cozying up in their beautifully decorated rooms or grabbing a delicious meal at the award-winning restaurant, LON's. The meticulously landscaped grounds, stunning views of Camelback Mountain, and prime location near Phoenix's Camelback Corridor can't be beaten.

The Spanish-themed ★ **Omni Scottsdale Resort & Spa at Montelucia** (4949 E. Lincoln Dr., 480/627-3200, www.omnihotels.com/hotels/Scottsdale-montelucia, $430-600) makes a convincing aesthetic tie between the Sonoran Desert and Andalucia's arid landscape and big skies. No expense was spared in creating this elegant mix of dark woods, Moroccan screens, and Moorish geometric patterns. The real attraction, however, is the resort's extraordinary views of the red-hued Camelback Mountain—particularly at sunset from the main pool—which makes reserving a room during high season worth the splurge. Inside, rooms start at 500 square feet and feature sunken tubs, walk-in showers, and high-tech hookups to link your laptop and iPod to the room's flat-screen TV and sound system. Also, kids will love the complimentary backpack gift filled with games and goodies as well as a delivery of milk and cookies on their first night's stay.

The Phoenician (6000 E. Camelback Rd., 480/941-8200, www.thephoenician.com, $550-600 d) is the grande dame of Valley resorts, having hosted royalty, heads of state, A-list actors, and rock stars. The 250-acre property sprawls across the base of Camelback Mountain, with a 27-hole championship golf course, its renowned Centre for Well-Being spa, and an 11-court "tennis garden." The resort's eight swimming pools include a 165-foot water slide and a signature pool inlaid with handcrafted mother-of-pearl tiles (plus, there's a splash pad for the teeny ones). This is the good life secluded in landscaped grounds, and you won't know that you are

Omni Scottsdale Resort & Spa at Montelucia

only a five-minute drive to Scottsdale Fashion Square. For some of the best views of the Valley, enjoy a cocktail on the lobby terrace or dinner at chef Jean-Georges Vongerichten's J&G Steakhouse.

When A-list actors and pop stars come to Scottsdale in search of style and discretion, they often hide away at ★ **Sanctuary on Camelback Mountain Resort & Spa** (5700 E. McDonald Dr., 480/948-2100, www.sanctuaryoncamelback.com, $400-729 d). Once a 1960s' tennis ranch, this chic resort maintains many of its architectural details, although it has benefitted from a sleek mod overhaul. Subtle Asian touches carry throughout the property, including the innovative restaurant and fashionable spa. The boutique resort's 105 luxury casitas—many with outdoor balconies, wood-burning fireplaces, and private outdoor soaking tubs—climb the side of Camelback, giving guests a cliffside view of Paradise Valley and Mummy Mountain. And in a tribute to the resort's history, Sanctuary offers daily clinics and personalized instruction at its five championship tennis courts.

Secluded in the elegant neighborhood of Gainey Ranch, the **Hyatt Regency Scottsdale Resort & Spa** (7500 E. Doubletree Ranch Rd., 480/444-1234, www.scottsdale.hyatt.com, $350-600 d) is a blissful retreat that combines a manicured resort setting with an unbeatable location 10 minutes from Old Town and Scottsdale Fashion Square. Most days, the lobby's glass walls slide open, providing the lounge and bar with a soft breeze and views of the turquoise pools, golf courses, and McDowell Mountains. Ditch the kids at Camp Hyatt and spend your day being pampered at the award-winning Spa Aviana or lounging by one of the 10 interconnected pools, 45 waterfalls, and a three-story water slide. In the evening, enjoy dinner at one of the eight on-site restaurants before taking a romantic gondola ride around the lagoon.

NORTH SCOTTSDALE $100-250

For visitors who would like to stay near Scottsdale WestWorld or the FBR Open's TPC golf course, there are a few affordable options in North Scottsdale. The **Sleep Inn at North Scottsdale Road** (16630 N. Scottsdale Rd.,

866/477-6424, www.sleepinn.com, $100-200 d) is within walking distance of the TPC golf course and a host of restaurants and bars. It may lack quirky character but the place is clean and they offer free daily breakfast, outdoor pool, and free Wi-Fi access.

The convenient **Holiday Inn & Suite Scottsdale North-Airpark** (14255 N. 87th St., 480/922-6500, www.ihg.com, $100-180 d) is just off Highway 101 and Thunderbird Road. It is another clean and cheap place to crash out after a long day of golf at the nearby TPC. Plus, this place has an outdoor heated swimming pool for year-round splashes.

Resorts

The sprawling **Fairmont Scottsdale Princess** (7575 E. Princess Dr., 480/585-4848, www.fairmont.com/scottsdale, $300-600 d) deftly marries luxury service with a casual atmosphere, making it an excellent choice for many. Kids love the Trailblazers Family Adventure Center, lagoon fishing, and multiple swimming pools—complete with towering slides—while their parents appreciate chef Michael Mina's fashionable Bourbon Steak and the two 18-hole championship golf courses, home of the boisterous FBR Open. The resort is also a popular getaway for couples and friends who prefer to spend their days at the must-be-seen-to-be-believed Well & Being Spa and their nights at The Plaza Bar.

The ★ **Four Seasons Resort Scottsdale at Troon North** (10600 E. Crescent Moon Dr., 480/515-5700, www.fourseasons.com/scottsdale, $425-500 d) overlooks the city from its stunning North Scottsdale perch at Pinnacle Peak, a 20-minute drive from Old Town. The adobe-inspired architecture and brilliant desert landscape create an elegant desert retreat, complete with two pools, a spa, and the popular Troon North Golf Club. The 25 casitas, each with a private balcony, were designed to showcase the colors of the Sonoran Desert and the multi-bedroom suites are perfect for families. Take advantage of the

unique programs they offer their guests, like desert stargazing, customized evening picnics, and weekly beer, wine, and margarita tastings. And for one of the best Scottsdale experiences, order a prickly pear margarita on the terrace of Onyx Bar & Lounge for a dazzling view of the Valley of the Sun.

If you're hoping for a vacation destination where your golf bag doesn't leave your side, **The Westin Kierland Resort & Spa** (6902 E. Greenway Pkwy., 480/624-1000, www.kierlandresort.com, $149-679 d) delivers. Kierland Golf Club's 27 holes will satiate any diehard golfer, and its personalized instruction and Foremax Training System provide a comprehensive approach to improving your score. Of course, there's more than the putting green at Kierland. The informal resort's surf simulator, monstrous water slide, and lazy river are popular with the kids, and the walls are lined with the mementos from Arizona history. The neighboring Kierland Commons and Scottsdale Quarter shopping districts offer shopping and dining options without having to get into a car.

You're not in Kansas anymore—or anywhere else on the planet, for that matter. **The Boulders Resort & Spa** (34631 N. Tom Darlington Dr., 480/488-9009, www.theboulders.com, $300-500 d) sits at the foot of its namesake 12-million-year-old rock formation, a stunning testament to the geological scale of the Sonoran Desert. Pathways wind through the 1,300-acre property, where you're likely to come across quail, jackrabbits, lizards, and even javelina. The luxury resort still offers all the amenities of Scottsdale: shimmering pools, two championship golf courses, tennis courts, and one of the finest spas in the world. The rooms have received a much-needed multi-million-dollar renovation to complete the experience for guests—and speaking of unforgettable experiences, rock-climbing clinics are available for thrill-seekers wanting to conquer those impressive boulders.

Information and Services

TOURIST INFORMATION

Experience Scottsdale (800/782-1117, www. experiencescottsdale.com, 9am-6pm Mon.-Sat., 10am-5pm Sun.) is a great resource, distributing useful information to help you plan a customized trip to the city. Visit the extensive website (with some of the most over-the-top promotional art you'll ever see) or stop by its Visitor Center at the **Galleria Corporate Centre** (4343 N. Scottsdale Rd., Ste. 170, 8am-5pm Mon.-Fri.) where over 400 brochures and interactive iPads await to help you plan your trip. You can also pick up materials from the Tourist Information Center at **Scottsdale Fashion Square** (7014 E. Camelback Rd., 9am-5pm Mon.-Sat., 10am-4pm Sun. Oct.-May, 10am-4pm daily Jun.-Sept.).

LIBRARIES

The five branches of the **Scottsdale Public Library** (480/312-7323, www.scottsdalelibrary.org) can be handy resources for visitors with some great free events if you're traveling with kids. The **Civic Center Library** (3839 N. Drinkwater Blvd., 9am-9pm Mon.-Thurs., 10am-6pm Fri.-Sat., 1pm-5pm Sun.) is a popular destination because of its super-convenient location near Old Town, frequent events, and large children's section that's decorated with imaginative structures. Further north, the architecturally stunning **Arabian Library** (10215 E. McDowell Mountain Ranch Rd., 9am-8pm Mon.-Thurs., 10am-6pm Fri.-Sat., 1pm-5pm Sun.) brings Desert Modernism to North Scottsdale. Its rusted, metal facade seems to emerge like small mountain from its rocky site, and the glass walls allow natural light to bathe its reading rooms.

HOSPITALS AND EMERGENCY SERVICES

The renowned **Mayo Clinic** (5777 E. Mayo Blvd., 480/515-6296, www.mayoclinic.org/scottsdale) has a branch in North Scottsdale, serving as an important center for medicine in the Valley. In fact, the large medical complex attracts patients from around the world because of its respected doctors, high-tech equipment, and clinical trials.

HonorHealth (www.honorhealth.com) has three hospitals scattered around the city, each with emergency rooms and a spectrum of services. **Scottsdale Osborn Medical Center** (7400 E. Osborn Rd., 480/882-4000) is conveniently located in Old Town, while the **Scottsdale Shea Medical Center** (9003 E. Shea Blvd., 480/323-3000) and **Scottsdale Thompson Peak Medical Center** (7400 E. Thompson Peak Pkwy., 480/324-7000) are found further north.

Transportation

AIR

Phoenix Sky Harbor International Airport (3400 E. Sky Harbor Blvd., 602/273-3300, www.skyharbor.com) is a short, 15-minute ride from downtown Scottsdale's restaurants, bar, and hotels. The airport serves as important regional hub for national and international flights, including direct flights to and from New York, London, and Mexico.

If you're able to fly by private jet, **Scottsdale Airport** (15000 N. Airport Dr., 480/312-2321, www.scottsdaleaz.gov/airport) is a handy, headache-free option. The North Scottsdale airpark is a frequent choice of celebrities and other heavy hitters flying into town for special events.

CAR
Rental Cars

In all likelihood, you'll need a vehicle to get around Scottsdale, especially if you want to explore both Old Town and North Scottsdale's attractions. At Phoenix's Sky Harbor International Airport, take the free shuttle from any of the terminals to the **Rental Car Center** (1805 E. Sky Harbor Circle, 602/683-3741). You'll find major companies, like **Budget** (602/261-5950, www.budget.com), **Hertz** (602/267-8822, www.hertz.com), and **Enterprise** (602/225-0588), which have convenient drop-off centers around Phoenix and Scottsdale. It can be hard to find a gas station near the airport's rental car center, so be sure to fill up before returning your vehicle.

Limos, Shuttles, and Taxis

Join a shared-van ride to your resort or hotel with the reliable **SuperShuttle** (877/215-9262, www.supershuttle.com). Its bright blue vans are easy to spot at all of Sky Harbor's terminals.

If you want a private sedan for your transportation, hit up **ExecuCar** (800/410-4444, www.execucar.com), which provides affordable and professional airport service. For anything from airport pickup to limo to party-bus rentals, try **Lux Transportation** (480/646-6250, www.luxtransportationaz.com).

You can also grab a taxi at Sky Harbor with one of three contracted companies: **Apache Taxi** (480/557-7000, www.apachetaxi.com), **AAA/Yellow Cab** (480/888-8888, www.yellowcabaz.com), and **Mayflower Cab** (602/955-1355, www.mayflowercab.com). Phoenix rejoiced in June 2016 when rideshare services like Uber and Lyft gained access to the airport's arrivals curb for passenger pickup.

And if you want to hit the town at night, try **Discount Cab** (602/200-2000, www.discountcab.com), which also offers service via text (send your address with city or zip code to 777222).

PUBLIC TRANSPORTATION
Trolley

If you're tired of driving or walking around downtown, the free **Scottsdale Trolley** (480/312-3111, www.scottsdaleaz.gov/trolley,

---

Valet of the Sun

One thing you'll notice about cities in the Southwest is the vast expanse of winding paved highways and roads that connect almost every inch of the city. It's expected that every destination should be accessible by car and that there should be convenient parking. While public transit and walking define urban life in many American cities, the citizens of Scottsdale (and the greater Valley) are constantly driving in their own cars and get easily flustered, confused, and enraged by anything less than a parking spot near the front door of their desired destination.

That said, older areas of town aren't equipped to accommodate such expectations. Downtown (aka Old Town) Scottsdale can become quite cramped with cars, so it's not uncommon to see a vulgar abundance of valet services. Here, valet is not considered fancy or out of league for the average earner. Although some flashy establishments in Scottsdale might have a valet filled with patrons' super expensive rides, most of the time, it's merely a matter of efficiency and a judge-free option for the common man.

Bottom line: Use the valet if you can and be sure to bring a $5 or $10 bill along for the tip ($20 if you're flashy).

routes and hours vary) shuttles visitors across the area, with stops throughout downtown and surrounding neighborhoods.

Bus

Scottsdale is a part of the **Valley Metro** (602/253-5000, www.valleymetro.org) public-transportation network, which connects the Phoenix metropolitan area. Its buses run throughout the city, but the new light-rail system, which links the communities of Mesa, Tempe, and Central Phoenix, doesn't stop in Scottsdale. Bus fares start at $2 for a single ride, and all day or multiday passes are available. Visit the website for a comprehensive schedule and map.

Vicinity of Scottsdale

CAVE CREEK

You're more likely today to find yuppie bikers and artist studios than cattlemen in Cave Creek, but the town is neck and neck with Scottsdale in managing to retain more of its Old West character than other Valley communities. In fact, there was a recent squabble between Scottsdale and Cave Creek as to which community was the "West's most Western town."

Who won? We're not going to get involved in answering that.

This hardscrabble outpost, first settled by miners and ranchers in the 1870s, has changed significantly. In the 1920s, tuberculosis camps first popped up in Cave Creek, as those suffering from lung ailments thought the dry desert air would cure them. By the 1940s and 1950s, dude ranches took over old homesteads and the visitors have been coming ever since.

Sights

You can get a sense of Cave Creek's Old West past and have a little tourist fun at **Frontier Town** (6245 E. Cave Creek Rd., 480/488-3317, www.frontiertownaz.com), an "1880s-style theme town." Sure, it's a little hokey, but you can't help but smile while walking the wooden boardwalks and dodging hitching posts and antique wagons on your way to grab a beer. In the 1930s and 1940s, the WPA set up camp here, providing living quarters for workers building Bartlett Lake and Horseshoe Dams.

Today, Frontier Town is home to restaurants with live music, gift shops, and even wedding chapel and reception pavilion.

For an authentic slice of the Old West, the **Cave Creek Museum** (6140 E. Skyline Dr., 480/488-2764, cavecreekmuseum.com, 1pm-4:30pm Wed.-Thurs., 10am-4:30pm Fri., 1pm-4:30pm Sat.-Sun., adults $5, children under 12 free) is just down the street from Frontier Town. You can see the last tuberculosis cabin in the state of Arizona, one of 16 cabins originally found in a 1920s camp, and the only operational 10 stamp gold stamp mill in Arizona.

Recreation

Cave Creek's **Spur Cross Stables** (11029 N. Spur Cross Rd., 480/488-9117, www.horsebackarizona.com) can get even the newest cowpokes into the saddle. The ranch, located on the site of an 1870s' gold mine, offers spectacular rides through the desert and mountain passes of Tonto National Forest. Customize your horseback adventure, or select from a menu of guided tours like the one-hour desert ride ($43) up to a half-day petroglyph tour ($123). Children will love the experience from start to finish as they are introduced to their horse as well as the mini Dexter cow, pigs, a tortoise, and donkey.

The par-70 **Rancho Mañana Golf Club** (5734 E. Rancho Mañana Blvd., 480/488-0398, www.ranchomanana.com) in Cave Creek will definitely wow you with its dramatic elevation changes and pristine desert surroundings. The rolling course's green fairways, sculptural cacti, and sweeping mountain views make it the most scenic course in the Valley. You can't help but enjoy yourself on this challenging course, and its high Sonoran Desert setting outside of the city means slightly cooler temperatures on warmer days.

If you're a hiker or mountain biker, don't pass up the opportunity to explore the desert in this area, because it is beee-uuu-ti-ful! The six-mile Go John Loop at **Cave Creek Regional Park** (37900 E. Cave Creek Pkwy., 623/465-0431, www.maricopacountparks. net, $6) is one of the most popular trails in town, and it's long enough that you'll experience plenty of solitude as you traverse the moderate trail with sweeping views of the area. The quaint **Spur Cross Ranch Conservation Area, Jewel of the Creek Preserve** (44000 N. Spur Cross Rd., www. maricopacountyparks.net) may not have the amenities of other trailheads but it offers some of the very best hiking in the Valley. Take the kids along the 1.7-mile Dragonfly Trail, which crisscrosses the actual Cave Creek and is teeming with riparian life. For a more serious trek, take the seven-mile Spur Cross and Elephant Mountain Loop, which traverses countless washes, dips into small canyons, climbs mountains, and passes by ancient ruins.

Shopping

Whether you arrive by car or motorcycle, the shops at **Cave Creek Frontier Town** (6245 E. Cave Creek Rd., www.frontiertownaz.com, 480/488-3317) will seem like another world compared to Scottsdale's high-end shopping centers. Join the "Creekers" and bikers who frequent the barbershop and saloon. Amble down the touristy wooden sidewalks, and pick up a few Arizona souvenirs at the Glory Bees Boutiques or Debra Ortega's Native American Jewelry & Arts. Other quirky shops include Udder Delight Mile Soaps & Creams and Suzanne's Hot Stuff.

Just down the street, **The Town Dump** (6820 E. Cave Creek Rd., 480/488-9047, www.towndump.net, 10am-6pm daily) is packed with furniture, old light fixtures, giant metal lizards, rusted gates, and brightly painted Mexican pottery. The shop almost lives up to its motto as "one of the world's most unusual stores."

Spur Cross Ranch Conservation Area

Food

Cave Creek may be famous for its cowboy steaks and burgers, but do not miss the casual **El Encanto** (6248 E. Cave Creek Rd., 480/488-1752, www.elencantorestaurants. com, 11am-9pm Mon.-Thurs., 11am-10pm Fri., 9am-10pm Sat., 9am-9pm Sun., $9-17) for legitimate Mexican cuisine. Outdoor tables line a pleasant lagoon where palm trees grow and ducks wait patiently for a reward. Many have chosen this site to pop the question, and while the ambience is above and beyond, the food falls in the "pretty good" category. Not that that's a bad thing—you can surely get your Mexican food fix here with their traditional menu including all the greats: fajitas, tacos, tamales, enchiladas, carnitas, and more. Try the Pollo Fundido, a roasted chicken breast with spices, onions, and peppers rolled in a flour tortilla and drizzled with jalapeño and cream-cheese sauce.

★ **Binkley's** (6920 E. Cave Creek Rd., 480/437-1072, www.binkleysrestaurantgroup. com, 5pm-9:30pm Tues.-Sat., $120-150) may be the best restaurant in Arizona. Chef Kevin Binkley, who trained with superstar chef Thomas Keller, brings style and culinary panache to his eponymous eatery, creating a menu that changes frequently to showcase fresh, seasonal ingredients. What's all the fuss about? Order the multi-course tasting menu and you'll see. The carefully arranged French-inspired new American dishes (like crispy seared foie gras with blood orange, sweet potato, and French toast, or the five spice-seared elk loin with charred broccoli and ponzu demi-glace) are punctuated by a series of *amuse-bouche* presentations. Be sure to make a reservation for this place because it fills up quick.

The Horny Toad (6738 E. Cave Creek Rd., 480/488-9542, www.thehornytoad.com, 11am-10pm Sun.-Thurs., 11am-11pm Fri.-Sat., $8-24) has been dishing out ribs and country fun long before tourists discovered Cave Creek. The Horny Toad is one of the few restaurants within riding distance of North Scottsdale where cowboy boots aren't

for show. This is a meat-lover's dream with a jam-packed menu filled with all walks of dead things. Come hungry for the juicy 12-ounce New York Strip or the vast Tijuana Torpedo Burger, which might require a cooling-off period. In addition to the full lineup of barbecue, you'll find plenty of poultry and seafood. If you splurged on some new boots during your visit, this is the perfect place to break 'em in.

Getting There

From downtown Scottsdale, hop on AZ-101-Loop north for about 13 miles. Take exit 34 and follow signs for Scottsdale Road. Take a right to head north on Scottsdale Road for another 10 miles until you reach AZ 74 W/ E Carefree Highway. Take a left to head west for just two miles. Turn right onto North Cave Creek Road heading north, and you have reached the main road in town.

CAREFREE

Residents of Carefree like to live the definition of their town name. This small community started out as a haven for retirees and although there's still a fair amount of those fine folks living it up, many artists have also flocked in to enjoy the laid-back vibe of this town.

Sights

The further you get out of the city, the better the desert will be. This is certainly true for the **Carefree Desert Gardens** (101 E. Easy St., 480/488-3686, carefree-desert-gardens.com, open 24/7, free), which features some of the most incredible desert fauna you'll see. The four-acre garden also houses the Carefree Sundial (the largest sundial in the U.S.), a playground, and public art.

Shopping

El Pedregal (34505 N. Scottsdale Rd., 480/488-1072, www.theboulders.com/el-pedregal, 10am-5:30pm Mon.-Sat., noon-5pm Sun.) means "a place with many stones." The name is more than fitting as the open-air

El Pedregal hosts outdoor concerts on the weekends.

shopping center sits among the dramatic rock formations that also inspired the name of the neighboring resort, The Boulders. El Pedregal features 30 upscale boutiques, art galleries, artisan-crafted goods, and other niche shopping opportunities (no department stores). Grab a bite at the handful of dining options on-site and stick around the amphitheater, which often hosts live music on the weekends.

Food

Café Bink (36899 N. Tom Darlington Dr., 480/488-9796, www.binkleysrestaurantgroup.com, 11am-9pm Mon.-Sat., 10am-9pm Sun., $12-38) is the sister restaurant to Cave Creek's Binkley's and more casual, featuring superb mountain views, a cozy patio, and French bistro-inspired fare. You'll find a few of the usual Parisian suspects—cheese and spinach quiche and mussels—although chef Kevin Binkley shakes things up with some inventive additions. Like duck eggs. You can add a duck egg to the Croque Madame or the pork mac 'n' cheese. Other choices include the delicious trout Meuniére with haricots verts, toasted almonds, and lemon brown butter.

Getting There

From downtown Scottsdale, hop on AZ-101-Loop north for about 13 miles. Take exit 34 and follow signs for Scottsdale Road. Take a right to head north on Scottsdale Road for another 10 miles and continue on to North Tom Darlington Drive for another two miles. You'll know you're in Carefree when you reach the roundabout.

FOUNTAIN HILLS

Fountain Hills is a funky little community established in 1970 and planned by none other than a Mr. Charles Wood Jr., the same guy who developed theme parks such as, oh, Disneyland (no big deal). You'll see his signature style throughout the area but most punctuated at the Fountain Lake. Fountain Hills has been a charming outpost for decades but is now more visited than ever by locals as Scottsdale's developments reach further and further north.

Sights

You can't go to Fountain Hills without seeing the famous fountain at **Fountain Park**

Fountain Park

(12925 N. Saguaro Blvd, www.fh.az.gov). You can see the fountain's water flying up in the air from miles away but there's nothing like witnessing it on the banks of the man-made lake that surrounds it. Every hour on the hour from 9am-9pm, a huge gush of water is thrust straight up, reaching 330 feet. Even without the jutting water, the park itself is quite lovely with playgrounds, a splash pad in the summer, picnic ramadas, interpretive signage, and an 18-hole disc golf course.

If you're really into the history of the Lower Verde River Valley, head to the **River of Time Museum** (12901 N. La Montana Blvd., 480/837-2612, www.rotmuseum.org, 10am-4pm Tues.-Fri., $5 admission), which boasts 5,000 square feet of exhibits showing the daily life of the ancient Yavapai people, the Fort McDowell U.S. Army post, the P-Bar Ranch, and famous explorers, through artifacts and displays. The history runs even deeper with educational exhibits showcasing the geology of the land.

Events

While Fountain Hills is considered way out of the way for most residents, folks are more than willing to make the drive every year for the **Fountain Festival of Arts and Crafts** (480/837-1654, www.fountainhills-chamber.com/fountain-festival, free). Every November, nearly 200,000 people visit the booths and makeshift shops of about 500 artisans displaying and selling fine art and crafts. With food vendors, live music, and beer gardens (yes!) this free event is not to be missed.

Getting There

From downtown Scottsdale, hop on AZ-101-Loop north for about six miles. Take exit 41 and turn right onto East Shea Boulevard, following it for just under nine miles before turning left onto North Fountain Hills Boulevard. Once you pass East Segundo Drive, you are in the heart of town.

Sedona

Sights 177

Entertainment and Events 181

Shopping. 185

Sports and Recreation 191

Food 200

Accommodations. 208

Information and Services 214

Transportation. 214

Getting There and Around. 214

Vicinity of Sedona 215

Many come to Sedona seeking spiritual beauty and internal truth by relaxing, exploring, or meditating among the town's iconic red-rock formations, which many claim hold mystic powers. To a cynic, the crystal-rubbing

Sedona fanatic might seem a little silly, but even the most logical minds will boggle with just one glimpse of the spectacular red-rock walls and spires dominating the horizon.

The red cliffs mark the southern rim of the Colorado Plateau, a massive expanse of land that rises 2,000 feet from the high-desert floor in Sedona and stretches into Utah, Colorado, and New Mexico. The variegated sandstone buttes, carved by wind and rain, feature a series of rounded formations and delicate spires that seem to defy gravity.

This evocative terrain attracts outdoor adventurers. Hikers, climbers, and mountain bikers of all skill levels come to scale or explore the colossal buttes as they kick up the region's iconic red dirt. For families, the neighboring Oak Creek Canyon's swimming holes and Slide Rock State Park make for fun-filled vacations. New Age followers come in search of vortexes, which they believe are invisible centers of spiraling cosmic energy.

For others, the scenery merely serves as a backdrop for golf games, Southwestern cuisine, and rejuvenating spa treatments. The inspiring beauty has led to the rich tradition of visual artists who live, visit, and create among the red rocks. Art fanatics can find plenty of art galleries to view or purchase a piece of this inspiration.

It can be hard at times to get past the hordes of tourists, streaming convoys of brightly colored Jeep tours, and touchy-feely New Age mystics—complaining about the development boom and resulting traffic is a pastime shared by both residents and visitors alike. But none of that can really distract or detract from the landscape. After all, no matter where you go or what you do in Sedona, the red rocks cast a powerful energy that's hard to ignore.

So, go ahead. Align your chakras, heal through your breath, and let out a hearty, "ommmm." It's okay. Really. Welcome to Sedona.

Previous: ballooning above the red rocks; Sedona's beautiful desert landscape. **Above:** Uptown Sedona.

Look for ★ to find recommended
sights, activities, dining, and lodging.

Highlights

★ **Chapel of the Holy Cross:** This iconic church appears to rise out the red rocks, creating a brilliant union of art, nature, and spiritualty (page 177).

★ **The Red Rocks:** The massive red-rock buttes that soar from the desert floor captivate with intricate spires and rich colors (page 179).

★ **Uptown Sedona:** Spend the afternoon walking, shopping, eating, and getting a psychic reading (page 186).

★ **Tlaquepaque Arts and Crafts Village:** Sedona's charming shopping center, inspired by small artisan villages in Mexico, features some of the city's best shops, galleries, and restaurants (page 187).

★ **Jeep Tours:** A guided Jeep trip is a fun way to explore out-of-the-way formations and learn about Sedona's unique geology and wildlife (page 192).

★ **Hiking:** Thanks to spectacular buttes, massive geological formations, and acres upon acres of protected land, there seems to be a world-class trail wherever you go (page 195).

★ **Oak Creek Canyon:** Drive the scenic highway through this leafy refuge north of Sedona. The quiet, wooded setting is an ideal place to take a hike—although kids will want to slip down the natural chute at **Slide Rock State Park** (page 215).

★ **Jerome:** Locals will tell you that this mining town is haunted. The narrow streets that

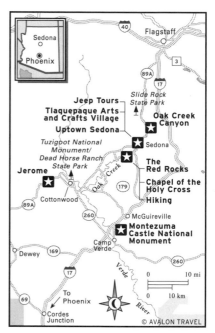
© AVALON TRAVEL

were once home to saloons and brothels now feature small restaurants, galleries, and shops (page 221).

★ **Montezuma Castle National Monument:** The five-story, 20-room pueblo, which clings to side of a limestone wall 75 feet above the ground, is an impressive testament to the ingenuity of the Sinagua people (page 227).

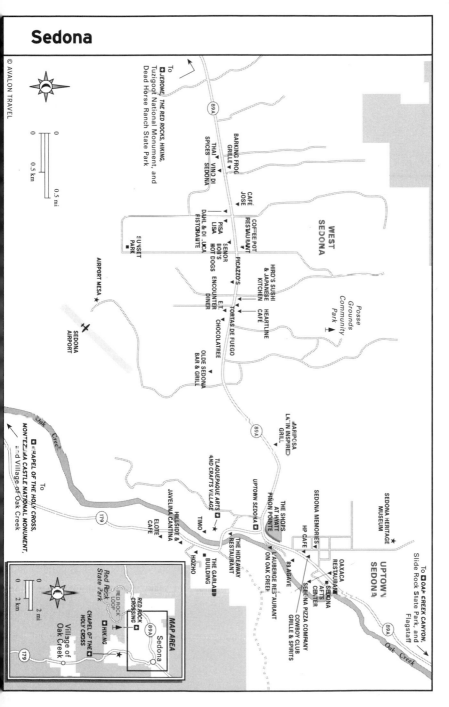

Sedona

© AVALON TRAVEL

SEDONA

0   0.5 mi
0   0.5 km

To
JEROME, THE RED ROCKS, HIKING,
Tuzigoot National Monument, and
Dead Horse Ranch State Park

89A

BARKING FROG
GRILLE ▼

THAI' VINO DI
SPICES SEDONA ▼

CAFE
JOSE ▼

COFFEE POT
RESTAURANT ▼

DAHL & DI LUCA
RISTORANTE ▼

PISA
LISA

SEÑOR
BOB'S
HOT DOGS ▼

SUNSET
PARK ■

WEST
SEDONA

Posse
Grounds
Community
Park

AIRPORT MESA ★

SEDONA
AIRPORT

PICAZZO'S ▼

HIRO'S SUSHI
& JAPANESE
KITCHEN ▼

ENCOUNTER
DINER ▼

E.T.
TORTAS DE FUEGO ▼

HEARTLINE
CAFE ▼

CHOCOLATREE ▼

OLDE SEDONA
BAR & GRILL ■

89A

MARIPOSA
LATIN INSPIRED
GRILL ▼

TLAQUEPAQUE ARTS
AND CRAFTS VILLAGE

UPTOWN SEDONA ■

HILLSIDE ■

JAVELINA CANTINA
& ELOTE
CAFE ▼

TIMO ★

HUZHO ▼

THE GARLAND ■
BUILDING

THE HIDEAWAY
RESTAURANT ▼

THE SHOPS
AT HYATT
PIÑON POINTE ■

HP CAFE ▼

SEDONA MEMORIES ▼

L'AUBERGE RESTAURANT
ON OAK CREEK ▼

88 AGAVE ▼

SEDONA
ARTS
CENTER

SEDONA HERITAGE
MUSEUM

OAXACA
RESTAURANT ▼

SEE SENA PIZZA COMPANY ▼

COWBOY CLUB
GRILLE & SPIRITS ▼

UPTOWN
SEDONA

To **OAK CREEK CANYON,**
Slide Rock State Park, and
Flagstaff

89A

Oak Creek

Oak Creek

To
CHAPEL OF THE HOLY CROSS,
MONTEZUMA CASTLE NATIONAL MONUMENT,
and Village of Oak Creek

179

0   2 mi
0   2 km

Red Rock
State Park

RED ROCK
LOOP

RED ROCK
CROSSING

CHAPEL OF THE
HOLY CROSS

HIKING

89A

Sedona

MAP
AREA

179

Village of
Oak Creek

Keeping Up Appearances

As Sedona has mushroomed from small town to tourist mecca, residents have become nearly fanatical in their determination to keep things "tasteful." When mounting road congestion called for traffic lights that could have marred the city's multi-million-dollar-earning views, planners solved the problem by constructing a series of roundabouts from the Village of Oak Creek to the Y intersection on Route 179. Even global powerhouse McDonald's had to conform to the town's strict zoning ordinances, changing its iconic golden arches to teal at its West Sedona location. And when the sun sets, there are also ordinances for "light pollution" to protect the nighttime sky for stargazing.

ORIENTATION

Situated about 90 minutes north of Phoenix, Sedona is merely a 19-square-mile city. Along with its neighboring communities, it can be broken into four distinct areas: Village of Oak Creek, Uptown, West Sedona, and Oak Creek Canyon.

Visitors driving from Phoenix on Route 179 will arrive in the Village of Oak Creek, a small suburb that has mushroomed in the last decade with a host of new shopping centers, hotels, and restaurants along the main drag. The village is a handy option for exploring the red rocks and, pleasantly, feels a bit less congested than the rest of Sedona.

Continue north on Route 179, and you'll see many of the area's most prominent rock formations along the seven-mile scenic drive. Once you cross over the leafy banks of Oak Creek, you'll hit the Y, a three-pronged roundabout that splits West Sedona and Uptown Sedona on Route 89A. Touristy Uptown commands impressive views of the rock formations and caters to visitors with a diverse selection of accommodations, restaurants, galleries, and shops. As well as locals, you'll find less-expensive hotels, popular bars, and bistros in West Sedona.

PLANNING YOUR TIME

Sedona is best experienced a few days at a time. Although it has grown with its legions of tourists in mind, it's still a small town. With lots to do in a compact area, your visit can include meandering through pedestrian-friendly shopping areas, sampling delicious restaurants, and viewing contemporary art at impressively diverse galleries—all surrounded by the red rocks.

Couples yearning for a quick romantic trip with minimal stress can easily pop up from Phoenix for an overnight stay at one of Sedona's charming resorts overlooking Oak Creek. More adventurous travelers, though, may want to stay two or three nights in order to enjoy the natural attractions and historic sites throughout the Verde Valley. The nearby Slide Rock State Park, small mining town of Jerome, and Native American ruins that dot the area make Sedona a convenient home base for side trips.

Outdoor lovers could easily tack on a few extra days to explore Sedona's hiking and biking trails, horseback ride, play golf or tennis, or appreciate the red rocks from a hot-air balloon or biplane.

No matter what time of year you visit, Sedona's landscape never fails to impress. Spring wildflowers and autumn leaves are irresistible incentives, not to mention balmy temperatures. Summer, on the other hand, is quite warm, with highs well above 90°F, but it cools off considerably at night. The occasional light snow in winter and annual holiday-light events make a winter trip to Sedona a compelling option.

HISTORY

Admittedly, Sedona suffers from the stucco extravaganza many new boomtowns tend to sport. The truth is, however, that settlers have been coming to Sedona and the Verde Valley for 6,000 years, lured by the dramatic landscape and mild climate.

As far as we know, the Sinagua were the first people to soak up the incredible views all the way back in AD 900. While it doesn't appear that they lived in present-day Sedona, ruins of their pueblos can be found throughout the valley, the most striking being the cliffside Montezuma's Castle. The civilization mysteriously disappeared sometime after 1350, and historians believe they blended into the Apache tribes that roamed northeast Arizona.

In 1876, the Apache were forced onto reservations by the U.S. government, and the first homesteader, John J. Thompson, arrived in Oak Creek Canyon. Additional ranching and farming families joined him, including T. C. Schnebly, an entrepreneurial settler who built his wooden house-turned-hotel where Tlaquepaque and the Los Abrigados Resort now stand. He established the area's first post office in 1902, which required him to submit a name for the burgeoning community. After the postmaster general in Washington rejected Schnebly Station and Oak Creek Crossing for being too long for a cancellation stamp, Schnebly followed his brother's advice and submitted his wife's name: Sedona. Isn't that sweet?

After the turn of the century, Arizona pioneers built a dusty stagecoach trail through town, connecting the communities of Flagstaff and Prescott, and bringing the first regular tourists to Sedona. More settlers began to stream into the Verde Valley, where they found work as farmers or in Jerome's ore-rich mines.

But it was the power of Hollywood that really made Sedona famous. Many classic Westerns were filmed against the backdrop of the massive rock formations, beginning with Zane Grey's *Call of the Canyon* in 1923. Since then, stars from John Wayne and Joan Crawford to Robert De Niro and Sharon Stone have shot nearly a hundred films in the area, and the rugged terrain is still attracting production companies.

People went nuts for the place following the big-screen attention and after World War II, its tourism industry took off as Americans began to explore their country by car. By the 1980s and 1990s, Sedona had exploded as a retirement and vacation destination (hence the stucco). Fortunately, more than half of the land in and around Sedona is protected by state and national parks, which has driven up real-estate values and pushed new residents into the neighboring Village of Oak Creek and Cottonwood. Still, some 11,000 people live in Sedona today—dwarfed by approximately 3.5 million visitors every year—and the community manages to retain plenty of its frontier-town character.

Sights

Hands down, the sights created by Mother Nature herself can't be trumped by any man-made structure. The red-rock buttes, evergreen pines, and blue skies dominate the horizon, while refreshing Oak Creek cuts through town, creating a peaceful, leafy axis. Make driving the scenic byways and hiking the numerous trails your top priorities. And after you've had your fill there, be sure to carve out some time to visit the city's cultural attractions, shops, and galleries.

UPTOWN
★ Chapel of the Holy Cross
With such beauty in its natural landscape, bulldozing to build would be an absolute crime. Thankfully, the design of the **Chapel of the Holy Cross** (780 Chapel

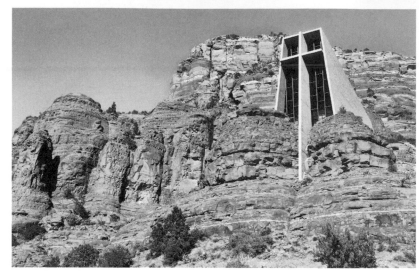

Chapel of the Holy Cross

Rd., 928/282-4069, www.chapeloftheholy-cross.com, 9am-5pm daily, free) works *with* Sedona's red rocks, not against them. The chapel's 90-foot-tall cross rises dramatically to the sky between two rock formations and is framed by a simple Modernist chapel. Perched high above Sedona and just south of Uptown proper, the elegant structure overlooks the valley's famed buttes and attracts visitors to its minimalist interior, embellished only by a floor-to-ceiling window behind the altar and flickering red votive candles lit by believers and visitors.

This inspiring edifice can be credited to the generosity and talents of Marguerite Brunswig Staude, a philanthropist and sculptor who envisioned a building that could glorify God through art. Her design was inspired by a trip to New York City in 1932, where she saw a cross in the steel-and-glass facade of the recently constructed Empire State Building. Early sketches of her glass cathedral impressed Lloyd Wright, son of architect Frank Lloyd Wright, but the archbishop of Los Angeles ultimately rejected them for a proposed cathedral. When Staude and her husband bought a ranch in Sedona in 1941, she found the perfect home for her calling. Her

plans were adapted, and the small chapel was completed in 1956.

Sedona Heritage Museum

Get a glimpse of how Sedona's early residents lived long before the tourists and art galleries arrived in Jordan Historical Park. Take a self-guided tour of the **Sedona Heritage Museum** (735 Jordan Rd., 928/282-7038, www.sedonamuseum.org, 11am-3pm daily, adults $5, children under 13 free, additional $2 for audio tour), located on the grounds of the original Jordan family farmstead to see the family's 1931 one-room cabin, restored with some of its original furnishings. The home's exhibits showcase life in early Sedona, from the rough work of farmers and cowboys to an old-fashioned schoolroom. Visitors can also learn about nearly a hundred movies filmed in the area, many shot during Hollywood's Golden Age of Westerns. Be sure to venture out to the Apple Packing Shed, which houses Walter Jordan's original apple-grading machine, an ingenious bit of frontier ingenuity that sorted his orchard's fruit by quality and size. Also at the museum is the Telegraph Office, which is a restored building once used on the set of John Wayne's *Angel and the Badman*.

Why So Red?

The red rocks' famous color is just part of the story that created this dramatic landscape. Much of the credit goes to the area's unique geology—and a few hundred million years of work. Over the eons, this part of Arizona has sat under the ocean, endured volcanic eruptions, and fluctuated between muggy swamp and Sahara-like desert. With each climatic and geological upheaval, a new layer of sediment was added, producing layer upon layer of limestone and sandstone.

Oak Creek began the work of exposing these layers, splitting the buttes from the massive Colorado Plateau, which extends well into the Four Corners region. Erosion, caused by wind and rain, did most of the shaping and sculpting of those buttes, creating the intricate formations and tall, slender spires seen today.

As for that trademark color; not surprisingly, the rusty-red rocks get their tint from dissolved iron that has drained through the porous sandstone layers. That classic mixture of iron and water produced iron oxide, staining the brilliantly colored buttes red. In most formations, you'll see rings that reveal each of Sedona's previous lives. The hard, white limestone formed at the bottom of the sea, while the porous, red sandstone was created from the dry sands that once blew across the landscape. To make things a bit more complicated, shifting tectonic plates caused some of the land to buckle, moving these layers. Fortunately for visitors, all of that work has resulted in one of the most beautiful landscapes on Earth.

Sedona Arts Center

Started in 1958 as a place for local artists to teach and share ideas, the **Sedona Arts Center** (15 Art Barn Rd., 928/282-3809, www.sedonaartscenter.com, 10am-5pm daily, free) has evolved to into one of the region's leading cultural forces, helping transform Sedona into an art mecca. Visitors can peruse galleries that feature local and regional artists, with rotating exhibitions that include fine art, jewelry, sculpture, textiles, and photography. The center's School of Arts offers more than a hundred art classes every year, for a host of media and skill levels. Its three- to five-day intensive art workshops and field expeditions are handy for artistically minded travelers in town for a short period of time.

★ THE RED ROCKS

Let's face it—it's all about the rocks. People go to Sedona because it's pretty much impossible not to experience breathtaking views of the red rocks at every turn. The mammoth buttes and prehistoric formations in electric hues dominate the horizon and bombard your vision. You'll see them everywhere: from the highway, through your hotel-room window, on the patio at a small restaurant, and even while you're getting a Watsu massage in an outdoor pool.

So why not get to know them a little better? Take a self-guided driving and hiking tour to seek formations named after shapes their silhouettes resemble—although you should expect a little creative license. Make the kids look up from their tablets long enough to spot the buttes from the road or, better yet, pull off the highway for a quick trek on one of the many hiking trails for an up-close view of these striking formations.

To view as many majestic rocks as possible in a short time, take a ride on Route 179, known as the **Red Rock Scenic Byway.** When driving northbound from Phoenix (from the I-17, take exit 298), you'll be treated to beautiful sights as you cruise through the Coconino National Forest, blanketed by evergreen pinion trees. Once you pass through the charming Village of Oak Creek, the landscape explodes with the glowing red-rock spires reaching to the sky. Keep a look out for several scenic pullouts and hiking trails as you drive by Bell Rock, Courthouse Butte, Cathedral Rock, and so many more incredible formations.

Village of Oak Creek

If you're driving north from Phoenix on Route 179, look east to see the first major butte; you'll soon recognize **Bell Rock,** the easiest formation to match to its namesake silhouette. Behind the Liberty Bell-shaped butte, you can spot the stout **Courthouse Butte.**

On the opposite side of the highway to the west, you'll discover the enormous **Castle Rock** as well as the more modest **Cathedral Rock,** a multi-spired formation that's probably the most photographed red rock of them all. Hop off Route 179 onto Back O'Beyond Road to hike the short and steep Cathedral Rock Trail to experience one of the most popular vortex sites. For views without a hike, pull off Route 179 and drive up Chapel Road to the Chapel of the Holy Cross, where you can get a clear view of three small formations: the beaked **Eagle Head Rock,** the double spires of **Twin Nuns,** and the charming **Mother and Child Rock.** To see the low-lying **Submarine Rock,** head east on Morgan Road and hike along the Broken Arrow Trail for a closer look.

Uptown Sedona

Once you drive into town, you can see **Thumb Butte and the Bench.** Kids will get a kick out of **Snoopy Rock** from the perspective of Uptown Sedona (looking southeast), where they'll recognize the famous beagle asleep on his back. If you continue north on Route 89A, you'll locate **Steamboat Rock** towering west of the road near Midgley Bridge.

West Sedona

Travel back down Route 89A to West Sedona and turn south on Airport Road, where you'll be treated to one of Sedona's best panoramic views on **Airport Mesa.** You can make out most of the major formations before exploring the short hiking trails (Airport Loop, Table Top, and Brewer Trails are all in the area) and one of Sedona's best-known vortexes.

Continuing west on Route 89A, look north

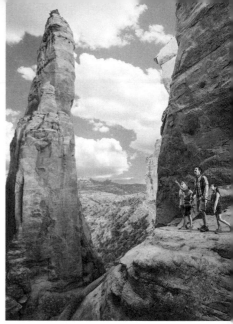
The red rocks of Sedona are unforgettable.

and you'll see the telltale spout of **Coffeepot Rock** and the spire of **Chimney Rock,** both connected by the domed **Capitol Butte.**

Parks and Recreation Areas

Sunset Park (665 Sunset Dr., 928/2827098, www.sedonaaz.gov, dawn-dusk, free) will be a daily visit for those of you traveling with kids. With the dramatic red rocks as a backdrop, the park has two shady playgrounds; a splash pad (operational 10am-6pm daily, May-Sept.); two tennis courts; hiking trails that connect to the Coconino National Forest, where you can hike in and among the red rocks; a large grass field; basketball court; and a super-long sentence in a travel book to describe all its amenities. It's definitely worth a visit. Dogs on a leash are welcome as long as you pick up their doo-doo.

Is this real life? That's what you'll wonder when you explore the **Crescent Moon Recreation Area and Red Rock Crossing** (928/282-4119, www.fs.usda.gov/coconino,

Crescent Moon Recreation Area

$10 per vehicle). This popular picnic spot sits near the cool waters of Oak Creek and gives postcard views of Cathedral and Castle Rocks. Don't you dare miss the hiking trail that kisses the creek and wanders through shady groves before opening up suddenly to dramatic views. Along the way, you'll find deep pools that are great for swimming with kids. It's just an easy mile in and packs more jaw-dropping beauty and romantically quiet corners than many of the trails in town. Go there. Seriously.

Oak Creek flows to the 286-acre **Red Rock State Park** (http://azstateparks.com/parks/rero, 8am-5pm, last entry 4:30pm, daily, $6 adult, $3 ages 7-13, children under 6 free) on the western edge of town. With a five-mile network of intersecting, family-friendly trails that are easy to follow thanks to excellent signage, visitors can hoof up the Eagle's Nest Trail for a 300-foot climb to a scenic vista or simply wander among the trails near Oak Creek, which cross back and forth over pedestrian bridges. The **Miller Visitor Center** (4050 Red Rock Loop Rd., 928/282-6907, 9am-4:30pm daily) offers restrooms, a gift shop, and fabulous educational displays. Maps are provided at the front gate and additional information can be found at the Visitor Center.

Entertainment and Events

Based on the attire of hiking sandals, workout garb, and minimal hair and makeup efforts, you'll take the hint pretty quick that Sedona isn't a "paint the town red" kind of place (besides, it's already red). Sedona is still a small town, and its slow pace and relaxed atmosphere mean you won't discover a ton of events or a buzzing nightlife. But that's not a bad thing. In fact, a quiet evening under the stars with a locally brewed beer in hand can provide a nice complement to a day full of hiking and exploring the red rocks.

NIGHTLIFE

Uptown

If you're the type who can't sit with a drink unless live music is filling your ears, then **Sound Bites Grill** (101 N. S.R. 89A, 928/282-2713, www.soundbitesgrill.com, 11:30am-10pm Sun.-Thurs., 11:30am-11pm Fri.-Sat.) is quite literally your "jam." Located in Uptown's Piñon Pointe shops, live bands are booked Wednesday through Sunday evenings. Check the website for events, upcoming performers, and cover prices.

West Sedona

The **Rooftop Cantina** (321 N. S.R. 89A, 928/282-4179, www.oaxacarestaurant.com, 11am-9pm daily) at Oaxaca Restaurant serves tasty margaritas and a fine menu of 50 tequilas. Best of all, the views of Snoopy Rock are as much fun as the atmosphere at this Uptown Mexican restaurant.

The **Olde Sedona Bar & Grille** (1405 W. S.R. 89A, 928/282-5670, www.oldesedona.com, 11am-2am daily) is a West Sedona mainstay. The self-described family restaurant may not have the best food in town, but its live music and funky Western atmosphere can't be beat. Grab a local brew at sunset and head to the second-story patio for a view of the red rocks. You could easily spend the rest of the night drinking, shooting pool, dancing, and listening to a blues band with new friends or catch a sports game during daytime hours.

You don't have to look far to find a decent beer in Red Rock Country. **Oak Creek Tap Room and Brewery** (2050 Yavapai Dr., 928/204-1300, https://oakcreekbrew.com, 4pm-11pm Mon.-Thurs., noon-1am Fri.-Sun.) in West Sedona serves up a slew of award-winning handcrafted beers, like its popular amber ale, pilsner-style gold lager, and refreshing Hefeweizen. Check out the cabinet where members stow their personal mugs before heading out to the patio to listen to live music, which ranges from rockabilly and bluegrass to "off-kilter jazz fusion."

Wine and beer connoisseurs, you have a home in Sedona! It's called **Vino di Sedona** (2575 W. S.R. 89A, 928/554-4682, www.vinodisedona.com, 4pm-9pm Mon., 11am-11pm Tues.-Thurs., 11am-midnight Fri.-Sat., 11am-9pm Sun.) and it has everything a serious wine and beer lover wants: contemporary decor, live entertainment, and a tasty menu. This, of course, is in addition to the beers on tap that range from Boddington's to Kilt Lifter, over 100 bottles of beer, a wine list curated by an owner with 30 years of experience in the industry, and wine bottles to purchase so you can continue your experience at home. The lovely wine bar is cozy and authentic—lacking the touristy feel that often plagues Sedona.

Locals and visitors rave about **The Sundowner** (37 Navajo Dr., 928/282-1858, 9am-11pm Sun.-Fri., 10am-11pm Sat.) and who could resist a place that calls itself "Sedona's only five-star dive bar"? The friendly staff includes a well-known bartender named Bertha, who is charming as heck and will make for a memorable visit. Grab some grub while you're there because the food is more than decent. Oh, and bring a wad of cash—just like any legit dive, the place is cash only.

You never know what you'll find at the spirited **Relics Restaurant & Roadhouse at Historic Rainbow's End** (3235 W. S.R. 89A, 928/282-1593, www.relicsrestaurant.com, 5pm-2am daily), a former homestead, general store, and stagecoach stop. Thankfully, the dance hall—which retains much of its rustic ambience and northern Arizona's largest wooden dance floor—is still attracting Sedonans with weekly events, including Johnny Cash tributes, Latino nights, and DJ dance parties that range from Motown to country. If the barroom looks a little familiar, you may have seen it in the 1965 Western, *The Rounders,* starring Henry Fonda and Glenn Ford.

Couples will find plenty of romantic restaurants in which to enjoy a glass of wine, although the big resorts expertly set the mood with cozy fireplaces and leafy patios. Make the 15-minute drive to **Enchantment Resort**

Oak Creek Showdown

Oak Creek Canyon. The Village of Oak Creek. Oak Creek.

Is anyone else confused?

When first planning a trip to Sedona, it's easy to mix up these three designations. Lucky for you, this explanation will clear it all up.

Working north to south, Oak Creek Canyon is the area that sits north of Sedona proper. So, basically, when you're driving north through Sedona on either Route 89A or 179, you'll hit the Y roundabout, where they converge. Just keep heading north on the 89A through the shopping area and BOOM, you're well on your way to Oak Creek Canyon. Within minutes, the highway will cut right into the beautiful canyon, carved out by the Oak Creek itself as it crisscrosses along the road. The whole area is fed by the creek and you can expect riparian trees and wildlife in the shadows of the red-rock canyon walls. Gorgeous.

Now, if you picture the geography of the area like a peanut-butter sandwich, Oak Creek Canyon is the top slice of bread and the Village of Oak Creek is the bottom slice (with Sedona being the peanut butter). The Village of Oak Creek is a small community of residents, hotels, shopping centers, and restaurants along Route 179 and located south of Sedona proper. It's less touristy and generally less expensive but still offers a lovely stay and is just a short drive away from all the action.

And then there's Oak Creek itself. It's the waterway that is pretty much responsible for everything wonderful about Sedona. The creek carved—and is still carving—Oak Creek Canyon over millions of years as it twists and turns its way down through Sedona, offering swimming holes, idyllic shoreline picnic spots, and inspiring scenery.

Got all that?

(525 Boynton Canyon Rd., 928/282-2900, www.enchantmentresort.com), which is nestled in the horseshoe-shaped Boynton Canyon.

Village of Oak Creek

Join the locals at **Full Moon Saloon** (7000 S.R. 179, 928/284-1872, www.thefullmoonsaloon.com, 1pm-2am daily) at Tequa Marketplace in the Village of Oak Creek. This place has everything you want for a casual night out: pool tables, tasty bar food, live music, and karaoke (check the website for event schedules). This place is committed to a good time and is open 365 days a year.

PJ's Village Pub & Sports Lounge (40 W. Cortez Dr., 928/284-2250, www.pjsvillagepub.com, 10am-2am daily) is a laid-back watering hole in the village that packs in locals with live music on Saturday nights and every other Wednesday. As at any good neighborhood bar, you'll find regulars jockeying at the jukebox, playing darts, foosball, or pool at their quarter tables.

PERFORMING ARTS

Chamber Music Sedona (928/204-2415, www.chambermusicsedona.org) presents an eclectic series of artists at venues throughout Sedona, often in intimate settings at private residences with local wine served. Check the website for performance dates and locations.

Although "performing arts" may not be the most accurate term for what **Sedona Creative Life Center** (333 Schnebly Hill Rd., 928/282-9300, www.sedonacreativelifel.com) has to offer, it's kind of related in that a group of people congregates to share an experience. Here, it could be anything from mentalists to healers to award ceremonies. Check the website for a calendar of events and keep an open mind for this roster.

Take in a film on the big screen or a live performance at the **Mary D. Fisher Theatre** (2030 W. S.R. 89A, 928/282-1177, www.sedonafilmfestival.com), which hosts regular screenings of films, plays, musicals, live on-screen Met Opera performances, and the annual Sedona International Film Festival.

FESTIVALS AND EVENTS
February

Sedona boasts a rich selection of outdoor festivals throughout the year. Serious runners converge in early February for the **Sedona Marathon** (www.sedonamarathon.com). Unlike big-city races with views of architecture and concrete jungles, the challenging run wends its course strategically to offering spectacular views of the natural surroundings and a few wildlife sightings. The full- and half-marathon runs, as well as the more manageable 5km option and youth runs, are open to runners of all levels.

Around the last week of February, the **Sedona International Film Festival** (2081 W. S.R. 89A, 928/282-1177, www.sedonafilmfestival.com) presents more than 100 movies from around the world, including big-budget features, documentaries, shorts, and student films. Some have even gone on to earn Academy Award nominations. The screenings are open to the public, with directors, producers, and stars frequently in attendance.

March

Bust out with your green threads and head to the **Sedona St. Patrick's Parade and Festival** (www.sedonamainstreet.com), which is just that—a parade and a festival. The free event along Jordan Road in Uptown is growing in popularity year over year with a parade by local businesses and dignitaries followed by the festival, which features family activities, food, and music.

July

If you're in the mood to really dive into the Wild West cowboy culture for a day, join the fun at Uptown for the **National Day of the Cowboy Celebration** (www.sedonamainstreet.com). This rowdy event happens late July and includes gunfights, roping, action shooting, re-enactments, musicals revue, storytelling, poetry, and a costume contest. It's just the kind of thing you can only find in the American Southwest and the kids will have a blast.

September

The **Red Rock Music Festival** (877/733-7257, www.redrocksmusicfestival.com) in late August and early September attracts classical-musical lovers for a vibrant showcase of

The Fiesta De La Tlaquepaque celebrates Mexican Independence Day.

chamber music. Concerts and events are held at venues throughout Sedona.

Celebrate Mexican Independence Day with class at the **Fiesta De La Tlaquepaque** (336 S.R. 179, 928/282-4838, www.tlaq.com), a traditional event in Sedona that has been running for more than 40 years. Along with the beautiful backdrop of this historic shopping center, enjoy delicious food, music, dance, and entertainment as well as arts-and-crafts exhibits showcasing the traditional and contemporary art of Mexico. **Sedona Winefest** (www.sedonawinefest. com). Need we say more? Wine lovers will be delighted at this weekend-long event that features food, live music, vendors, and views. And, of course, an impressive array of Verde Valley and Southern Arizona wines are available for tasting.

October

Look for a sea of white tents in West Sedona the second weekend of October. The **Sedona Arts Festival** (995 Upper Red Rock Loop Rd., 928/204-9456, www.sedonaartsfestival.org) assembles more than a hundred juried artists for a showcase of contemporary paintings and sculpture, colorful jewelry, and multi-media works by artists and craftspeople. Children can create their own masterpieces from paint, glitter, beads, and feathers in the Kid Zone.

The **Sedona Plein Air Festival** (928/282-3809, www.sedonapleinairfestival.com) in late October attracts painters from around the country to create art "in the open air," a technique made famous by the French Impressionists. The weeklong event—at trailheads, creeks, and parks throughout town—includes demonstrations and workshops for painters hoping to develop their technical abilities as well art lovers who would like a behind-the-scenes peek.

December

Sedona does the holidays right. Every year the city transforms itself in December into **Holiday Central Sedona** (www.holidaycentralsedona.com), which basically means the whole place gets super-duper Christmas-y by decorating storefronts and drenching the town in light strings. A robust calendar of events like photos with Santa, Jingle Bell Run, and performances of The Nutcracker is updated online. And to see a unique Southwestern holiday tradition, visit Tlaquepaque Arts and Crafts Village for the **Festival of Lights** (336 S.R. 179, 928/282-4838, www.tlaq.com) in mid-December. Some 6,000 glowing luminarias—small paper bags filled with sand and a single lit candle—flicker in the charming shopping complex.

Shopping

What do American tourists love to do? Buy stuff! Shopping is probably Sedona's most popular activity, with the vast majority of stores targeting the out-of-state visitors who flock here for a taste of Arizona—or to experience the New Age energy. Small specialty stores selling cactus jellies, cowboy boots and hats, colorful pottery, and mystical gemstones line Highways 179 and 89A. And you won't have to search long to find Native American arts and crafts such as handmade Navajo rugs and kachina dolls.

Sedona's thriving gallery scene also attracts serious collectors as well as first-time buyers. The 50-some galleries range from mammoth, light-filled spaces selling large-format bronzes and contemporary pieces to intimate studios specializing in Western-themed canvases. Even if art isn't your thing, the gallery scene is a quintessential part of Sedona and shouldn't be missed.

You'll find the greatest concentration of souvenir shops, metaphysical boutiques, and galleries in Uptown. If you're looking for gifts for friends and family back home, the gourmet salsas, outdoor wind sculptures, silver jewelry, and "healing" crystals can be fun and a little kitschy. You may even want to consider splurging on a handcrafted piece of furniture or canvas to remember your trip.

★ UPTOWN
Shopping North of the Y

Okay, so "Uptown Sedona" includes the area around the Y intersection of Routes 179 and 89A, and "Uptown Uptown Sedona" is the bustling area north of the Y on Route 89A, which is famous for tourist foot traffic. With a series of small shopping centers lining both sides of the road, travelers can park their cars and hop out for a whirlwind of boutiques, Jeep tours, museums, restaurants, and aura readings.

BOUTIQUES AND SPECIALTY SHOPS

Blink and you'll miss the **Sedona Candle Gallery** (276 N. S.R. 89A, 928/204-0688, 9am-7pm daily), which is a teeny, tiny shop churning out some special and beautiful candles. Watch as the resident candle-maker creates these small masterpieces that make for reasonably priced, one-of-a-kind gifts.

If you've got a sweet tooth that won't be satisfied by the cactus candy sold at the endless blur of souvenir shops, stop by the **Sedona Fudge Company** (257 N. S.R. 89A, 928/282-1044, www.sedonafudgecompany.com, 10am-9pm daily) for cookies, chocolate-dipped fruit, and crazy-delicious fudge.

In the market for an American Flag button-down Western shirt? Then head to **Cowboy Corral** (219 N. S.R. 89A, 928/282-2040, www.cowboycorral.com, 10am-7pm daily). Inside the stone-facade building, wannabe desperados and cowgirls can buy reproduction badges, leather holsters, spurs, fringed jackets, and even replica non-firing guns (don't take that on the airplane ride home). Splurge on one of the cowboy hats or a lariat especially sized for a child.

NEW AGE

If you want to start your spiritual journey, **Sedona Crystal Vortex** (300 N. S.R. 89A, 928/282-3388, www.sedonacrystalvortex.com, 9am-8pm daily) is a must-visit. Here you'll find crystals and gemstones alongside feng shui supplies, angelic gift items, jewelry, and cards. Receive some TLC for the soul with the on-site psychic readers and massage therapists, who accept walk-in customers.

If you're looking to amp up your rock collection to keep your inner peace at its best, pop into **Spiritstone Gems** (301 N. S.R. 89A, 928/204-2100, www.spiritsonegems.com, 10am-6:30pm daily) to grab handfuls of crystals, geodes, and stones with influential properties. The store also offers divine jewelry, healing tools, and a friendly staff available for energy healing, chakra balance, and other guidance.

ARTS AND CRAFTS

You're practically tripping over Native American goods in Sedona, but only **Joe Wilcox Indian Den** (320 N. S.R. 89A, Ste. J, 928/282-2661, www.joewilcoxsedona.com, 9:30am-8pm daily) offers such a vast array of gifts and souvenirs. The Sinagua Plaza boutique features authentic jewelry crafted by Navajo, Zuni, and Hopi artists, and goodies include Zuni fetishes and Navajo pottery, kachinas, sand paintings, and alabaster carvings. Shoppers also will find Southwestern wall art, housewares, wind chimes, and a vast collection of holiday ornaments year-round.

And if your desire for Southwest tchotchkes hasn't been sated, duck into **Zonie's Galleria** (215 N. S.R. 89A, 928/282-5995, www.zonies-galleria.com, 9:30am-7pm daily). The tiny shop's Southwestern housewares, sculpture, pottery, and wind chimes may be just what you are looking for.

JEWELRY

For jewelry "traditionally inspired but with a contemporary flair," peruse the selection

SINAGUA PLAZA

UPPER LEVEL
TOUCHSTONE GALLERY
UP WEST LEATHER
OPEN RANGE GRILL & TAVERN
ANIMA'S TRADING CO
NEW WINE
SEDONA TALK OF THE TOWN
GRAND CANYON HARLEY DAVIDSON

LOWER LEVEL
SEDONA OFFROAD ADVENTURES
SPARKLE GEMS BOUTIQUE
KOKOPELLI TRADING
HOPI HILLS FACTORY DIRECT
EZ
LITTLE TIBET
GEDION GALLERY
JOE WILCOX INDIAN DEN
SAAD SILVER
SEDONA PIZZA COMPANY
LOCK, STOCK & BARREL
WHISKERS BARKERY

Visit Joe Wilcox Indian Den at the Sinagua Plaza.

at the **Blue-Eyed Bear** (299 N. S.R. 89A, 928/282-1158, www.blueeyedbear.com, 10am-6pm daily). The Uptown shop specializes in handmade pieces crafted from sterling silver, gold, and semiprecious stones, all designed by Native American and Southwestern artists. The necklaces, bracelets, and earrings evoke Arizona's indigenous roots while the clean lines and bold color give the work a modern feel.

Turquoise jewelry has made a major fashion comeback in recent years and there's no better place to find this classic Southwestern blue-green stone than at the **Turquoise Buffalo** (252 N. S.R. 89A, 928/282-2994, www.turquoisebuffalo.com, 9am-6pm daily.), which stocks more than 1,700 unique pieces. The helpful staff guides buyers—and curious browsers—through dozens of varieties of turquoise specimens available, from the green-veined Lone Mountain and the copper-flecked Morenci to the creamy white variations. It's a fascinating stop even if you haven't considered buying a piece.

The Shops at Hyatt Piñon Pointe

187

On a small bluff overlooking the Y intersection of Routes 179 and 89A, **The Shops at Hyatt Piñon Pointe** (101 N. S.R. 89A, 928/254-1006, www.theshopsathyattpinonpointe.com) include some interesting independent boutiques along with a few chains, which are quickly creeping into Sedona. For the manly man in your life, head to **West Fork Mens** (928/282-8708, www.sedonaclothing.com, 10am-6pm daily), which stocks a fine collection of sophisticated men's clothing and accessories with a Southwest flair (but not full on cowboy). **Rock and Rouge** (928/282-7623, www.rockanrouge.com, 10am-5pm Mon.-Sat., 11am-4pm Sun.) is a sweet little boutique with trendy active-wear for the ladies as well as accessories, skin care, and makeup. **George Kelly Fine Jewelry** (928/282-8884, www.sedonafinejewelry.com, 10am-5pm daily) carries imaginative and contemporary necklaces and rings. And for a tasty souvenir or gift, pick up a bottle of Arizona vino at **The Art of Wine** (928/203-9463, www.artofwinesedona.com, 11am-7pm daily).

★ Tlaquepaque Arts and Crafts Village

Say this out loud: tuh-LAH-kuh-PAH-kee. Try it again. Okay, you are now ready to visit **Tlaquepaque Arts and Crafts Village** (336 S.R. 179, 928/282-4838, www.tlaq.com, shops open 10am-5pm daily) without embarrassing yourself with a mispronunciation. This charming shopping center is considered a Sedona landmark. Tlaquepaque was the mission of Abe Miller, who bought the 4.5-acre homestead on the banks of Oak Creek in the early 1970s, promising its original owners that he would do his best to preserve the property's mature sycamore grove.

Miller envisioned an artists' enclave where visitors could see craftspeople at work and traveled around Mexico with an architect and designer, visiting towns and villages to observe how shoppers and artisans interacted

SEDONA
SHOPPING

in the small plazas and markets. He replicated the colonial-style buildings and courtyards, decorating them with colorful tiles and flowers, and incorporating truckloads of iron work, carved doors, clay pots, and lanterns that he had shipped north from Mexico. He was particularly proud of the chapel, a romanticized confection of stained-glass windows, hand-carved leather pews, and adobe walls, which now hosts weddings year-round.

True to his word, Miller built the complex around the property's old sycamore and cypress trees, giving the shopping village a timeless feel. And although his vision of a live-work artists' village didn't come to full fruition, Tlaquepaque—which means "best of everything"—now houses many of Sedona's finest boutiques, galleries, cafés, and restaurants. Expect to spend an afternoon sauntering through the beautiful property and popping into its 45-plus retailers. Yes, it can be overwhelming, but here are a few to get you started.

ART GALLERIES

Sedona's galleries of glass, paintings, photography, and sculpture are certainly fabulous, but all that fabulousness has a tendency to blur. A memorable stop at Tlaquepaque is **Azadi Navajo Rugs** (928/203-0620, www.

azadifinerugs.com), which features an outstanding collection of incredible Navajo rugs. Bold colors, traditional patterns, and phenomenal quality make this gallery a must-visit. Azadi has several stores nationwide and a second store in Tlaquepaque, **Azadi Fine Rugs** (928/203-0400), but it's the Navajo rugs that will knock your socks off.

Renee Taylor Gallery (928/282-7130, www.reneetaylorgallery.com) regularly draws celebrities and serious art collectors with an eclectic mix of contemporary paintings, jewelry, and sculpture. The abstract works and unique jewelry are particularly strong.

For a colorful collection of hand-blown glass art, visit **Kuivato Glass Gallery** (928/282-1212, www.kuivatoglassgallery.com). The delicate glass sculptures, wall art, and light fixtures sparkle brilliantly, tempting many buyers to ship one of the fragile pieces home.

Tlaquepaque's **Andrea Smith Gallery** (928/203-9002, www.andreasmithgallery.com) features "uplifting" pieces from cultures around the world, including colorful Native American-inspired canvases, an impressive collection of sculpture from southeast Asia, and one of the largest collections of carved amber west of the Mississippi.

Tlaquepaque Arts and Crafts Village

Sedona's Artistic Tradition

Sedona's sculptural rock forms and bold color palette of deep-scarlet rocks, cerulean-blue skies, and forest-green ponderosa pines have provided powerful inspiration to many visitors and residents. Sedona didn't emerge as an artistic haven, though, until Hollywood's epic Westerns first publicized the vivid landscape in big-screen, Technicolor glory. Surrealist Max Ernst was among the first to arrive, briefly making his home here in the 1940s. Before long, a growing artistic community would help shape the town and define its identity. In fact, it was a sculptor, Marguerite Brunswig Staude, who would give Sedona its most iconic landmark, the Chapel of the Holy Cross.

The burgeoning art scene really began to take hold in 1958, when Egyptian Nassan Groban and a few like-minded artists established the "Canyon Kiva" at the old Jordan Apple and Peach Packing Barn in Uptown Sedona. This studio/exhibition space, where artists could gather and teach, evolved into the Sedona Arts Center. A few years later, cowboy artist Joe Beeler arrived in Sedona, brandishing his Western canvases and sculpture. He met with Charlie Dye, George Phippen, Robert MacLeod, and John Hampton in 1965 at the Oak Creek Tavern (now the Cowboy Club Grille & Spirits), where they formed the Cowboy Artists of America, a Western school of art still highly sought by serious collectors.

Soon galleries began popping up across town, with the growing hordes of tourists eager to take home a Sedona souvenir. Even today, the expanded Sedona Arts Center continues its mission to serve as a resource for local artists, providing gallery and classroom space as well as hosting festivals and events year-round. To temporarily immerse yourself in the art scene, join the First Friday Gallery Tour evening art walk. Many of Sedona's galleries feature both contemporary and Southwestern art; they host receptions and technique demonstrations between 5pm-8pm. The Sedona Trolley offers free transportation between galleries. For more information, contact the **Sedona Gallery Association** (928/282-3865, www.sedonagalleryassociation.com).

Eclectic Image Gallery (928/203-4333, www.eclecticimage.com) specializes in travel photography, canvases, and print work. The black-and-white landscapes and brilliantly colored images of Arizona's canyons, rivers, and forests make terrific souvenirs.

You'll find South American folk art at **El Picaflor** (928/282-1173, www.elpicaflor.com), a quirky gallery that stocks handcrafted ceramics, intricate patchwork tapestries, and beautifully woven garments made from Peruvian alpaca wool.

BOUTIQUES AND SPECIALTY SHOPS

There aren't very many clothing boutiques at Tlaquepaque but gurrrl, **Just Us Girls Sedona** (928/282-0571, www.justusgirlssedona.com) has got you covered for some serious Sedona style. There are colorful dresses, chunky jewelry, breezy scarves, and hats. Top off the look with a poncho—why not? You'll look like a local in no time.

On the other hand, **Bennali Outdoor Gear** (928/282-1295, www.bennalioutdoorgear.com) is a perfect stop if you're in the market for some new hiking gear (or maybe a cozy headband to keep your ears warm while you visit all the shops at Tlaquepaque as you research a travel book—yeah, perfect for that, too). The small shop sells active-wear for men and women including hats, shoes, and jackets. And cozy headbands.

One of Abe Miller's original tenants, **Cocopah** (928/282-4928, www.beadofthemonthclub.com) bills itself the "oldest bead store in Arizona," and also carries an impressive array of Art Nouveau and Art Deco estate jewelry, antique Tibetan beads, and Native American jewelry and accessories.

If you have a small adorable child with you, take them to **Tlaquepaque Toy Town** (928/282-1087, tlaqtoytown.com). This comes with a warning—they will seriously lose their little mind in this incredible toy shop. The small space is jam-packed floor to ceiling with beautiful, eco-friendly and educational toys all made in the U.S.A.

If you're nutty about Christmas, check out **Feliz Navidad** (928/282-2752, www.merry-christmassedona.com), which specializes in handmade Christmas decorations created by Sedona natives and artisans worldwide.

The Garland Building

Just south of the Y, you'll find **The Garland Building** (411 S.R. 179), the first of a strip of small art galleries and Southwestern-looking shopping centers lining Route 179 that is also known as Gallery Row. For an elegant selection of Native American arts and crafts, visit **Garland's Navajo Rugs** (928/282-4070, www.garlandsrugs.com, 10am-5pm daily). The large stone building houses an incredible selection of Navajo rugs, including antique pieces and hard-to-find large floor rugs. Garland's offers an extensive assortment of tastefully displayed Navajo sand paintings, hand-carved kachina dolls, pueblo pottery, and hand-woven baskets. While poking around the building, don't miss a visit to **Mary Margaret's Sedona Pottery** (928/282-1192, www.sedonapotter.com, 10am-5pm Mon.-Sat., 11am-5pm Sun.), which features incredible pottery and sculpture made by Mary Margaret, a committed artist who established her pottery shop in Sedona in the 1960s. Often you can see her working in her studio at the shop, creating vessels, dishes, mugs, and wall art.

Hozho Distinctive Shops & Galleries

The Santa Fe-style **Hozho Distinctive Shops & Galleries** (431 S.R. 179) offers a small collection of galleries and shops. Seasoned hikers and hikers-to-be will enjoy a visit to **The Hike House** (928/282-5820, www.thehikehouse.com, 9am-6pm Mon.-Sat., 9am-5pm Sun.) where boots, hats, bandanas and gear can be purchased for your Sedona hikes. Then pop into their Energy Café for a cup of coffee and a chat with the staff, who can give you great trail suggestions and directions.

Pick up a map or a travel book there because they have really excellent books (um, like this one). Art collectors and shoppers will find Native American canvases, sculpture, and jewelry at **Turquoise Tortoise Gallery** (928/282-2262, www.turquoisetortisegallery.com, 10am-6pm Mon.-Sat., 11am-5pm Sun.). **Lanning Gallery** (928/282-6865, www.lanninggallery.com, 10am-6pm Mon.-Sat., 11am-5pm Sun.) features more contemporary oils, acrylics, and encaustics, as well as ceramics and handmade furniture.

Hillside Sedona

The neighboring **Hillside Sedona** (671 S.R. 179, www.hillsidesedona.net), an upscale shopping center overlooking Oak Creek, features unique restaurants, galleries, and shops. Probably the biggest crowd pleaser for the casual art observer is **ALT Gallery** (928/554-7840, www.altgallerysedona.com, 10am-6pm daily), which showcases contemporary art glass, paintings, and (here's where the crowd-pleaser part comes in) the Art of Dr. Seuss. Be sure to check out **James Ratliff Gallery** (928/282-1404, www.jamesratliffgallery.com, 10am-6pm Mon.-Sat., 11am-5pm Sun.), which has called Sedona its home for over 30 years and sells high-end bronzes, colorful canvases, and modern Southwestern works.

Route 179

Drive a few minutes south of the Y on Route 179 and you can't miss one of Sedona's best stores, **Son Silver West Gallery** (1476 S.R. 179, 928/282-3580, www.sonsilverwest.com, 9am-7pm daily). The kitschy shop manages to avoid a touristy feel, selling brightly colored glassware and ceramics, bells and wind chimes, imported Mexican crafts, and dried chili peppers. Meander through a pleasant outdoor pottery garden, where contemporary and Southwestern pots are stacked alongside some spectacular cow skulls.

Shoppers looking for a sweeping survey of art should pop into **Exposures International Gallery of Art** (561 S.R. 179, 800/526-7668, www.exposuresfineart.com, 10am-5pm daily), the largest fine-art gallery in Arizona. The sprawling indoor-outdoor exhibition space showcases paintings, photography, wall art, fountains, glass, sculpture, and jewelry.

WEST SEDONA
Boutiques and Specialty Shops

On an unassuming road tucked behind large sycamore trees just south of the Y, **Hummingbird House** (100 Brewer Rd., 928/282-0705, www.hummingbirdhouse-sedona.com, 10am-5pm Mon.-Sat., 11:30am-4pm Sun.) offers shoppers a nostalgic slice of old Sedona. The quaint building used to be Hart General Store, Sedona's first store built in 1926. Today, it has been preserved and refurbished to hold a delightful collection of country knickknacks, antiques, garden accents, home accessories and custom furniture. It's the perfect one-stop shopping trip for unique and homey gifts.

For housewares and furnishings with a "south of the border" look, stop into **Mexidona** (1670 W. S.R. 89A, 928/282-0858, www.mexidona.com, 10am-5pm daily). Shoppers can order rustic-looking furniture or browse the extensive collection of Talavera pottery, richly painted in deep blues, golds, and reds, similar to the tiles that decorate Tlaquepaque Arts and Crafts Village.

New Age

A name like **Mystical Bazaar** (1449 W. S.R. 89A, 928/204-5615, www.mysticalbazaar.com, 9am-9pm daily) could mean any number of things, but this shop sells unique jewelry as well as a host of metaphysical items, including New Age books, music, tarot cards, and a diverse selection of gemstones and crystals. The shop also offers aura photography, psychic readings, healing sessions, massages, and private spiritual tours. Talk to a team member if you'd like assistance in finding the right combination of tools and experiences for a mystical journey.

Explore Sedona's New Age side at **Crystal Magic** (2978 W. S.R. 89A, 928/282-1622, 9am-9pm Mon.-Sat., 9am-8pm Sun.), "a resource center for discovery and personal growth." Take home some healing crystals or stock up on aromatherapy oils and candles, feng shui supplies, incense, books, or music. If you want a more personalized experience, pop in to see Ray for a psychic reading.

Native American Arts and Crafts

Kachina House (2920 Hopi Dr., 928/204-9750, www.kachinahouse.com, 8:30am-4:30pm Mon.-Fri., 8:30am-2:30pm Sat., 10am-2pm Sun.) is Arizona's largest distributor of Native American arts and crafts, many for rather reasonable prices. The Native American emporium sells hundreds of kachina dolls, Navajo rugs, painted hides, baskets, and pottery, all made by Native American artisans.

Sports and Recreation

For some of us, merely viewing Sedona's majestic red rocks from the roadside or the comfort of a hotel balcony doesn't quite cut the mustard. Luckily, there are plenty of ways to get outside and get a little dirty. Hikers and bikers could spend weeks, if not months, exploring the miles and miles of trails that wind through Sedona's protected state and national parks. The region's deep canyons, meandering creeks, and ponderosa pine forests can be irresistible, and the diverse topography and wildlife frequently surprise visitors.

A Jeep tour is one of Sedona's must-dos. The bumpy and occasionally dusty trips are a lot of fun, giving visitors a taste of how the pioneers who arrived by stagecoach more than a century ago must have felt. Of course, there are more refined ways to sneak in your time outdoors: a round of golf, an alfresco massage at a four-star spa, or a hot-air balloon trip.

No matter what you do, be sure to wear sturdy shoes, a hat, and sunscreen when you venture outside. Despite the shady trees, this is still the high desert, and the sun can be brutal, especially for visitors who underestimate its power. Also, bring water—and lots of it—as it's not uncommon to dehydrate quickly in this arid climate.

TOURS
★ Jeep Tours

Taking a ride with iconic **Pink Jeep Tours** (204 N. S.R. 89A, 800/873-3662, www.pinkjeeptourssedona.com) is the most popular way to romp over Sedona's red rocks. Charismatic guides describe the geology and ecosystem surrounding Sedona as they drive beefed-up Jeep Wranglers over steep boulders and occasionally treacherous passes. The tours provide excellent photo opportunities and, surprisingly, a deeper appreciation for the animals, fauna, and red-rock vistas surrounding the city center. Several tours are offered with full descriptions online. The popular Broken Arrow Tour ($95 adults, $71.25 ages 12 and under) explores the submerged-below-the-treetops Submarine Rock

and scouts out postcard-perfect views. For a little history with your nature, the three-hour Ancient Ruins Tour ($76 adults, $57 ages 12 and under) stops at an ancient cliff dwelling and a close look at the Honanki Heritage Site. Plush motor coach tours to the Grand Canyon are also available ($140 adults, $112 ages 12 and under). Advanced reservations are recommended, although there's no harm in asking for a same-day tour.

Red Rock Western Jeep Tours (301 N. S.R. 89A, Ste. G, 928/282-6667, www.redrockjeep.com) offers four-wheeling excursions and much more. The cowboy guides may look like cheesy anachronisms, but these local experts enrich a traveler's appreciation for Sedona's complex geology and wildlife. Red Rock's various outings range from romping with wine tasting and romantic private tours *à deux* to Western-themed treks that trace Apache and cowboy trails. The company also provides horseback riding, ranch cookouts, and sunset trips to the Grand Canyon. Basic Jeep tours are about $50 per person. Parties of 10 or more may qualify for group rates.

Adventure Tours

If you're not content letting the scenery pass you by from the seat of a Jeep, **Sedona**

See the red rocks with Pink Jeep Tours.

Adventure Tours (928/204-6440, www.sedonaadventuretours.com) leads tours that explore Sedona's waterways. Try the most decadent of guided tours offered with the Classic Water to Wine Tour ($109 per person), which spends about 90 minutes floating down the Verde River on a Ducky Kayak and is followed by a wine tasting at Alcantara Vineyards. Reservations are simple: Book online and they'll send you an email with a meet-up time and place.

Oh man, for a truly one-of-a-kind and zany tour of Sedona, consider **Sedona Segway** (411 Forest Rd., 928/282-4611, www.sedonasegway.com) for a Segway tour (Segways are those goofy two-wheeled, battery-powered transports as seen in the movie *Paul Blart: Mall Cop*) of Uptown, Sedona art galleries, or the Chapel of the Holy Cross. Call to make your reservations and you may talk to a kind soul named "Pancake," who will happily cater your tour to your desires. The family-run business is charming, to say the least, with prices ranging from $65-$100 at 1-2 hours. Is this for real? Yes, yes it is.

Helicopter and Biplane Tours

If you're game for hopping in a helicopter, why not do it in one of the most beautiful places in the world? **Hillsboro Aviation** (1200 Airport Rd., 928/282-8903, www.sedonahelitours.com) skims the massive buttes and green forests that proliferate the area, descending into canyons and climbing over rugged mountains. The Rim Dancer tour ($99) surveys the area's best-known formations, like Bell and Cathedral Rocks, as well as the Chapel of the Holy Cross and Bear Wallow Canyon in just 12-15 minutes. For a look at ancient Sinagua cliff dwellings, take the Ancient Spirit Tour ($149), which visits Secret, Boynton, and Long canyons. Or go big with the Sinagua Majestic Deluxe tour ($199) that combines all the sites of the aforementioned smaller tours with a full 30-plus minutes of tour time.

Take to the skies in a helicopter or airplane with **Sedona Air Tours** (1225 Airport Rd., 928/204-5939, www.sedonaairtours.com).

Tours range in price and length and the company will customize a trip for your unique needs like special-destination tours, fishing excursions, or whitewater-rafting trips. For a quick but memorable experience, try the 15-minute Bear Wallow Run Helicopter Tour, which is described as a "sampler" of the red rocks, including Three Nuns and Snoopy Rock as well as the beautiful Bear Wallow Canyon ($99 per person). If you're up for it, go for the Grand Canyon Airplane Tour, a three-hour flight through Sedona and Oak Creek Canyon, over the San Francisco Peaks to the Little Colorado River ($229 per person). Those are just a couple of the trips offered, so shop on the website for your adventure.

Astronomy Tours

Sedona's dark skies provide the perfect backdrop for shimmering planets, galaxies, and star clusters. **Evening Sky Tours** (928/853-9778, www.eveningskytours.com, $60 adults, $35 children, ages 6-12) survey the nighttime canopy with telescopes that offer so-close-you-can-touch-it views of sights like the Moon, meteor showers, and even Saturn's rings (when possible). The astronomers are educational and entertaining, guiding you around the night sky without getting too technical.

BALLOONING

While the "worm's-eye view" is spectacular for sure, Sedona's landscape begs to be seen from every angle possible. A gentle hot-air balloon flight seems perfectly fitting. That said, only a handful of ballooning companies are permitted by the Coconino National Forest to fly in the red-rock area, so be sure to check when booking a tour operator not listed here.

Northern Light Balloon Expeditions (928/282-2274, www.northernlightballoons.com, $220 per person) is the oldest and largest ballooning company in Sedona, offering red-rock air tours since 1973. The sunrise flights provide visitors with one of those "only in Sedona" experiences—and this one's

Did You Feel That? It Could Be a Vortex.

Some say you can find a vortex by looking for trees that have grown in a twisted fashion.

They're as ubiquitous as the red rocks and pink Jeeps, but not nearly as easy to spot. Sedona's vortexes embody much of the city's New Age culture: An ever-present phenomenon that earns curiosity from locals and visitors alike. For believers, vortexes are spiraling centers of cosmic energy that lead to heightened self-awareness and spiritual improvement. You may be familiar, though, with more common vortexes, like tornadoes, whirlwinds, or water going down a drain.

In Sedona, these funnels of the Earth's inner-energy are prime spots for meditation. Depending on who you speak to, numerous sites are scattered around town, but there are four well-known and easy-to-reach vortexes near Airport Mesa, Boynton Canyon, Bell Rock, Red Rock Crossing, and Cathedral Rock. Some feature a masculine energy, improving strength and self-confidence, while others are more feminine, boosting patience and kindness.

If you'd like a guided journey, contact **Sedona Vortex Tours** (150 S.R. 179, 928/282-2733, www.sedonavortextours.com, $89-239 per person), where guides can customize a trip to multiple vortexes and explain about medicine wheels, power points, and ley lines. Staff at New Age bookstores and crystal shops will also make recommendations.

topped off by a champagne picnic breakfast after landing. Unlike other balloon companies that maintain a fleet of balloons holding 12 people, most of Northern Light's balloons only hold up to seven passengers, making for a quiet and intimate experience. Call for reservation availability as it changes depending on the weather.

Red Rock Balloon Adventures (273 N. S.R. 89A, Suite M&N, 800/258-3754, www.redrockballoons.com, $220 adults, $195 children ages 12 and under) offers stunning sunrise tours. The 60- to 90-minute adventures—depending on weather—drift through Sedona skies and conclude with a picnic. Brides and grooms may want to consider the Wedding Package ($2,500), which can accommodate up to six people on a private flight and includes a "commemorative picnic" with wedding cake.

★ HIKING

The hiking in Sedona is…breathtaking? Heart-stopping? Stunning? Bonkers? Yes, all of those things and more. It's hard to convey just how rich and dynamic Sedona's landscape is, especially when explored on foot. Thanks to spectacular buttes, massive geological formations, and acres upon acres of protected land, there seems to be a world-class trail wherever you pull over your car in Sedona. And, even if you're not a hiker, there are plenty of simple paths in an convenient parking that offer a view with minimal effort.

If you're a hard-core hiker looking to research the very best trail for your particular skill level and desires from a trail, pick up a trail map at tourist centers and outdoor stores or visit www.redrockcountry.org for some ideas. Of course, one quick search online will yield dozens of options for Sedona hiking books with trail reviews and maps.

Beginners may want to consider the **Bell**

Red Rock Pass

Before you set out to explore Sedona's famous buttes and hiking trails, be sure to purchase a **Red Rock Pass,** which is required to park your vehicle in national forest areas. Most of the pull-offs on Highways 89A and 179 will require the pass, as well as parking lots at trailheads. The pass must be displayed on the windshield of your vehicle, although it is not required if you are simply pulling over for a quick stop or photo-op. You can purchase the $5 daily and $15 weekly passes at visitor centers, many hotels, Sedona Chamber of Commerce, and automated kiosks at parking areas and trailheads, including Bell Rock and Boynton Canyon. Money generated from the passes is used to maintain and protect this "high-impact recreation area." For more information, call 928/203-2900 or visit www.redrockcountry.org.

Rock Pathway (the round-trip is three miles), the single best introductory trail in Sedona. It's wide, flat, well signed, and easy to navigate. So easy, in fact, that the trail can get quite crowded on holidays and weekends. Conveniently located just north of the Village of Oak Creek on Route 179, the trail is popular for good reason: it's beautiful. The leisurely trek traces the delicate Bell Rock and nearby Courthouse Butte, making for ample selfie opportunities for families and first-time hikers.

About a mile north on Route 179, turn into the Back O'Beyond housing development, where the **Cathedral Rock Trail** (a 1.5-mile round-trip) offers a bigger challenge. The short but steep hike to the "saddle" of Cathedral Rock can be tough, but the rewarding views of the multi-spired formation are incredible. Follow the basket cairns (stacked-rock markers) and be prepared to use hands and feet to climb a small portion of the rock. At the top of three-quarters of a mile, many believe a vortex swirls with cosmic energy.

For panoramic views of Sedona and its red-rock buttes, the 3.5-mile **Airport Mesa Trail** provides a host of camera-ready vistas. Just be aware that you're following along a trail on the slope of a mesa with airplanes soaring overhead so it's not great for families, dogs, or small children. It's best to hit this trail early in the morning before the parking lot—just off of Route 89A in West Sedona—fills up. If you're not up for the entire loop, it can easily be cut short because after a quick walk uphill (and by "quick" we mean you basically walk up one flight of stairs) the view hits hard and so does a vortex.

From Route 89A in West Sedona, take Dry Creek Road north to Forest Road 152, where you'll need a four-wheel-drive vehicle to access the trailhead for **Devil's Bridge Trail** (two miles round-trip), which leads to a natural stone arch. Halfway through the moderate, mile-long hike (one-way), the trail splits, with the right trail going to the top of the soaring Devil's Bridge and the left winding below the arch. A warning for those with a fear of heights: Be prepared to climb the well-used stone stairs, which do not have handrails. Have a friend snap a photo of you on Devil's Bridge and then continue on the main trail until it ends at about a mile in.

Farther north on Dry Creek Road, you'll find two stunning canyon trails on Boynton Pass Road. Park just outside Enchantment Resort to trek the **Boynton Canyon Trail,** an easy to moderate hike that traverses several different terrains, from cactus-dotted desert to pine-shaded forest. The hike is about a five-mile round-trip and you'll pass Native American ruins in cliffside caves as you make your way up the canyon. Unlike some of the other panoramic trails that offer sweeping views of Sedona, the cocooning box canyon feels more intimate. Plus, its reputation as a vortex site and the belief by the Apache that the canyon was the birthplace of their ancestors gives the area a spiritual vibe. At the beginning of the trail, look for the tall, elegant spire called Kachina Woman Rock, which watches over the canyon.

Just west on Boynton Canyon Road, you'll come across the trailhead for **Fay Canyon Trail.** Oak and pine trees shade parts of this flat, easy hike, which runs about two miles round-trip to the canyon's red sandstone walls. This trail is absolutely perfect for folks traveling with small children and babies as it has a wide path, hardly any cacti, and no scary cliffs. Oh, and it's super gorgeous.

Cathedral Rock

BIKING

Strap on your helmet and get ready for some of the best off-roading in the country. Mountain bikers will find a terrain every bit as diverse and challenging as meccas in Moab, Utah, and Durango, Colorado—although far less crowded. The single-track trails lure diehards and beginners alike, thanks to challenging combinations of dirt, sand, and slick rock.

Many of Sedona's hiking trails allow biking, the most notable exceptions being designated wilderness trails where it is strictly forbidden. Consult signage at trailheads before starting. Also, the terrain can be a bit unpredictable, so exercise caution on rock formations and near cliff sides. As always, be courteous and communicative with hikers!

For an introductory ride, try **Bell Rock Pathway and Courthouse Butte Loop** (a four-mile loop) just north of the Village of Oak Creek on Route 179. This combo makes a loop around (you guessed it) Bell Rock and Courthouse Butte. Portions of the trail offer bypass pathways that help a biker avoid the main shared trail with hikers.

The **Jim Thompson Trail** (5.4 miles round-trip) can be accessed from the end of Jordan Road in Uptown Sedona or a couple of miles north at the Wilson Canyon Trailhead at the Midgley Bridge on Route 89A. Thompson built the trail in the 1880s as a wagon road to his home, which is why it tends to be a bit wider than most trails in these parts. Loose rocks cover much of the terrain, and the ride is pleasant.

Okay, bikers, get ready to freak out, because Sedona is building its own **Bike Skills Park** (525 Posse Ground Road). As of press

Total Cairnage

a row of cairns

And here we are with another write-up about rocks. Only this time, we're talking about the little rocks, not the big, giant ones on the horizon. Specifically, the little rocks that make up cairns.

Cairns are stacks of rocks traditionally used as directional aids along hiking and biking trails. Typically, the stack is made from flat, smooth stones that decrease in size as each layer is added. These little things are everywhere along the trails in Sedona, although they seem to occur randomly. In some instances, you'll stumble upon a miniature city of cairns. So what's the deal?

Many visitors and residents create the cairns as a part of personal ritual or spiritual action. Seems innocent enough, right? Not so. In recent years, anti-cairn advocates have voiced concerns about the practice, claiming the removal and placement of rocks disrupts the natural habitat and can cause erosion.

It's important to note, however, that there are helpful cairns in Sedona that come without controversy. As you explore the Sedona trails, you'll see a different style of cairn: large, wire baskets encasing rough red stones. These cairns are legit—meaning they are strategically placed by the trail planners to reassure hikers that yes, they are following a maintained trail.

time, plans and bids were underway to start the first phase of building the 13-acre bike haven, which will eventually include a pump park, flow trails, gravity trails, jump area, skill zone, and dual slalom trail. Fingers are crossed all over Sedona that the park (or at least a portion of it) will be open by late 2016. For the most recent information, call Sedona Parks and Recreation at 928/282-7098 or visit www.sedonaaz.gov.

If you need to rent some wheels, **Sedona**

Bike & Bean (75 Bell Rock Plaza, 928/284-0210, www.bike-bean.com, 8am-5pm daily) in the Village of Oak Creek offers convenient access to trails near Bell, Courthouse, and Cathedral rocks. The laid-back shop rents mountain and road bikes starting at $30 for two hours and same-day reservations are welcome on any bike for any length of time. The coffee's pretty darn good, too, and makes a great way to fuel up on caffeine before or after a ride. Talk to the helpful staff to get the best trail suggestions…especially if you need to include that information in, say, a travel book.

Over the Edge (1695 S.R. 89A, 928/282-1106, www.otesports/locations/sedona.com, 9am-6pm daily) offers a robust bike-rental package that includes your choice of bike, helmet, choice of pedals, spare tube, and personalized fit. The enthusiastic staff will set up suspension according to your weight and even swap stems or saddles if need be. They can also hook you up with detailed mountain bike trail maps and free, up-to-date trail advice.

BIRDING

More than 300 bird species flock to the Verde Valley's lush riparian areas and protected forests, making Sedona a prime spot for bird watching. Throughout the year, it's not uncommon to see a host of colorful birds perched on the ponderosa pine and cottonwood trees, including bald and golden eagles, herons, orioles, hawks, and even Canadian geese in the winter. Black hawks populate the **Red Rock State Park** (4050 Red Rock Loop Rd., 928/282-6907, http://azstateparks.com/parks/rero, $6 adult, $3 per children ages 7-13, children under 6 free) and the habitats are designated by signs as you hike the trails. If you're really into birding, plan your trip for April to catch the **Verde Valley Birding and Nature Festival** (928/282-2202, www.birdyverde.org) with workshops, speakers, and guided explorations. For birding year-round, check in with **Jay's Bird Barn** (2360 S.R. 89A, Suite B-1, 928/203-5700, www.jaysbirdbarn.com) where you'll find other bird enthusiasts. Pick up binoculars and other supplies at the store and sign up for their weekly guided bird walks.

GOLF

For those who appreciate the pleasure of a golf course's natural landscape as much as the thrill of a challenging game, Sedona won't disappoint. The lush fairways provide a brilliant contrast to the crimson buttes that surround the area's courses. Unprotected land that can be developed is at a premium in Sedona, so

expect slightly shorter drives and imaginatively designed tees and greens.

One of the best golf courses in the state, **Seven Canyons** (755 Golf Club Way, 866/367-8844, www.sevencanyons.com) has earned much critical acclaim, including being named one of America's 50 Greatest Golf Retreats by *Golf Digest Index* and one of the Top 100 Modern Courses by *Golfweek* magazine. Tom Weiskopf designed the par-70 course to emphasize the natural topography of the landscape, with tees that take advantage of changes in elevation, naturally rolling fairways, and small, quick greens. The rock walls, water features, bridges, mature trees, and high-desert landscaping are eclipsed only by the red-rock formations that surround the course. The instructional Performance Center and two-tiered Practice Park—which features a 20,000-square-foot teeing space, four target greens, and a chipping area with a practice bunker—round out the world-class facility. Keep in mind, however, that Seven Canyons is a private club with non-member access exclusively through Enchantment Resort and Mii amo Spa.

The par-3 executive course at the **Poco Diablo Resort** (1752 S.R. 179, 928/282-7333, www.pocodiabloresort.com) provides an excellent opportunity to work on your short game while taking in some impressive views along Oak Creek. The duck ponds, willow and pine trees, and the low-key atmosphere offer a refreshing break from Uptown's crowds. The water hazards and fast greens can be challenging, but the real draw to this 9-hole course is its manageable size, offering a quick and affordable way to fit in a game of golf on a short trip to Sedona.

If the scenery looks familiar at the **Sedona Golf Resort** (35 Ridge Trail Dr., 928/284-9355, www.sedonagolfresort.com), you may recognize it from one of the classic Westerns that were filmed here in the 1930s and 1940s, long before the carefully manicured greens and sandy bunkers arrived. The championship course in the Village of Oak Creek features long, rolling fairways and scenic vistas—the view of the red rocks at the par-3 10th hole can be particularly distracting while teeing off. *Golf Digest* regularly bestows the 6,646-yard, par-71 course with a well-deserved four-star rating. And for duffers in need of a quick refresher or extensive instruction, the clubhouse offers clinics, private and group lessons, and even a club-fitting analysis. Before you leave, be sure to check out the remains of the red-rock wall from an early homestead between the first and 18th holes.

Another top course can be found in the Village of Oak Creek. The par-72, 18-hole **Oakcreek Country Club** (690 Bell Rock Dl, d., 990/991 1090, n n n.oakcreekcountry club.com) will appeal to purists who prefer a traditional layout: tree-lined fairways that dogleg, slightly elevated greens, and lakes that pose the occasional hazard. Robert Trent Jones Sr. and Robert Trent Jones Jr. designed the championship golf course to be a tough play, and the signature fourth hole, which is complemented by terrific views of the red rocks, will push most golfers to earn a par 3.

SPAS

Therapy on the Rocks (676 N. Hwy. 89 A, 928/282-3002, www.myofascialrelease.com, 9am-5pm daily) takes a holistic approach to massage therapy or what they call "hands-on bodywork." The four-story cliff house, just north of Uptown on Oak Creek, specializes in the myofascial release, a massage technique practitioners say relieves pain and increases range of motion. There are hour-long and half-day sessions as well as comprehensive two-week programs for people with chronic pain conditions. If it's warm enough, you can enjoy a creek-side treatment or the outdoor whirlpool on the sun deck. Customized treatments vary from person to person. Call ahead for individual treatment prices.

One of the finest spas in the world, **Mii amo** (525 Boynton Canyon Rd., 888/749-2137, www.miiamo.com, 6am-10pm daily) regularly tops magazine "best of" lists for its comprehensive treatments, chic decor, and incredible setting in Boynton Canyon. The

one downside: The luxury spa is only open to guests staying at Mii amo or its sister resort, Enchantment. If you're a diehard spa-goer, consider splurging on a stay here—you won't be disappointed. Mii amo's design and treatments are inspired by Native American, Asian, and New Age practices. You'll want to spend days relaxing by indoor and outdoor pools, enjoying a fitness class on the yoga lawn, or taking a moment for quiet contemplation in the Crystal Grotto, which perfectly aligns with the sun's light during the summer solstice. Day packages for registered Enchantment guests start at $430, and prices for an all-inclusive three-day journey for guests at Enchantment Resort begin at $2,520.

Younger spa-goers may appreciate **The Spa at the Sedona Rouge Hotel** (2250 W. S.R. 89A, 928/203-4111, www.sedonarouge. com/spa, 10am-7pm daily.). The modern, boutique option offers a bit of style and substance as therapists are trained in a host of techniques, including Ayurvedic services, Thai massage, cranial sacral reflexology, and cupping massage. Wellness guru Deepak Chopra hosted his five-day SynchroDestiny Retreat here in 2006. In addition to gender-specific steam rooms and alfresco whirlpools, guests can enjoy the co-ed tranquility room and garden. Massages start at $120.

Sedona's New Day Spa (3004 W. S.R. 89A, 928/282-7502, www.sedonanewdayspa. com, 9am-7pm Mon.-Sat., 11am-5pm Sun.) is a favorite among travelers and locals alike, being voted the best day spa for eight years running. This stand-alone spa doesn't share priorities with a resort or hotel, making the spa experience their number-one priority. The service list is extensive, offering everything from desert-nature body treatments to massage, facials, nail care, waxing, and "soul journeys" at fair prices (massages start at $65). The friendly staff will gladly set up an entire day of bliss for you, filled with treatments that use Native American traditions and organic, wild-crafted indigenous products.

Sedona Spa (160 Portal Ln., 928/282-5108, www.sedonaspa.com, 6am-9pm Mon.-Sat.,

8am-6pm Sun.) at Los Abrigados Resort offers an impressive selection of therapeutic massages that begin at $95, as well as acupuncture and full-body polishes, herbal wraps, and soothing mud masks. Get to the spa early to relax in the eucalyptus steam room, sauna, or to fit in a game of tennis or Pilates class. Remodels and upgrades in spring 2016 allow full accessibility for wheelchair-bound spa-goers.

Sedona Athletic Club (90 Ridge Trail, 928/284-6900, www.hiltonsedonaresort. com, 5:30am-9pm Mon.-Fri., 7am-8pm Sat.-Sun.) is a rather unpretentious facility that boasts a devoted local membership. The 25,000-square-foot facility includes three tennis courts, an outdoor heated lap pool, a fully equipped gym, and fitness classes that range from basic cardio to tai chi, Kundalini yoga, and qigong. Be sure to try one of the massages starting at $127 before taking advantage of the separate men's and women's steam rooms, saunas, and rooftop sun decks.

Food

Sedona's dining options range from the sublime to the ridiculously expensive. Hole-in-the-wall cafés, mom-and-pop diners, crowded brewpubs, and four-star restaurants duke it out for your taste buds—and your money. You'll want to sample Sedona's Mexican and Southwestern cuisine for a taste of authentic Arizona, and fortunately, there are delicious options for every price range. Also, be sure to splurge at least once while you're in Red Rock Country at one of the romantic dining spots that make a stay in Sedona such a treat.

UPTOWN
American

When you're in the hustle bustle of Uptown, you may feel a bit cut off from the red-rock views. What a crime! Pop into **Open Range Grill and Tavern** (320 S.R. 89A, 928/282-0002, www.openrangesedona.com, 11am-9pm daily, $9-33), for an eyeful through their floor-to-ceiling windows. Grab a burger, steak, or nachos as you soak it up. Be assured that all the beef is Arizona raised without hormones or any scary stuff. And choose from an impressive wine list with bottles from Chile to Italy.

As you walk the shops in Uptown, consider **HP Café** (269 S.R. 89A, 928/282-7761, www.hpcafesedona.com, 7am-8pm Tues.-Sat., 7am-3pm Sun.-Mon., $10-26) for your dining needs whether it be breakfast, lunch, or dinner. Expect American classics with inspired dishes from cuisines around the globe. So while you may enjoy your Eggs Benedict for a late breakfast, a friend might opt to start with tempura garlic pickles followed by a burger. Dinner includes seafood entrées, steak, or a unique dish like the apricot and nut-brown braised pork shoulder. Vegetarians will appreciate the Farm-Table Vegetarian dish, which includes local vegetables and pasta.

Enjoy Sedona's very own award-winning microbrew at ★ **Oak Creek Brewery & Grill** (336 S.R. 179, 928/282-3300, www.oakcreekpub.com, 11:30am-8:30pm daily, $11-26). The casual second-floor pub at Tlaquepaque has a darn good menu of sandwiches, salads, pastas, burgers, and "fire-kissed" pizzas such as the feta-and-artichoke Oak Creek Greek Pizza. The BBQ Pork Ribs Red Rock Rack with house-made sauce or the rotisserie lemon chicken are always good choices. Check out the delicious ales and pilsners brewing in copper tanks behind the bar before heading out to the large patio, which has a nice view of Snoopy Rock.

Pizza, sandwiches, and salads are in abundance at **Spoke and Wheel Tavern** (160 N. Portal Ln., 928/203-5334, www.spokeandwheeltavern.com, 11am-9pm daily, $11-30) at Los Abrigados Resort and Spa. The food is decent and the ambience is super-casual, with multiple rooms for seating, a large bar, and a pool table. Oh, and about 20 flat-screen televisions to watch your favorite sports game as you chow on their Margarita pizza. The food's nothing to scream about (either from joy or agony) but certainly decent. Choose from an extensive wine list or local beers on tap and join the rowdy crowd as they cheer and jeer for their teams.

Also located inside Los Abrigados Resort and Spa, **Timó** (160 N. Portal Ln., 928/203-5334, www.timocentral.com, 4pm-9pm Wed.-Sun., $7.50-40), which offers a posh dining experience that won't kill your travel budget. With wine tastings from 4pm-5pm, after which the full menu is available for the remainder of the evening, it's the perfect place to leisurely ease into the dinner hour. The interior is dark and modern and the menu includes tasty small plates and tapas like elk and buffalo meatballs, escargots, or Maine lobster tail, which can be shared and accompanied by a wine sampling. If you're not in a sharing mood, get yourself your own plate of N.Y. steak or lamb adobo with red curry.

If you're not inclined toward the fancy life offered at L'Auberge de Sedona's reservation-only restaurant, Cress on Oak Creek, perhaps the resort's more casual dining option, **Etch Kitchen & Bar** (301 L'Auberge Ln., 888/759-0083, www.lauberge.com/dining, 7am-10:30am breakfast, 11:30am-2:30pm lunch, 5:30pm-9pm dinner Mon.-Sat., 9am-2pm brunch, 5:30pm-9pm dinner Sun., $12-18 breakfast, $15-24 lunch, $18-42 dinner) is more your style. The sleek, recently remodeled design of this contemporary hang-out welcomes a casual crowd filled with many who are still kicking off dust from their hiking boots for breakfast, lunch, and dinner. Serving cuisine that ranges from pancakes in the morning to scallops for lunch to three-cheese tortellini for dinner, all guests will find a satisfying dish. The unique cocktail menu is a nice touch and during the "off hours" one can still order from a menu of tapas-style snacks.

Asian

Chinese Restaurant. Sushi Bar. Cocktail Lounge. Pretty much everything you might want in an Asian dining experience is at **Szechuan** (1350 W. S.R. 89A, 928/282-9288, www.szechuansedona.net, 11am-9:15pm Sun.-Thurs., 11am-9:45pm Fri.-Sat., $11.50-20.50) including beautiful decor and atmosphere. The extensive menu has what you'd expect for traditional Chinese cuisine, with beef, chicken, and shrimp noodle and rice dishes. The same can be said about the sushi menu, with all the favorite sashimi, nigiri, and sushi rolls represented. The drink menu, on the other hand, has some exciting mixed cocktails like the Geisha Girl and the Blue Ninja, as well as an impressive collection of Asian beers and sake. Dine in for a pleasant experience or do take-out to enjoy the tasty dishes.

If you've got the craving for sushi, head to **Hiro's Sushi Bar & Japanese Kitchen** (1730 W. S.R. 89A, 928/282-8906, www.hirosedona.com, 11:30am-1:30pm, 5pm-close Tues.-Fri., 5pm-close Sat.-Sun., $16.50-25), a restaurant that proves you can get good seafood in the middle of the desert. Customers really love the sushi with a menu that includes all the standards for nigiri, maki, and sashimi (in other words, slices of fish and rolls). If sushi isn't your thing, no biggie. They've also got entrées like delicious teriyaki chicken, tempura, and toppanyaki. Try the green tea or azuki bean ice creams for dessert and partake in some sake served hot or cold.

Breakfast and Lunch

Finding an inexpensive lunch in Uptown can be a challenge. Fortunately, the sandwiches at **Sedona Memories** (321 Jordan Rd., 928/282-0032, 10am-2pm Mon.-Fri., $4.50-7.75) are cheap and delicious. Expect generous portions and fresh ingredients at this cash-only, mom-and-pop shop. There are a few tables outside, although you may want to order a picnic to go.

The laidback **Secret Garden Café at Tlaquepaque** (336 S.R. 179, 928/203-9564, www.sedonasecretgardencafe.com, 8am-5pm daily, $11-16) is a pleasant place to enjoy breakfast, especially outside by the charming fountain. Order a cup of the Kona coffee and try the fluffy French toast dipped in Grand Marnier batter or the filling breakfast burrito. In the afternoon, the café serves salads, sandwiches, hearty quiches, and burgers that get the job done (but don't expect anything exceptionally tasty here). And if you were thinking about indulging in a red-rock picnic, you can get your order to go at the counter.

Desserts

How Sweet It Is (336 S.R. 179, 928/282-5455, 10am-5pm daily) sells delicious chocolates, fudges, ice cream, and unique candies. Kids will have a field day perusing the rows of candy and confections in this small sweet shop, and you may want to treat yourself to a fresh fruit smoothie or homemade lemonade.

French

In a city of spectacular views, ★ **Cress on Oak Creek** (301 L'Auberge Ln., 866/584-0804, www.lauberge.com/dining, 5:30pm-9pm Sun.-Thurs., 5pm-9pm Fri.-Sat., $80-140), part of L'Auberge de Sedona resort, stands out. The patio of the elegant restaurant creeps right up the banks of Oak Creek, creating a leafy, romantic setting. The menu's seasonal ingredients reflect the changing scenery, from pine-smoked venison and kobe beef in winter to dishes made with locally grown vegetables and herbs in the summer. Dining here is by reservation only and the dinner menu is fixed and priced for a three- or four-course meal.

The formal dining room at **René at Tlaquepaque** (336 S.R. 179, 928/282-9225, www.renerestaurantsedona.com, 11:30am-8:30pm Sun.-Thurs., 11:30am-9pm Fri.-Sat. pm-8:30pm, $10-55) attracts locals and visitors celebrating weddings, anniversaries, and birthdays, although it's the French New American cuisine that keeps them coming back. Feast on traditional Gallic treats like escargots, onion soup, and steak au poivre, or try surprising dishes like carpaccio of

one of the stunning dishes at René at Tlaquepaque

antelope, thinly sliced antelope with aioli, bruschetta, and crispy fried onions.

Italian

If you're looking for traditional, no frills, red-sauce-and-meatball-style Italian food then **The Hideaway House** (231 S.R. 179, 928/202-4082, www.sedonahideawayhouse.com, 11am-9pm Sun.-Thurs., 11am-10pm Fri.-Sat., $7-30) is for you. Tucked inside a small shopping center across the way from Tlaquepaque, the multi-level restaurant has a cozy, homey feel. Grab a table on the patio for nice view or snag a chair at the bar for mingling. They've got all the Italian standards like Caesar salad, pizza, and lasagna as well as American dishes including grilled fish, rib eye steak, burgers, and sandwiches.

Mexican and Southwest

Oaxaca Restaurant (254 N. S.R. 89A, 928/282-4179, www.oaxacarestaurant.com, 11am-9pm daily, $8-14) boasts a healthy approach to south-of-the-border fare. The menu was designed by a dietician and provides many guilt-free entrées, like grilled Arizona cactus with a zesty sauce of roasted tomatoes, red peppers, chilies, and almonds. The restaurant's patio offers stunning views of Sedona's red rocks, and there is great people watching along the city's main drag. If you just want to sip a margarita while you feast on nature's eye candy, this is the place, as the views are better than the food.

Your other choice to fill a craving for Mexican food on the main strip is **89Agave Cantina** (321 N. S.R. 89A, 928/282-7200, www.89agave.com, 11am-9pm daily, $16-23), formerly known as Taos Cantina. The restaurant underwent an extensive renovation from the decor to the menu, and although the prices can be a bit, well, pricey (this is probably the only Mexican restaurant on the face of the earth that charges for chips and salsa), the food is tasty, with the standard favorites you'd expect plus a few unique treats like the sweet corn *sopa*, a creamy white sweet corn soup with chili and lime topped with corn relish and *cotija* cheese (yum!). Hit it during happy hour from 3pm-5pm to take full advantage of cheaper eats and their crowd-pleasing margaritas. Being in the heart of all the action, it's a perfect stop for patio chatting while people watching.

If you ventured all the way to Sedona to find some good Mexican food, look no further than ★ **Elote Cafe** (771 S.R. 179, 928/203-0105, www.elotecafe.com, 5pm-9pm Tues.-Sat., $13-20). Chef Jeff Smedstad has traveled through Mexico for more than 15 years, creating a flavor distillation of the country's diverse cuisine that runs deeper than tacos and refried beans. Be gluttonous and order an appetizer, entrée, and dessert so you can experience as much as possible of this crazy-delicious menu. The *elote* is an absolute must: fire-roasted corn with spicy mayo, lime, and *cotija* cheese. Try the jicama and orange salad, and follow it up with the sweet-and-spicy lamb adobo or the super-popular smoked pork cheeks. The restaurant's flavors will make a lasting impression on you.

If you're shopping at Tlaquepaque and the urge for classic tacos or quesadillas strikes, hit up **El Rincon** (336 S.R. 179, 928/282-4648, www.elrinconrestaurant.com, 11am-4pm Mon., 11am-9pm Tues.-Sat., 11am-8pm Sun., $5-15). The Mexican-village atmosphere of Tlaquepaque provides a pleasant backdrop for the Arizona-style Mexican cuisine that most Americans will recognize, like shredded-beef burritos, green chili and cheese enchiladas, and sweet corn tamales, served enchilada style with red or green chili sauce. The combination platters are a convenient way to taste a few highlights from the menu—complemented by a prickly pear margarita or Mexican beer, of course. We wouldn't call this destination dining but the ambience is pleasant and the service is quick.

Javelina Cantina (671 S.R. 179, 928/282-1313, www.javelinacantinasedona.com, 11:30am-8:30pm daily, $10-18) isn't out to set the world on fire with an original menu but after tasting their great food, you'll be like, "Who needs that fancy business anyway?" With the comfort of predictable choices like quesadillas, nachos, burritos, enchiladas, fajitas, and every single other traditional Mexican dish you can think of on the menu, no one will leave unsatisfied. Many say this place serves the best fajitas in town and, of course, they arrive sizzling on a hot skillet just as you'd expect. This popular restaurant in the Hillside Sedona Shops is spacious but can get busy with families and large parties around dinnertime. And it's no wonder that business is booming—you can spy some serious red-rock scenery from almost every seat in the house.

Steakhouses and Barbecue

Where else can you get cactus fries and rattlesnake? Slip into one of the big booths at **Cowboy Club Grille & Spirits** (241 N. S.R. 89A, 928/282-4200, www.cowboyclub.com, 11am-10pm daily, $11-36) and admire the "second-largest set of Longhorn horns in the United States" while digging into the buffalo chili, fresh seafood, and wild-game entrées.

This is definitely the place to go for cowboy-worthy steaks and ribs. Next door, the more upscale sibling, **Silver Saddle Room** (5pm-9pm daily, $11-36), features a more elegant experience with a few small additions to the menu in a less-touristy atmosphere.

WEST SEDONA
American

Okay, so you must forgive this writer for constantly talking about the view at all of these restaurants. And it's happening again here because at ★ **Mariposa Latin Inspired Grill** (700 W. S.R. 89A, 928/862-4444, www.mariposasedona.com, 11am-2.30pm, 4pm-9pm daily, $7.50-58), the view is just spectacular. Perched on a hill off Route 89A, this drop-dead gorgeous restaurant is designed with a huge patio and indoor dining room with the most stunning view looking north to the red rocks. To match this beauty is a menu with impeccable food like Aquacate Frito (fried avocados with aioli), gazpacho, and delicious steak. Vegetarians will be happy with plenty of thoughtful options. Everything on the menu is delicious and diners really can't go wrong. The staff is eager to make your dining experience decadent and wonderful. They are successful so, um, eat here (and make reservations if you want a table at dinner).

Food, wine, glowing red rocks, and a spectacular Arizona sunset is what you can expect at **Mesa Grill** (1185 Airport Rd., 928/282-2400, 7am-9pm daily, $8-39). Oh, and the occasional smell of jet fuel. The contemporary American restaurant has a robust menu that delivers. The ingredients are fresh and the flavors are good but the real spectacle here is the location. The minimalistic restaurant and bar sits next to the runway of the Sedona Airport, so watch planes take off and land as you enjoy a great tasting dish like the calamari panko, braised short rib, or vegan tempeh salad. The restaurant serves through breakfast, lunch, happy hour, and dinner so no matter what the time, you can get a great meal here.

If you like options, head to **Heartline Café** (1610 W. S.R. 89A, 928/282-0785, www.

heartlinecafe.com, 4pm-9pm Mon.-Fri., 8am-2pm, 4pm-9pm Sat.-Sun., $8.50-29), which serves breakfast, lunch, and dinner with each meal featuring a sizeable menu. The hard-to-categorize restaurant features Southwestern flavors, Asian touches, and a little continental flair, like butternut squash and roasted pear soup with spiced pecans or tea-smoked chicken dumplings with peanut sauce. There is seafood, pasta, and vegetarian dishes on the menu, with plenty for meat eaters.

Señor Bob's Hot Dogs (2015 W. S.R. 89A, 928/204-2627, 11am-6pm daily, under $10) sports all-beef hot dogs, homemade buns, and a bar of fixin's that can't be beat. If you like hot dogs—which, let's face it, most of America does—you have to grab one here. Try their $5.99 deal for the Hebrew National dog with unlimited toppings, fries, and drink. P.S. Their freshly prepared, homemade fries can't be beat.

Don't let the location next to the Super 8 fool you, **The Golden Goose American Grill** (2545 W. S.R. 89A, 928/282-1447, www.goldengoosegrill.com, 7am-8pm Mon.-Sat., 8am-8pm Sun., $6-40) is surprisingly upscale-ish. The interior decor is contemporary and although it may feel a little fancy, the fairly priced menu and welcoming staff will make you feel at ease (even if you show up in dusty hiking clothes with a grumpy toddler on a busy day when you've been trying to pack in as much activity as possible because maybe you're a travel-book writer). The breakfast, lunch, and dinner menu has all the American standards like pancakes, burgers, sandwiches, salads, and steaks. The ingredients are fresh and the dishes are well prepared. And if you're up for a little culinary adventure, try their exotic burgers like buffalo, kobe, or ostrich.

Breakfast and Lunch

If you're into irony and kitsch, the **E.T. Encounter Diner** (1655 W. S.R. 89A, 928/282-6070, 11am-9pm Mon.-Fri., 8am-9pm Sat.-Sun., $8-19) is for you. It's a 1950s'-diner-meets-outer space motif that serves diner-quality American fare for lunch and dinner (a breakfast menu is available on the weekends). Oddly enough, they have a full bar to add to this surreal dining experience. No joke—look for the UFO out front and old signage that reads "Red Planet Diner."

Locals have been making ★ **Coffee Pot Restaurant** (2050 W. S.R. 89A, 928/282-6626, www.coffeepotsedona.com, 6am-2pm daily, $3.50-11.25) a morning ritual for years, and the small breakfast joint is exactly what you pay for. It's cheap and it gets the job done. You'll find all the morning staples, like pancakes, bacon, and eggs. And more eggs. And more eggs with their list of 101 omelets. The place is bustling most mornings and it there's a wait for your table, a small gift shop is great for browsing. Try to get a table on the patio for a view of the diner's namesake, Coffee Pot Rock.

Euro Deli (3190 W. S.R. 89A, 928/282-4798, www.eurodelisedona.com, 8am-5pm Mon.-Fri., 9am-3pm Sat., closed Sun.) is the perfect stop to or from a hike as they can whip up a hearty sandwich for you to take with or enjoy on their small, pet-friendly patio. The small grocery and deli can get packed quickly if more than three people show up at once but it will be well worth it when you taste their popular Ruebens, Bavarian bratwurst sandwich, or authentic Polish sausage and kraut. They even have a section on the menu solely dedicated to vegetarians, with options like veggie burger, veggie wrap, and veggie quesadilla. Bonus: They serve breakfast all day.

Italian

Order an Oak Creek Nut Brown beer and dive into **Picazzo's** (1855 W. S.R. 89A, 928/282-4140, www.picazzos.com, 11am-9pm Sun.-Thurs., 11am-10pm Fri.-Sat., $16-30) epic menu. Ingredients range from the meaty (sausage, pepperoni, Canadian bacon) to the cheesy (ricotta, parmesan, mozzarella) to the spicy (yellow peppers, red chili flakes, fresh jalapeños). Or you can go the gourmet route with creamy brie, applewood-smoked bacon, and dates. Or, heck, create your own

pizza using their massive list of topping options. They've even got more on the menu like pastas, salads, appetizers, quinoa bowls, and desserts.

★ **Dahl & Di Luca Ristorante Italiano** (2321 W. S.R. 89A, 928/282-5219, www.dahlanddiluca.com, 5pm-9pm daily, $14-36,) is always packed with locals and visitors, who swear by fresh pasta and organic, local ingredients. Be sure to start with the incredible antipasti menu, which includes arancini risotto balls served crispy and delicious calamari fritti. There's often a lively atmosphere in the bar as well as a Tuscan-inspired dining room and patio.

Brought to you by the same owners as Dahl & Di Luca, **Pisa Lisa** (2245 W. S.R. 89A, 928/282-5472, www.pisalisa.com, 11:30am-close Mon.-Sat., noon-close Sun., $10-23) brings the same fine quality of food to a more casual atmosphere. The pop music-themed decor in the small pizzeria is an odd choice but you won't care once you bite into their delicious wood-fired pizzas. Super fresh ingredients and contemporary flavors throughout a robust menu make for a fine culinary experience. The Margherita pizza is sure to please and the vegan Deluxe Semplice is very tasty and cleverly created—no weird fake cheese is used (yay!). Mediterranean-inspired appetizers like the hummus plate with a very fine, mild hummus, tabouli, dolmas, and olives are yummy and the salads are hearty enough to stand on their own as an entrée. The Arizona beers on tap are a nice touch, as is the popular gelato bar. So, yeah, eat here.

Another great pizza spot is **Famous Pizza** (3190 W. S.R. 89A, 928/282-5464, www.azfamouspizza.com, 11am-9pm Sun.-Thurs., 11am-10pm Fri.-Sat., $11-22). With two locations (one in Sedona, one in Oak Creek) the place has got all one would expect in a local pizza shop with a variety of pies, subs, and wings. Try the Sedona-inspired Buddha Beach pizza with mozzarella, pesto, chicken, sun-dried tomatoes, artichokes, and feta. The real perk to hitting this pizza shop is their beer menu, which features a rotating list of craft beers on tap from Dogfish Head, Four Peaks, and THAT breweries.

For tasty Italian food in hefty portions, head to **Bella Vita Ristorante** (6701 W. S.R. 89A, 928/282-4540, www.bellavitasedona.com, 4pm-9pm Sun.-Thurs., 4pm-10pm Fri.-Sat., $15-30), which serves up all the Italian standards like Caesar salad, fettuccine Alfredo, and chicken parmesan. Located at the Sedona Pines Resort, the cozy restaurant is decked out in Italian decor with an indoor fireplace. Everyone loves the delicately prepared calamari so be sure to start with that and then dig in to the vast menu filled with fresh pasta dishes.

Mexican and Southwestern

Tamale lovers, you're in luck. **Tamaliza** (40 Soldier Pass Rd., 928/202-9056, www.sedonatamaliza.com, 11am-7pm Tues.-Sat.) offers daily made, fresh tamales to go and boasts a menu that is sourced from local, organic farms without any processed ingredients. The small store churns out take-out only dishes from a simple menu of tamales and chili rellenos. While the prices are a little steep ($5 per tamale), the quality ingredients and flavor are worth the cost. They've also got vegetarian and vegan tamale options.

With so many choices for Mexican food, it's easy to be overwhelmed. But probably the best authentic Mexican cuisine in all of Sedona is at ★ **Tortas de Fuego** (1630 W. S.R. 89A, 928/282-0226, 8am-9pm daily, $5-14). This pay-at-the-counter eatery has all the indications that you're at the right place. It's small, clean, and filled with Spanish speakers in and out of the kitchen. The extensive menu is sure to please with breakfast, lunch, and dinner options. Tacos, burritos, *chilaquiles,* salad, tostadas…you name it, it's here. Don't miss the tortas, which are made with delicious bread and served with fries or chips. There's even a whole section of vegetarian options and kid's menu. Need more to convince you? This should do it: Choco-flan.

The colorful and relaxed **Plaza Bonita** (164 Coffee Pot Dr., 928/282-2728, www.

casabonitaaz.com, 11am-10pm Sun.-Thurs., 11am-11pm Thurs.-Fri., $9-24) is a favorite with locals, and although it may not look like much, it's hard to beat the tasty margaritas, fresh salsa, and refreshing escape from the tourists of Uptown. The homey, reasonably priced restaurant is hidden in a grocery store plaza and its diverse menu includes chicken *poblano* and bacon-wrapped shrimp smothered in a flavorful cream sauce.

Named for the croaking amphibian that lives in southeastern Arizona, **Barking Frog Grille** (2620 W. S.R. 89A, 928/204-2000, www.barkingfroggrille.com, 11am-9pm daily, $7-24) serves Southwestern favorites for lunch and dinner. The food is good but not spectacular, and given the price, one might expect a little more. Still, it's a sure crowd pleaser with an extensive menu. Kick off happy hour with a prickly pear mojito and stay for dinner to enjoy the chicken tortilla soup, fish tacos, or enchiladas. If you're looking for something more filling, try the cowboy pot pie or the Southwest fried chicken. Conclude the night with the house-made churros.

Vegetarian

If you want to embrace Sedona's crunchy peaceful vibe inside and out, then **Chocolátree Organic Eatery** (1595 W. Hwy 89A, 928/282-2997, www.chocolatree.com, 9am-9pm daily, 11am-9pm second Wednesday of every month, $6-12) is your destination. No animals or hippies were hurt in the creation of their dishes, which are 100 percent organic, locally grown, gluten free, non-GMO, and vegetarian and vegan friendly. The food is more about philosophy than flavor although the recreations of contemporary favorites like the Caesar salad, veggie burger, and Mediterranean wrap are decent. The real win here is the extensive dessert menu, impressive selection of chocolates, and seemingly endless options for beverages. Dining in is best if you're in the mood for hot tea and something sweet. Just make sure you ask to sit on the peaceful back patio in a vibrant garden.

Thai Spices (2611 W. S.R. 89A,

928/282-0599, www.thaispices.com, 11:30am-9pm Mon.-Sat., $8-13) is a well-loved choice of Sedona vegetarians. The healthy Thai cuisine features hot noodle dishes, fresh spring rolls, and flavorful soups. It's good, the ingredients are fresh, and the prices are fair. The inexpensive lunch specials are quite popular, and meat eaters will find several chicken and shrimp dishes.

VILLAGE OF OAK CREEK
American

With a name like **Schoolhouse Restaurant** (7000 S.R. 179, 928/284-2240, 5pm-9pm daily, $11-30), you might expect a cafeteria like cuisine. Not so! This place has a contemporary American menu that includes thoughtful dishes like pan-seared diver scallops with a chardonnay sauce made from roasted carrot and organic apple. Lamb shoulder, demi-braised pork, beef tenderloin, and the ever-popular chicken and waffles are some of the meatier options, and there are also vegan and vegetarian dishes on the menu. Head in for their happy hour from 4:30pm-6pm at the bar to taste a sample of appetizers that include Dr. Pepper chicken wings with a creamy *Sriracha* dipping sauce.

For delicious, no-fuss steak sandwiches and Reubens, join the locals at **PJ's Village Pub** (40 W. Cortez Dr., 928/284-2250, www.pjsvillagepub.com, 10am-2am daily, $8-14). You'll find bikers, hikers, and golfers huddled around the closely packed tables or at the popular bar. The tavern is known for its specials—Taco Tuesdays, Prime Rib Saturdays—and the Friday-night fish fry's have become a weekly ritual in the Village of Oak Creek. Hit the happy hour (3pm-6pm) for cheap eats or order from the pub grub menu for small bites. As if that all weren't enough, there's live music every Wednesday and most Saturdays. Party!

Breakfast and Lunch

Hidden away in a small strip center, the down-home **Blue Moon Café** (6101 S.R. 179, 928/284-1831, www.bluemooncafe.us, 7am-9pm daily, $6-15) is a great way to start your day before a hike or round on the links at the Sedona Golf Resort. They've got all the American breakfast standards served all day. You can also stop by after your adventures to refuel with the hearty Philly sandwiches, subs, burgers, and hand-tossed pizzas. You'll find a few Southwestern specialties and a decent beer and wine list. And if you're not in the mood to go out, they deliver.

Admittedly, there's no shortage of breakfast and lunch cafés in the Village of Oak Creek but that shouldn't sway you from hitting up the **Red Rock Cafe** (100 Verde Valley School Rd., 928/284-1441, 6:30am-2pm Mon.-Fri., 7am-2pm Sat.-Sun., $7-16). You, they serve breakfast all day. Yes, it's got American and Mexican food options. Yes, it's reasonably priced, has friendly service, good-tasting food, and serves alcohol. And, yes, it's got the biggest darn cinnamon roll you'll ever encounter that will make you wish you could say no.

Although it serves breakfast, lunch, and dinner, **Miley's Café** (7000 S.R. 179, 928/284-4123, 6:30am-8pm daily, $8-16) is a scrumptious option for breakfast served all day. The menu is comfortable and teeming with American and Mexican food options. The dishes are well priced and taste great and there's a casual atmosphere and good service. Oh, and there's beer, wine, and margaritas.

Italian

★ **Cucina Rustica** (7000 S.R. 179, 928/284-3010, www.cucinarustica.com, 5pm-close daily, $14-34) is a crowd-pleaser and is brought to you by chef Lisa Dahl, the same one who delivers incredible meals at Sedona's Dahl & DiLuca, Mariposa Latin Inspired Grill, and Pisa Lisa (dang, she's good!). The salads, soups, and meat dishes are delicious, but it's the fresh, homemade pasta that has made the restaurant a hit with Sedona diners. Try the linguine bolognese, tortellini with button mushrooms and truffle cream sauce, or the penne jambalaya with spicy Calabrese sausage and jumbo prawns. Eat at the bar or have a seat in the dining room, which is drenched in

a tasty dish at Cucina Rustica

Renaissance Italian decor. Reservations are recommended, especially on the weekend.

Middle Eastern

Organic international cuisine with a Moroccan influence? Sign me up! **A Taste of Marrakech** (25 Bell Rock Plaza, 928/284-4356, www.atom-organic.com, 11am-3pm, 5pm-8pm Tues.-Sat., $9.50-12) is a refreshing change of pace for the restaurants in Sedona. The menu changes seasonally because the chefs rely on the availability of fresh produce. That said, some of the dishes they're known to create are elk sliders, falafel flatbread tacos, or lamb gyro (just to name a few). The preservative-free, clean food allows you to indulge without feeling over-indulgent. The portions are small and the prices are super-reasonable for Sedona, so your group can enjoy sampling the flavorful menu alongside a decent selection of beer, wine, and teas.

Accommodations

T.C. and Sedona Schnebly built the town's first hotel in 1900, a cozy homestead that is now the location of the Tlaquepaque shopping plaza. More than a century later, visitors are still flocking to Sedona, and although there are a host of motels, hotels, resorts, and inns to suit every taste, its specialty is the romantic getaway—something about those red rocks really get the juices flowing. Accommodations tend to be steep year-round, with rates peaking in winter and spring. Still, there are bargains to found in Sedona, but they tend to be occasionally moderate prices at the more expensive hotels and resorts. No matter where you stay, however, you can almost be guaranteed a room with a view.

UPTOWN
$50-100

Star Motel (295 Jordan Rd., 928/282-3641, www.starmotelsedona.com, $86-186 d) is an ideal spot for budget travelers looking for affordability with a little character and its prime locale in pedestrian-friendly Uptown can't be beat. The converted 1955 homestead maintains many of the original home's retro features, and its 11 units are bright and clean. The hospitable owner, Anne, couldn't be sweeter. Those staying for several nights will love the second-floor suite's king bed, full kitchen, and private patio with views of the red rocks. The ground floor unit in the original home features two bedrooms, a kitchen, and a living room.

$100-250

Best Western Plus Arroyo Roble Hotel & Creekside Villas (400 N. S.R. 89A, 928/282-4001 or 800/773-3662, www.bestwesternsedona.com, $179-299 d) may be a mouthful to say, but the five-story hotel next to Sedona Arts Center has a lot to offer, providing a host of amenities you typically would find at a large resort: tennis and racquetball courts, a fully equipped exercise room, and indoor and outdoor swimming pools. The rooms are spacious and well decorated—some even have fireplaces and jetted tubs. The 1,300-square-foot, two-bedroom creek-side villas offer a posh stay. Although you're staying at a chain hotel, the complimentary full breakfast and the hotel's incredible setting—complete with red-rock views and private paths on the banks of Oak Creek—make for a unique experience.

The Matterhorn Inn (230 Apple Ave., 928/282-7176, www.matterhorninn.com, $139-189 d) sits right in the heart of Uptown, which means you can explore many of Sedona's shops, galleries, and restaurants without having to get into your car. The rooms are nice, and thanks to the hotel's hillside location, all rooms have a private balcony or terrace with panoramic views of the red rocks.

You can't beat the Uptown location of **Orchards Inn** (254 N. S.R. 89A, 928/282-2405, www.orchardsinn.com, $159-389 d). Perched hillside, every room overlooks the valley, with patios and decks that offer spectacular views of Snoopy Rock and the surrounding buttes. If a "room with a view" is a priority and budget is a concern, this hotel tucked behind a row of shops on Sedona's main street may be an ideal place to hang your hat. Plus, most of Uptown's shops, restaurants, and bars are just outside your front door. The rooms received a beautiful renovation in 2015 and feature a subtle palette to complement the red rock views.

Centrally located one block south of the Y, ★ **The Sedona Motel** (218 S.R. 179, 928/282-7187, www.thesedonamotel.com, $100-150 d) is an excellent value. Visitors are more than satisfied with the simple rooms that are clean, modern, and comfortable. The

The Matterhorn Inn

rooms include a few unexpected perks for a motel, including HBO, Wi-Fi, refrigerator, microwave, and commanding views of the red rocks from the terraced patio. It's the perfect place for visitors interested in exploring the town who want a bargain but like to hit the hay in a nice place.

Los Abrigados Resort & Spa (160 Portal Ln., 928/282-1777, www.diamondresorts.com, $135-250 d) used to be Sedona's gold standard for top accommodations. And although it has been eclipsed by more luxurious options, the resort sits quite literally in the heart of Sedona, next to the Tlaquepaque shopping center and Oak Creek. Walking the 22-acre, beautifully landscaped resort, you'll find plenty of diversions: swimming pools, tennis and basketball courts, a fitness center, and a creek-side miniature golf course. Plus, you really can't beat a stroll on the banks of Oak Creek while feeding the resident ducks. The one- and two-bedroom rooms underwent remodeling in 2015, and they have brought a refreshing dose of style back to the resort. Be aware: Online reviewers warn against a time-share sales pitch. Just say no and then get on with your vacation.

Creekside Inn at Sedona (99 Copper Cliffs Dr., 928/282-4992, www.creeksideinn.net, $199-329 d) is a delicately decorated bed-and-breakfast adorned with period antiques, and its cheerful rooms are bright and clean. The mammoth, ceiling-high walnut bed in the Creekview Suite is a showstopper, and the room's French doors, private deck, and large bathroom overlooking Oak Creek provide an ideal setting for a romantic weekend. Guests can pass the time by fishing in the creek, relaxing on the porch with a glass of wine, or taking the short walk to Gallery Row.

Over $250

Thanks to a $25 million renovation and expansion, ★ **L'Auberge de Sedona** (301 L'Auberge Ln., 800/905-5745, www.lauberge.com, $325-395 d) continues to seduce guests, many of whom return annually for romantic pilgrimages along the banks of Oak Creek.

The intimate resort feels hidden away under giant sycamores, and the morning duck feedings and relaxing spa feel a world away from the congestion and crowds just up the hill in Uptown. Cozy rooms are available in the main lodge, although the creek-side cabins are worth the splurge. The hillside cottages are refreshingly modern, boasting outdoor showers and large observation decks. You can't help but appreciate the warm and social atmosphere, which is helped along by stargazing sessions on Tuesday, Thursday, and Friday evenings.

The charming ★ **El Portal Sedona** (95 Portal Ln., 928/203-9405, www.elportalsedona.com, $250-350 d) is one of Arizona's finest hotels, marrying Arts and Crafts-period design with Southwestern hacienda architecture. Owners Connie and Steve Segner have created an intimate, luxury inn, and even the smallest details reflect their vision, like rough-hewn beam ceilings, cozy fireplaces, 18-inch thick adobe walls, and a grassy central courtyard. Each of the 12 unique rooms echoes El Portal's eclectic historical style—the vaulted log-beam Grand Canyon and handsome Santa Fe suites are particularly exquisite. Situated next to the Tlaquepaque shopping center, the inn is conveniently located near some of Sedona's best restaurants and galleries, but you may not want to leave this elegant hideaway. The Segners welcome four-legged friends, and they're happy to recommend pet-friendly trails and parks.

For big city interior design among the natural beauty of small-town Sedona, try **Amara Resort and Spa** (100 Amara Ln., 928/282-4828, www.amararesort.com, $180-450 d). This location is unbeatable. It's a creek-side property that is nestled along a canyon wall right off the main drag of Uptown. One minute, you're walking the Uptown streets with the tourists and with just a stroll down a hill, your temporary home is a quiet respite away from the hustle and bustle. The 100 rooms range from patio guest rooms to 720 square-foot creek-side studio spa suites, all furnished and decorated in a sleek, contemporary style.

Private patios with views of the infinity zero-edge pool are commonplace. Amenities include all the regulars (high-speed Internet, fitness center) as well as a few extras like complimentary transportation within a one-mile radius and public bikes free to all guests.

WEST SEDONA
$50-100

Cheap, clean, and convenient, **Sugar Loaf Lodge** (1870 W. S.R. 89A, 928/282-9451, www.sedonasugarloaf.com, $60-90 d) provides the basics just off Route 89A and even throws in a pool, free Wi-Fi, and in-room refrigerators. The motel is absolutely no-frills, but its low price is hard to beat, as is the convenient access to neighboring hiking and mountain biking trails. And if you're planning on bringing your pooch to Sedona, Sugar Loaf has a few pet-friendly rooms.

$100-250

The Santa Fe-style **Southwest Inn at Sedona** (3250 W. S.R. 89A, 928/282-3344, www.swinn.com, $95-185 d) is a terrific value if you're looking for a quiet, comfortable place to sleep between hiking, shopping, and visiting galleries. The converted motor lodge has been nicely updated with excellent bedding and gas fireplaces, but don't expect a resort-like setting. Be sure to ask for a room with a view of the red buttes.

Sky Ranch Lodge (1105 Airport Rd., 888/708-6400, www.skyranchlodge.com, $135-290 d) is funky and quirky, which is about what you'd expect from a hotel next to a small airport. The clean rooms feature new furniture and fixtures but are still quite outdated. Small ponds, bridges, and grassy lawns dot the six-acre property, with quaint stone paths leading to quiet gardens, a secluded swimming pool, and an on-site wine bar. Best of all, the inn is perched on Airport Mesa, 500 feet above Sedona, providing elevated views of the town and its red-rock formations and green valleys. And when you're ready for a little excitement, a five-minute drive will drop you back in the heart of Uptown. Be sure to ask for a private deck when you make a reservation.

Visitors who appreciate a more modern style may want to check in at the **Sedona Rouge Hotel & Spa** (2250 W. S.R. 89A, 928/203-4111, www.sedonarouge.com, $179-1,500 d). The hotel combines clean lines and Sedona's distinctive color palette of warm earth tones and deep-red accents. The comfortable rooms are well appointed and range from one room with two queen beds up to a two-bedroom suite with four beds. Sedona Rouge has a more urban vibe than some of its competitors, but you'll still get amazing views of the red rocks, particularly from the Observation Terrace, which is open at night for stargazing. Plus, you'll find other amenities, like a large outdoor seating area with fireplace, a heated swimming pool and Jacuzzi, and a topnotch spa.

The Lodge at Sedona (125 Kallof Pl., 928/204-1942, www.lodgeatsedona.com, $219-349 d) is tucked away in West Sedona. The quaint stone-and-timber lodge features Arts and Crafts-style decor, Mission furnishings, and cozy, fireside seating areas. Make time to explore the gardens, which include water features and red-rock views, before heading out to the meditative rock labyrinth that is based on Native American traditions. The handsome Star Gazer suite features a large deck with garden views and an outdoor shower, while the Red Rock Crossing king suite offers a jetted in-room tub that's perfect for a romantic weekend.

The red-stucco ★ **Alma De Sedona Inn** (50 Hozoni Dr., 928/282-2737, www.almadesedona.com, $189-309 d) is a lovely bed-and-breakfast for those who appreciate a little privacy with their red-rock views. The 12 large rooms have king-size beds, gas fireplaces, and two-person tubs (one room forgoes the tub for a large, handicap-friendly shower). The grounds are well maintained and feature a meditation pond, labyrinth, and medicine wheel. You may take a dip in the seasonally heated pool and enjoy your breakfast poolside during the summer.

The **Sedona Reăl Inn & Suites** (95 Arroyo Pinon Dr., 928/282-1414, www.sedonareal.com, $140-285 d) lacks character, but the clean, spacious rooms and suites are a nice option for families and big groups, especially for the price. You also get some perks not found at budget competitors: free high-speed Internet, an outdoor pool and spa, free continental breakfast, private balconies, and pet-friendly rooms.

The **Best Western Plus Inn of Sedona** (1200 W. S.R. 89A, 928/282-3072, www.innofsedona.com, $150-250 d) offers views that would cost you a pretty penny anywhere else in the world. Although the rooms are clean and comfortable you'll want to spend most of your time on the communal balconies, which feature panoramic views of the red rocks. There's also plenty of convenient parking and a pool, as well as a free shuttle to and from Uptown, and pet-friendly rooms.

Over $250

With a name like **Boots and Saddles** (2900 Hopi Dr., 800/201-1944, www.oldwestbb.com, $220-295 d), you can expect a heavy dose of cowboy style at this popular bed-and-breakfast. The innkeepers have created a rabid following, thanks to their warm hospitality and gourmet breakfasts. Each of the six suites is unique, decorated in Western themes like Ghost Rider and El Dorado, and with amenities that vary from fireplaces and outdoor air-jet tubs to telescopes for stargazing. The 600-square-foot City Slickers room includes a sunrise nook with a large window, a cheery place to read the paper and enjoy a morning cup of coffee.

Subtlety isn't a word that is used at **Adobe Grand Villas** (35 Hozoni Dr., 928/203-7616, www.adobegrandvillas.com, $325-699 d). The 16 over-the-top, bigger-is-better villas start at 850 square feet, and each has at least one king-size bed, two fireplaces, and styles ranging from French to Tuscan to Desert Oasis. Some rooms feature tubs for two and steam showers, while others offer red-rock views, private patios, and wood-beam ceilings.

You won't find a hotel in Sedona with a more stunning backdrop than **Enchantment Resort** (525 Boynton Canyon Rd., 928/282-2900, www.enchantmentresort.com, $350-450 d). Situated 10 minutes outside of town, the resort is nestled into the horseshoe-shaped Boynton Canyon and its soaring cliff walls envelop the resort, creating a sense of seclusion. The casita-inspired design features 218 rooms scattered across the property, which began as a homestead before being transformed into a tennis ranch and later a luxury resort. Guests have exclusive access to swimming pools, tennis courts, private hiking trails, and the Mii amo spa, one of the finest facilities in the world. Kids will enjoy Camp Coyote, which explores the surrounding natural environment and Native American culture.

★ **Mii amo** (525 Boynton Canyon Rd., 928/282-2900, www.miiamo.com) sets the bar for destination spa-going, blending holistic wellness treatments, Native American traditions, and luxury pampering. The resort creates three-, four- and seven-night all-inclusive packages and then creates "personal journeys" that are tailored to a guest's goals: de-stress, healthy body balance, spiritual exploration and so on. The total price includes accommodations in one of 16 spa guest rooms and suites, three meals a day, and two spa treatments every day, as well as the use of fitness classes, spa facilities, swimming pools, and activities like tennis, hiking, and mountain biking. The intimate, communal setting is perfect for solo travelers who want to balance personal time and socializing with new friends. Mii amo's seamless indoor/outdoor design blends chic, modern style with the Boynton Canyon's soaring red walls and the desert landscape. Rates begin at $3,150 for a three-night package for a solo traveler.

VILLAGE OF OAK CREEK
$50-100

Adobe-inspired **Wildflower Inn** (6086 S.R. 179, 928/284-3937, www.sedonawildflower-inn.com, $85-200 d) is bit a nicer than your standard motel fare, and its prime location across the street from Bell Rock…well, rocks. A remodel in 2014 spruced the place up well and the rooms are very clean. Expect a few pleasant perks like flat-screen TVs and free Wi-Fi, and be sure to call the motel directly for any late-breaking deals.

$100-250

Loaded with character, **Adobe Village Graham Inn** (150 Canyon Circle Dr., 928/284-1425, www.adobevillagegrahaminn.com, $200-250 d) promises a bit of "rustic luxury" and doesn't disappoint. The boutique inn's unique rooms and villas earn kudos for their Western decor and romantic ambience. Try to reserve the Sundance Room, which offers a fireplace, wood plank flooring, king-size canopy bed, and large bathroom with a rainforest shower and jet tub. For a real splurge, go with the Wilderness Villa, a picturesque gem with log walls, a charming periwinkle-blue sleigh bed, and a river-rock fireplace that connects the bedroom with a two-person tub. The small gardens and incomparable views of Bell, Cathedral, and Courthouse rocks make this bed-and-breakfast a real find.

★ **Adobe Hacienda Bed & Breakfast** (10 Rojo Dr., 928/284-2020, www.adobe-hacienda.com, $199-239 d) bills itself as "Sedona's most authentic Southwest-style bed-and-breakfast inn," and it may just be. The small bed-and-breakfast's six guest rooms are each decorated with traditional Southwestern touches, like lodge pole beams, Saltillo tile floors, Native American rugs, hand-painted Mexican sinks, and cozy Pendleton blankets. Owners Russ and Aurora Mulder are the consummate hosts, happy to point you in the direction of an easy hiking trail or to serve up a hearty breakfast on the flagstone patio overlooking the adjacent golf course and the red rocks. Call for last-minute discounts or to request a specific room.

Families will appreciate the $8.5-million renovated **Hilton Sedona Resort at Bell Rock** (90 Ridge Trail Dr., 928/284-4040, www.hiltonsedonaresort.com, $180-300 d), which provides an impressively diverse assortment of amenities for its price, including a championship golf course, an athletic club, a full-service spa, and multiple pools. Guest rooms and one-bedroom suites—which can accommodate up to five people—are tastefully decorated with locally inspired symbolic objects with contemporary accents and boast gas fireplaces and small balconies. The helpful and friendly staff is happy to provide recommendations on local restaurants, tours, and hiking trails. Perched on a hill overlooking the Village of Oak Creek and Bell Rock, the hotel's location far from the crowds of Uptown can provide a nice change of pace.

Las Posadas of Sedona (26 Avenida de Piedras, 928/284-5288, www.lasposadasofsedona.com, $199-279 d) calls itself a "boutique inn" and the sprawling property and all-suite hotel feels like a large condo complex. It's not a bad choice if you are planning to spend more than a few days in Sedona and need a home away from home. The chef goes above and beyond every morning to create made-to-order Southwestern-themed breakfasts each morning, and some of Oak Creek's best restaurants are within walking distance.

About halfway between Uptown and the Village of Oak Creek, **Poco Diablo Resort** (1752 S.R. 179, 928/282-7333, www.pocodiabloresort.com, $150-200 d) offers travelers a hint of luxury without breaking the bank. Aside from red-rock views and lots of nearby hiking, the "Little Devil" lures its visitors with a fitness center, a swimming pool, a nine-hole golf course, and pristine tennis courts. Worried about catching your ZZZ's after all that action? Don't be. The standard room is clean and comfy, and for a few bucks more you can relax in your own private whirlpool bath.

Information and Services

TOURIST INFORMATION

The **Sedona Chamber of Commerce** (331 Forest Rd., 928/282-7722 or 800/288-7336, www.visitsedona.com, 8:30am-5pm daily) has a convenient office in Uptown that supplies visitors with maps, directions, and suggestions for getting the most out of your time in Sedona. You can also purchase a Red Rock Pass here. The **Red Rock Visitor Center and Ranger Station** (8375 S.R. 179, 928/203-2900, www.fs.usda.gov/coconino, 9am-4:30pm daily), just south of the Village of Oak Creek, may be a more convenient option if you are driving in from Phoenix.

LIBRARIES

It's kind of crazy how everything in Sedona is beautiful. This includes the gorgeous **Sedona Public Library** (3250 White Bear Rd., 928/282-7714, www.sedonalibrary.org, 10am-6pm Mon.-Tues., Thurs., 10am-8pm Wed., 10am-5pm Fri.-Sat.) with stone-clad architecture that allows natural light to bathe the stacks. A second branch, the **SPL in the Village** (51 Bell Rock Plaza, 928/284-1603, www.sedonalibrary.org, 1pm-5pm Mon.-Fri., 10am-2pm Sat.) has opened up in the Village of Oak Creek. Be sure to check the library events for educational gatherings and happenings, including fabulous reading and singing groups for your kids.

HOSPITALS AND EMERGENCY SERVICES

Hopefully, you won't have to consult this section of the book. But, if you're in need of medical care, the **Verde Valley Medical Center Sedona Campus** (3700 W. S.R. 89A, 928/634-2251, www.nahealth.com) offers 24-hour emergency services in West Sedona, as well as primary and specialty health care.

You can also opt for the local **NextCare Urgent Care** (2530 S.R. 89A, 928/203-4813, www.nextcare.com, 8am-6pm Mon.-Fri., 9am-5pm Sat., 9am-4pm Sun.). This multistate clinic service treats illness, minor injury, and pediatrics.

Transportation

Sedona is a small town, and almost all of the area's natural attractions, cultural sights, and restaurants can be reached within a 10-minute drive of Uptown. And with so much neck-craning scenery, you won't mind your time behind the wheel. Beware the weekend traffic, which can turn that ten minutes into an hour (we're not kidding), especially during holidays. The scenic drive between the Y intersection in Uptown and the Village of Oak Creek on Route 179 is particularly inspiring. Plan to pull over more than a few times to check out the mammoth formations and charming metaphysical shops.

AIR

You'll need to fly into **Phoenix Sky Harbor International Airport** (3400 E. Sky Harbor Blvd., 602/273-3300, www.skyharbor.com) and in all likelihood drive the 90 minutes north to Sedona on I-17 to Route 179. If you don't want to rent a car, try Arizona Shuttle (800-888-2749, www.arizonashuttle.com, $50 one way), which offers a shuttle service from Sky Harbor to Oak Creek and Sedona. Also, chartered jet services are available to **Sedona Airport** (235 Air Terminal Dr., 928/282-4487, sedonaairport.org).

CAR
Rental Cars

To really explore Sedona, Red Rock Country, and the Verde Valley, you'll need a car. At Phoenix's Sky Harbor International Airport, take the free shuttle from any of the terminals to the **Rental Car Center** (1805 E. Sky Harbor Circle, 602/683-3741). You'll find major companies, like **Budget** (602/261-5950, www.budget.com), **Hertz** (602/267-8822, www.hertz.com), and **Enterprise** (602/225-0588), which has convenient drop-off centers around Phoenix. If you're the outdoorsy type, you may want to consider renting a vehicle with four-wheel drive, especially as many of Sedona's off-highway hiking and biking destinations go off-road.

TROLLEY

If you're tired of driving, catch the **Sedona Trolley** (276 S.R. 89A, 928/282-4211, www.sedonatrolley.com, $15 adults, $10 children ages 12 and younger) at its Uptown depot for one of two hour-long, narrated tours. Take the creatively titled "Tour A," which visits Gallery Row and Tlaquepaque Arts and Crafts Village before making a stop at the Chapel of the Holy Cross. Or try the "Tour B," which visits the west side of town and then heads into Dry Creek Valley for some gorgeous views of Boynton and Long canyons.

Vicinity of Sedona

Have you heard about Sedona's red rocks? Let's talk about them some more! The red rocks steal a lot of attention, but there's plenty to see outside of Sedona, which makes an excellent home base to explore some of the region's other notable natural attractions and historic sites. Within 10 minutes of Uptown Sedona, you can drive Arizona's first officially designated scenic highway through the leafy forests of Oak Creek Canyon. Head 25 minutes south, and you'll find one of the country's most impressive Native American ruins, the cliffside Montezuma Castle. And if you travel 30 minutes east, you'll land in the historic—and haunted—mining town of Jerome. Even if you're in Sedona for just a few days, be sure to make some time to visit one of these areas.

★ OAK CREEK CANYON

Drive north from Uptown Sedona on Route 89A and you'll discover one of Arizona's most picturesque drives. Oak Creek Canyon may not offer the scale of the Grand Canyon or the sculptural beauty of Sedona's red-rock formations, but its intimate scale is far more approachable and equally fun to explore. The scenic highway, which meanders from Sedona to Flagstaff through a series of lingering turns, traces much of the 12-mile-long river gorge. Running water along a geological fault line formed the canyon, creating sheer walls that range from 800-2,000 feet tall.

The wooded canyon was first made popular—like Sedona—in the 1920s and 1930s when Hollywood arrived. Films like Jimmy Stewart's *Broken Arrow* captured its red-rock walls, leafy forests, and cascading waters. Today, Oak Creek Canyon attracts visitors in search of some rest and relaxation—although you won't escape the crowds, especially in summer. Fall is particularly lovely, when many of the sycamore trees turn golden yellow, shimmering against the evergreen pines and red rocks. No matter the time of year, it's still possible to find a quiet area for a picnic or hike without running into other people. Much of the area is part of the Coconino National Forest or state park land, ensuring its protection from development.

Slide Rock State Park

When the temperatures start to climb in late spring, the cool waters of Oak Creek can be irresistible. Take the plunge at Arizona's best swimming hole in **Slide Rock State Park** (6871 N. Hwy. 89A, 928/282-3034, https://az-stateparks.com, hours change seasonally with minimal hours of 9am-5pm, fees change seasonally with a range of $10-30 per vehicle; website reflects current hours and fees), situated seven miles north of Sedona. Glide down the 80-foot-long natural rockslide, which was carved into the granite and red sandstone canyon floor by Oak Creek. The chilly water that started as snowmelt on neighboring mountains can be a little brisk—and the ride can be a little hard, so be sure to bring an old pair of sneakers to navigate the slick rock. There are small wading pools for a more relaxed swim or you can sunbathe like a lizard on one of the warm red rocks. The **Slide Rock Market** (10am-4pm Sat.-Sun. Nov.-Mar., 10am-6pm Mon.-Fri. Apr.-Oct.) sells snacks and water, although you may want to bring a picnic and cooler if you plan to stay the day.

Like any well-loved attraction, Slide Rock has become too popular for its own good in recent years. Families from Phoenix and across Arizona descend upon the park on weekends and during holidays in the summer, causing temporary closings when the parking lots fill up or when daily water tests reveals high levels of E. coli bacteria. In the fall and winter, the park can be blissfully quiet, providing a nice opportunity to explore the former homestead's historic buildings and apple orchard.

Picnic Areas

A little bit closer to Sedona and just over Midgely Bridge, you'll find **Grasshopper Point Swimming and Picnic Area** (928/203-2900 www.fs.usda.gov, 8am-dusk, $8 per vehicle), another popular swimming hole and picnic area. In the summer, be sure to get there early before it gets too crowded, as the deep pool attracts cliff-jumpers on the weekends. Follow Allen's Bend Trail, which heads north for about a half mile, if you're in the mood to hike along the creek. To get there, head down the access road off Route 89A and follow the signs.

And there's more. Route 89A is speckled with various recreation and picnic areas (928/203-2900 www.fs.usda.gov, 8am-dusk, $8 per vehicle) but be warned, not all are open year-round. Working your way five miles north from Midgely Bridge along the 89A, you'll encounter **Encinoso Picnic Area** close to Oak Creek and offering fishing and water play. If you're in a hiking mood, try the steep North Wilson Mountain Trail to a bench to catch some views (about a four-mile

Oak Creek Canyon

Vicinity of Sedona

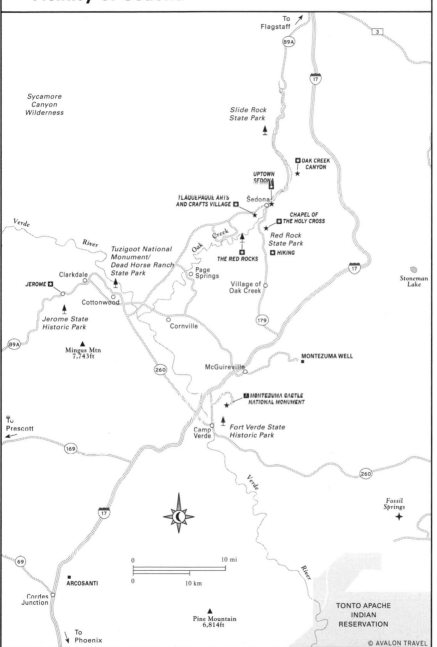

To Flagstaff

89A

3

17

Sycamore Canyon Wilderness

Slide Rock State Park

OAK CREEK CANYON

UPTOWN SEDONA

TLAQUEPAQUE ARTS AND CRAFTS VILLAGE

Sedona

CHAPEL OF THE HOLY CROSS

Red Rock State Park

HIKING

Verde

River

Creek

Oak

THE RED ROCKS

Tuzigoot National Monument/ Dead Horse Ranch State Park

Page Springs

Village of Oak Creek

17

Stoneman Lake

Clarkdale

JEROME

Cottonwood

Cornville

179

Jerome State Historic Park

89A

Mingus Mtn 7,743ft

260

McGuireville

MONTEZUMA WELL

MONTEZUMA CASTLE NATIONAL MONUMENT

To Prescott

169

Camp Verde

Fort Verde State Historic Park

260

Verde

Fossil Springs

17

0   10 mi

0   10 km

69

ARCOSANTI

Cordes Junction

To Phoenix

Pine Mountain 6,814ft

River

TONTO APACHE INDIAN RESERVATION

© AVALON TRAVEL

round-trip). Next on the list is **Halfway Picnic Area,** followed by **Banjo Bill Picnic Area**. Both offer the basics of picnic tables near the creek in a beautiful setting. Then there's the **Bootlegger Day-Use Site,** another picnic area with a few more features like a fishing hole and access to the A. B. Young Trail, which is a relentless series of switchbacks up the side of the canyon and totaling close to a five-mile round-trip.

Rainbow Trout Farm

Hungry for trout? Well, then get some your darn self! While many anglers visit the waters of Oak Creek, the **Rainbow Trout Farm** (3500 N. S.R. 89A, 928/282-5799, www.sedonarainbowtroutfarm.com, 9am-5pm daily) gives you a guaranteed catch of trout raised in sparkling clean spring water for just $1 per person. The two ponds are absolutely teeming with trout and the facility has fishing rods and nets ready for you. The staff will clean the fish for you (for just 50 cents) then you can grill it up right on the property at their propane grills and picnic tables or have them pack it in ice to be enjoyed later. You'd be hard pressed to find fresher fish in this land-locked state.

West Fork of Oak Creek

There are plenty of great hiking spots in Oak Creek Canyon, but **West Fork of Oak Creek Trail** is by far the best and no doubt one of the best trails in the state. The trail, which starts in a small meadow, follows the creek through lush riparian areas and shady groves before it slices into a narrow slot canyon. The large trees and 200-foot-tall canyon walls provide lots of shade, which is a blissful relief during the hot summer. The initial three-mile trek will suit most visitors, and even first-time hikers will enjoy the easy, flat trail. Serious and well-experienced explorers, though, can penetrate even farther into the deep, forested canyon, where they'll need to wade into the creek—and even swim in some spots. The vegetation gets thicker and the trail less defined, and it takes at least a full day to make the additional 11 miles. If you're down for that, be

sure to talk to a ranger or consult the website for a detailed guideline on preparation and supplies.

To find the trail, take Route 89A between mile marker 385 and 384 to the **Call of the Canyon Day-Use Area** ($10 per vehicle, 928/203-2900, www.fs.usda.gov, 8am to dusk), named after the classic novel written by Zane Grey after a visit to the area.

Shopping

Two classic Native American trading posts can be found in Oak Creek Canyon. Step inside **Garland's Indian Jewelry** (3953 N. S.R. 89A, 928/282-6632, www.garlandsjewelry.com, 10am-5pm daily), and you'll see walls of intricately crafted silver-and-leather belts, woven baskets, kachina dolls, and jewelry. The designs lean toward the traditional, although you'll find some impressively modern pieces like chunky bracelets inlaid with colorful stones and necklaces with simple patterns made of turquoise. The store sells antique pieces as well as new designs by emerging artisans from the Hopi, Navajo, and Zuni tribes.

For more than 60 years, **Hoel's Indian Shop** (9589 N. S.R. 89A, 928/282-3925, www.hoelsindianshop.com, 9:30am-5pm daily) has bought directly from Native American artisans, and their first-rate inventory is a testament to this tradition. The shop specializes in Native American arts and crafts, including jewelry, hand-carved kachina dolls, hand-woven baskets, and Navajo rugs and blankets. The innovative pottery designs are especially rich. The one-of-a-kind retail experience is located in the owner's home, inside a large vault.

Food

If you're cruising through the canyon and you want fresh, delicious food at a reasonable price, pop into **Garland's Indian Gardens Café & Market** (3951 N. S.R. 89A, 928/282-7702, www.indiangardens.com, $7-12). The small deli and market prepares fresh sandwiches, salads, and baked goods. With super-fresh ingredients and thoughtful flavor combinations in their simple dishes like the breakfast burrito or the vegetarian pita, you will walk away full and satisfied. You can also stock up on lunchtime essentials like water, soda, and chips, as well as fresh brewed coffee and craft beer.

The elegant dining room at **Garland's Oak Creek Lodge** (8067 N. S.R. 89A, 928/282-3343, www.garlandslodge.com, $45-50) serves up a communal culinary experience. A single prix-fixe menu is presented each night, with a changing gourmet lineup that may include coconut crabmeat chowder, rack of lamb, or grilled salmon with sweet corn and bacon relish. Guests share tables, creating a warm atmosphere. Cocktails are served at 6pm by the fire or out on the lawn, depending on the weather, and the dinner bell rings at 7pm. Reservations are required, and the restaurant is open daily from early February through mid-November.

Stop by **The Butterfly Garden Inn Cafe** (9940 N. S.R. 89A, 855/255-8244, www.thebutterflygardeninn.com, 7am-5pm Sun.-Thurs., 7am-6pm Fr.-Sat., $8-10) at The Butterfly Garden Inn for a simple but delicious menu of breakfast burritos, salads, burgers, sandwiches, quesadillas, and flatbread pizzas. Each of the menu items cleverly comes in three styles: the All American, the Southwest, and the Fancy Schmancy sure to please all visitors.

Accommodations

If you want peace, quiet, and idyllic grassy meadows where sheep frolic (that's not an exaggeration), try the ★ **Briar Patch Inn** (3190 N. S.R. 89A, 928/282-2342, www.briarpatchinn.com, $239-425 d). Its 19 country cottages are furnished with rustic wood tables, old rocking chairs, and brightly colored Native American blankets and rugs, all lovingly cared for by the incredibly friendly and hardworking staff. The accommodations range from cozy one-room hideaways to the sprawling four-bedroom Ponderosa cabin, which is large enough to sleep up to nine, but has meeting space for up to 39 people. Wood-burning fireplaces and hearty morning

breakfasts inspire true relaxation. Splurge for a cottage that overlooks Oak Creek, where you can fish for trout and jump into the private swimming hole during summer. Be sure to make time to meet Briar Patch's permanent guests, Wooly and Bully, two sheep that tend the property's meadow.

Small and pleasantly rustic, **Canyon Wren Cabins** (6425 N. S.R. 89A, 928/282-6900, www.canyonwrencabins.com, $165-185 d) attracts guests seeking refuge from technology (no television or Wi-Fi and cellular reception is spotty). Just six miles north of Uptown, its three chalet-styled cedar cabins are recently updated and designed to accommodate two people comfortably with a small living room, kitchen, Jacuzzi bathtubs, an eco-friendly electric fireplace downstairs, and an open loft bedroom with a queen bed upstairs. The Honeysuckle Log Cabin is a bit smaller, but it can be a fun way to live out your Zane Grey fantasies for a week. The very sweet proprietors Milena and Mike provide a substantial continental breakfast with homemade muffins, eggs, fresh fruit, juice, and coffee, and they are happy to recommend tips for sightseeing and shopping.

Garland's Oak Creek Lodge (8067 N. S.R. 89A, 928/282-3343, www.garlandslodge.com, $325 per cabin) provides guests with the romance of a cabin in the woods and all the style of a small resort. The 1908 homestead is a well-kept Arizona secret, although you may have a hard time getting a reservation for one of the 17 cabins. And like any good summer hideaway, the lodge's on-site restaurant—simply called The Dining Room—will keep you coming back night after night. Breakfast and dinner are included with your stay. The resort is open daily from early February through mid-November. If possible, book one of the large cabins with a fireplace.

Escape into the woods at the quirky **Forest Houses Resort** (9275 N. S.R. 89A, 928/282-2999, www.foresthousesresort.com, $120-165 per house). The 16 cabins, A-frame homes, and stone cottages are scattered on 20 wooded acres. Updates to the cabins are ongoing, but they're all a lot of fun. Try to reserve one of the creek-side cottages, the charming Rock House, or the arty Studio, a former sculpting workshop that overlooks a grassy meadow. The homes range in size, accommodating up to 10 people. Be sure to ask about the resort's charming history—there's a monkey involved.

CAMPING

Many get hung up on the expense of accommodations in both Sedona and Oak Creek Canyon but a much, much, much cheaper option is camping. Along Route 89A in Oak Creek Canyon, you can find multiple campsites just off the road. From north to south, you'll first find **Pine Flat** campground, which offers drinking water with tent and trailer camping. **Cave Springs** offers a bit more luxury, with many campsites located on the banks of Oak Creek, access to hiking trails and showers. And **Manzanita**, closest to Sedona and the toughest to claim a spot, provides the basics with running water and tent camping only. Each campsite costs $20 per night, with some reservations available by calling 877/444-6777. Pine Flat and Cave Springs adopt a season from early spring through mid-fall (or first snowfall) but the Manzanita campground is open year-round. As mentioned, the campsites are near the street, so you may have to put up with cars zooming by, especially during daytime hours. The real trick here is to snag a spot, because in spite of the roadside location, the sites seem constantly full. Check out www.fs.usda.gov/activity/coconino/recreation/camping-cabins/ or call 928/203-2900 for more information.

Getting There

Oak Creek Canyon just sort of happens before you know it as you drive along Route 89A. Simply head north of Uptown Sedona on Route 89A; in minutes, you'll be wending your way through one of Arizona's most beautiful forests, with roadside views of red-rock formations and cool, running waters. The drive to Slide Rock should take less than 20 minutes from Sedona (assuming it's not a holiday weekend), and with another 20 minutes or so in the car, you can reach the mountain retreat of Flagstaff, the unofficial capital of northern Arizona. Keep in mind it's a two-lane, super-squiggly road without many chances to turn around if you miss your destination—an easy thing to do when the scenery is so spectacular!

THE VERDE VALLEY

One thing Arizona is not particularly known for is the color green. When 16th-century Spanish explorers first rode into this valley, they were struck by the tall, green *(verde)* grasses and mighty cottonwoods flanking the banks of its small river. The conquistadors named the area Verde Valley, a testament to its contrast against the brown Sonoran Desert.

The Sinagua had known of this temperate oasis for hundreds of years, making their homes in cliffside dwellings and hilltop pueblos until they disappeared in the 1400s. By the late 19th century, Anglo settlers arrived and clashed with the Apache Indians who roamed the land, prompting the construction of Fort Verde. In their zeal to appease the settlers, though, Fort Verde's civilian and military commanders changed the landscape forever. Local pioneers took full advantage of the Native Americans' relocation to reservations and moved wave after wave of cattle and farms onto the land. So many head of cattle were brought in that the waist-high grasses that gave the Verde Valley its name were soon gone. The topsoil washed away, leaving much of the land so denuded that the hard cacti and low grasses seen today were all that survived.

Fortunately, however, you can still see the vestiges of Verde Valley's green landscape and reminders of its dramatic history. Visit the national monuments at Montezuma Castle and Tuzigoot to see the protected pueblo villages of the Sinagua. Learn what life was really like in the Old West by exploring the haunted mining town of Jerome or the frontier military installation at Fort Verde. And be sure to see how the valley earned its green moniker at Dead Horse Ranch State Park, a lush riparian reserve between Sedona and Jerome.

the town of Jerome

★ Jerome

Jerome is one of the funkiest places to visit in all of Arizona. It's a rough-and-tumble town with a colorful history and penchant for surviving disaster. Once dubbed the "Wickedest Town in the West," the hillside community has endured the ravages of fire, landslides, and an influenza epidemic—not to mention Prohibition and the boom-and-bust business of mining.

There is a whole lot of history packed into Jerome, despite its small, walkable size. The town was founded in 1876 after prospectors Angus McKinnon and M. A. Ruffner filed the first mining claims. Six years later, entrepreneur William Andrews Clark established the

United Verde Copper Company mine. It became the richest individually owned mine in the world, and Clark made a fortune. Workers arrived in droves, and Jerome became a melting pot of cultures, with Irish, Greek, and Chinese immigrants appearing in search of jobs and opportunity.

In its heyday, its population topped at 15,000. Saloons, opium dens, and brothels lined the streets and transformed the mining camp into a lively boomtown. Jerome flourished for decades, but after more than $1 billion had been milked from the mines, the bust came to town. The UVCC mine closed for good in 1953, having produced enough copper to put 13 pounds of it into the hand of every person living at the time. Jerome became a ghost town overnight. It wasn't until the 1970s that settlers started to return, but this time they were hippies and artists who found the quaint atmosphere and cheap rent appealing.

Small shops, bars, and hotels still cling to the side of Cleopatra Hill, although today they mainly cater to tourists. The winding streets are filled with visitors on the weekends—and they're not alone. Jerome is rumored to be haunted by a slew of ghosts, including the

Who Is Jerome?

The city was named for New Yorker Eugene Murray Jerome, a United Verde Copper Company investor and cousin to Winston Churchill's mother. Jerome never visited his namesake, believing the camp and the "rabble" that worked in it would be too crude for his refined tastes.

spirit of Jennie Banters, a former madam who was once considered the wealthiest woman in northern Arizona. She was murdered by her opium-addict boyfriend in 1905. Banters was a beloved figure in Jerome—at least in part because she was often the first to rebuild after the repeated fires that consumed local businesses.

Plan to spend a couple of hours in Jerome, a National Historic Landmark. Explore the narrow streets and alleys that climb the steep slopes and pop into its small galleries and stores. The must-see **Mine Museum** (200 Main St., 928/634-5477, www.jeromehistoricalsociety.com, 9am-5pm daily, adults $2, children free) is small but jam-packed with information, giving a great overview of Jerome's sordid past. Exhibitions trace the complex hierarchy of prostitutes, immigrants, and shopkeepers who made their home in Jerome, and the displays of rusty old tools quickly school onlookers in the rigors of life in the mines.

Out front, bikers frequently park their hogs on **Main Street** while, inside the saloons, they compete with tourists for space at the bar and a view of the band.

WINE TOUR

In recent years, local vineyards have made Jerome famous for fine, Arizona-grown wines. Take a mini wine tour of your own while walking the funky streets in town. First, try out **Passion Cellars** (417 Hull Ave., 928/649-9800, www.passioncellars.com, 11am-6pm Sun.-Thurs., 11am-7pm Fri.-Sat.), which sports wines sourced from the family's Verde Valley vineyard. Next, try out the tasting room for **Cellar 433** (240 Hull Ave., 928/634-7033, 11am-6pm Thurs.-Sun., 11am-5pm Mon.-Wed.), which serves cheese and fruit with your tastings as well as a small selection of bottle micro-brews. Perhaps saving the most memorable for last, head to **Caduceus Cellars and Merkin Vineyards Tasting Room** (158 Main St., 928/639-9463, www.caduceus.org, 11am-6pm Sun.-Thurs., 11am-8pm Fri.-Sat.) to sample wines created by Maynard James Keenan, the front man for

1990s' rock band Tool. The guy is passionate and intense and well known in Arizona for his vineyards and wines.

SHOPPING

If you're in the leather market, check out **Altai Leather Designs** (415 Main St., 800/213-8112, www.moonshineleather.com, 10am-6pm daily) with original, handmade leather goods like briefcases, handbags, journals, belts, and clothing. Only a place like Jerome would be fitting for **Nellie Bly** (136 Main St., 928/634-0255, www.nelliblyscopes.com, 9:30am-5:30pm Sun.-Thurs., 9:30am-6pm Fri.-Sat.), the "largest kaleidoscope store in the world," which includes kaleidoscopes made by international artists as well as glass art. Down the street, **Laughing Mountain** (116 Main St., 928/634-8764, www.jeromechamber.com/businesses/laughing-mountain, 10am-5pm daily) offers expansive views of Verde Valley, along with Southwestern gifts of every variety that are perfect for AZ-themed gifts for your return home. Want to pick up something in Jerome that will literally last a lifetime? How about a tattoo (come on, do it!)? Head into **Jerome Tattoo Company** (403 Clark Street, 928/649-2143, typically open 11am-close Wed.-Sun.), where skilled artists can hook you up with a beautiful design while you soak up the Old West ambience of the shop.

FOOD AND DRINK

Jerome has a Y of its own, where the main road splits and **The Flatiron** (416 Main St., 928/634-2733, www.theflatironjerome.com, 7:30am-3pm Thurs.-Mon., $8-12) is located in the beautiful building crammed into the wedge of streets. This teeny-tiny café serves coffee, breakfast, and lunch in just 380 square feet. The menu is never fixed and relies on local, fresh, whole foods.

The casual **Mile High Grill & Inn** (309 Main St., 928/634-5094, www.milehighgrillandinn.com, 8am-4pm Sun.-Thurs., 8am-8pm Fri.-Sat., $7-12) is one of Jerome's best bets for a good meal. Breakfast creations

The Grape Escape

Take that, California! Arizona has its very own wine country and although much (much!) smaller, its undiscovered nature makes for a more intimate, humble experience as you sip, swish, and spit among the dramatic northern Arizona landscape. Between Cottonwood, Jerome, Sedona, and other surrounding communities, pioneering wineries are working the land to birth what many believe will become an area as well-known as Napa…someday.

For now, take your own tour along the **Verde Valley Wine Trail,** which connects seven wineries with eight tasting rooms. The trail is best taken by car (elect a designated driver, please!) with stops every 5-10 miles. Most stops can be found along Routes 89A and 260 between Jerome and Cottonwood. Plan a day of touring the towns along the way, grabbing some bites to eat, and taking home a few bottles of the good stuff.

For a full description list of wineries, and a Verde Valley Wine Trail map, visit www.vvwinetrail. com.

include baked oatmeal with blueberries, cinnamon, and candied ginger served with walnut brittle and cream. Yum, right? If you're in for lunch, try the hand-pressed burgers, the signature pork chili stew, or one from a range of fresh salads.

Don't let the exterior fool you, as the historic English Kitchen building really does house **Bobby D's BBQ** (416 Main St., 928/634-6235, www.bobbydsbbqjerome. com, 11am-6pm Sun.-Thurs., 11am-8pm Fri.-Sat., $11-30), which is a lively restaurant with friendly staff and meat, meat, meat as

far as the eye can see. Try their St. Louis-style ribs in half or full rack, pecan-smoked chicken, or the pulled-pork sandwich. Go over the top by starting with the chili cheese fries and cactus-tini made with prickly pear cactus juice.

You can't leave Jerome without having a drink at **The Spirit Room** (166 Main St., 928/634-8809, www.spiritroom.com, 11am-1am daily). Beers and bands abound at this town mainstay, which feels every bit as bad as the old saloons that used to serve up whiskey to miners after a long day underground.

The Spirit Room

During the daytime the place is bustling and on a weekend night, the dance floor gets crazy (you'll love it).

The Asylum Restaurant and Lounge (200 Hill St., 928/639-3197, www.theasylum.biz, 11am-9pm daily, $7-31) at the Jerome Grand Hotel has earned rave reviews for its Southwestern-inspired dishes, like prickly pear barbecue pork tenderloin and the vegetarian sesame tofu and roasted butternut squash. The New American cuisine is complemented by a terrific view of Verde Valley and an extensive wine list, which has earned kudos from *Wine Spectator* magazine.

ACCOMMODATIONS

The Miner's Cottage (553 Main St., 928/254-1089, www.theminerscottage.com, $950 per week, $125-150 d) is a sophisticated throwback to Jerome's Victorian past, with two master suites available for rental by the week. Shorter stays are available upon request.

Ghost City Inn Bed and Breakfast (541 Main St., 888/634-4678, www.ghostcityinn.com, $105-150 d) is a charming bed-and-breakfast that was originally built around 1890 as a boarding house for copper miners. The eight available rooms range from cozy one-bedrooms to suites with full kitchens. Each room has its own themed décor, like Northern Exposure or the red, white, and blue Americana. Updated private bathrooms put the perfect touch on this popular favorite.

The 12-room **Hotel Connor** (160 Main St., 928/634-5006, www.connorhotel.com, $105-165 d), built in 1898 by David Connor, is incredibly charming with an old-timey vibe in its decor and furnishings. Eight of the rooms offer respite from the high-spirited happenings in the Spirit Room saloon below, with four of them located right above all the action.

For a truly unique stay, try **John Riordan House** (34 Magnolia Ln., 480/892-0603, www.johnrioridanhouse.com, $215 d), a fully restored, two-bedroom home that was originally built in 1898 but was buried for decades. Literally. Because a mudslide hit it in 1953. In 2012, restoration and reconstruction began and now the beautiful house features all modern conveniences but is full of authentic antique features like a wood-burning stove, hand-crank Victrola record player with discs, and a Julius Audra wall phone from 1914.

A National Historic Landmark, the haunted **Jerome Grand Hotel** (200 Hill St., 928/634-8200, www.jeromegrandhotel.com, $155-520 d) sits high above town on Cleopatra Hill. Staying here will give you a dominant view of Jerome and the Verde Valley. You can opt for the ghost-hunting package to help with the ongoing investigation of the paranormal activities around the hotel.

GETTING THERE

To make the easy road trip to Jerome from Sedona, take Route 89A west to the Cottonwood. The highway drifts south before looping north through town. You can stay on Route 89A straight through to Jerome, where it winds up the side of Cleopatra Hill, or you can opt for the more scenic drive through Old Town Cottonwood on Highway 260, which is also called Main Street. Highway 260 passes by exits for Dead Horse Ranch State Park and Tuzigoot as well as through the town of Clarksdale, where it rejoins Route 89A to make the ascent up to Jerome.

Tuzigoot National Monument

Sitting on the summit of a desert hilltop, **Tuzigoot National Monument** (off Broadway between Clarksdale and Old Town Cottonwood, 928/634-5564, www.nps.gov/tuzi, 8am-5pm daily, $10 adults, children ages 15 and younger free) was once the home of the Sinagua people, who lived in the 110-room village between AD 1125 and 1400. The three-story pueblo ruins were constructed from limestone and sandstone rocks and formed an intricate complex of living, cooking, and storage spaces used by Sinaguan farmers who traded with communities hundreds of miles away. Visitors can explore the ruins up close and trace the well-preserved walls, which rise a few feet high. The largest room at the top of the complex has been reconstructed, giving views of the surrounding landscape and a sense of what it must have been like living in this close-knit community. Be sure to check out the nearby tailings pond, where Jerome's United Verde Copper Mine used to deposit leftover minerals and sediment. The impact on the landscape is quite extraordinary.

GETTING THERE

From Sedona, head south on Route 89A for about 17 miles, then hang a right onto East Mingus Avenue in Cottonwood. Follow Mingus Avenue for about six miles and turn

Tuzigoot National Monument

right onto North Main Street. Follow signs for Tuzigoot National Monument, which will lead you to turn right onto Tuzigoot Road; follow this road to the end.

Dead Horse Ranch State Park

To catch a glimpse of what the Verde Valley looked like before the settlers and cattle herds arrived, head to **Dead Horse Ranch State Park** (675 Dead Horse Ranch Rd., 928/634-5283, https://azstateparks.com, 8am-5pm daily, $7 per car), a nearly pristine stretch of Verde River that offers camping, hiking, mountain biking, fishing, and equestrian areas. Don't let the name fool you. This is some of the most verdant land in the area. Officially classified as a cottonwood and willow riparian gallery forest—one of only 20 such ecosystems left in the world—the 423-acre park protects one of the last stretches of free-running river in the Sonoran Desert and more than 100 species of migrating birds, including black hawks and golden eagles, which come every year to feast on the trout released into the river.

GETTING THERE

From Sedona, take Route 89A southwest to Cottonwood. Once you enter the town, the highway loops north and turns into Main Street. At the Y intersection, stay on Main Street, which is also called Highway 260. Turn right on 10th Street and head north. Make a right at Dead Horse Ranch Road, where you'll see the entrance to the park.

Old Town Cottonwood

Enjoy a bit of roadside charm on a quick ride through **Old Town Cottonwood,** a terrific throwback to the 1950s' small towns you would expect to find off Route 66. The district's quaint Main Street—which is also called Old State Route 89A or Highway 260 depending on the sign—is a pleasant drive, especially for travelers on their way from Sedona to Jerome, Tuzigoot, or Dead Horse Ranch State Park. Many of its storefronts are restored as Cottonwood tries to recapture a bit

of its former glory. And although the town of 11,000 residents has strong agricultural roots that are still alive, modern Cottonwood also serves as a bedroom community for people priced out of expensive Red Rock Country.

FOOD

Hankerin' for an Old West cookout? Well, even if themed dining isn't your thing, **Blazin' M Ranch** (1875 Mayberry Ranch Rd., 928/634-0334, www.blazinm.com, 5pm-8:30pm Wed.-Sat., closed Jan., adults $35.95, children ages 3-12 $19.95, seniors $32.95) serves up darn good "cowboy vittles, stories, tomfoolery," and it's a destination in its own right for many Sedona tourists. Arrive at 5pm when the gates open so that you can enjoy the full Wild West experience, including a shooting gallery, train ride, petting zoo, and roping. The dusty streets and wooden sidewalks may not be authentic, but it's hard to resist browsing the old-fashioned shops—or dressing up as rough-and-tumble cowboys and saloon madams for an "Olde Tyme" photo. The dinner bell rings at 6:30pm, when you'll find chuckwagon grub barbecued ribs and chicken, cowboy beans, prickly pear coleslaw, homemade biscuits, and dessert. After supper, the Blazin' M Cowboys carry on the Old West tradition of twangy music and storytelling. Call for reservations.

Old Town Red Rooster Cafe (901 N. Main St., 928/649-8100, 8am-4pm daily, $8-13) gets more than just a job well done for breakfast and lunch. The contemporary menu serves up well-prepared items like pancakes and *huevos rancheros* for breakfast and then showers guests with excellent choices for lunch. Sandwiches include the Cuban, made with grilled Black Forest ham, turkey, and gruyère cheese, all drizzled in mustard aioli. And the coffee ain't half bad, either.

The bustling **Nic's Italian Steak & Crab House** (925 N. Main St., 928/634-9626, www.nicsaz.com, 5pm-9pm daily, $13-29) packs in Cottonwood residents with solid seafood dishes and topnotch steaks. If there's a wait, grab a drink at the saloon-like bar and consider whether to start with the New Zealand green mussels sautéed in wine and garlic with tomatoes and pesto or the baked Crabby Mac 'n' Cheese, pasta tossed in a cheddar-and-Alfredo sauce with sweet lump crab. And as at any good Italian restaurant, you can't go wrong with the eggplant parmesan, classic lasagna, or lemon-and-caper chicken piccata.

ACCOMMODATIONS

You'll find a few chain motels in Cottonwood, but frankly, you're better off staying in Sedona or Jerome. If you need to say in town, though, **Pines Motel** (920 S. Camino Real, 928/634-9975, www.azpines-motel.com, $69-99) is better than your average roadside hotel and is located in the middle of Wine Country in Verde Valley. Its clean, bright rooms are cheery and the accommodations are great for larger groups or big families.

GETTING THERE

A quick day trip to Cottonwood is just 25 minutes away, and it's a great place for a meal in between stops at Tuzigoot National Monument or Dead Horse Ranch State Park. From Sedona, take Route 89A west. You'll notice the landscape changes quite starkly from red-rock buttes, high-desert cacti, and ponderosa pines to tawny grasslands and flat plains. Once you get into Cottonwood, the highway loops north and turns into Main Street or Highway 260. You can opt to take Highway 260 south to Camp Verde and Montezuma Castle.

★ Montezuma Castle National Monument

Walking up the shady, creek-side path to **Montezuma Castle National Monument** (I-17 Exit 289, 928/567-3322, www.nps.gov/moca, 8am-5pm daily Sept.-May, 8am-6pm daily Jun.-Aug., $10 adults, children ages 15 and younger free), you can't help but imagine what it must have been like to live in the five-story pueblo, one of the best-preserved cliffside dwellings in North America.

From about 1125 to the 1400s, the 20-room village served as a home of the Sinagua people, who cultivated the land along Beaver Creek by day and scaled tiered ladders 75 feet above the ground every night. The Sinagua used the mud, stone, and wood-timbered rooms and balconies for sleeping, preparing food, weaving, and storing the goods they traded with surrounding communities.

Montezuma Castle National Monument

The vertical limestone cliff wall also functioned as a natural defense against rivals.

As many as 35 people lived in the structure, with an additional 100 people living in the 45-room "Castle A" at the bottom of the cliff. Montezuma Castle—built into a deep, carved-out recess in the cliff and sheltered from the elements—is in much better shape than Castle A and the hundreds of other Sinaguan sites throughout the Verde Valley. A 1997 stabilization project added a fresh, chestnut-brown layer of mud to the facade. Incidentally, there is no connection to Montezuma; American explorers who discovered the site in the 1800s speculated that the Aztecs and their legendary emperor had built the impressive structure. The small museum at the visitor center provides a nice overview of the site and the Sinagua people.

MONTEZUMA WELL

The Sinagua were experts at making the most of the Verde Valley's natural landscape. Just 11 miles north of Montezuma Castle, you can witness their ingenuity at another of Arizona's natural wonders, **Montezuma Well** (I-17 Exit 293, 928/567-4521, 8am-5pm daily Sept.-May, 8am-6pm daily Jun.-Aug., $5 adults, children free). Small cliffside ruins and canals are clustered around the site, which once provided a vital source of water to the agrarian community. Underground springs still feed 1.5 million gallons of water every day into the well, which actually is a large sinkhole, 365 feet across and 55 feet deep. The constant supply of 74°F water has created a distinct ecosystem, with several plants and animals not found anywhere else in the world. Unique species of crustaceans, water scorpions, and turtles thrive in the warm, carbon dioxide-rich water that is inhospitable to most fish and aquatic life. Walk through the forested grounds to the water's edge, where the temperature can be as much as 20°F cooler than in the surrounding grasslands. There are also ruins of small pit houses built by the Southern Sinagua, who first constructed the canals—they're still running—in the 8th century.

GETTING THERE

If you're coming from Sedona, head south on Route 179 to the I-17. Take Exit 289, and drive east through two roundabouts for less than a mile, where you turn left on Montezuma Castle Highway. Plenty of signs will make navigating the narrow two-lane road quite easy. From Phoenix, follow the I-17 north for about an hour and a half and turn right at Exit 289, where signs will direct you through two traffic circles to the monument's entrance. To reach Montezuma Well, drive the I-17 to Exit 293, which is four miles north of the turnoff for Montezuma Castle. Follow the signs through the towns of McGuireville and Rimrock to the park's entrance.

Fort Verde State Historic Park

Wyatt Earp never shot it out with lawless gunslingers on its dusty streets, but **Fort Verde State Historic Park** (125 E. Hollamon St., 928/567-3275, https://azstateparks.com/Parks/fove/, 9am-4:30pm daily, $5 adults, $2 children ages 7-13, free children ages 6 and under) is the place to go for a glimpse of the real Old West—especially of life among the soldiers sent out West after the Civil War. Originally built in 1871, the fort housed as many as 300 soldiers, who were stationed here to protect Anglo settlers from Apache and Yavapai raids. What remains of the old fort today is considered the best-preserved example of Indian Wars-era military architecture in the state.

The territorial-style houses that line the dusty parade ground look more like the remains of a Midwestern main street than the stockade-fenced forts seen in old Westerns. The three surviving historic houses are decorated with 1880s'-period furnishings, and the former Administration building now houses a visitor center with interpretive exhibits, period military artifacts, and history on the Indian Scouts and Indian Wars era. Exhibitions describe how many of the area's Native Americans were eventually confined to a reservation in the Verde Valley, then evicted wholesale to the San Carlos Apache reservation in 1875.

Today, more than 10,000 people live in the modern town of Camp Verde. The main drag is lined with a few forgettable antique shops and restaurants, although the fort is a good stop if you need a break between Phoenix and Sedona.

GETTING THERE

From Sedona, drive south on Route 179 through the Village of Oak Creek to the I-17, where you'll merge right and head southwest. Take Exit 289 for Middle Verde Road and turn left. Stay on Middle Verde Road through two traffic circles and then continue onto Montezuma Castle Highway for about three miles. Turn left onto Finnie Flat Road, then take an immediate left onto Main Street. Turn left onto Turner Street, followed by another immediate left onto Woods Street, which will turn right onto Hance Street. The fort is on the right.

If you are driving from Phoenix, simply take the I-17 north to Exit 285 for General Crook Trail. Turn right onto General Crook Trail for 1.3 miles. Then turn left onto Main Street for just over half a mile. Turn right onto Turner Street, followed by immediate left onto Woods Street, which will turn right onto Hance Street, with the fort on the right. From there, you'll follow Highway 260 south to Finnie Flats Road and Camp Verde.

Arcosanti

The utopian village of **Arcosanti** (928/632-7135, www.arcosanti.org, 9am-5pm daily) was designed and built by Italian architect Paolo Soleri as the embodiment of his principles of "arcology"—a mixture of architecture and ecology. Soleri's goal is to create a "lean alternative" to the wastefulness of modern cities by making them more compact and

self-sustaining. His real-world experiment began in 1970, more than two decades after he first came to the Southwest to study with Frank Lloyd Wright at Taliesin West. Today, Arcosanti is perched in rural splendor on a bluff in Arizona's high desert and is home to just a few hundred people at any one time. From a distance, it looks like an unlikely combination of Italian hill town and sci-fi movie. But up close, the small, hand-crafted details of its buildings and the community's perfectly human scale make it a delight to visit, not to mention a pioneering example of urban sustainability. Daily guided tours have a suggested donation of $10.

GETTING THERE

From Phoenix, drive north some 60 miles on I-17. Take Exit 262 for Route 69 toward Prescott and turn right on Cordes Lakes Road. From there, signs for Arcosanti should direct you left on Stagecoach Trail, which is unpaved after a brief asphalt stretch, then onto Cross I Trail.

From Sedona, head south on Route 279 to I-17. Take it 36 miles south to Exit 262 for Route 69 toward Prescott and turn right on Cordes Lakes Road. Signs for Arcosanti will direct you left on Stagecoach Trail and then onto Cross I Trail.

Rock Springs

Mention **Rock Springs Café** (35769 South Old Black Canyon Hwy., 623/374/5794, www.rocksprings.cafe, 7am-9pm Mon.-Fri., 7am-10pm Sat.-Sun., $4.50-$19) to any Arizonan and watch their face light up. Then they'll immediately tell you which pie is the best (ahem, the Jack Daniels Pecan Pie) and then tell you that you need to go to try your favorite pie and then grab their keys because, "Hey, why don't we all just hop in the car right now?" Way before this whole pie thing happened, the quirky little stop along I-17 was an encampment for the Yavapai Indians. Enter the expansion of the American West territory in the late 19th century and it became a water stop for miners, cattle drivers, and travelers on the Black Canyon Trail. Fast-forward to 1917 and a young entrepreneur built a canvas-covered store, then a hotel, and next a general store. Today, Rock Springs Café is a restaurant, store, and producer of the aforementioned delicious pies. So delicious that many Phoenicians have been known to make the drive just to fulfill a craving (that is, before they started shipping the pies, making the world a better place). They have a restaurant, too, that serves breakfast, lunch, and steak dinners. And pie. The store sells whole pies that only cost a little over $20. Don't forget to try the pie. Oh, did we mention the amazing pie?

GETTING THERE

From Phoenix, drive north some 35 miles on I-17. Take Exit 242 for Velda Rose Road and turn left to cross under the I-17. Turn left onto Old Black Canyon Highway and you'll see Rock Springs Café on the right.

From Sedona, head south on AZ-279 to I-17. Take it 55 miles south to Exit 242, then turn right onto Velda Rose Road, followed by an immediate left onto Old Black Canyon Highway. Rock Springs Café will be on the right.

Background

The Landscape 232

Plants and Animals 237

History 241

Government and Economy 246

People and Culture 248

The Landscape

If the word "desert" conjures up images of sand dunes, camels, and parched, monochromatic landscapes, then get ready for a surprise. Phoenix and Scottsdale sit in the northeastern corner of the Sonoran Desert, the most ecologically diverse desert region on the planet. It stretches more than 100,000 square miles from central Arizona south into Mexico and west into California, and is home to more than 1,000 native species of plants, 60 species of mammals, 350 kinds of birds, 20 amphibians, and 100 or so reptiles. It's also the only place in the world where the towering saguaro cactus—made famous in so many Western movies—grows naturally. Sure, it's a desert that's usually hot from May to September and sunny most of the year, but Lawrence of Arabia would be lost here.

GEOGRAPHY AND GEOLOGY

The Phoenix metro area is ringed with mountains, deep canyons, and broad, alluvial valleys watered by rivers that can go from shallow trickles to raging torrents in a matter of minutes. This landscape is part of the vast basin and range zone born 15 million years ago, when the Earth's crust beneath what is now the western United States was pulled apart by shifting tectonic plates. It stretched as much as 50 percent, pushing up and pulling down the land to form a regular pattern of small but steep mountains and broad, flat valleys. Today, a ring of such mountain ranges around metro Phoenix gives the area its nickname: the Valley of the Sun. The major ranges surrounding the Valley are the White Tank Mountains to the west, the Sierra Estrella to the southwest, the Superstitions to the east,

and the McDowell Mountains to the northeast. Smaller ranges also ring the center of the city, including the Phoenix Mountains, South Mountain, and the Papago Buttes. Most of the rock that forms these craggy hills is volcanic, but they were created less by geysers of lava than by the inexorable seismic shifting that tilted up huge blocks of the Earth's crust.

To the north lies the high, flat Colorado Plateau. Sedona sits in the southwestern part of this high-desert region, which covers the Four Corners area where northeastern Arizona, southeastern Utah, southwestern Colorado, and northwestern New Mexico meet. But to get there from Phoenix, you have to climb the Mogollon Rim, a long, snaking cliff that bisects the state from east to west. This dramatic drop-off separates the low desert surrounding Phoenix from the grasslands and ponderosa pine forests of this vast plateau, and the trails along its edge offer fabulous views of the Sonoran Desert below. The area around Sedona is known as Red Rock Country, thanks to the red-tinged sandstone cliffs towering above Oak Creek Canyon. The color comes from iron deposits that rust as the rock weathers and exposes them to air and water. But the majestic formations, called "fins," came to be owing to a much simpler process: the combination of weak ground and flowing water. Oak Creek tumbles down from the north through a fault line. Over the millennia, thousands of small earthquakes fractured the ground above the fault, and water seeped in and carried away layer after layer of rock to form Oak Creek Canyon. The strongest rock formations stood up to this liquid attacker and now soar far above the canyon floor.

Previous: the valley's desert landscape; cacti.

RIVERS AND LAKES

Phoenix owes its very existence to the Salt River (or Rio Salado as it is called in Spanish). The snaking stream runs 200 miles from the White Mountains in eastern Arizona to join the Gila River about 15 miles west of downtown Phoenix, and farmers from ancient times to the present have come to the Valley of the Sun for its life-giving water. A series of dams has left the lower half of the riverbed mostly dry since the first, the Roosevelt Dam, was built in 1911, but the Salt's natural flow is more than 2,500 cubic feet per second, about three times the amount of water in the Rio Grande. Except for overflow released after storms, most of this water now goes into hundreds of miles of irrigation canals scattered around the region, and the dams themselves provide flood control and produce electricity. The one exception to this is the two-mile-long Tempe Town Lake, created in 1999 by building two inflatable dams in the bed of the Salt River and filling the area between them with a combination of upstream storm runoff and treated wastewater. Perhaps not surprisingly, no swimming is allowed, but kayaking, rowing, sailing, and paddle-boating are all popular pastimes, and the lake is stocked with fish regularly.

Central Arizona's other major river, the Gila, is even longer and more powerful than the Salt. It flows almost 650 miles from the White Mountains near the border with New Mexico all the way to the Colorado River, which forms the border between Arizona and California. Dams and irrigation diversions reduce the river to a trickle in several areas, but in its natural state, the Gila carries more than 6,000 cubic feet of water per second and once was navigable from the Colorado nearly to the New Mexico border. For five years, from the end of the Mexican War to the Gadsden Purchase in 1853, the Gila River actually formed the border between the U.S. and Mexico. Today, significant portions of the river run through Native American communities.

All the dams on the Salt and Gila rivers have created a surprising number of lakes. An oft-repeated but completely unverified statistic that Arizonans love to repeat is that Maricopa County has one of the highest per capita rates of boat ownership in the nation. Whether or not this is true, the somewhat incongruous sight of a large pickup truck towing a water-ski or fishing boat through the desert is surprisingly common, and it's possible to learn how to sail, kayak, and even scuba dive

Tempe Town Lake is one of many lakes created along the Salt River through a series of dams.

at Lake Pleasant and a few of the other large lakes in the area.

CLIMATE

It's probably the Valley of the Sun's greatest claim to fame: the near-perfect weather—well, at least for a good portion of the year. In February, blue, sunny skies and balmy temperatures (averaging 70-80°F) delight residents and visitors alike. The good times last well into April, as hiking trails, golf courses, and restaurant patios fill up with people hoping to spend every last second soaking in the spring nirvana. And because this is the desert, the arid climate's low humidity means nighttime temps fall between 20-30°F, providing a cool counterpoint to the warm days.

The Sonoran Desert heats up quickly in May, and its reputation for sizzling summer temps isn't an exaggeration, with an average high well over 90°F and lows above 70°F. Still, the low moisture means that it actually feels quite a bit cooler than comparable days in New York, Miami, or Houston. By July, though, watch out. It's hot—as in a 115°F kind of hot. Phoenix has the warmest climate of any major metropolitan area in the country, and its record high of 122°F on June 26, 1990, caused even the toughest of desert-tested Phoenicians to break out in one heck of a sweat. Most people cope by switching to an early morning or nocturnal schedule in the summer, as overnight lows drop to around 80°F. There are frequent breaks from the scorching heat and constant sunshine in late summer, when the monsoon storms roll into the city from the desert. These afternoon showers, caused by a seasonal change in weather patterns, can be sudden and torrential, stranding motorists and even mountainside hikers. The dramatic bolts of lightning force golfers off the course and swimmers out of the pool. Of course, residents love every second of it.

By October, a "second spring" emerges with lush, green plants and colorful wildflowers. The triple-digit heat becomes a memory with fall temperatures dropping back to 80-87°F, which means you'll be able to fit in plenty of outdoor time. In the high deserts of Sedona, which is typically 15-20°F cooler than Phoenix throughout the year, the sycamore trees along Oak Creek begin to turn, revealing golden yellow and fiery red leaves against the green ponderosa pines.

Believe it or not, there is a winter in the Sonoran Desert. Don't laugh—there is. The 60-65°F highs and 40-45°F lows chill Phoenicians to the bone. OK, the weather is darn-near perfect, and residents love nothing more than calling up snowed-in relatives in other parts of the country to gloat. Still, nighttime lows do fall below freezing a few times a year, and a rare light snow does happen, especially in Sedona.

ENVIRONMENTAL ISSUES

Former Mayor Phil Gordon announced an ambitious plan in 2009 to make Phoenix "the greenest city in America." Although admirable, the plan will have to solve at least two of the metro area's most daunting environmental problems if it's to be more than rhetoric—air pollution and suburban sprawl. In winter, a brown cloud of dust, car exhaust, and other particulates often hangs over the city for days at a time thanks to the surrounding mountains, which block the wind and trap warmer air near the ground. In summer, strong sunlight and extreme heat interact with chemicals in car exhaust to form ozone, a colorless pollutant that affects breathing and often leads to warnings from health officials that people with respiratory illnesses should stay inside. It's a problem that defies easy solution in a metro area that sprawls over more than 1,000 square miles and forces residents to drive almost everywhere.

But that's not the only problem with the way one of America's fastest-growing cities is planned and built. The new subdivisions, office parks, and shopping malls sprouting up on the edge of town are paving over the desert at an alarming rate. This destroys wildlife habitat and native plants (although damaging or even moving a saguaro cactus without a

Monsoon Madness

Triple-digit heat is to be expected during the summer months in Phoenix, but there's a weather phenomenon in the desert Southwest that makes the sweltering afternoons slightly unpredictable. The Arizona monsoon season begins June 15 and ends September 30, bringing volatile afternoon storms that can range from blowing dust to torrential downpour. The term "monsoon" is taken from the Arabic word for season, *mausim,* referring to a seasonal shift in wind flow. In Arizona, the typically westerly winds shift to a southerly flow, which pulls in moisture from the Gulf of California. Combine that moisture with the intense afternoon heat, and you get thunderstorms.

In May, the average afternoon high temperature is about 95°F, with relative humidity averaging 15 percent. By July, the mercury will rise each afternoon to about 106°F, and relative humidity doubles to an average of about 30 percent. That makes it tougher for the human body to cool down during the sweltering heat. But heat is only one of the dangers of the monsoon.

About a third of Phoenix's yearly rainfall occurs in the summer, and sometimes it comes dangerously quickly. The sandy desert floor cannot absorb rainfall that sometimes amounts to an inch or more in just a few hours. Flash-flooding becomes a problem as normally dry washes fill with water and careless drivers attempt to cross them. Traffic is often halted on highways too, as massive dust storms sweep across town. This happens when we see dry thunderstorms. Their strong winds pick up the dry desert soil and push it into town, sometimes bringing visibility to near zero (we call these massive dust clouds "haboobs"). Finally, thunderstorms often send hikers and golfers hurrying for cover, as lightning lights up the desert horizon.

Monsoon thunderstorms are most likely during the afternoon and evening hours but can erupt any time of the day. They are more common the further south and east you go in Arizona. Although they can be very dangerous, they're essential to the desert ecosystem. Many desert creatures, including tarantulas, toads, and quail, have adapted their breeding cycles to benefit from the monsoon rain. And in May and June you will notice saguaro cacti blooming with beautiful white flowers, letting their fruit seeds ripen just in time to soak up the summer rains. For the humans who call this place home, monsoons are a well-loved thrill—and often the only thing that is loved about spending the summer months here.

permit can result in hefty fines and even jail time), not to mention the views of pristine desert that draw so many people to Arizona in the first place.

Water and where to get it has always been a top concern in the desert, but metro Phoenix has fewer problems in this area than might be expected. Rivers and streams that flow out of the mountains to the north and east fill roughly half the metropolis's water needs, while a 350-mile canal from the Colorado River delivers the other half. Local officials say the billions of dollars spent on this water infrastructure can supply more than the area currently needs, but a long drought could create serious problems. The complicated legal agreement that apportions water from the Colorado River to states along its banks is actually based on historically high levels of water, and with California at the front of the line, Arizona cities could get very thirsty if the mountain snows that feed all the rivers around the state get much lighter. Draining rivers so completely also creates a slew of environmental problems. Even under current conditions, very little of the water from the Salt and the Gila rivers makes it to the Colorado, and the mighty river itself now dries up long before it reaches its mouth at the Sea of Cortez.

Another major problem comes from wildfires sparked by lightning, campers, and other human activities. Huge blazes in recent years have charred hundreds of square miles at a time. Although none of the fires have caused devastation to Phoenix or Scottsdale, the surrounding suburbs in the northeast valley have been affected, with some homes destroyed as fires have traveled through its neighboring Tonto National Forest.

State and local officials are trying to address these problems by changing the way people live and travel in the region. A light-rail line running through Phoenix, Tempe, and Mesa opened in 2008. It surpassed ridership expectations in its first six months, and has since become a well-used means of travel in a city that was previously dominated by vehicle transportation only. Phoenix was one of the first cities in the state to adopt a Climate Action Plan, aiming to reduce greenhouse gas emissions from city operations. The plan was a great success in surpassing its original goal of five percent reduction in five years when, three years ahead of schedule, the greenhouse gas emissions were reduced by 7.2 percent. Further ambitious goals have been set as a part of the Climate Action Plan that involve methane capture at landfills, alternative fuels, LED streetlights, and various city solar power projects. In fact, the city has completed almost 30 solar projects from 2007 to 2014 located at light-rail stops, public libraries, fire stations, and community centers. Increasing a culture of sustainability will hopefully attract high-paying engineering jobs to a metro area that's always been big in computer-chip manufacturing and engineering. But they may also help bring the next wave of technology to a place that's been uniquely affected by it. From the precise levels used by the Hohokam to build ancient irrigation canals from the Salt River to the air-conditioning-inspired real-estate boom of the 1950s and 1960s, metro Phoenix has always been affected by new ideas and products—and there's no reason to think that the future won't repeat the cycle.

Plants and Animals

PLANTS
Cacti

They may seem prickly at first, but the Sonoran Desert's cacti are quite lovable once you get know them. These ingenious plants are prime examples of form meeting function in Arizona's harsh environment, having developed resourceful means to mitigate the hot, arid climate. In fact, many of their well-known features are simply an effort to conserve water. Their leaves have evolved into hard, slender spines that provide shade and defend against animals foraging for food and water. Their trunks have become spongy repositories to store water, and their green skins have taken on the duties of photosynthesis.

The saguaro (pronounced "sah-WAH-roh") cactus is the king of the Sonoran Desert, an iconic figure that can only be found in this part of the world. The spiny giant can grow up to 60 feet tall and live to be more than 150 years old, with some of the oldest specimens living two centuries. Its clever root system tunnels only a few feet deep but radiates out to a distance equal to the saguaro's height,

allowing the camel-like plant to capture the maximum amount of water possible after a rainstorm. These slow-growers can take up to 50-75 years to develop branches, or arms, with some growing as many as 25 and others never producing any. The saguaro is an important resource to the desert's ecosystem. In late spring, the cactus blooms with white flowers at night, taking advantage of nocturnal pollinators like moths and bats. They produce sweet, red fruits, which have been eaten by animals and indigenous people for thousands of years. The saguaro's thick trunk also often provides a home for a burrowing Gila woodpecker—or the occasional desert owl that takes over an abandoned "apartment." Native people once used the plant's wooden ribs in the construction of their shelters, and desert animals still take up residence in their dry skeletons.

Of course, there are other barbed species in the desert. The paddle cactus, more commonly known as the prickly pear, has flat, rounded pads that are quite edible once cooked. The cactus produces a sweet, pink

Prickly Pear is easy to recognize with its flat paddles and fruit.

fruit, or fig, that is often used to make candy, jelly, and even a syrup that flavors the popular prickly-pear margarita. The stout barrel cactus can be found along desert washes, growing 1-3 feet wide and 2-4 feet high. The barrel-shaped body is easy to recognize, although you won't want to get too close to its fishhook spines. Interestingly, the cactus is also called the "compass barrel," as older plants frequently lean toward the southwest. The cholla cactus is also a common inhabitant of the Sonoran Desert, a shrubby-looking plant that comes in 20 varieties, like buckhorn cholla and the deceptively cuddly teddy bear cholla, aka the "jumping cactus," which doesn't so much jump as cling stubbornly to anything that touches it.

Trees and Bushes

First-time visitors to Arizona may be familiar with the Sonoran Desert's cacti but they are often surprised by the numerous native trees and bushes found in the area. The green-barked palo verde tree is a gorgeous example. The drought-deciduous tree, which is often found in floodplains and washes, sheds its tiny leaves during dry spells, leaving its "green wood" to take over photosynthesis. In the spring, the canopy blooms in an explosion of tiny yellow flowers. The hardy mesquite tree easily adapts to limited water conditions, thanks in part to a deep taproot that can easily tunnel 25-50 feet underground. Generations of pioneers or artisans have used the hard, dense wood in furniture and as a smoky flavoring in barbecues. There are also several varieties of acacia, including the whitethorn acacia, which produces fuzzy, yellow flowers. Farther north, in Sedona and Oak Creek Canyon, you'll see dark-green ponderosa pines, as well as white and Douglas firs, leafy oaks, old sycamores, and distinctive species like the scaly alligator juniper.

There are smaller shrubs to enjoy, too. The waxy creosote bush, a prevalent sight throughout the desert, produces a unique, herbal scent after much-appreciated rainstorms. In the spring, the silver-leafed brittlebush blooms

The desert explodes in spring with incredible wildflowers.

with delicate yellow flowers, while the woody jojoba produces a nut that cosmetic companies covet for its natural oil. The long, slender ocotillo, which is also called vine cactus, is easy to spot. Its cane-like stems grow from the desert floor, and bright-red, tube-shaped flowers appear on the tips. Also, the ornamental agave is used as a decorative plant in many gardens. The thick leaves grow from a central core, often in a symmetrical pattern, and end in a sharp point. The slow-growing agave produces a single flower only once, on a tall mast that grows from the center of the plant, which, like a romantic Western tragedy, dies after it blooms.

Wildflowers

Nothing dispels the misperception of a lifeless, beige landscape in the Sonoran Desert like wildflower season, when a torrent of psychedelic colors washes across the desert floor. Thanks to *Arizona Highways* magazine, the Grand Canyon State is famous for its vibrant wildflowers, which typically appear after a rainstorm in late February or March and can last well into April or early May. Get your camera ready for the apricot-colored globemallow, desert lavender, golden desert sunflower, violet purplemat, red-flowered chuparosa, and lemon-yellow desert senna. It's not hard to find these seas of color, as any of the mountain preserves that surround the city will teem with polychromatic life, although the best spots are east of Phoenix at the far end of Highway 60 in the Superstition Mountains, or in North Scottsdale in the McDowell Mountains and Cave Creek. You can also catch a secondary round of blooms in the fall, when summer's hot weather gives way to spring-like temperatures.

ANIMALS
Reptiles and Amphibians
Only the tough survive in the Sonoran Desert, and the millennia-old reptile family has adapted to the harsh landscape like no other animal. The rattlesnake may be the area's most famous resident, with some 20 species slithering around Arizona's rocky canyons and dusty desert floors, including the Arizona ridge-nosed rattlesnake (the state's official reptile), the western diamondback, tiger, and sidewinder. They're best known for their ominous rattles, a series of hollow segments made of keratin—like fingernails—that rub against one another at the end of their tails. When threatened, the snakes strike a defensive posture and shake their tails to warn predators of their potent venom, which has an enzyme that paralyzes nerves and destroys tissue and blood cells. What is rarely appreciated about the rattlesnake, though, is its heat-sensing pits. These sensory organs near the eyes and nostrils produce a "heat image" that allows them to spot prey in the pitch black of a desert night. You may also come across other desert snakes, like the banded sand snake, king snake, or gopher snake.

Lizards scurry around the desert as well, consuming insects, leaves, and springtime blossoms. Visitors are likely to see some of these harmless creatures sunning themselves on mountainsides and rocks, or even searching for shade on patios. The dozens of varieties include the Sonoran collared lizard and desert iguana, as well as whiptails, geckos, chuckwallas, and spiny lizards. North America's only venomous lizard, the Gila monster, also makes its home in Arizona. This large reptile, which can grow up to two feet long, spends most of its life underground. These black lizards are covered in spots or bands in shades of pink,

Seeing a desert tortoise in the wild is a rare treat.

orange, yellow, or red. A host of toads, frogs, and desert tortoises also inhabit Arizona.

Mammals

Despite the extreme heat, many warm-blooded mammals thrive in the desert, like mountain lions, bighorn sheep, and desert cottontail rabbits, a common sight in arid landscapes in and around the city. Bobcats look very similar to domestic cats, although they're about two to three times larger and extremely fierce, as they are able to hunt down rabbits, squirrels, rodents, and even pronghorn antelope and mule deer. Don't be surprised if you see coyotes roaming the deserts at night—or at least hear these small canines howling in the distance. Their tan-and-beige coats, along with their keen hearing and sense of smell, help them hide from predators in the day and search for prey at night. Additionally, brown, furry javelinas roam the desert in groups, searching for leaves, cacti, and grasses.

Bats, nature's only flying mammal, serve an important role in the desert's ecosystem. Migrating species, such as the lesser long-nosed bat from Mexico, travel to Arizona in the spring to pollinate plants and cacti such as the saguaro. Some 18 species live in caves throughout the deserts of the Southwest and the hungry bat colonies eat many of the small insects that would otherwise plague the region.

Birds

Arizona is a bird-watcher's paradise, with more than 100 avian species soaring across the state's blue skies, including cardinals, finches, eagles, hawks, hummingbirds, and sparrows. And as Arizona resident Stevie Nicks once sang, "Just like the white-winged dove sings a song," you can actually hear these birds, which flock to the desert every spring to pollinate blooming saguaro cacti. And they're not alone. Arizona's state bird, the brown-and-white cactus wren, is a frequent guest in backyard trees and on patios throughout the Valley of the Sun. There are also a half-dozen species of owl in the desert, including the ghost-faced barn owl and the great-horned owl—although a more apt name would be the "great-eye-browed owl."

Beep beep! If we've learned anything from cartoons, it's that where there are wily coyotes, there are speedy roadrunners. The long-legged cuckoos dash across the desert, happily chasing down lizards and insects. Their unique feet—four toes on each foot, two facing forward and two facing backward—make their "x"-shaped tracks easy to recognize. And although you won't find that other great cartoon bird, Woody the Woodpecker, the Gila woodpecker burrows into trees and cacti in the Sonoran Desert. Its black-and-white-striped wings help distinguish the bird from other species, as does the small red "cap" on the top of the male's head. The ground-dwelling Gambel's quail, crowned by a curled "top-knot," is often seen in the late spring with its small chicks following in an orderly line.

Insects, Arachnids, and Centipedes

These creepy, crawly creatures may be the earliest residents of the Sonoran Desert, and once you get over the initial heebie-jeebies, you may be able to appreciate Arizona's insects. The easiest to love, of course, are the graceful butterflies that populate the desert in the spring or those that migrate from Mexico in late summer and early fall. The great purple hairstreak, orange sulphur, and painted lady are colorful specimens to keep an eye out for. It may be a bit harder, though, to channel the warm fuzzies for the giant desert centipede and the cactus longhorn beetle, which feasts on the *cholla* and prickly pear cacti.

There are also a few spiders lurking in the desert, like the Arizona blond tarantula and the more common desert tarantula. Typically, they hide underground in their silk-lined holes, but like Scottsdale club-goers, they do come out in search of mates. The same is true of the unnerving scorpion, which causes even the toughest of travelers (and cowboys) to halt. Luckily, of the 30 species in Arizona, only the bark scorpion produces venom that can be lethal. Stingers aside, tracking down these pinchers is a bit of a sport in Arizona, and hunters search for the scorpions with an ultraviolet "black" light that causes their bodies to glow, or fluoresce.

History

ANCIENT CIVILIZATIONS

Despite its inhospitable appearance, the Sonoran Desert has proven an irresistible temptation for waves of settlers, beginning with early Native American hunters and followed by a succession Spanish explorers, Catholic missionaries, 19th-century miners and ranchers, and modern-day pioneers, all searching for opportunity. These generations of immigrants define much of Arizona's history, beginning 12,000 years ago when the first humans roamed the area. These Paleo-Indian people followed big game around the region, hunting them in small groups. However, it wasn't until 300 BC that permanent civilizations began to form, thanks in large part to the development of agriculture, which requires a long-term, communal effort.

Two major groups emerged during this time, leaving a lasting legacy. The Hohokam laid the foundations for modern Phoenix. They migrated from Mesoamerica (present-day Mexico) just before the birth of Christ, bringing with them crops like corn and beans. Small groups settled along the banks of the Salt River, and over time, they dug miles and miles of canals to create a dependable source of water for their fields. Villages developed and residents lived in pit houses, igloo-like structures that were built over holes 1-2 feet deep and covered by a dome of sticks and brush, before being plastered with mud. As the population grew, a complex culture developed, with elaborate pottery, organized competitions on ceremonial ball courts, and a sophisticated understanding of mathematics and astronomy, which allowed them to expanded their canals and track crop cycles.

Just north, the Sinagua people were developing their own civilization, having expanded from northern Arizona into the Verde Valley and Sedona region in about AD 900. This complex society sustained itself by hunting, farming, and gathering indigenous plants. They constructed large hilltop villages made of rock and mud, as well as cliffside dwellings to shelter their communities. Unlike the earthen mounds of the Hohokam, these pueblo ruins still dot the high Sonoran Desert, as well as rocky outcroppings near Flagstaff. The Sinagua thrived from about 1100 to 1350, as they sat at the crossroads of several trade routes that stretched from California to the

petroglyphs

Four Corners region and the Hohokam villages in the south.

This Golden Age came to an abrupt end, however. Around 1400, the Hohokam and Sinagua civilizations began to collapse. The cause is a bit murky, although it may have been triggered by a combination of drought, floods, and perhaps internal strife. Some anthropologists have suggested that the civilizations had grown too large, too complex, and too interdependent to sustain themselves. With as many as 50,000 people living in Phoenix alone, the desert's resources may have been stretched beyond their limits. By the end of the 1400s, the Hohokam and Sinagua had abandoned their pueblos and canals, with some establishing compact farming villages scattered across the region and others blending into smaller tribes. The modern Pima (Akimel O'odham) trace their roots to the Hohokam, as do the Papago (Tohono O'odham), while the Hopi, Yavapai, and six other tribes consider the Sinagua to be their ancestors.

THE EUROPEANS ARRIVE

Spanish explorers, who first swept through the Sonoran Desert in the 16th century, seemed initially to be unimpressed with the region. That is, until tales of the Seven Cities of Gold began to circulate. In 1539, the viceroy of New Spain (now Mexico) organized a small expedition that included Friar Marcos de Niza, who returned with stories of a golden city that had homes decorated with jewels and semiprecious stones. A second expedition, headed by Francisco Vázquez de Coronado, was quickly dispatched and the two-year odyssey stretched to the Grand Canyon and as far away as present-day Kansas. In the end, it revealed the legendary golden cities to be nothing more than myths.

Coronado's failed expedition fizzled most interest in Arizona for 150 years, with the exception of a few explorers and missionaries, the most famous being Father Eusebio Francisco Kino, an Italian Jesuit who began his lifelong calling in 1687 to spread Catholicism through the Sonoran Desert. He introduced Native Americans to European plants, animals, and farming methods as he built a string of colonial missions, two of which became the first permanent European settlements in present-day southern Arizona. It was Padre Kino who mapped and named Phoenix's Salt River (Rio Salado), a moniker earned because of the salty taste of the water's high mineral content.

Mexico gained its independence from Spain in 1821 and a couple decades later, the Mexican-American War broke out. It ended in 1848, with Mexico ceding what is now the American Southwest, including most of Arizona, as a part of the Treaty of Guadalupe Hidalgo. The new Mexican-American population shaped much of the state's art, culture, and cuisine.

THE TERRITORIAL BOOM

In 1849, the California Gold Rush broke out. Prospectors, eager to strike it rich, flooded across Arizona, which was officially part of the New Mexico Territory. Boomtowns sprung up overnight, and calls to make Arizona a separate territory went unheeded as the country plunged into the Civil War. In 1862, residents made the bold move to form the Confederate Arizona Territory, which stretched across the southern half of the New Mexico Territory, giving Confederate troops in Texas access to California. However, Union troops easily seized control of the desert renegades, prompting the U.S. Arizona Territory, with its current boundaries, to be established the following year.

In 1867, former Confederate soldier Jack Swilling passed through the Salt River valley and decided that it looked like a good place for farming. The broad, fertile landscape was filled with desert grasses, mesquite, willow, and cottonwood trees, all fed by a wide, winding river, prompting the one-time scout, gold miner, cattle rancher, and saloon owner to return home to Wickenburg, a mining town about 50 miles northwest of present-day Phoenix, to seek financial backing. He got it from a group of local residents and organized a company to dig irrigation canals and establish farms. It wasn't long before he and the dozens of settlers who followed discovered that digging up the Hohokam canal system was an easier way to bring water to their fields than starting from scratch. It was his friend, British-born Lord Darrell Duppa, who suggested they name their new town Phoenix for the mythical bird that rises from its own ashes after being consumed by flame, a poetic tribute to the city's Hohokam roots.

It was still very much the Wild West in the Arizona Territory, however. Fort Verde was built in 1871 to house as many as 300 soldiers, who were stationed at the military outpost to protect Anglo settlers from Apache and Yavapai raiders, who at that time were being forced onto reservations. Just north, Jerome was founded in 1876 after prospectors filed the first mining claims. Workers arrived in droves, and soon saloons and brothels lined the streets, transforming the mining camp into a lively boomtown. By comparison, Swilling's Phoenix seemed a "proper" Victorian town, so much so that Arizona's territorial capital moved from Prescott in 1889, and in just a decade, the young city's population grew to 5,554. Shortly after the turn of the century, Arizona pioneers built a dusty stagecoach trail through the new town of Sedona, connecting the communities of Flagstaff and Prescott, and bringing the first regular tourists to the area.

STATEHOOD

By the early 20th century, Arizonans were clamoring for statehood. After rejecting a 1906 congressional decision that Arizona and New Mexico enter the Union as a single state, they took political matters into their own hands. In 1910, they elected 52 delegates (41 Democrats and 11 Republicans) to a state constitutional convention. Many of the representatives—who included Arizona's first governor, George W. P. Hunt, as well as Barry Goldwater's grandfather—had progressive, populist leanings. They drew up one of the nation's most liberal state constitutions, with provisions meant to give greater political voice to average Arizonans, including voter initiatives, referendums, and recalls. President William Howard Taft, who thought recalling judges would compromise judicial independence, threatened to veto Arizona's admission unless the provision was removed. It was, and Arizona was granted statehood. Voters, however, had the last laugh when they passed a constitutional amendment in the state's first general election in November 1912 that restored the controversial measure. It was Wild West democracy in action.

The Western landscape also created problems. Snowmelt and rain regularly sent the Salt River over its banks. Luckily, President Theodore Roosevelt was ready to ride to the rescue with a bold plan and several million dollars. Roosevelt tasked the newly formed federal Bureau of Reclamation with building a hydroelectric dam on the Salt River in 1911 to control flooding and generate electricity. It was the first project the new agency tackled, and the Roosevelt Dam tamed the free-flowing river by diverting the whole flow from its banks into an expanded canal system, leading to one of the city's first big boom periods. With an economy fueled by the "Five C's"—citrus, cotton, cattle, copper, and climate—Phoenix's population mushroomed to nearly 30,000 people by 1920, then added almost 20,000 more by 1930, matching the Hohokam's previous record of 50,000 inhabitants in just 50 years.

The state came of age during World War II with the bombing of the USS *Arizona* at Pearl Harbor. The Sonoran Desert's terrain was an ideal spot for training soldiers to fight in the deserts of North Africa, and thanks to the state's blue skies and open stretches of land, new airfields were constructed, 60 in all by the end of the war. Moreover, the large, land-locked state also provided space for the 23 prisoner-of-war camps scattered around Arizona, including one at Phoenix's Papago Park, which saw the largest mass escape of POWs in the U.S. during the war. When they weren't escaping, the German POWs helped with projects like canal maintenance and harvesting cotton crops. Also, due to the state's proximity to large Japanese-American populations in California, several Japanese relocation and work camps were built, including one just south of Phoenix on the Pima-Maricopa Indian reservation.

During this time, one of the most important pieces of legislation in American history was drafted by an Arizona senator, Ernest W. McFarland. The World War I veteran witnessed the poverty many servicemen were forced to endure after returning home and fought to pass a bill that granted tens of thousands of veterans financial assistance for education and housing. As the primary sponsor of the GI Bill, McFarland was a major force behind its unanimous passage in the Senate and House, although it's unlikely he anticipated the sweeping effects it would have on the nation when President Franklin D. Roosevelt signed the bill into law in 1944. McFarland eventually served in the state's three highest offices: U.S. senator, governor, and chief justice of the Arizona Supreme Court.

THE NEW LAND RUSH

In its early days, downtown Phoenix served as the city's commercial and residential district, surrounded by thousands of square miles of farmland and undeveloped desert. Its churches, theaters, and department stores attracted distant farmers and ranchers who would "go into town" for supplies and entertainment, all of which lent itself to a lively downtown familiar to most American cities. The postwar building boom changed all of that. Many servicemen, captivated by Arizona's climate and landscape while stationed at its many military training facilities, returned to Phoenix after the war with their Midwestern families and 1950s' expectations of a three-bedroom home and a green lawn. The Valley of the Sun's burgeoning housing industry was happy to oblige, and developers conjured up cookie-cutter track housing and large master-planned communities with amenities like parks and golf courses that appealed to young families as well as retirees.

As air-conditioning became widely available and early technology-manufacturing companies also moved to the city in search of cheap land, the population grew past 100,000 by 1950 and neared an almost-unimaginable 440,000 by 1960. Former agricultural land was quickly consumed by thousands of ranch houses, forcing new home-buyers further and further out into the suburbs. All of this sprawl and, some would argue, poorly managed growth has created a few unexpected consequences. A brown smog cloud often chokes the Valley's famed blue skies in the winter, and the dry desert air that once attracted health-seekers suffering from asthma and tuberculosis is now burdened in the spring with pollen from non-indigenous plants brought in from other parts of the country. Formerly independent towns and suburbs now blend from one into another, with regional malls and business districts that have sapped away much of downtown Phoenix's urban appeal.

Things are changing, however. Some 1.5 million people live in Phoenix, making it the country's sixth-largest city, and the U.S. Census Bureau estimates 4.1 million residents in all of Maricopa County. Many of these folks are driven by the same optimism and pioneering spirit that attracted the waves of settlers who preceded them, pushing these new Arizonans to dream up solutions to 21st-century problems. Phoenix, Scottsdale, and Sedona now seemed determined to harness their growth responsibly, forcing developers to be mindful of the desert landscape and developing green-minded enterprises like solar-powered energy. Downtown Phoenix is once again a center of activity, thanks to projects costing billions that include condos and hotel towers, restaurants, stadiums, museums, and a 20-mile light-rail system that many hope will curb the city's love affair with the automobile. And it's anyone's guess what seemingly impossible feats the residents of this dynamic city will tackle next—a looming water crisis likely tops the list. Nevertheless, Arizona's landscape has sparked hope, art, and opportunity for generations. Now its citizens are working to ensure it inspires generations more.

Barry Goldwater:
The Good, the Bad, and the Ugly

Arizona has had its share of rough-and-tumble politicians. At the top of the list stands the Grand Old Man of the Republican Party, Barry Goldwater, who brought Arizona into the national spotlight in the 1960s. The politically inclined might notice the famed U.S. senator's name etched onto the Phoenix airport's busiest terminal, but Goldwater's legacy extends far beyond the state's front door.

THE GOOD

Goldwater, with his trademark horn-rimmed glasses, ascended to the U.S. Senate in 1953. During his five terms and 30 years in Washington, the senator espoused a new form of conservatism. His politics carried a libertarian flare. Like most good Republicans, he valued a strong military and held a profound mistrust of the Soviet Union during the Cold War Era. But he did not defer to the Republican politics of personal choice and religion that so often define the GOP. He famously said of one well-known evangelist, "I think every good Christian should kick [Jerry] Falwell right in the ass."

THE BAD

In 1964, Goldwater proved his star status when he snagged the Republican nomination for president. Opposition was fierce; Lyndon B. Johnson branded Goldwater as an extremist and critics said he would bring the country to the brink of a nuclear war. Black voters turned on Goldwater after he voted against the Civil Rights Act of 1964, and the damage was done. Goldwater won his home state of Arizona, but only five others in the South, and the election ended in a landslide in Johnson's favor. After the drubbing, pundits said the Republican Party was doomed, fractured, and conservatism all but dead. Goldwater left office for four years after the election and remained largely out of the spotlight after his return to Washington.

THE UGLY

Barry Goldwater reemerged, however, during the Watergate crisis. As the call for Richard Nixon's resignation grew louder, Goldwater applied the pressure that presumably helped tip the scale. The senator visited Nixon at the White House and told the president that Congress could do nothing to stop his impeachment. Goldwater broke the news that few Senate Republicans still backed the president. He later said of the disgraced president, "Nixon was the most dishonest individual I have ever met in my life. He lied to his wife, his family, his friends, his colleagues in the Congress, lifetime members of his own political party, the American people, and the world."

THE LEGACY

Goldwater left the Senate for the final time in 1986. Twelve years later, at the age of 89, he died at his Paradise Valley home, in the early stages of Alzheimer's disease. Goldwater will be remembered for his individualism—as the one of the few politicians who was unafraid to speak his mind, even if it meant criticizing the power structure of his own party. Historians say that Goldwater's credo paved the way for Ronald Reagan's ascent to the White House in 1980. It's believed that a speech Reagan delivered on behalf of Goldwater during the 1964 campaign helped spark the future president's political career and ultimately allowed the next generation of conservatism to thrive. Today, numerous think tanks bear the senator's name, including the Goldwater Institute in Phoenix. These groups recall Goldwater's staunch belief in the Constitution and his principles of limited government as they shape public policy more than 50 years after Goldwater's rise.

Contributed by Peter O'Dowd, reporter/host, KJZZ

Government and Economy

GOVERNMENT

In its relatively short history, Arizona has experienced no shortage of political milestones, defining moments, or shameful antics. For instance, more than 80 years before Bush versus Gore, the state faced its own contentious court battle for chief executive. A gubernatorial battle broke out in 1916 when Arizona's first governor, George W. P. Hunt, demanded a recount after his challenger, Thomas Campbell, was declared the winner by 30 votes. Hunt refused to vacate the governor's chair and both men took the oath of office. The Arizona Supreme Court eventually settled the case, declaring Hunt the winner. However, both men would go on to serve multiple—and individual—terms as governor.

By the 1960s, Arizona's political titans were working hard to transform the Grand Canyon State into a national player. Morris "Mo" Udall took office in 1961 after winning the U.S. House seat vacated by his brother, Stewart, who had been appointed Secretary of the Interior by President John F. Kennedy. The Udall brothers, Representative John Rhodes, Senators Barry Goldwater and Carl Hayden, and Governor Paul Fannin formed a bipartisan group of political giants who reached across party lines and used their collective power to turn the state from a never-has-been into a united political power.

That's not to say there hasn't been scandal. When former car dealer Evan Mecham was removed from office in 1988, it extinguished a political firestorm that ignited almost as soon he was sworn in a year earlier. During his brief-but-infamous tenure, Mecham rescinded the Martin Luther King Jr. holiday, defended the use of the word "pickaninny," blamed women who worked for increasing divorce rates, and managed to insult most minority groups. With his impeachment came one bright spot: Arizona swore in its first female governor—and only the 10th in U.S.

history—Rose Mofford. Strangely, it wasn't her first time in the chair. During the early days of Governor Bruce Babbitt's 1988 presidential bid, Mofford served as acting governor while he campaigned out of state.

In fact, true to the state's Wild West roots, women have enjoyed a great deal of independence and opportunity in Arizona. They were granted the right to vote in the year of Arizona's statehood in 1912, eight years before the Nineteenth Amendment. In 1981, President Ronald Reagan made history—and fulfilled a campaign promise—when he appointed the first female Supreme Court Justice, Arizonan Sandra Day O'Connor. Following her groundbreaking confirmation, O'Connor emerged as one of the most influential voices on the Court, serving as a swing vote in many of its most controversial and closely watched cases, from abortion to affirmative action. Nearly two decades later, in 1998, Arizona made national headlines again when voters elected the country's first all-female line of succession: governor, secretary of state, attorney general, treasurer, and superintendent of public instruction. The media dubbed the unprecedented lineup the "Fabulous Five," which included then-Attorney General Janet Napolitano, who would later serve as governor and U.S. Secretary of Homeland Security.

Another important constituency has emerged. The release of the 2010 U.S. census heralded a demographic shift and strong new political voice in Arizona. Latinos accounted for 40 percent of Arizona's population that year, soaring from 25 percent in 2000, and the numbers are still on the rise. Latino voters will likely flex ever-more-considerable political influence in the coming decades, which is why they are being courted by both Republicans and Democrats. This group could prove to insert some blue into this state, which has historically remained staunchly red.

Arizona's Political Titans

ARIZONANS WHO MADE (UNSUCCESSFUL) BIDS FOR PRESIDENT

- Barry Goldwater, Republican: 1964
- Morris "Mo" Udall, Democrat: 1976
- Bruce Babbitt, Democrat: 1988
- John McCain, Republican: 2000 and 2008

CABINET MEMBERS

- Morris "Mo" Udall, Democrat: Secretary of the Interior, Kennedy Administration
- Bruce Babbitt, Democrat: Secretary of the Interior, Clinton Administration
- Janet Napolitano, Democrat: Secretary of Homeland Security, Obama Administration

SUPREME COURT JUSTICES

- William Rehnquist
- Sandra Day O'Connor

INFLUENTIAL POLITICAL AND MILITARY FIGURES

- Geronimo, Apache chief
- César Chávez, labor leader
- Pat Tillman, NFL football player and Afghanistan Silver Star recipient
- Gabriel Giffords, U.S. Representative

ECONOMY

The "Five C's"—copper, cotton, cattle, citrus, and climate—fueled Arizona's early economy, signifying the state's early reliance on agriculture and mining as its main economic engine. The Valley of the Sun became an important farming center, thanks to the canals originally built by the Hohokam and resurrected by Jack Swilling—so much so that, at one time, the state was the country's largest producer of cotton. Even the small farming community of Gilbert—now a Phoenix suburb of almost 250,000 people—produced enough alfalfa in its fields during World War I to earn the title "Hay Capital of the World." Today, Arizona can still call itself the "Copper State," with its mammoth open-pit and underground mines producing about two-thirds of nation's total yield of the peachy-gold metal.

Thanks to over 300 days of sunshine a year, it's possible to grow oranges and grapefruit, but the endless sunny days also mean dining alfresco, lying by the pool, and playing golf year-round—in short, tourism, which accounted for $21 billion in 2015. The sun may even be the basis of a new sustainable solar economy as the country searches for energy independence—a particularly critical need for this region, which is dependent on air-conditioning during the triple-digit summer months. High-tech innovation in the desert isn't new, though. After World War II, early technology manufacturing companies set up shop in Phoenix, including Motorola, which opened a research and development laboratory in 1948. Other computer-chip manufacturers and engineering firms followed, and within the past decade, Arizona political and business leaders have enticed medical research and biotechnology firms, such as TGen, to take the state's economy—and its health care—to new heights.

People and Culture

Phoenix is a city of immigrants, and that, perhaps more than any other factor, save the unrelenting sun, has shaped the city's character. Sydney has its convicts and Boston its Puritans. However, Phoenix was founded by a different breed: the pioneer. These trailblazing optimists left their homelands for the Wild West, an open frontier where opportunity and the promise of a better life outweighed the difficulties of a harsh terrain. And these expatriates continue to arrive in thousands every year, lured by warm winters or jobs in the high-tech and hospitality industries. They're all driven by a thirst for more and an independent spirit that's best embodied by the state's original icon, the cowboy, a figure that has come to represent not only Arizona, but also the Western attitude of "live and let live."

So many people have pulled up stakes and moved to the Valley of the Sun that residents like to joke that a native Phoenician is hard to find. Some newbies are initially tempted by the warm climate, moving to Phoenix to attend school at Arizona State University or to spend their years on the golf course. Even visitors popping in to see their college kids or retired parents can be easily seduced to make a move, not to mention the millions of tourists who travel to the state every year.

More than half of Arizona's 6.8 million residents live in the Greater Phoenix Metropolitan Area, and according to the 2010 U.S. Census Bureau results, about half are white, reflecting the city's changing demographics. Latinos make up most of the other half of the population. And although the city

Traditional Mexican mariachi music is revered in Phoenix.

Arizona State Facts

- **State Nickname:** The Grand Canyon State
- **Statehood:** February 14, 1912
- **Capital:** Phoenix
- **Area:** 113,998 miles
- **State Flower:** Saguaro cactus flower
- **State Bird:** Cactus wren
- **State Tree:** Palo verde
- **State Fossil:** Petrified wood
- **State Gemstone:** Turquoise
- **State Amphibian:** Arizona tree frog
- **State Reptile:** Arizona ridge-nosed rattlesnake
- **State Neckwear:** Bolo tie
- **Famous Arizonans:** Singer-songwriter Michelle Branch; actress Lynda Carter; rock star Alice Cooper; novelist Zane Grey; professional golfer Phil Michelson; jazz composer Charles Mingus; singer-songwriter Stevie Nicks; singer-songwriter Linda Ronstadt; comedian Garry Shandling; comedian David Spade; singer-actress Jordin Sparks; director Steven Spielberg; actress Emma Stone; and architect Frank Lloyd Wright

casinos, which have expanded in recent years to include resorts, restaurants, golf courses, amusement parks, and museums. Among them, the Gila River Indian Community spans 584 square miles south of Phoenix, from the Sierra Estrella in the West Valley to the communities of Florence and Coolidge in the east. The 11,000 members are from the Pima (Akimel O'odham) and the Maricopa (Pee-Posh) tribes. Its most famous son, Ira Hayes, was one of the five Marines depicted in the iconic 1945 photograph "Raising the Flag on Iwo Jima."

The Pima and the Maricopa also make their home on the Salt River Pima-Maricopa Indian Community just east of Scottsdale. Over 9,000 individuals are enrolled as tribal members, living on 52,000 acres surrounded by Scottsdale, Tempe, Mesa, and Fountain Hills. The adjacent Fort McDowell Yavapai Nation is bordered by McDowell Mountain Park and the Tonto National Forest. Its 950 members are one of three Yavapai tribes in Arizona. Just north, in the Verde Valley near Sedona, the Yavapai have also aligned with the Tonto Apache at the Yavapai-Apache Nation, where many of its 750 residents (out of 2,440 total enrolled tribal members) live on four non-contiguous parcels of land.

RELIGION

Arizona has a rich religious tradition, beginning with the spiritual practices of Native Americans who first worshipped in the region thousands of years ago. European missionaries introduced Catholicism to the Southwest in the 16th century, with Franciscan and Jesuit priests traveling throughout the Sonoran Desert to convert many of its indigenous people. Today, about 21 percent of Arizonans identify themselves as Catholic, according to the Pew Center, due in large part to the sizable Latino population. There are still cultural reminders in Arizona of the Southwest's unique style of Catholicism, which incorporates indigenous customs, such as Día de los Muertos, or Day of the Dead. Some Latino families celebrate the holiday October 31

still attracts retirees, only 16.4 percent of the population is over age 65. With job opportunities and cheap (by comparison to other major cities) real estate, younger people are moving to the Valley, which may help explain Scottsdale's vibrant nightlife scene.

Several Native American communities govern tribal land around Phoenix and Sedona. These sovereign tribes act in many ways like independent nations, with the right to form their own governments, try legal cases within their borders, and levy taxes. Although these communities still cling to their agricultural roots, many now own and operate successful through November 2 by visiting the graves of their ancestors or building small altars decorated with sugar skulls, artwork, flowers, and favorite foods. At Christmastime, luminarias, or small votive candles in paper bags, are lit to celebrate the holiday season.

As for the rest of Arizona, more than a third of the state is Protestant. About five percent of the population is Mormon, or members of the Church of Jesus Christ of Latter-day Saints. Mormon pioneers settled the East Valley town of Mesa in 1878, and the Valley of the Sun has the nation's largest concentration of Mormons outside of Utah. Also, there are small Jewish, Muslim, Buddhist, and Hindu populations throughout the state, but these account for just six percent of its population. New Age followers have flocked to Sedona in recent years as well, citing the area's "spiritual energy" and Native American traditions.

LANGUAGE

Language can be a hot topic in the Arizona desert, fueled largely by the controversial immigration debate that flares up on a regular basis in this border state. About 75 percent of Arizonans speak only English at home, with 13 percent speaking Spanish. In 2006, voters passed Proposition 103 to establish English as the official language for the state. Historically, the public school system's English as a Second Language (ESL) program often faced opposition and produced mixed results. Today, some schools offer language immersion programs that speak both English and Spanish, encouraging a bilingual approach for all students, although sadly these are few and far between. Travelers will hear Spanish spoken throughout the state, particularly in Phoenix, where Spanish-language media and billboards are fairly commonplace. Native American languages may be heard on Indian lands although almost all Native Americans in urban areas speak English.

THE ARTS

Arizona has been called lot of things—the Wild West, retirement haven, desert oasis, sweltering inferno—but "cultural hotbed" is not one of them. Oh, how wrong reputations can be. Even among the air-conditioned locals who frequent malls and big-box stores chains, the state's rich artistic tradition seems hidden, if not forgotten. The truth is, Arizona's rich cultural tradition reaches back thousands of years, beginning with the state's original inhabitants, Native Americans. Some of the 20th century's greatest artists produced work here, from Ansel Adams and Max Ernst to Frank Lloyd Wright, having been inspired by the dramatic Sonoran Desert landscape.

Today, there is a scrappy group of young artists who populate downtown Phoenix and Roosevelt Row; they fight tooth and nail to legitimize Phoenix and Arizona as home to a burgeoning art scene. You can see the fruits of their labor by visiting one of the art walks that take place on the first and third Fridays of every month, when galleries showcase local and national artists.

Arts and Crafts

Arizona's arts and crafts trace their origins back to the earliest Native American residents, who decorated rocks and everyday objects with graceful patterns and anthropomorphic images. Today, artisans continue the tradition, creating work that is firmly rooted in their tribal customs. That wasn't always the case, though. Following the postwar tourism boom, some Native American artisans began producing work that sightseers expected to see, such as spearheads, teepees, and mass-produced baskets. Fortunately, most have now abandoned this practice and are once again creating artwork in styles unique to their individual tribes. Some contemporary artists are moving beyond traditional imagery, which they dismiss as kitsch, and are pushing the definitions of Native American art by imagining innovative, contemporary pieces.

Buyers shopping for authentic Native American arts and crafts should keep a few things in mind. First, when possible, buy directly from the designer. There are markets and festivals throughout the year that feature

Native American artists, such as the Heard Museum's annual Indian Fair and Market. Ask about the materials and how pieces were made and be sure to get a certificate of authenticity. Quintessential arts and crafts include hand-woven baskets, turquoise jewelry, pottery, Navajo rugs and sand paintings, and Hopi kachina dolls, which have become more elaborate in recent years due to their popularity.

Architecture and Design

Arizona, and Phoenix in particular, suffered for years from a dearth of quality, geographically relevant architecture. Beginning with the Victorian buildings constructed in the original 1870s' Phoenix townsite, architects have tried to impose misappropriated styles onto the Sonoran Desert. It took one of the greats, Frank Lloyd Wright, to break them of the habit—or at least introduce them to relevant ways of designing for the desert. Wright took his cues from the architecture of ancient Native Americans, building with materials from the desert and designing buildings around the sun's orientation.

Phoenix grew big, quickly, and developers responded to demand by building large, faceless ranch houses in many of parts of the Valley. By the 1990s, though, architects—inspired by Wright and a group of midcentury Modernist designers like Al Beadle and Bennie Gonzales—pioneered a new style, Desert Modernism, which respected Phoenix's harsh summer climate. These minimalist buildings blend indoor and outdoor spaces, use innovative materials, and embrace the desert's hallmark light and space. The best-known example, the Will Bruder-designed Burton Barr Central Library, features a rectangular, rusted-steel facade that resembles a red-hued mesa. On the equinox, the sun shines directly through overhead skylights in the fifth-floor reading room, lighting its graceful, white columns.

Interior designers are also employing many of Wright's design techniques, banishing the howling coyotes, flute-playing Kokopelli icons, and pastel colors that had come to define Southwestern design in the 1980s. Instead, many of the Valley's best designers are now employing a subtler style that incorporates light as a central element. Large glass windows, natural stone and wood elements, and polished concrete floors that remain cool in the summer are turning posh restaurants and resorts into showplaces for chic desert style.

Literature

The myth of the West has proven to be a fertile source of literary inspiration. For generations, stories were often related orally, heightening their romance and intimacy. Native Americans would pass their histories and folklore from one generation to the next, while cowboys shared stories over campfires or whiskies. Novelist Zane Grey may not have been the first to put these tales to paper, but he was certainly one of the most prolific, having produced 60 books, from which 110 films were made. Many of them were set in Arizona and filmed in Sedona, like *Call of the Canyon*. Grey's popular stories portrayed an idealized version of the Old West, with big heroes and bigger landscapes.

Author and environmental essayist Edward Abbey, the "Thoreau of the American West," extolled the virtues of the Southwest and the occasionally radical means one might take to protect it in his works, *The Monkey Wrench Gang* and *Desert Solitaire*. These days, a new breed of Arizona writer is building on Grey's frontier legacy, with equally adventurous stories, albeit not in very different settings; examples include adventure writer Clive Cussler and Stephenie Meyer, author of the *Twilight* vampire series.

Essentials

Transportation................ 253

Travel Tips..................... 254

Health and Safety.............. 256

Information and Services 258

Transportation

AIR

Most visitors to the Valley of the Sun arriving by air land at **Phoenix Sky Harbor International Airport** (3400 E. Sky Harbor Blvd., 602/273-3300, www.skyharbor.com). It's one of the country's ten busiest airports in terms of traffic, with some 120,000 passengers arriving and departing every day. **American Airlines** (800/433-7300, www.aa.com) and **Southwest Airlines** (800/435-9792, www.southwest.com) account for most of Sky Harbor's traffic, although 14 other carriers provide service, including international airlines like **British Airways** (800/247-9297, www.britishairways.com) and **Air Canada** (888/247-2262, www.aircanada.com). The PHX Sky Train® connects Terminals 2, 3, and 4 (Terminal 1 was demolished in 1990), and visitors can also catch buses to the rental-car center and the light rail stop at 44th Street. Sky Harbor sits smack-dab in the middle of the Valley, just three miles east of downtown Phoenix and 20 minutes from Old Town Scottsdale. Two entrances link the airport to the city: one on the west side that connects to I-10 and 24th Street, and another on the east side that joins Highways 143 and 153 (44th Street) and Highway 202 (Loop 202).

Travelers arriving by private jet can use **Scottsdale Airport** (15000 N. Airport Dr., 480/312-2321, www.scottsdaleaz.gov/airport), a handy, headache-free option. This North Scottsdale airpark, a frequent choice of celebrities, is one of the busiest single-runway airports in the country. **Phoenix-Mesa Gateway Airport** (6033 S. Sossaman Rd., 480/988-7600, www.phxmesagateway.org) in east Mesa serves as a small hub for regional carrier **Allegiant Air** (702/505-8888, www.allegiantair.com), with service to northern parts of the country. As the Valley continues to grow, the airport will likely relieve growing congestion at Sky Harbor.

CAR

The car, in some ways, continues the grand tradition of exploring the West on horseback or by stagecoach, as it gives travelers the solitary experience of seeing the wide-open spaces that stretch between Arizona's towns and cities. That's the romantic take, at least. In truth, most visitors to Phoenix and Scottsdale will need a car, especially those planning to make the trip to Sedona. The Valley of the Sun is expansive, and unlike densely populated centers in New York and San Francisco, there is too much space and too little public transportation to see it all in an efficient manner. Embrace the spirit of the Great American Road Trip, and be prepared to spend some time behind the wheel when plotting trips to Jerome, Oak Creek Canyon, and Montezuma Castle.

Phoenix and Scottsdale were built with the car in mind. The streets follow an efficient and easy-to-navigate grid pattern that is interconnected by a large web of highways. The I-10 snakes from the southern part of the city, through downtown Phoenix, before heading to the West Valley. Highway 60, also called the Superstition Freeway, provides an important artery to the East Valley, which is encircled by Highway 202 (Loop 202). Its counterpart, Highway 101 (Loop 101), wends from Chandler to Tempe and Scottsdale, where it turns west and travels to the West Valley communities of Peoria and Sun City, before veering south through Glendale and connecting to the I-10. Finally, "the 51" freeway connects Central Phoenix to the northern part of the city and Highway 101 (Loop 101).

ESSENTIALS
TRANSPORTATION

Previous: the Valley Metro Light Rail in Phoenix; driving through Sedona.

This book covers only a small portion of the Grand Canyon State, and there is plenty to see within few hours' drive of Phoenix. Further afield, the I-10 connects Phoenix to Tucson in the south and Palm Springs and Los Angeles in the west. The scenic I-17 crosses Phoenix into the high deserts and grasslands of Camp Verde and Flagstaff, where you can catch other highways to the Grand Canyon and Las Vegas or to the other Four Corners states of New Mexico, Colorado, and Utah.

BUS

Greyhound (2115 E. Buckeye Rd., Phoenix, 602/389-4200, www.greyhound.com) provides bus services to major cities throughout the state and Southwest, although you will not find terminals in Scottsdale or Sedona. To reach Red Rock Country without a car, you can catch a shuttle service from Phoenix's Sky Harbor International Airport. **Arizona Shuttle** (800/888-2749, www.arizonashuttle.com) offers a direct link to the Village of Oak Creek and West Sedona.

Travel Tips

ECOTOURISM

It's only natural that tourists be mindful of the environment when visiting Arizona, as the state's main attraction is its rugged, yet surprisingly delicate, landscape. Increasingly, ecotourists—travelers who are drawn to a natural locale and try to minimize their environmental impact—are choosing to explore the Sonoran Desert. To capitalize on this movement and ensure that future generations are able to appreciate the desert, Arizona's tourism community has started to make green-minded changes to how they operate. For a statewide online resource with environmentally conscious travel ideas, including cultural attractions and outdoor activities, visit www.visitarizona.com/sustainability.

FOREIGN TRAVELERS

International travelers should expect a warm welcome to Arizona, although you will encounter some long lines and a little paperwork at immigration when entering the country. Citizens from most North American, European, and Latin American countries do not need a visa for stays up to 90 days. However, all international visitors, including Canadians, are required to show a passport valid for at least six months after your planned departure from the United States. For more information about visas and requirements to enter the U.S. through the Visa Waiver Program, visit the U.S. State Department's website at www.travel.state.gov.

Travelers exchanging foreign currency can do so at small kiosks inside the airport (two are located in Terminal 4) or at most banks. ATMs (automated teller machines) are also an option offering decent exchange rates but they often charge a small fee for the convenience. Be sure to inquire with your home bank to see if they charge an exchange fee, which usually ranges 1-2 percent. You'll find ATMs at a host of locations, including banks, shopping centers, and gas stations.

TRAVELERS WITH DISABILITIES

In the Valley of the Sun and Sedona, hotels, restaurants, attractions, and public transportation are easy to access, thanks in large part to the Americans with Disabilities Act. However, the Sonoran Desert's rugged terrain can be difficult to navigate. That said, many state and city parks have developed barrier-free, ADA-accessible trails, like the new **Gateway Trailhead at the McDowell Sonoran Preserve** (18333 N. Thompson

Ethical Travel

Travel is perhaps the most valuable means by which we learn about the world and our place in it. But as we explore red-rock buttes and marvel at ancient ruins, our consideration of the impact we make on the cultures and landscapes we encounter becomes increasingly important. Observe a responsible and sustainable approach to travel by following these guidelines:

· **Plan ahead and prepare:** Arriving with a sense of the social, political, and environmental issues at your destination makes your travels more meaningful. Educate yourself about the region's geography, customs, and cultures, and remember to respect local traditions.

· **Minimize your environmental impact:** Always follow designated trails. Do not disturb animals, plants, or their natural habitats. Learn about and support local conservation programs and organizations working to preserve the environment. Obey signage that designates closed areas.

· **Leave what you find:** Take only photographs. Leave only footprints. The impact of one person may seem minimal, but the global effect of removing items from their native place can be decimating.

Peak Rd., 480/998-7971, www.mcdowell-sonoran.org) in Scottsdale. Up north, Sedona's Jeep tours offer an excellent opportunity to explore Red Rock Country's monolithic buttes up close. The off-the-highway trails can get quite bumpy, so those with disabilities may want to request a front seat, which offers some neck and back support. The National Parks Service also offers free admission to visitors with permanent disabilities. The lifetime **America the Beautiful—National Parks and Federal Recreational Lands Pass Access Pass** (www.nps.gov) includes Arizona sights like Montezuma Castle. The passes are available at all national parks or through the mail, and documentation is required.

TRAVELING WITH CHILDREN

With summer comes the all-important family vacation, and travelers with children shouldn't let the heat detour them from planning a trip to Arizona. In fact, most kids will revel in the season's prime attraction: the swimming pool. Families can easily spend days by the pool or at the Valley's three major water parks, which offer mammoth wave pools, multistoried slides, and lazy rivers for tubing. Most of the big resorts have built their own water parks, and the hotels offer adults a bit of respite thanks to well-organized kids' camps, which pack days full with morning hikes, arts and crafts, trips to the pool, and games in air-conditioned clubhouses. The whole family can enjoy a rafting trip on the Salt River, northeast of Phoenix. These outdoor adventures are nothing more than a leisurely float, as the rapids never exceed a Class I (almost no white water). There are also kid-approved museums like the interactive Arizona Science Center and the Children's Museum of Phoenix.

In the cooler months, the state's parks and easy hiking trails can be fun to explore, especially on horseback. Phoenix Zoo delights kids with birds, slithering reptiles, and furry mammals as well as a small petting area and the walk-through Monkey Village. For a taste of the Wild West, Rawhide Western Town delivers 1880s'-themed family fun, with stunt shows, stagecoach rides, and old-fashioned chuck-wagon cookouts under the stars. And if you plan to head north, Sedona may not wow the little ones, but older kids and teenagers will appreciate the bouncy Jeep tours and dozens of mountain-biking trails.

SENIOR TRAVELERS

Arizona's blissfully warm weather makes the state a popular destination for seniors, particularly active travelers who hit tennis courts, swimming pools, and the more than 200 golf courses. In the summer, people can avoid the extreme heat at the half-dozen casinos scattered around the Valley on Native American lands. Most Phoenix, Scottsdale, and Sedona attractions offer discounts for seniors, including the Desert Botanical Garden, which is an excellent opportunity to survey the Sonoran Desert's diverse plant life without having to leave paved sidewalks. Travelers aged 62 and older can obtain a **Senior Pass** that grants lifetime access to all national parks from the National Park Service. It can be purchased for $10 at any national park (www.nps.gov), online, or through the mail.

GAY AND LESBIAN TRAVELERS

Like most major metropolitan areas, the Valley has an active gay community centered around Central Phoenix, where travelers will find many of the city's gay-friendly restaurants and bars, including those on Central and 7th Avenues, between Indian School and Camelback Roads. The **Greater Phoenix Gay & Lesbian Chamber of Commerce** (602/266-5055, www.phoenixgaychamber. com) is a convenient resource for travelers, producing an online business directory that lists hotels and restaurants, as well as a thorough relocation guide for new transplants. *Echo Magazine* (www.echomag.com) provides news and information on upcoming events.

Health and Safety

SUN AND HEAT

Phoenix is called the Valley of the Sun for good reason. With more than 300 days of sunshine a year, the warm rays of light can be hard to avoid—not that winter visitors trying to escape frozen climates find that a problem. Still, the Sonoran Desert's powerful sun shouldn't be underestimated, particularly in the summer, when in late afternoon the sun's UV rays are most intense, causing fair skin to burn in less than 10 minutes. Excessive exposure can cause real, and potentially fatal, health problems. Fortunately, it's all quite avoidable.

Shield yourself from the sun by covering up. Try to wear protective clothing, like long-sleeved shirts and pants. The sun easily damages sensitive skin on your face and neck, so be sure to bring a broad-rimmed hat and sunglasses when you are planning to spend extensive time outside, like on the golf course or while hiking. Poolside, long sleeves and pants may seem unreasonable, which makes a sunscreen with a high SPF a crucial ingredient. Be

sure to slather on a thick coat 15 minutes before going out and reapply throughout the day. Also, seek shade when possible and get out of the sun occasionally. It's best to avoid the sun during the hottest part of the day, from 11am to 3pm, when the UV rays are at their peak.

Although everyone is at risk of getting **sunburnt,** no matter the skin tone, fair-skinned people and children are particularly susceptible. In fact, those with light skin, blue or green eyes, blond or red hair, freckles, or moles are at a greater risk of skin cancer. Should a burn occur, cool the skin by applying ice or taking a cold shower or bath. Apply an alcohol-free aloe vera gel and stay out of the sun.

The desert's hot, arid climate can take its toll on the body in other ways. You may not even feel particularly sweaty in Arizona, especially compared to more humid climates, but perspiration evaporates quickly in the dry air, depleting the body of moisture and leading to **dehydration.** Drink lots of water, about a gallon a day in the summer or when outside for long periods of time. Many Phoenicians carry a bottle of water with them and instinctively drink throughout the day. On the golf course, you'll see lots of drinking fountains and giant water coolers—take advantage of them. Again, try to limit exertion during the hottest parts of the day.

Should you find yourself dizzy, weak, or nauseated, it may be **heat exhaustion,** which is caused when the body is unable to replace fluids. Other symptoms include sweating profusely, paleness, muscle cramps, headaches, and fainting. Find a cool place immediately, sit down, and drink a beverage with electrolytes, like Gatorade. If the body is unable to cool down, it may suffer from **heatstroke,** a potentially fatal form of hyperthermia. Heat stroke is often marked by the body reaching 104°F and an inability to sweat or release heat. The skin may be red or hot to the touch. Also, look for an increased heart rate, dizziness, fatigue, unconsciousness, or convulsions. Get immediate medical help, and try to cool the body down with water, ice, or cold compresses. Staying hydrated and avoiding the extreme heat will stave off these serious ailments. Bottom line: If you are out in the heat and start feeling weird, get yourself hydrated immediately and into a cooler environment.

Heat exhaustion can turn to heatstroke very quickly and it's nothing to take lightly.

FLOODS, LIGHTNING, AND DUST STORMS

The Sonoran Desert's weather, like its landscape, can be severe. Blue, sunny skies can quickly turn ominous when a storm rolls across the horizon, with sheets of rain and forked bolts of lightning. During monsoon season, a wall of dust may even move in from the desert and sweep across the city with impressive speed, with not a drop of rain despite a perceptible increase in moisture. These powerful storms are intense displays of the desert's strength, and they can leave motorists, golfers, and swimmers scurrying for cover. Should one of these climatic events occur, don't take any chances. Immediately get out of a swimming pool or any body of water if you see lightning or even hear thunder. You should also abandon any mountain biking or hiking expeditions (heights!) or rounds of golf (metal clubs!).

Even residents fail to use their best judgment and learn from the experiences of others. Quick deluges can dump inches of rain on the dry desert floor, which is unable to absorb that much water so quickly. As a result,

ESSENTIALS HEALTH AND SAFETY

A dust storm rolls into Phoenix

usually dry washes become swiftly moving rivers, trapping cars that attempt to cross them. Freeways can become makeshift canals, filling with water and stranding commuters. When pouring rain or dust storms limit visibility, pull over to the side of the road and wait for conditions to improve, as most storms sweep through quickly.

REPTILES, SCORPIONS, AND BEES

Most travelers don't mind a little sun or rain, but nothing makes a tourist second-guess a trip to Arizona more than the creepy-crawlies that bite (or sting) in the Sonoran Desert. If you stay on trails and use good judgment when hiking, a painful encounter with a snake or insect is unlikely. Keep an eye out for rattlesnakes, although you may be more likely to hear their rattling tails first. They usually don't attack unless they are foolishly provoked, so simply keep a safe distance from the slithering desert dwellers and move along.

Scorpions tend to hide under rocks or in holes, and they typically sting people when they are inadvertently touched. If you're particularly concerned about scorpions, shake out your shoes before putting them on and pay attention to what you grab when exploring the desert. Gila monsters are also venomous, but bites from these slow-moving creatures are rare. In fact, many natives can live a lifetime in the desert without ever seeing a Gila monster.

Many people fear scorpions and reptiles but the reality is, bees are the bigger threat. You'll notice signs along hiking trails marking areas that are heavy with bees. Especially in the spring, hives and swarms can pose a threat to outdoor adventurers. If you're allergic, carry that epinephrine auto-injector (epi-pen). If you have the misfortune of being caught in an attack by a bee swarm, your best bet is to cover your head and run as fast as you can toward safety.

If you're stung or bitten by any poisonous desert dweller, don't panic. Remove constricting jewelry and limit movement of the affected area in order to minimize venom from flowing into the rest of the bloodstream. Seek medical attention immediately.

Information and Services

MAPS AND TOURIST INFORMATION

The **Arizona Office of Tourism** (1110 E. Washington St., Ste. 155, Phoenix, 602/364/3700, www.visitarizona.com) is happy to help visitors plan a trip to the Grand Canyon State, and its comprehensive guide and website, which includes videos and slide shows, are excellent resources for tailoring a trip to your individual interests. The **Greater Phoenix Convention & Visitors Bureau** (602/254-6500, www.visitphoenix.com) offers loads of information for visitors and new residents about the Valley of the Sun. It's located in the **Downtown Phoenix Visitor Information Center** (125 N. 2nd St., Ste. 120, 8am-5pm Mon.-Fri.), conveniently situated in the heart of downtown.

In Scottsdale, **Experience Scottsdale** (800/782-1117, www.experiencesscottsdale.com) distributes useful information to help you plan a customized trip to the city. Visit the extensive website (with some of the most over-the-top promotional art you'll ever see) or stop by its Visitor Center at the **Galleria Corporate Centre** (4343 N. Scottsdale Rd., Ste. 170, 8am-5pm Mon.-Fri.), where over 400 brochures and interactive iPads await to help you plan your trip. You can also pick up materials from the Tourist Information Center at **Scottsdale Fashion Square** (7014 E. Camelback Rd., 9am-5pm Mon.-Sat.,

Local Media

NEWSPAPER

- *The Arizona Republic*
- *Phoenix New Times (Alt Weekly)*

NATIONAL PUBLIC RADIO

- KJZZ 91.5 FM

TELEVISION

- 3 KTVK (Independent)
- 5 KPHO (CBS)
- 8 KAET (PBS)
- 10 KSAZ (FOX)
- 12 KPNX (NBC)
- 15 KNXV (ABC)
- 45 KUTP (FOX)
- 61 KASW (CW)
- 39 KTAZ (Telemundo)

10am-4pm Sun. Oct.-May, 10am-4pm daily Jun.-Sept.).

The **Sedona Chamber of Commerce** (331 Forest Rd., 928/282-7722 or 800/288-7336, www.visitsedona.com, 8:30am-5pm daily) has a convenient office in Uptown that supplies visitors with maps, directions, and suggestions for getting the most out of their time in Sedona. You can also purchase a Red Rock Pass here. The expanded **Red Rock Visitor Center and Ranger Station** (8375 S.R. 179, 928/203-2900, www.fs.usda.gov/coconino, 9am-4:30pm daily), just south of the Village of Oak Creek, may be a more convenient option if you are driving in from Phoenix.

Arizona's top attraction is its incredible landscape, and there seems to be a stunning formation or unique geological feature off every highway exit. To chart out the state's national parks and monuments, visit the website for the **National Park Service** (www.nps.gov/state/az). Not to be outdone, the **Arizona State Parks** system (602/542-4174, www.azstateparks.com) is among the best in the country. Learn more about the parks' diverse habitats and natural attractions by visiting the website.

AREA CODES AND TIME ZONES

The Grand Canyon State has five area codes, three of which are dedicated to the Phoenix metropolitan area: 602 for Phoenix proper, 623 for the West Valley, and 480 for the East Valley, including Scottsdale. Sedona and the rest of northern Arizona are assigned 928, while Tucson and southern Arizona were given 520.

Free-spirited Arizona is never one to be told what to do by the rest of the country, and that sentiment extends to something as basic as time. Officially, the state is a part of the Mountain Standard Time (MST) zone, along with Utah, Colorado, New Mexico, Wyoming, Idaho, and Montana. Unlike the rest of its western brethren, however, Arizona does not observe daylight saving time, and instead of its clock springing forward in March, it instead syncs up with Pacific Daylight Time (PDT). Why the difference? Well, in the hot desert, the last thing Arizonans need is more daylight. The extra hour of darkness at night means residents can take advantage of cooler temperatures earlier in the evening. With this arrangement, the clock never changes during the year in Arizona.

There is one exception to the exception: The Navajo reservation, which takes up a sizable portion of the northeastern part of Arizona, does observe daylight saving time, so that all of its land, which stretches into the neighboring Four Corners states, is on the same schedule.

Resources

Glossary

Arizona shares a border with Mexico and has a shared history with native peoples. With that comes delicious food and gorgeous customs and a whole lotta hilarious mispronunciations of many words. Here's a guide to build your confidence when navigating these southwest towns (and their restaurant menus).

adobe (ah-DOH-bee): earthen building material, usually formed into bricks and dried in the sun

agua fresca (AH-wa FRES-cah): literally, "fresh water," referring to a beverage made with an infusion of mashed fruits or herbs and lightly sweetened

Anasazi (Ah-na-SAH-zee): a prehistoric farming culture in the Four Corners region; Ancestral Puebloan is preferred

ancho chile (AHN-cho CHILL-ee): a dried poblano chile that has turned a deep black-red color; its smoky-sweet flavor is found in many dishes

arroyo (ah-ROH-yo): a dry gully or small wash

asada (ah-SAH-dah): broiled over hot coals or roasted, such as carne asada

bajada (ba-HA-da): a sloping plain formed by the gravelly runoff that fans out from the base of a desert mountain range

camarón (cah-mah-ROHN): shrimp

carne (CAR-nay): meat, usually beef

cerveza (ser-VAY-sah): beer, the most popular Mexican brands in Arizona being Corona, Dos Equis, Modelo, Pacifico, and Tecate

ceviche (seh-VEE-chay): citrus-marinated seafood, raw or cooked, and tossed with spices and vegetables, like onions, chilies, and tomatoes

chile relleno (CHILL-ee ray-YAY-no): a mild green chile stuffed with cheese, lightly fried, and topped with a spicy red sauce

chimichanga (chih-mee-CHAHN-gah): a deep-fried burrito filled with meat and typically garnished with lettuce, salsa, sour cream, and guacamole

chipotle (chih-POHT-lay): a hot, smoke-dried jalapeño chile pepper

cholla (CHOY-ah): any of several shrubby cactus with cylindrical stems that drop segments easily (also known as "jumping cactus"

chorizo (CHOH-ree-zoh): a spicy pork (or sometimes beef) sausage, flavored with chilies and spices

cilantro (SIH-lahn-troh): a fresh, slightly spicy herb used in salsas and as garnish

cotija (coh-TEE-ha): an aged, crumbly white Mexican cheese

elote (eh-LOH-tay): roasted corn on the cob, often topped with butter, *cotija* cheese, lime juice, and chile pepper

empanada (em-pah-NAH-da): a baked pastry filled with meat, cheese, or fruit

enchiladas (en-chih-LAH-das): corn or flour tortillas, dipped in red sauce and wrapped around shredded beef, chicken, or cheese; they are topped with more red sauce and cheese, and then baked

fajitas (fah-HEE-tas): grilled beef or chicken, served on a sizzling platter with onions and green peppers; warm flour tortillas and fresh tomatoes and lettuce accompany the dish

flauta (FLOU-tah): a flour or corn tortilla

stuffed with chicken or beef, then deep-fried

frijoles (free-HO-lays): beans, typically pinto or black; most dishes come with a side of frijoles, the most common being refried beans, which are fried, mashed, and "refried" with lard

Gila (HEE-lah): Probably a mix of Spanish and Yuman, Gila refers to a river that flows across Arizona, its valley or region, and the Indian reservation along part of the river.

habanero (hah-bah-NEH-roh): Mexico's hottest pepper, used sparingly; adds a feisty kick to salsas and dishes

helado (eh-LAH-do): ice cream

Hohokam (ho-HO-kum): Arizona's prehistoric desert culture, from the Pima (Akimel O'odham) *huhugam*, meaning "all used up"

horchata (or-CHAH-tah): a sweet, vanilla-and-cinnamon-flavored drink made with ground rice and water or milk

huevo (WAY-voh): egg

huevos rancheros (WAY-vose rahn-CHAIR-ohs): eggs, ranch-style—fried or scrambled eggs, topped with a red chile sauce or chunky salsa; served with tortillas and beans

huitlacoche (weet-lah-CO-chay): corn smut or corn truffle, a delicacy that is sometimes used as a taco stuffing

machaca (mah-CHA-ca): shredded beef

mariscos (mah-REE-skos): seafood, usually shellfish

masa (MAH-sah): a traditionally stone-ground corn dough, used in tamales

menudo (meh-NOO-doh): a spicy, chunky soup flavored with chiles, tripe, onion, and spices; routinely served with warm tortillas and fresh avocado and lime

mesa (MAY-sah): literally, "table," referring also to a flat-topped landform

mole (MOH-lay): a rich, dark sauce made with chilies, Mexican chocolate, nuts, fruit, spices, and vegetables

nopales (noh-PAHL-lays): prickly pear cactus pads that are stripped of their spines and then grilled or boiled; they're added to soups, served like fries, or stuffed into tacos

paleta (pah-LAY-tah): ice pops, a frozen treat often made with fruit

panela (pah-NAY-lah): cane sugar

panadería (pah-nah-day-REE-ah): a Mexican-style bakery

pico de gallo (PEE-coh dah GUY-yoh): a fresh chunky salsa, made from chopped tomato, onion, chiles, and cilantro

poblano (POH-blah-no): a dark-green, fresh chile pepper that is very mild

pollo (POY-yoh): chicken

posole (pah-SOHL-lay): a hearty, moderately spicy soup with pork or chicken, hominy, onions, and spices; a delicious red stew sometimes garnished with cabbage, radish, onion, avocado, and lime juice

pueblo (PWEB-loh): literally, "people," but also used to refer to a village

puerco (PWEAR-coh): pork

queso (KAY-soh): cheese

saguaro (sah-WAH-ro): a columnar and often branched cactus growing up to 60 feet tall, endemic to the Sonoran Desert

serrano chile (seh-RAH-no chill-ee): a small green chile from northern Mexico that can be quite hot; used in moderation in a host of dishes and salsas

slickrock: bare rock, usually sandstone

talus: loose rocks, usually sloping

tamale (TAH-mah-lay): masa dough, stuffed with meat or vegetables, wrapped in a corn-husk and steamed

taquería (tah-kay-REE-ah): a casual restaurant that specializes in Mexican "street food" like tacos and burritos

tomatillo (toh-mah-TEE-yo): a fruit similar in appearance to a small, green tomato; its bright, acidic flavor adds a pleasant punch to many dishes and salsas

torta (TORR-tah): a crusty Mexican sandwich, served hot or cold, and filled with any number of ingredients

tostada (tos-TAH-dah): a flat, fried corn tortilla topped with layer of beans, meat, lettuce, tomato, cheese, and salsa

Suggested Reading

HISTORY

Buscher, Linda, and Dick Buscher. *Historic Photos of Arizona*. Nashville, TN: Turner Publishing Company, 2009. See how early pioneers, soldiers, and frontier families lived in the Wild West. The collection of 200 rare and historical images begins with Arizona's territorial days in 1850s and moves through statehood and the postwar population boom.

Dutton, Allen A. *Arizona: Then & Now*. Englewood, CO: Westcliffe Publishers, 2002. Get a sense of Arizona's dramatic evolution from the 19th century to the 20th. Historical photographs, stories, and essays document the Grand Canyon State's cities and towns, mining industry, and railroads, as well as the ranching and farming traditions.

Johnson, James W. *Arizona Politicians: The Noble and the Notorious*. Tucson, AZ: University of Arizona Press, 2002. A former University of Arizona journalism professor sketches colorful portraits of the politicians who shaped the state and the country, including Barry Goldwater, Mo and Stewart Udall, Bruce Babbitt, John McCain, William Rehnquist, Sandra Day O'Connor, and disgraced former governors Evan Mecham and Fife Symington.

Lauer, Charles D. *Arrows, Bullets, and Saddle Sores: A Collection of True Tales of Arizona's Old West*. Phoenix, AZ: Golden West Publishers, 2005. The Wild West was built on a rich tradition of storytelling, from Native American myths to cowboy yarns. Learn about the events from the real West, including street-clearing gunfights, outlaw gangs, fatal poker games, stolen gold, and dirt-floored prisons.

Martin, Douglas D. *An Arizona Chronology: The Territorial Years, 1846-1912*. Tucson, AZ: University of Arizona Press, 1963. They didn't call it the Wild West for nothing. Learn how Arizona evolved from Mexican territory to America's 48th state.

Trimble, Marshall. *Roadside History of Arizona*. Missoula, MT: Mountain Press Publishing Company, 2004. Arizona's state historian takes a road-trip approach to exploring the Grand Canyon State's past. Because it's organized geographically and along highways, travelers can easily cruise to cultural sites, like old missions and Civil War battlefields.

NATIVE AMERICANS

Betancourt, Marian, Michael O'Dowd, and Jack Strong. *The New Native American Cuisine: Five-Star Recipes from the Chefs of Arizona's Kai Restaurant*. Dallas, TX: Three Forks Press, 2009. Only a handful of restaurants in the U.S. have earned AAA's Five Diamond rating and Mobil's Five Star designation, but it's little surprise given the innovative and elegant cuisine at Kai Restaurant at the Sheraton Grand at Wild Horse Pass Resort. Try out some of the Native American-inspired recipes at home, including those for cocktails, soups, salads, deserts, and entrées like grilled elk chop with truffles and sweet corn panna cotta with venison carpaccio.

Circle of Light Navajo Education Project. *Our Fathers, Our Grandfathers, Our Heroes... The Navajo Code Talkers of World War II: A Photographic Exhibit*. Gallup, NM: Circle of Light Navajo Education Project, 2004. This rich collection of photographs chronicles the incredible story of the Navajo Code Talkers, who transmitted U.S. Marine Corps messages in their native language during World War II. See the letters documenting the program's inception, newspaper clippings, a guide to the Navajo language, and historic photos of recruitment visits to the reservation and scenes from the Pacific Theater battlefields.

Hodge, Carle. *Ruins Along the River: Montezuma Castle, Tuzigoot, and Montezuma National Monuments.* Tucson, AZ: Western National Parks Association, 1986. Explore the rich history and heritage of the Sinagua people and how they were able to build a series of impressive monuments that still stand as a testament to their sophisticated civilization.

LITERATURE AND MEMOIRS

Guerrero, Pedro E. *Pedro E. Guerrero: A Photographer's Journey with Frank Lloyd Wright, Alexander Calder, and Louise Nevelson.* New York, NY: Princeton Architectural Press, 2007. Guerrero, a Mexican-American and Arizona native, documents the lives and work of some of the giants of the 20th-century art world. Here, 190 black-and-white photographs—some of them iconic images—tell the stories of these artists and the midcentury modernist movement that flourished during the photographer's heyday as well as Guerrero's incredible, seemingly impossible life.

McCain, John, and Mark Salter. *Worth the Fighting For.* New York, NY: Random House, 2002. Following his release from imprisonment in Vietnam, John McCain returned home to the U.S. and launched his formidable political career, which has included two-plus decades in Congress and two bids for the presidency. In this autobiography, the Grand Canyon State's senior senator shares profiles of the mavericks who inspired him: Theodore Roosevelt, Ernest Hemingway, Ted Williams, and Marlon Brando.

Notaro, Laurie. *The Idiot Girls' Action-Adventure Club: True Tales from a Magnificent and Clumsy Life.* New York, NY: Villard, 2002. The hilarious writer chronicles a world of hourly

wage jobs, Phoenix's subcultures, high-school reunions, and hangovers that leave her surprised she woke up in the first place.

O'Connor, Sandra Day, and H. Alan Day. *Lazy B: Growing up on a Cattle Ranch in the American Southwest.* New York, NY: Random House, 2005. The former Supreme Court justice and her brother recount their lives growing up on an Arizona ranch near the New Mexican border, highlighting how their parents, fellow cowhands, and the environment taught them hard lessons and fundamental values. The warm, engaging memoir demonstrates how the Arizona landscape forged one of the country's greatest minds.

NATURE

Bearce, Neil R. *Minerals, Fossils, and Fluorescents of Arizona: A Field Guide for Collectors.* Tempe, AZ: Arizona Desert Ice Press, 2006. Arizona's vast mineral wealth is a dream for rockhounds, and this guide to the state's geological treasures provides advice and maps on where to find agates and geodes, amethysts and malachite. For those new to rock hunting, there are photos and a thorough outline of mineral basics, like shape, size, and color as well as a how to primer on scavenging.

Johnson, Tom, and Hoyt C. Johnson. *Sedona: The Most Uniquely Beautiful Site on Earth.* Sedona, AZ: Sedona Publishing Company, 1998. A picture's worth a thousand words, and it's the only way to truly comprehend Sedona's incredible beauty on the printed page. Discover the region's red rocks, stunning formations, and craggy canyons as well as its fall leaves and springtime flowers.

Epple, Anne Orth, John F. Wiens, and Lewis E. Epple (photographer). *Plants of Arizona.* Guilford, CT, and Helena, MT: Falcon Guides, 2012. Full-color photographs organized by the color of flower; there's no easier way to navigate the many plants in the state.

This is an essential guide for all plants and includes a complete section specific to cacti.

Menconi, Lilia. *Take a Hike Phoenix*. Berkeley, CA: Avalon Travel, 2013. Hiking is a huge attraction in Phoenix and this guide offers the best "to-do" list available, with over 80 hikes within a two-hour drive of the city. It also includes a chapter for high-country hikes including the Sedona, Flagstaff, Prescott, and Payson areas.

PHOENIX

Ellin, Nan. *Phoenix: 21st Century City*. London, UK: Booth-Clibborn Editions, 2006. The richly photographed book chronicles Phoenix's evolution into a cosmopolitan metropolis, replete with cutting-edge architecture, a burgeoning fashion scene, modern design, and vibrant public art. Local writers, photographers, and designers create a rich tapestry that documents the city's cultural evolution.

Scharbach, Paul, and John H. Akers. *Phoenix: Then and Now*. San Diego, CA: Thunderbay Press, 2005. A fascinating before-and-after look at the Valley's growth, the well-illustrated book contrasts historical images against contemporary shots of Phoenix, Tempe, Mesa, and Glendale. The consistent theme: growth.

Talton, Jon. *A Brief History of Phoenix*. Charleston, SC: Arcadia Publishing and The History Press, 2015. Phoenix was once home to one of the most advanced prehistoric societies. Fast-forward to today and it's the sixth-largest city in the United States. This quick history tells how the desert was tamed to support the two cultures (and everyone in between).

TRAVEL

Kramer, Jon, Julie Martinez, and Vernon Morris (illustrator). *Arizona Journey Guide: A Driving & Hiking Guide to Ruins, Rock Art, Fossils, and Formations*. Cambridge, MN: Adventure Publications, Inc., 2007. A full-color photographic and illustrated guide to the "greatest hits" of sights the state has to offer. Most destinations listed can be reached by car and the book offers a comprehensive list for sites of amazing archaeology, geology, and paleontology.

Lindahl, Larry. *Secret Sedona: Sacred Moments in the Landscape*. Phoenix, AZ: Arizona Highways, 2005. Sedona's red-hued landscape takes center stage in this lavishly illustrated book, with stunning photography and poetic descriptions that showcase the region's massive formations, ancient Native American history, and rich geology and wildlife.

Lowe, Sam. *Arizona Curiosities: Quirky Characters, Roadside Oddities, & Other Offbeat Stuff*. Guilford, CT: The Globe Pequot Press, 2007. Lowe, a former Arizona newspaperman, provides a humorous survey of the Grand Canyon State's kooky history, people, and roadside attractions. Most Arizonans don't know even half of the oddball stories, which cover concrete religious shrines, alien abductions, and "wild" burros that roam the streets of one town.

Naylor, Roger. *Boots and Burgers: An Arizona Handbook for Hungry Hikers*. Tucson, AZ: Rio Nuevo Publishers, 2014. This small guide outlines the best of the best, assuming you're a hiker and carnivore, that is. Roger Naylor presents some fabulous destinations for hitting the dirt then hitting a nearby diner to fuel up. With his entertaining voice and enthusiasm for Arizona, the guide covers the entire state.

Treat, Wesley. *Weird Arizona: Your Travel Guide to Arizona's Local Legends and Best Kept Secrets*. New York, NY: Sterling, 2007. Uncover the Wild West's weird and wacky side, from outlaws and outhouses to rattlesnake-inspired bridges.

Internet Resources

TOURISM SITES

Arizona Office of Tourism
www.arizonaguide.com
Featuring video tours, itinerary options, travel deals, and a calendar of events, the AOT website is a valuable resource and great place to start planning your visit.

Arizona State Parks
azstateparks.com
A guide to the Grand Canyon State's myriad parks, plus volunteer programs, events, and reservations for campsites. Also includes weather-forecast information and directions on obtaining an annual parks pass.

Jerome Chamber of Commerce
jeromechamber.com
For all things Jerome, check this site to help guide you on your day or overnight trip to this tiny ghost town. Upcoming events, history, hotels, restaurants, and more are on the site.

Visit Phoenix
www.visitphoenix.com
Visit Phoenix provides news and information on everything from golf to accommodations to LGBT resources. The site also hosts a blog called The Hot Sheet, which will "help you experience our city like a true Phoenician."

Experience Scottsdale
www.experiencescottsdale.com
A comprehensive website for all things Scottsdale: attractions, shopping, resorts, and hotels as well as special packages available year-round. Visitors can book their entire trip at this one-stop shop.

Sedona Chamber of Commerce
www.visitsedona.com
The definitive site for visiting Red Rock Country. You'll also find helpful information and assistance if you plan on getting married in Sedona.

Sedona Verde Valley Tourism Council
sedonaverdevalley.com
This visitor guide and information center covers the area surrounding Sedona, including Jerome and Camp Verde, and provides suggestions for arts and cultural activities, along with news on events and festivals, hotels, dining, shopping, and tours.

NEWS AND CULTURE

Arizona's Family
www.azfamily.com
Local television station 3TV's website features news, entertainment, and weather and traffic information. Slideshows and readers' photos make this hometown site a real Arizona "family" affair.

azcentral
www.azcentral.com
The website for *The Arizona Republic* newspaper, azcentral covers news in the nation and the world, along with the latest in local sports, food, and the weather, plus a "Things to Do" link that serves as an essential resource for tourists.

KJZZ
www.kjzz.org
Phoenix's National Public Radio station (KJZZ 91.5 FM) offers this multimedia website, a great resource to learn more about the city's news, politics, people, and culture.

The Phoenix New Times
www.phoenixnewtimes.com
For those seeking news in the alt-weekly style, this website for *The Phoenix New Times* weekly newspaper fits the bill. For travelers, its food, music, and art pages will feature the latest in events and places worth visiting.

Index

A

Ahwatukee: 50-51
Airport Mesa: 180
Airport Mesa Trail: 195
air travel: 253
amusement parks: 41
animals: 239-241
Annual Arizona Renaissance Festival and Artisan
    Marketplace: 61, 109
Annual Festival of Lights (Globe): 112
Apache Junction: 109
Apache Lake: 111
Apache Trail: 107-114; map 108
Arcadia Farms: 14, 22, 150
architecture: 251
architecture, Phoenix: 34-35
Arcosanti: 229
area codes: 259
Arizona Canal: 70
Arizona Capitol Museum: 32
Arizona Cardinals (football): 81
Arizona Coyotes (hockey): 81
Arizona Diamondbacks (baseball): 80
Arizona Museum of Natural History: 17, 49-50
Arizona Opera: 60
Arizona Rock'N'Roll Marathon: 60
Arizona Science Center: 17, 38
Arizona State Capitol: 16, 32, 36
Arizona State Fair: 62
Arizona State University: 47, 49
Arizona State University Art Museum: 49
arts and crafts: 20, 250-251
ATMs: 254
auto travel: 253-254
AZ88: 14, 127
AZ Heritage Center at Papago Park: 43

B

Bajada Nature Trail: 15, 144
Ballet Arizona: 60
ballooning: see hot-air ballooning
Banjo Bill Picnic Area: 218
Barrett-Jackson Collector Car Auction: 132
Barrio Café: 14, 86, 88
Bartlett Lake: 142
beer/breweries: Phoenix 58, 61, 86, 96; Scottsdale
    131, 156; Sedona 182, 200
Bell Rock: 17, 180
Bell Rock Pathway: 15, 195, 196
Bench, The: 180

Besh Ba Gowah Archaeological Park: 112
bicycling: Phoenix 50, 70-72; Scottsdale 141-142,
    168; Sedona 196-198, 226
Big Surf: 18, 80
Bike Skills Park: 196
Biltmore Fashion Park: 14, 24, 64, 66
birds/bird-watching: 198, 226, 240
Black Mesa Loop: 113
boating: 47
Bobby's Rock Trail: 74
Bondurant Racing School: 80
Bootlegger Day-Use Site: 218
botanical gardens/arboretums: 44-45, 113
Boulder Canyon Trail: 114
Bourbon Steak: 22, 159
Boyce Thompson Arboretum State Park: 113
Boynton Canyon Trail: 196
Breakfast Club: 19, 150
Breakfast Joynt: 14, 156
Brown's Ranch Trailhead: 144
Burnt Corral Recreation Site: 111
Burton Barr Central Library: 14, 17, 35, 41
bus travel: 254

C

Caduceus Cellars and Merkin Vineyards Tasting
    Room: 222
Café Monarch: 22, 148
Caffe Boa: 17, 98
Call of the Canyon Day-Use Area: 218
Camelback Mountain: 13, 19, 42, 73-74, 78
Camelback Ranch: 78
camping: Phoenix 110, 111; Sedona 220, 226
Canyon Lake: 110
Capitol Butte: 180
Carefree: 169-170
Carefree Desert Gardens: 169
Carraro Cactus Garden: 46
car travel: 253-254
Castle Rock: 180
Cathedral Rock: 17, 19, 180
Cathedral Rock Trail: 15, 195
Cave Creek: 19, 20, 167-169
Cave Creek Museum: 167
Cave Creek Regional Park: 168
Celebration of Fine Art: 133
Celebrity Theatre: 60
Cellar 433: 222
Central Phoenix: 42-43; map 65
Central Scottsdale: 123-125

Challenger Space Center: 52
Chamber Music Sedona: 183
Chapel of the Holy Cross: 17, 23, 177-178
Charles M. Christiansen Memorial Trail 100: 15, 71
Chase Field: 80
Children's Museum of Phoenix: 17, 38-39
children, traveling with: 255
Chimney Rock: 180
Chloe's Corner: 19, 21, 156
Cholla Trail: 74
Chuckbox, The: 16, 97
churches/temples: Phoenix 36; Sedona 177-178
Cibo Urban Pizzeria: 17, 87
CityScape: 14, 18, 24, 63, 75
Civic Space Park: 16, 20, 36
climate: 234, 235
climbing: Phoenix 72-74; Scottsdale 144-145
Cobre Valley Center for the Arts: 112
Coffee Pot Restaurant: 19, 205
Coffeepot Rock: 180
Comerica Theatre: 60
Copper Square: 32
Cosanti: 20, 22, 35, 124
Courthouse Butte: 15, 17, 180, 196
Cowboy Ciao: 14, 148
Crescent Moon Recreation Area: 19, 180-181
Cress on Oak Creek: 23, 202
currency exchange: 254

D
Dayton Fowler Grafman Atrium: 132
Dead Horse Ranch State Park: 19, 226
Deem Hills Recreation Area: 72, 74
Deer Valley Petroglyph Preserve: 51-52
Delux: 13, 86, 89
Desert Botanical Garden: 13, 21, 44-45
Desert Broom Library: 35
Desert Classic: 71
design: 251
Devil's Bridge Trail: 195
Dia de los Muertos: 62
disabilities, travelers with: 254-255
Downtown Phoenix: 32-33, 38-42; map 33
Downtown Scottsdale: 120-123; map 121

E
Eagle Head Rock: 180
East Valley: 47-50; map 48
Echo Canyon Recreation Area: 42, 73
Echo Canyon Summit Trail: 15, 73
Ecinoso Picnic Area: 216
economy: 247-248
ecotourism: 254
El Encanto: 19, 23, 169
Elote Cafe: 19, 203

emergencies: Phoenix 105-106; Scottsdale 165; Sedona 214
Encanto Park: 16, 40-41
Enchanted Island Amusement Park: 16-17, 41
Enchantment Resort: 23, 212
environmental issues: 234, 236

F
families, activities for: 16-17, 19
Farm at South Mountain: 17, 95
fauna: 239-241
Fay Canyon Trail: 196
Festival of Lights (Tlaquepaque): 185
Fiesta Bowl: 60
Fiesta Bowl Parade: 60
Fiesta De La Tlaquepaque: 185
First Friday Art Walk: 64
fish/fishing: Phoenix 43, 47; Sedona 216, 226
flora: 237-239
foreign travelers: 254
Fort Verde State Historic Park: 228-229
Fountain Festival of Arts and Crafts: 171
Fountain Hills: 170-171
Fountain Park: 75, 170
Four Peaks Brewery (Phoenix): 13, 58, 86, 96
Four Peaks Grill & Tap (Scottsdale): 156
Four Seasons Resort Scottsdale at Troon North: 21, 164
Frontier Town: 19, 167, 168

G
Gammage Auditorium: 49, 60
Garland's Indian Gardens Café & Market: 23, 218
gay and lesbian travelers: 256
Geisha A Go-Go: 14, 128
geography: 232-233
geology: 232
Geordie's at the Wrigley Mansion: 55
Glendale Glitters: 62
Globe: 112
Goldfield Ghost Town: 109
Goldwater, Barry: 245
golf: Phoenix 40, 43, 76-77; Scottsdale 142-144, 167-168; Sedona 198-199
Goodyear Ballpark: 78
government: 246
Grasshopper Point Swimming and Picnic Area: 216
Great Arizona Beer Festival: 61

H
Halfway Picnic Area: 218
Hall of Flame Fire Museum: 47
Hanny's: 35
Hayden Flour Mill: 47

health: 256-258
Heard Museum: 14, 17, 20, 39
Heard Museum Guild Indian Fair & Market: 61
Herberger Theater: 60
Heritage Square and Science Park: 17, 34, 36, 38
Hidden Valley: 15, 74
Hieroglyphic Trail in the Superstition Mountains: 18, 114
hiking: general discussion 15; Phoenix 42, 43, 50, 71, 72-74, 109-110, 111, 113-114; Scottsdale 144-145, 168; Sedona 180-181, 195-196, 216, 218, 226
history: 241-245
Hoel's Indian Shop: 23, 218
Hohokam Stadium: 78
Hole-in-the-Rock: 13, 44
Hole-in-the-Rock Trail: 15, 74
Holiday Central Sedona: 185
horseback riding: Phoenix 50, 77; Scottsdale 145, 167; Sedona 226
hot-air ballooning: Phoenix 70; Scottsdale 140; Sedona 193-195
Hotel San Carlos: 34

IJ
Indian Bend Wash Greenbelt: 142
itineraries: 13-24
Jack's Landing: 111
Jade Bar: 22, 131
Japanese Friendship Garden: 41-42
Jay's Bird Barn: 198
Jerome: 19, 20, 221-225
Jerome Mine Museum: 19, 222
Jewel of the Creek Preserve: 168
Jim Thompson Trail: 196
jogging: see running/jogging
Joya Spa: 18, 146

KL
kayaking/canoeing: 193
Kierland Commons: 22, 137-138
Kiwanis Trail: 74
La Grande Orange: 13, 86, 89
lakes: 233-234
language: 250
Las Noches de las Luminarias: 62
lesbian and gay travelers: 256
literature: 251
Little Red Schoolhouse: 122
Lo-Lo's Chicken and Waffles: 14, 85, 86
LON's at the Hermosa Inn: 22, 155
Lost Dog Wash Trailhead: 144
Lost Dutchman State Park: 109-110, 113
Lost Leaf, The: 14, 54
Luhrs Tower: 34

Macayo's Depot Cantina: 16, 98
Main Street Scottsdale: 14, 138-139
maps and tourist information: 258-259
Margaret T. Hance Deck Park: 41
Mariposa Latin Inspired Grill: 23, 204
Marlen Gardens: 35
Marshall Way: 14, 138-139
Mary D. Fisher Theatre: 183
Maryvale Stadium: 78
Matt's Big Breakfast: 16, 85, 86
McCormick-Stillman Railroad Park: 19, 124-125
McDowell Gateway Trailhead: 144
McDowell Mountain Regional Park: 24, 141, 144-145
McDowell Sonoran Preserve: 141, 144-145
media: 259
Mesa Arts Center: 60
Mesa Golfland-Sunsplash: 18, 80
Mesa Grande Cultural Park: 49-50
Miami: 112
Mii amo Spa: 23, 212
Mile High Grill & Spirits: 19, 222
Mill Avenue: 17, 47, 68
Miller Visitor Center: 181
Mine Museum: 19, 222
Mint Ultra Lounge: 14, 129
Mission, The: 14, 151
money: 254
monsoon season: 235
Montezuma Castle National Monument: 17, 227-228
Montezuma Well: 17, 228
Mormon Trail: 15, 74
Mother and Child Rock: 180
Musical Instrument Museum: 23, 43
Mystery Castle: 17, 20, 51

NO
National Day of the Cowboy Celebration: 184
National Trail: 71, 74
National Trail Trek: 72
newspapers: 259
North Mountain Visitor Center: 73
North Phoenix: 43, 74
North Scottsdale: 125-126
Oak Creek Brewery & Grill: 19, 200
Oak Creek Canyon: 18, 19, 215-216, 218-220
Oak Creek Tap Room and Brewery: 182
Old Adobe Mission: 14, 22, 122-123
Old Town Cottonwood: 226-227
Old Town Scottsdale: 14, 19, 22, 24, 120-122
Old Town Tortilla Factory: 19, 151
Orpheum Theatre: 35, 60
Ostrich Festival: 61

P

packing tips: 12
Palo Verde Branch Library: 35
Pane Bianco: 14, 92
Papago Park: 13, 16, 21, 43-47, 74; map 44
Parada del Sol Rodeo: 133
Paradise Gardens: 35
Paradise Valley: 22, 123-125
parks and gardens: Phoenix 36, 40-43, 47, 50-51;
    Sedona 180-181
Passion Cellars: 222
Peach Festival: 62
Pemberton Trail: 141, 145
Peoria Sports Complex: 79
Peralta Trail: 114
Phoenix: 25-107; maps 28, 33, 37, 44, 48, 65
Phoenix Art Museum: 14, 17, 20, 39-40
Phoenix Arts District: 32-33, 38-42; map 33
Phoenix City Hall: 34
Phoenix Comicon: 62
Phoenix Film Festival: 61
Phoenix Financial Center: 35
Phoenix Indian School: 41
Phoenix International Raceway: 80
Phoenix Mercury (basketball): 81
Phoenix Mountains Preserve: 72-73
Phoenix, Scottsdale and Sedona, map of: 2-3
Phoenix Sky Harbor International Airport: 13, 16,
    21, 86
Phoenix Summit Challenge: 72
Phoenix Suns (basketball): 81
Phoenix Symphony: 60
Phoenix Symphony Hall: 60
Phoenix Zoo: 16, 18, 45
Piestewa Peak: 13, 15, 24, 73
Pima Road: 142
Pizzeria Bianco: 14, 17, 87, 92
planning tips: 10-12
plants: 237-239
politics: 246, 247
Praying Monk: 42
public art tour, Scottsdale: 126
Pueblo Grande Museum and Archaeological Park:
    13, 16, 34, 45-46

QR

Racing Adventures: 80
radio: 259
Rainbow Trout Farm: 218
Rawhide Western Town: 17, 51
Red Rock Cafe: 17, 207
Red Rock Crossing: 180-181
Red Rock Music Festival: 184
Red Rock Pass: 195
Red Rocks: 20, 179-181

Red Rock Scenic Byway: 179
Red Rock State Park: 19, 181, 198
religion: 249-250
resources: 260-265
River of Time Museum: 171
rivers: 233-234
Roaring Fork: 22, 152
Rock Springs: 229-230
Roosevelt Dam and Lake: 111
Roosevelt Row: 20, 63
Rosson House: 34, 38
running/jogging: Phoenix 60, 70-72; Sedona 184

S

safety: 256-258
Salt River: 18, 19, 75, 145
Salt River Fields at Talking Stick: 79
Scottsdale: 19, 115-167; maps 118, 121
Scottsdale Arabian Horse Show: 134
Scottsdale Arts Festival: 134
Scottsdale Beer Company: 131
Scottsdale Center for the Performing Arts: 132
Scottsdale City Hall: 121
Scottsdale Civic Center Amphitheater: 132
Scottsdale Civic Center Mall: 120
Scottsdale Culinary Festival Weekend: 134
Scottsdale Fashion Square: 19, 22, 135-136
Scottsdale International Film Festival: 134
Scottsdale Museum of Contemporary Art
    (SMoCA): 20, 22, 24, 123
Scottsdale Stadium: 79, 145
Scottsdale Trolley: 19, 166
Sedona: 17, 23, 172-215; maps 175, 215
Sedona Arts Center: 179
Sedona Arts Festival: 185
Sedona Creative Life Center: 183
Sedona Gallery Association: 189
Sedona Heritage Museum: 178
Sedona International Film Festival: 184
Sedona Marathon: 184
Sedona Memories: 23, 201
Sedona Plein Air Festival: 185
Sedona St. Patrick's Parade and Festival: 184
Sedona Winefest: 185
senior travelers: 256
Siphon Draw Trail to the Flatiron: 113
Slide Rock State Park: 18, 19, 215-216
Sloan Park: 78
Snoopy Rock: 180
Sonoran Preserve: 72, 74
South Mountain Antenna Farm: 51
South Mountain Environmental Education
    Center: 51
South Mountain Park and Preserve: 17, 50-51, 74
South Phoenix: 50-51
Southwest Shakespeare Company: 60

Spa at the Boulders Resort: 21, 147, 164
Spa at the Four Season Resort Scottsdale: 21, 147
spas: Phoenix 81-82; Scottsdale 146-148; Sedona 199-200
spectator sports: Phoenix 60, 78-79, 80-81; Scottsdale 133, 145-146
spring training: 78-79
Spur Cross Ranch Conservation Area: 168
Spur Cross Stables: 22, 167
Stage 2: 132
Stand Up Live: 59
state parks: Phoenix 109-110, 113; Sedona 181, 215-216, 226
Steamboat Rock: 180
Steele Island School Park: 41
Stellar Adventures: 19, 24, 140
St. Mary's Basilica: 36
Submarine Rock: 180
Sugar Bowl: 19, 150
Sunrise Trailhead: 144
Sunset Park: 18, 180
Superior: 112
Superstition Mountains: 107-114
Surprise Recreation Campus: 79
Sweet Republic: 14, 86, 94
swimming: Phoenix 40, 75; Sedona 216

T

Taliesin West: 14, 19, 23, 35, 125-126
Talking Stick Resort Arena: 81
television: 259
Tempe: 13, 47-50; map 48
Tempe Beach Park: 47
Tempe Center for the Arts: 47, 60
Tempe Diablo Stadium: 78
Tempe Festival of the Arts: 62
Tempe Improv: 59
Tempe Municipal Building: 47
Tempe Town Lake: 13, 16, 47, 75
Third Friday Art Walk: 64
Thumb Butte: 180
time zones: 259
Tlaquepaque Arts and Crafts Village: 19, 23, 187-188
Tom's Thumb Trail: 15, 145
Tonto National Monument: 111-112
Tortilla Flat: 110-111

tourist information: 258-259
Tovrea Castle: 46
transportation: 253-254
Troon North Golf Club: 21, 143
Tuck Shop: 14, 83
Turf Paradise: 81
Tuzigoot National Monument: 225-226
Twin Nuns: 180

UV

University of Phoenix Stadium: 81
Uptown Sedona: 177-179
Valle Vista Road: 72
Valley Bar: 14, 53, 55
Valley of the Sun: 31
Verde River: 19, 193
Verde Valley: 220-230
Verde Valley Birding and Nature Festival: 198
Verde Valley Wine Trail: 223
Vig, The: 13, 56
Village of Oak Creek: 180
Virginia G. Piper Theater: 132
visas: 254
VNSA Book Sale: 60
vortexes: 194

WXYZ

Waste Management Phoenix Open: 133
water parks: 18, 75, 80
weather: 234, 235
Wells Fargo History Museum: 36
Western Spirit: Scottsdale's Museum of the West: 122
West Fork of Oak Creek: 15, 218
Westgate Entertainment District: 61
West Valley: 51-52
Westward Ho: 34
Wet 'n' Wild: 18, 75, 80
Wiener Mania: 61
wildlife/wildlife-watching: general discussion 239-241; Phoenix 73, 110; Scottsdale 144, 169
Windy Hill Recreation Site: 111
wine/wineries: 185, 193, 222, 223
Zinc Bistro: 22, 157
ZooLights: 62
zoos and animal parks: 45

List of Maps

Front Map
Phoenix, Scottsdale & Sedona: 2-3

Discover Phoenix, Scottsdale & Sedona
chapter divisions map: 10

Phoenix
Phoenix: 28
Downtown Phoenix: 33
The Arts District: 37
Papago Park: 44
Tempe: 48
Central Phoenix: 65
Apache Trail Scenic Loop: 108

Scottsdale
Scottsdale and Vicinity: 118
Downtown Scottsdale: 121

Sedona
Sedona: 175
Vicinity of Sedona: 217

Photo Credits

Title Page: sunset in the McDowell Sonoran Preserve courtesy of Experience Scottsdale; page 4 Parada del Sol courtesy of Experience Scottsdale; page 5 (top) view of the Superstition Mountains © Lilia Menconi, (bottom) crystals for sale in Sedona courtesy of Sedona Chamber of Commerce & Tourism Bureau/www.visitsedona.com; page 6 (top left) courtesy of Desert Botanical Garden, (top right) courtesy of Sedona Chamber of Commerce & Tourism Bureau/www.visitsedona.com, (bottom) courtesy of Experience Scottsdale; page 7 (top) courtesy of Desert Botanical Garden, (bottom left) courtesy of Experience Scottsdale, (bottom right) courtesy of Sedona Chamber of Commerce & Tourism Bureau/www.visitsedona.com; page 8 courtesy of Experience Scottsdale; page 9 (top) © Lilia Menconi, (bottom left) courtesy of Experience Scottsdale, (bottom right) courtesy of Sedona Chamber of Commerce & Tourism Bureau/www.visitsedona.com; page 11 courtesy of Sedona Chamber of Commerce & Tourism Bureau/www.visitsedona.com; page 12 (top) © Lilia Menconi, (bottom) © Scott Griessel | Dreamstime.com; page 13 © Lilia Menconi; page 14 (left) courtesy of Desert Botanical Garden, (right) © Lilia Menconi; page 15 courtesy of Experience Scottsdale; page 16 © Twildlife | Dreamstime.com; page 17 © Joseph Morelli | Dreamstime.com; page 18 courtesy of Sedona Chamber of Commerce & Tourism Bureau/www.visitsedona.com; page 19 courtesy of Sedona Chamber of Commerce & Tourism Bureau/www.visitsedona.com; page 20 © Lilia Menconi; page 21 courtesy of Experience Scottsdale; page 22 courtesy of Experience Scottsdale; page 23 © Wollertz | Dreamstime.com; page 24 James Turrell, *Knight Rise,* 2001/Venetian plaster, neon, steel/commissioned by Scottsdale Public Art/photo by Sean Deckert; page 25 (top) © Lilia Menconi, (bottom) © Lilia Menconi; page 27 courtesy of Desert Botanical Garden; page 34 © Lilia Menconi; page 35 © Lilia Menconi; page 38 © Lilia Menconi; page 39 courtesy of Experience Scottsdale; page 40 © Lilia Menconi; page 42 © Lilia Menconi; page 45 © Lilia Menconi; page 46 courtesy of Pueblo Grande Museum and Archaeological Park; page 49 © Lilia Menconi; page 50 © Lilia Menconi; page 53 © Lilia Menconi; page 59 © Lilia Menconi; page 61 courtesy of Experience Scottsdale; page 63 © Lilia Menconi; page 68 © Lilia Menconi; page 73 © Lilia Menconi; page 79 © Lilia Menconi; page 87 © Lilia Menconi; page 90 © Lilia Menconi; page 94 © Lilia Menconi; page 100 © Lilia Menconi; page 102 courtesy of Experience Scottsdale; page 106 © Lilia Menconi; page 110 © Lilia Menconi; page 115 (top) courtesy of Experience Scottsdale, (bottom) James Turrell, *Knight Rise,* 2001/Venetian plaster, neon, steel/commissioned by Scottsdale Public Art/photo by Sean Deckert; page 117 courtesy of Experience Scottsdale; page 122 © Derrick Neill | Dreamstime.com; page 123 courtesy of Experience Scottsdale; page 124 © Lilia Menconi; page 125 courtesy of Experience Scottsdale; page 127 © Lilia Menconi; page 130 © Lilia Menconi; page 133 courtesy of Experience Scottsdale; page 135 courtesy of Experience Scottsdale; page 136 courtesy of Experience Scottsdale; page 139 © Art One Gallery, Inc.; page 141 courtesy of Experience Scottsdale; page 143 courtesy of Experience Scottsdale; page 144 © Lou Kummerer; page 146 courtesy of Experience Scottsdale; page 152 courtesy of Experience Scottsdale; page 153 © Lilia Menconi; page 155 courtesy of Experience Scottsdale; page 161 © The Saguaro Scottsdale; page 163 courtesy of Experience Scottsdale; page 168 © Lilia Menconi; page 170 courtesy of Experience Scottsdale; page 171 © Lilia Menconi; page 172 (top) courtesy of Sedona Chamber of Commerce & Tourism Bureau/www.visitsedona.com, (bottom) © Lilia Menconi; page 173 © Lilia Menconi; page 178 © Tom Dowd | Dreamstime.com; page 180 courtesy of Sedona Chamber of Commerce & Tourism Bureau/www.visitsedona.com; page 181 © Lilia Menconi; page 184 courtesy of Sedona Chamber of Commerce & Tourism Bureau/www.visitsedona.com; page 187 © Lilia Menconi; page 188 courtesy of Sedona Chamber of Commerce & Tourism Bureau/www.visitsedona.com; page 192 © Pink Adventure Group; page 194 © Kirsten Mouritsen; page 196 courtesy of Sedona Chamber of Commerce & Tourism Bureau/www.visitsedona.com; page 197 courtesy of Sedona Chamber of Commerce & Tourism Bureau/www.visitsedona.com; page 202 courtesy of Sedona Chamber of Commerce & Tourism Bureau/www.visitsedona.com; page 208 courtesy of Sedona Chamber of Commerce & Tourism Bureau/www.visitsedona.com; page 209 courtesy of Sedona Chamber of Commerce & Tourism Bureau/www.visitsedona.com; page 216 courtesy of Sedona Chamber of Commerce & Tourism Bureau/www.visitsedona.com; page 221 © Sebcanuto | Dreamstime.com; page 223 courtesy of Sedona Chamber of Commerce & Tourism Bureau/www.visitsedona.com; page 224 © Donna Chesler; page 225 courtesy of Sedona Chamber of Commerce & Tourism Bureau/www.visitsedona.com; page 226 © Donna Chesler; page 231 (top) © Lilia Menconi, (bottom) © Lilia Menconi; page 233 © Lilia Menconi; page 235 © Lilia Menconi page 237 courtesy of Sedona Chamber of Commerce & Tourism Bureau/www.visitsedona.com; page 238 courtesy of Experience Scottsdale; page 239 © Lilia Menconi; page 241 © Lilia Menconi; page 248 courtesy of Desert Botanical Garden; page 252 (top) © Lilia Menconi, (bottom) © Imantsu | Dreamstime.com; page 257 © Lilia Menconi

Also Available

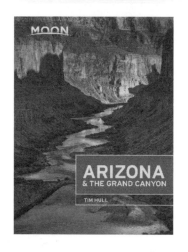

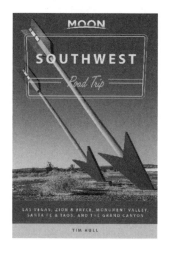

MAP SYMBOLS

▦▦▦ Expressway	★ Highlight	✗ Airfield	⚲ Golf Course
▦▦▦ Primary Road	○ City/Town	✗ Airport	🅿 Parking Area
▦▦▦ Secondary Road	◉ State Capital	▲ Mountain	◣ Archaeological Site
▪▪▪ Unpaved Road	⊛ National Capital	✛ Unique Natural Feature	♦ Church
- - - - Trail	★ Point of Interest		
·········· Ferry	• Accommodation	⟋ Waterfall	⬭ Gas Station
▪▪▪ Railroad	▼ Restaurant/Bar	♠ Park	⬮ Glacier
▦▦▦ Pedestrian Walkway	▪ Other Location	⬛ Trailhead	⬓ Mangrove
▥▥▥ Stairs	⋀ Campground	⛷ Skiing Area	▨ Reef
			▨ Swamp

CONVERSION TABLES

°C = (°F - 32) / 1.8
°F = (°C x 1.8) + 32
1 inch = 2.54 centimeters (cm)
1 foot = 0.304 meters (m)
1 yard = 0.914 meters
1 mile = 1.6093 kilometers (km)
I km = 0.6214 miles
1 fathom = 1.8288 m
1 chain = 20.1168 m
1 furlong = 201.168 m
1 acre = 0.4047 hectares
1 sq km = 100 hectares
1 sq mile = 2.59 square km
1 ounce = 28.35 grams
1 pound = 0.4536 kilograms
1 short ton = 0.907/18 metric ton
1 short ton = 2,000 pounds
1 long ton = 1.016 metric tons
1 long ton = 2,240 pounds
1 metric ton = 1,000 kilograms
1 quart = 0.94635 liters
1 US gallon = 3.7854 liters
1 Imperial gallon = 4.5459 liters
1 nautical mile = 1.852 km

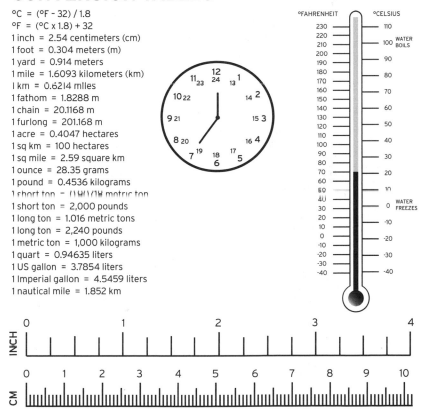

MOON PHOENIX, SCOTTSDALE & SEDONA
Avalon Travel
An imprint of Perseus Books
A Hachette Book Group company
1700 Fourth Street
Berkeley, CA 94710, USA
www.moon.com

Editor: Rachel Feldman
Series Manager: Kathryn Ettinger
Copy Editor: Sasha Heseltine
Graphics and Production Coordinator: Elizabeth Jang
Cover Design: Faceout Studios, Charles Brock
Interior Design: Domini Dragoone
Moon Logo: Tim McGrath
Map Editor: Mike Morgenfeld
Cartographers: Brian Shotwell, Austin Ehrhardt
Indexer: Greg Jewett

ISBN-13: 978-1-63121-340-3
ISSN: 2151-6138

Printing History
1st Edition — 2010
3rd Edition — May 2017
5 4 3 2 1

Front cover photo: rock formation in Sedona © DeepDesertPhoto/Getty Images

Back cover photo: hot air balloon over Phoenix © Danny Raustadt | Dreamstime.com

Printed in Canada by Friesens

KEEPING CURRENT

If you have a favorite gem you'd like to see included in the next edition, or see anything that needs updating, clarification, or correction, please drop us a line. Send your comments via email to feedback@moon.com, or use the address above.

AUTHOR

nconi

0 01 00 9083025 7

© LOU KUMMERER

a Phoenix gal through and through. She was born
oenix, with the famous Camelback Mountain visible
rd. While she enjoyed the occasional day hike with
g her childhood, she truly fell in love with the city's
adult.

_ward-winning writer whose work has appeared in
local publications, including *Phoenix New Times*, *Arizona Republic*,
and *Generation Health AZ*, and on the blog The Broke-Ass Bride.
She loves her day job as a communications coordinator and feels
lucky to accept additional work as a freelance writer and blogger.
She happily lives and works in Phoenix with her husband and two
adorable cats.

About Moon

Moon travel guidebooks are published by Avalon Travel, an imprint of Perseus Books, a Hachette
Book Group company. Moon was founded by Bill Dalton in 1973 with the publication of his own
legendary *Indonesia Handbook*, soon followed by Handbooks to Japan, the South Pacific, and
Arizona. Today, Moon specializes in guides to the United States, while also publishing books on
Canada, Mexico, the Caribbean, Latin America, Europe, Asia, and the Pacific. The Avalon Travel
office is in Berkeley, California, and our authors call places all over the world home.

Make Your Escape

Wander world-class museums in Phoenix. Relax in Scottsdale's famous spas. Hike the red rocks of Sedona. The Valley of the Sun proves just how hospitable the desert can be.

This book tells you what you need to know to plan the perfect trip for you:

- Where to find the best hikes—to red rocks, water-carved canyons, and mountain peaks

- Advice on outdoor recreation, including golfing, biking, climbing, and kayaking

- Highlights of the art scene, from Native American exhibits to contemporary galleries

- The best places for fine living, including five-star resorts, world-class spas, and gourmet restaurants

- What to do after dark, from stargazing in the desert to clubbing in Scottsdale

MOON.COM

THIRD EDITION   AVALON TRAVEL
An imprint of Perseus Books
A Hachette Book Group company

PUBLISHED MAY 2017
TRAVEL   US $17.99 CAN $23.49 UK £11.99

ISBN 978-1-63121-340-3

51799

9 781631 213403